Finance, Growth and Inequality

NEW DIRECTIONS IN POST-KEYNESIAN ECONOMICS

Series Editors: Louis-Philippe Rochon, *Laurentian University, Sudbury, Canada* and Sergio Rossi, *University of Fribourg, Switzerland*

Post-Keynesian economics is a school of thought inspired by the work of John Maynard Keynes, but also by Michal Kalecki, Joan Robinson, Nicholas Kaldor and other Cambridge economists, for whom money and effective demand are essential to explain economic activity. The aim of this series is to present original research work (single or co-authored volumes as well as edited books) that advances Post-Keynesian economics at both theoretical and policy-oriented levels.

Areas of research include, but are not limited to, monetary and financial economics, macro and microeconomics, international economics, development economics, economic policy, political economy, analyses of income distribution and financial crises, and the history of economic thought.

Titles in the series include:

Post Keynesian Theory and Policy
A Realistic Analysis of the Market Oriented Capitalist Economy
Paul Davidson

Inequality, Growth and 'Hot' Money
Pablo G. Bortz

The Financialization Response to Economic Disequilibria
European and Latin American Experiences
Edited by Noemi Levy and Etelberto Ortiz

Crisis and the Failure of Economic Theory
The Responsibility of Economists for the Great Recession
Giancarlo Bertocco

A Modern Guide to Rethinking Economics
Edited by Louis-Philippe Rochon and Sergio Rossi

Monetary Policy and Crude Oil
Prices, Production and Consumption
Basil Oberholzer

Finance, Growth and Inequality
Post-Keynesian Perspectives
Edited by Louis-Philippe Rochon and Virginie Monvoisin

Finance, Growth and Inequality

Post-Keynesian Perspectives

Edited by

Louis-Philippe Rochon

Full Professor of Economics, Laurentian University, Canada and Founding Editor Emeritus, Review of Keynesian Economics, *and co-editor,* Review of Political Economy

Virginie Monvoisin

Associate Professor, Grenoble Ecole de Management, France

NEW DIRECTIONS IN POST-KEYNESIAN ECONOMICS

Edward Elgar PUBLISHING

Cheltenham, UK • Northampton, MA, USA

Published by
Edward Elgar Publishing Limited
The Lypiatts
15 Lansdown Road
Cheltenham
Glos GL50 2JA
UK

Edward Elgar Publishing, Inc.
William Pratt House
9 Dewey Court
Northampton
Massachusetts 01060
USA

A catalogue record for this book
is available from the British Library

Library of Congress Control Number: 2019947176

This book is available electronically in the **Elgar**online
Economics subject collection
DOI 10.4337/9781788973694

MIX
Paper from responsible sources
FSC® C013056

ISBN 978 1 78897 368 7 (cased)
ISBN 978 1 78897 369 4 (eBook)

Typeset by Servis Filmsetting Ltd, Stockport, Cheshire
Printed and bound in Great Britain by TJ International Ltd, Padstow

Contents

Contributors

Arpita Bhattacharjee is currently a Research Fellow in the Economics Division at the Leeds University Business School, working on the EPSRC Self-Repairing Cities Project to investigate how artificial intelligence and robotics stand to alter the socioeconomic and cultural landscapes of cities. She received her PhD in Economics from the University of California, Riverside in 2017. Her current research encompasses applied empirical and theoretical microeconomics, specifically focused on analysis of social inequalities in labour markets, education, and health, and empirical investigation of policies targeted at mitigating inequalities.

Bruno Bonizzi is Lecturer in Political Economy at the University of Winchester, UK. He did his undergraduate studies at Bocconi University in Milan, Italy, before moving to London to do his MSc and PhD at SOAS, University of London. He has taught at City University and the University of East London. His doctoral research focused on pension funds and their investments in emerging market economies. Financialisation, pension funds and developing countries feature prominently in his current research projects. A macro-financial economist by background, he is keen on reaching out to the fields of political economy in addressing these issues.

Pablo G. Bortz holds a BA from the University of Buenos Aires, an MA from the Latin American Faculty of Social Sciences (FLACSO), and a Doctorate degree from the Delft University of Technology. He is currently professor of Advanced Macroeconomics at the MA in Economic Development (IDAES-National University of San Martin), of which he is the co-director. He also teaches at the National University of General Sarmiento (UNGS). He is a grantee of the National Council for Scientific Research (CONICET) in Argentina. He has published in several journals such as *Development and Change*, the *Review of Keynesian Economics* and the *European Journal of Economics and Economic Policies*.

Hasan Cömert is an Assistant Professor of Economics at the Department of Economics at Trinity College, US. He received his PhD from University of Massachusetts at Amherst in 2011. His research interests include central banking, financial markets, financial flows, developing countries and the Turkish economy. He is the author of *Central Banks and Financial*

Markets: The Declining Power of US Monetary Policy (Edward Elgar, 2013), and co-author (with Rex McKenzie) of *The Global South after the Crisis* (Edward Elgar, 2016). He has published several articles in Turkish and in English at peer-reviewed journals including *Cambridge Journal of Economics*. He has contributed as a researcher to different working packages of FESSUD and FEUTURE, European Union-funded projects conducted by the consortiums of many universities.

Óscar Dejuán is a Full Professor of Economics at the University of Castilla-La Mancha, Spain. He obtained his PhD in economics from the New School for Social Research. He is also a Doctor in Law from the University of Barcelona where he got an MA in Economics and Law. In his theoretical research he has combined the Classical-Sraffian theory of value and distribution with the Keynesian theory of output and money. In his applied research he has used Leontief's input–output analysis. He has authored and edited books with Edward Elgar and Routledge. He has published in a variety of journals including *Economic Systems Research*, *Review of Political Economy*, *Journal of Post Keynesian Economics*, *Review of Keynesian Economics*, *Metroeconomica*, *Energy Policy*, *Energy Economics*, *European Journal for the History of Economic Thought* and *Cambridge Journal of Economics*.

Hélène de Largentaye received her PhD in economics from the University of Cambridge in 1986 after receiving a diploma from the Paris Institut des Etudes Politiques, in 1971, and a Masters in Economics (1972) from University of Paris 1. She worked as an economist at the Paris Chamber of Commerce (1974–1997), as Secretary General of the Council of Economic Advisers (1997–2001) founded by Lionel Jospin, Prime Minister of France (1997–2002), and as an economic adviser to Bertrand Delanoë, Mayor of Paris (2001–2014). She co-authored 'Équilibre et Instabilité' (1987, *Economica*), a selection of articles by Nicholas Kaldor, translated into French. She organised the Keynes Conference at King's College (2016) for the 80th anniversary of the publication of Keynes's General Theory. She wrote the preface of the 2017 French edition of Keynes's General Theory published by Payot and translated several essays by Keynes, also published by Payot the same year (*La fin du laissez faire*).

Cristiano Boaventura Duarte has a PhD in Economics, double diploma: Institute of Economics, Federal University of Rio de Janeiro (IE/UFRJ – Brazil) and Centre d'Économie de l'Université Paris-Nord, Université Paris 13 (CEPN/UP13 – France). He has previously worked at the Brazilian Institute of Geography and Statistics (IBGE) and in the Brazilian main oil and gas Company (Petrobras). He is currently an economist at the Central

Bank of Brazil where he works in the International Affairs Department, with the team responsible for performing analysis of the global economy. The views presented on the article are his own, and do not represent those of the Central Bank of Brazil.

Renaud du Tertre is Associate Professor Emeritus, at Paris Diderot – Paris 7 University, and is a member of the Ladyss Research Laboratory. He worked as a scientific counsellor at the Commissariat Général du Plan (2002–2008) and as Director of Studies at the Institut de Recherches Économiques et Sociales, an institute related to trade unions (2009–2010). His research focuses on uncertainty and price-making of capital, on the impact of finance on the multinational firms' strategy, and on the growth regime of developed capitalist economies. He is coauthor with Olivier Passet of *Rentabilité et risque dans le nouveau régime de croissance, rapport du Commissariat général du Plan*, 2002; and with Yann Guy 'Stratégie de valorisation actionnariale et gouvernance des grands groupes cotés', in Michel Aglietta (ed.), *La transformation du régime de croissance* (2018).

Gary Dymski is Professor of Applied Economics at the Leeds University Business School, a position he took up in 2012 after 21 years in the University of California system. His research focuses on discrimination and redlining in credit markets, urban economic development, financial crisis, the subprime and Eurozone crises, banking and financial regulation, and urban development. His research projects at Leeds include one on inequality and finance in Europe, and another on how the robotic transition can be done without worsening inequality. He is involved in two UK-wide network projects, one aimed at rebuilding macroeconomics and the other focused on a region-first approach to the UK productivity puzzle.

Alicia Girón is the coordinator of the University Program of Asian and African Studies – National Autonomous University of Mexico (UNAM), and member of the United Nations High Level Panel for Women's Economic Empowerment. She is a researcher at the Economic Research Institute, and a professor at the Faculty of Economics and tutor of the Economics, the Latin American Studies, and the Administration Sciences Postgraduate degree programs at UNAM. Her main research interests include fiscal and financial economics, as well as gender economics in relation to financial circuits at a macroeconomic and microeconomic level. She was the Director at the Economic Research Institute (1994–2002) and of 'Problemas del Desarrollo. Revista latinoamericana de Economía' (2010–2018).

Diego Guevara is Assistant Professor in Heterodox Macroeconomics at the National University of Colombia. He did his undergraduate studies in engineering and then a MSc and PhD in economics. He has taught at the University of La Sabana and Javeriana University, in Bogotá, Colombia. His doctoral research is about financialisation and income distribution, and currently his research interests are on financialisation for emerging economies, and financialisation and history of economic though. He has also been advisor for CUT (Workers Union) in the minimum wage negotiations with the government during 2016 and 2017, and is a regular columnist for one of the main Colombian newspapers, *El Espectador*.

David Leadbeater is an Associate Professor of Economics at Laurentian University/Université Laurentienne in Sudbury (Canada), located on the traditional Anishinaabe territory of the Atikameksheng Anishnawbek and Wahnapitae First Nation. His work focuses on the fields of regional economic development, labour economics, and urban economics, and on critiques of globalization and impoverishment. He holds degrees from the University of Alberta, Oxford University, and the University of Toronto. He is editor of *Resources, Empire and Labour: Crises, Lessons and Alternatives* (Fernwood, 2014) and *Mining Town Crisis: Globalization, Labour and Resistance in Sudbury* (Fernwood, 2008).

Joëlle Leclaire is Associate Professor of Economics and Finance at SUNY College at Buffalo, where she teaches Macroeconomics, Economic Statistics, and Money and Banking. Her research looks at the connection between the real and financial sectors of the economy and the role of private and public debt on financial and economic macro-stability. She has presented her work at numerous conferences and graduate summer schools around the world, has served on international expert bodies such as the INET Private Debt Initiative, and has organized international conferences. Leclaire has published articles in the *Journal of Post-Keynesian Economics*, the *International Journal of Political Economy*, and the online Post-Keynesian Forum. She has authored one book, *The Great Deficit Debacle* (2008) and published one edited volume *Heterodox Analysis and Financial Crisis and Reform* (2011).

John S. L. McCombie is Professor Emeritus of Regional and Applied Economics and Emeritus Senior Fellow of the Department of Land Economy at the University of Cambridge. He is also Director of the Centre for Economic and Public Policy; Emeritus Fellow in Economics of Downing College and Director of Studies in Land Economy, Christ's College, Downing College and Girton College. He was formerly a member of the Economics Departments at the University of Hull and at the University of Melbourne. He is a Fellow of the Regional Studies Association and Fellow of the Academy of Social Sciences. He has been a consultant to the World Bank and the Asian Development Bank and a Special Advisor to a House of Lords Special Committee. His research interests include regional economics and post-Keynesian economics and he is currently researching into income inequality and political philosophy and the methodological and other economic implications of the sub-prime financial crisis.

Gabriel Michelena is currently a PhD candidate in Economics at the Universidad de Buenos Aires, where he teaches Quantitative Methods. He is also the author of several articles and publications on trade-related topics presented at congresses and published in different issues of the *Argentine Journal of International Economy* (RAEI) and *Realidad Economica*. He currently works as a Director at the Ministry of Production in Argentina in the impact assessment of public policies. His areas of specialization are applied econometrics, computational models, macroeconomics, and international trade.

Virginie Monvoisin is an Associate Professor at the Grenoble École de Management in the department of People, Organizations and Society. She also teaches at the Grenoble Alpes University or Sciences Po Grenoble. She obtained her PhD at the University of Burgundy with top honors. Her PhD dissertation was one of the first French theses on endogenous money. Before moving to Grenoble, she taught at Laurentian University (Canada) as an Assistant Professor. More broadly, her research interests are in the areas of monetary economics, macroeconomics and economic systems. She is currently working on banking systems and their alternative and ethic dimensions. She has published in French and International academics journals and books in her main field of research. Recently, she co-edited *L'économie post-keynésienne: Histoire, théories et politiques* (Editions du Seuil).

Max Nagel is a PhD candidate in Political Science and Sociology at Scuola Normale Superiore, Italy. His dissertation looks at institutional change of depoliticized policy fields, analyzing the development of monetary policy frameworks of central banks after the financial crisis 2007 in a comparative case study. He looks particularly at the role of ideas in policymaking by making use of insights from the sociology of knowledge. He has degrees in Economic and Financial Sociology from Goethe University Frankfurt, and International Economics & Development from Bayreuth University.

Jonathan Perraton is Senior Lecturer in Economics at the University of Sheffield, UK, and Associate Fellow of the Sheffield Political Economy Research Institute. He obtained an MA in Economics from Cambridge

University and a PhD from Nottingham University. He has published on economic globalization, balance of payments and growth, political economy and economic methodology, including papers in the *Cambridge Journal of Economics*, *International Review of Applied Economics*, *Journal of Economic Methodology*, and *New Political Economy*. His current research interests are in European economic models and development under globalization. He is a past co-ordinator of the UK Post-Keynesian Economics Study Group.

Nathan Perry is an Associate Professor of Economics at Colorado Mesa University. His research interests include money and banking issues such as the determinants of inflation and endogenous money. He has also published empirical work in Economic History and has conducted several regional economic grant studies in the state of Colorado, as well as publishing teaching modules on Deficits and Debt with Global Development and the Environment (GDAE). He teaches Money and Banking, Econometrics, Macroeconomics, and upper division statistics courses.

Louis-Philippe Rochon is Full Professor of Economics at Laurentian University, Canada. He obtained his doctorate from the New School for Social Research, in 1998, earning him an award for outstanding dissertation. He is the founding editor (now emeritus) of the *Review of Keynesian Economics*, and is currently co-editor of the *Review of Political Economy*. He is the author of over 125 articles in journals and books, and has written or edited 26 books. He has been guest-editor of the *Journal of Post Keynesian Economics*, the *International Journal of Pluralism and Economics Education*, the *European Journal of Economic and Social Systems*, and the *International Journal of Political Economy*. He has published on monetary theory and policy, post-Keynesian economics, and fiscal policy. He is on the editorial board of *Ola Financiera*, *International Journal of Political Economy*, the *European Journal of Economics and Economic Policies: Intervention*, and *Problemas del Desarrollo, Cuestiones Económicas*, and *Credit and Money*. He has been a visiting scholar or professor in Australia, Brazil, France, Italy, Mexico, Poland, South Africa, and the United States, and has additionally lectured in Colombia, Ecuador, Italy, Japan, Kyrgyzstan, and Peru. His forthcoming books include *A Short History of Economic Thought* (Edward Elgar Publishing, 2017, co-edited with Hassan Bougrine), *Employment in the Age of Austerity* (Edward Elgar Publishing, 2017, co-edited with Brian MacLean and Hassan Bougrine), as well as two volumes honouring the work of Marc Lavoie and Mario Seccareccia (co-edited with Hassan Bougrine).

Carlos Schönerwald is a Professor of Economics at the Department of Economics, Universidade Federal do Rio Grande do Sul (UFRGS) – Brazil. His current research interests include macroeconomics, econometrics and history of economic thought. One of his recent papers was co-authored with Matias Vernengo, 'Microfinance, Financial Inclusion, and the Rhetoric of Reaction: The Evolution and Limitations of Microfinance in Brazil', and published in *Latin American Policy*, 7 (2), December, 2016.

Marcia Solorza is Professor of Economics in the Faculty of Economics of the National Autonomous University of Mexico (UNAM), at both the graduate and undergraduate levels. She lectures on the history of economic thought, monetary policy and theory, and on financial crises. She completed her PhD in Economics (UNAM) and focused on the monetary circuit and foreign banking in the late 19th and early 20th centuries. She is currently leading a research project on 'Monetary Theories and Policies in Developing Countries in the early XXIst Century.' She has participated as a speaker in numerous seminars and round tables on monetary and financial issues, and has authored and co-authored a number of articles, book chapters, and specialized books on economic history and monetary and financial economics.

Marcello Spanò is Assistant Professor in the Department of Economics, at the University of Insubria, Italy, where he teaches International Economics. He completed a PhD in Economics from the University of York (2004). He has worked on risk management through derivatives for non-financial companies, analysing theoretical and empirical aspects (*Journal of Business Finance & Accounting*, *Rivista Italiana degli Economisti*, *Journal of Corporate Finance*); he has examined emerging markets accumulation of foreign reserves in connection with foreign and domestic finance, foreign exchange risk, real investments and growth (Panoeconomicus). His current research focuses on financialisation and sectoral imbalances, with an empirical focus on European countries (*Journal of Post Keynesian Economics*).

Hanna K. Szymborska is a lecturer in economics at the Open University, UK. Her research interests include economics of inequality, household finance, financial macroeconomics, and history of economic thought. She has previously worked as a teaching assistant at the University of Leeds, assistant economist at the UK Department of Health, and research assistant at SOAS, University of London, and at London School of Economics and Political Science. She has published in peer-reviewed journals, co-authored articles in policy magazines, contributed to policy reports and chapters in monographs including *Michal Kalecki in the 21st Century*

(Palgrave Macmillan, 2014), *Rosa Luxemburg: A Permanent Challenge for Political Economy* (Palgrave Macmillan, 2017), *Financialisation and the Economy* (Routledge, 2017), and *Challenges of Financialisation in the Latin American-led Growth Model* (Routledge, forthcoming). She has also co-edited the translation of Tadeusz Kowalik's *Rosa Luxemburg: Theory of Accumulation and Imperialism* (with J. Toporowski, Palgrave Macmillan, 2014).

Matthias Thiemann is an Assistant Professor of European Public Policy. His more recent work analyses the ideational change after the financial crisis and its impact on financial regulations. He recently published a book on the growth of shadow banking (Cambridge University Press, 2018). His articles on financial regulation have been published in the *American Journal of Sociology*, the *Review of International Political Economy* and the *Cambridge Journal of Economics*, among others.

Fernando Toledo is Professor of International Open Economy Macroeconomics in the Faculty of Economic Sciences, National University of La Plata, Argentina. He teaches International Open Economy Macroeconomics in the MA in Economic Development at the High Social Studies Institute, San Martín University, Argentina. He holds a MA in Economics from National University of La Plata, Argentina. His main research interests are in the fields of development macroeconomics, income distribution and international open economy macroeconomics. He has published several articles in books edited by ILO, UNDP and the Ministry of Finance in Argentina.

Acknowledgements

This book is the result of talks held at the Université de Grenoble, Alpes, in December 2017. A number of individuals helped make this happen. We would like to thank Guillaume Vallet, Adrien Faudot, and Gaëlle Despierre Corporon. We would also like to thank the wonderful staff at Edward Elgar for their continued support.

Introduction: moving forward

Louis-Philippe Rochon and Virginie Monvoisin

The financial crisis that began in 2007 has generally shown the weaknesses of neoclassical theories and policies, in particular by highlighting the irrelevance of modern macro models such as the Dynamic Stochastic General Equilibrium (DSGE) model and its microfoundations, which has come under considerable attack in the last few years, even from the mainstream. Indeed, as Lavoie (2018, p. 15) observes, "there is considerable dissatisfaction with the current state of mainstream macroeconomics", leading *The Economist* (2009) to refer to the "turmoil among macroeconomists".

As early as 2009, Krugman (2009a, Internet) was claiming "[t]he economics profession mistook beauty, clad in impressive-looking mathematics, for truth". More recently, he once again criticised the quest for microfoundations (see 2013, Internet), arguing "so the truth was that microfoundations in macroeconomics had its moment, but failed utterly at the one thing it was sold, above all, as being able to do – namely, give a better explanation of why nominal shocks have real effects. Time, you might think, to reconsider the project". A few years earlier, Solow, in a 2010 address to the United States Congress, disapprovingly claimed "I do not think that the currently popular DSGE models pass the smell test" (see Solow, 2010).

More recently, the *Oxford Review of Economic Policy* has dedicated two entire issues to the mainstream criticism, although a careful reading of the various contributions reveals the schism is not as deep (see Rochon and Rossi, 2018). Indeed, most articles are of the opinion that the problem with the DSGE model and its failure to predict the crisis or to suggest any meaningful policies since, is because of the lack of the right kind of microfoundations, or what King (2012, p. 150) describes as a debate over "our [microfoundations] are better than yours". There is no general call for the abandonment or replacement of DSGE models. Far from it. Rather, many are proposing amending the model and nothing more. Indeed, there are calls for the introduction of financial frictions, and other such imperfections, all in the aim of moving away from the RARE (rational expectations, representative agent) DSGE model (see King, 2012). Yet, attempts to introduce more realistic microfoundations hardly change the picture. As Solow (2008, p. 244) claimed a decade ago, "adding some realistic frictions does not make it any more plausible that an observed economy is acting out the desires of a single, consistent, forward-looking intelligence". King (2012) has called this the "microfoundations delusion". In this sense, Vines and Wills's (2018, p. 2) candid admission that it is "no longer clear what macroeconomic theory should look like", should not be interpreted as the mainstream's *mea culpa*, certainly not in the same way as post-Keynesians would mean it.

Yet, while the criticism in those articles may at times appear to be rather tame, there is nonetheless a general conclusion that emerges, one that may give hope to heterodox economists: many authors are calling for greater openness in the conduct of macroeconomic and monetary economics, and for the acceptance of parallel models.

For instance, among the most critical papers, Wren-Lewis (2018, p. 55) wishes to see parallel models exist alongside each other, rather than abandoning the DSGE model itself: "Just as microfoundations hegemony held back macroeconomics on that occasion, it is likely to do so again. Macroeconomics will develop more rapidly in useful directions if micro-founded models and more traditional SEMs work alongside each other, and are accorded equal academic respect". Wren-Lewis (2016, p. 27) made a similar statement two years earlier:

> The problem as I see it is more that in becoming the only accepted way of doing serious macroeconomic research and policy analysis, it [DSGE] (quite deliberately) crowded out other more traditional approaches that – had they persisted – might have left the discipline in a better position to understand the impact of the financial crisis. Furthermore, these alternative approaches might have encouraged the development of DSGE models in what we now know to be more fruitful directions.

Blanchard (2018, p. 51) takes a similar view. His solution is to have "different types of macro models" co-existing at the same time (2018, p. 44): a theory model (DSGE model) but also a number of policy models (data driven models), each with their respected strengths and weaknesses: "Not all models have to be explicitly microfounded. While this will sound like a plaidoyer *pro domo*, I strongly believe that *ad hoc* macro models, from various versions of the IS–LM to the Mundell–Fleming model, have an important role to play in relation to DSGE models. They can be useful upstream, before DSGE modelling, as a first cut to think about the effects of a particular distortion or a particular policy" (Blanchard, 2018, p. 48).

The bigger question, from a post-Keynesian perspective, however, remains to be seen: does this openness toward the existence of parallel models include post-Keynesian and heterodox models, most notably the agent-based or stock-flow consistency type? This is not an easy question to answer. One thing is certain, what these authors consider "traditional" is what post-Keynesians would call "neoclassical" or "mainstream", irrespective of whether these are microfounded or not.

THE NEXT CHAPTER

The observation that mainstream economic theory and policy seem to be at best at an eclectic place is not surprising. But in their desperation to appear more relevant and increasingly reflecting of the real world, mainstream authors are increasingly turning to ideas that have traditionally been the purview of post-Keynesians and other heterodox scholars. For instance, the recognition by New Consensus authors that central banks really control the rate of interest rather than the monetary based is a case in point, as is the increasing attention given to the income distributive nature of monetary policy (see Inui et al., 2017). To be sure, this intellectual encroachment is not limited to mainstream dissenters, but seems to be well spread.

Yet, in this new research, post-Keynesians are never, or rarely, cited: mainstream authors are peddling the illusion of scientific discovery. In this sense, there is a growing need to ensure that our views get heard. But how do we do that?

The post-Keynesian relationship with the mainstream is a complicated one, and has always been so. As King (2012, p. 1) explains, we can "fight them, cooperate with them, or ignore them". And while post-Keynesians have done all three with varying degrees of success, the conclusion remains the same: failure. The irony, of course, is that today while post-Keynesians remain marginalized, our ideas are nothing but and are being discovered by the mainstream.

The various authors in Lee and Lavoie (2011) propose a number of ways of engaging with the mainstream, by engaging with research departments in non-academic institutions like the IMF, or with faculty in business departments. But 8 years appears to be a long time: since that book was edited, we believe the time may be right to attempt to reach out (again?) to those doing research in overlapping areas of research, and engaging in a dialogue. The crisis has created an opening that seems to be right and which has not existed before. Of course, post-Keynesians should abandon neither their criticism of neoclassical economics nor the integrity of their work, but the continuous animosity between "us" and "them" is certainly a cause of our continued obscurity. If the argument rests in showing the mainstream that we matter, that there does exist an alternative, then the very idea that they are discovering long-held post-Keynesian views should make things easier. To be clear, this is not a call to dilute the post-Keynesian message, to the contrary if anything, we need to push the boundaries of heterodox economics even further.

Of course, the mainstream discovery of so many post-Keynesian ideas is wrapped in an unsavoury model, and there is little chance to convince them to abandon their cherished microfoundations. But one thing is certain, however: if we don't attempt a dialogue, we would have missed an enormous opportunity. A few examples of such an openness, for instance, is Wren-Lewis publishing in both the *International Journal of Political Economy* and the *Review of Keynesian Economics*; or Rochon's idea for a meeting on the 50th anniversary of Friedman's 1968 Presidential Address, subsequently published in the *Review of Keynesian Economics* (2018), containing articles by both established mainstream authors, such as Solow, De Long, Laidler, Gordon, Farmer and Forder, and some post-Keynesians.

To accomplish this, post-Keynesians must engage more in policy work and less in methodological navel gazing, such as eternal divisive debates and internal critiques, or never ending exegeses of structuralism and horizontalism.

The above comments will certainly generate further debate and questions, but at the heart of these ongoing reflections is the one, fundamental question "Where do we go from here?"

STRUCTURE OF THE BOOK

This book is the result of a get-together held in Grenoble, France, in December 2017. As editors, we chose a number of papers presented around three overall themes: finance and financialization, distribution and growth, and monetary policy.

The first part of the book on post-Keynesian views on finance and financialization focuses largely on issues of debt, financial flows, financialization and inequality.

In the opening chapter of the first section on finance, Marcello Spanò proposes an analysis of the composition of the yearly changes that occurred in sectorial balance sheets in fourteen founder countries of the European Union, from 1995 to 2015. He proposes a methodology based on stock-flow consistent accounting to analyze how superfluous financial flows grow and how they are allocated between sectors with different functions (purchasing power creators vs. users) and between different activities (real production vs. wealth appropriation), while also examining the impact of market revaluations on sectorial balance sheets.

He reaches three important conclusions. First, an increasing amount of credit creation has not been allocated to the generation of real income; second, a prevalent and growing share of the excess finance has circulated within the domestic and foreign financial sector only. Third, financial asset revaluations, which are of the same order of magnitude as private sector transaction flows, have a high incidence on the sectorial net financial position.

In Chapter 2, Óscar Dejuán and John McCombie discuss how credit explosions leading to asset bubbles and an increasing burden of debt are an endemic disease of advanced capitalism. Indeed, even the traditional originate-to-hold model of banking is not free from such a virus. The novelty of the originate-to-distribute model of finance, based on the securitization of mortgage loans, is that it has assembled the machinery to accelerate the process. The limit to credit expansion derives from the potential (full capacity) growth of output. If there is a systematic gap between both rates, the credit-led growth will eventually become a debt-burdened growth.

In Chapter 3, Bruno Bonizzi and Diego Guevara elaborate on the links between financialization and private pension funds in emerging economies. Firstly, they show how public pension systems (PAYGO) began to be replaced by private pension funds (AFP) under the mainstream argument that savings generate investment. In the second part of the chapter, the authors show how the promises of the AFPs in the emerging countries have not been accomplished in terms of coverage, low pension values and reductions of fiscal pressures. Finally, they analyze how AFP can be understood as a financialization enhancer in emerging economies, by increasing risk and dependence of global financial markets on local economies.

Chapter 4, by Alicia Girón and Marcia Solorza, is part of a greater study to explain how Argentina, Brazil and Mexico, through the processes of deregulation, liberalization and reform of the financial systems structure, were enrolled worldwide in the process of financialization, while the national banking industry insertion in the international financial circuits went deeper. Their research contextualizes the financialization process in the period after the breach of the Bretton Woods Agreement of the international monetary system, and the presentation of the degree of financial opening reached by those countries. The growth of financial services, current regulatory standards, and the levels of capital market deepening are analyzed.

In Chapter 5, Jonathan Perraton begins by acknowledging the growing recent literature examining the macroeconomic implications of household debt linking it to rising inequality across developed economies, which in turn contributes to stagnant or declining real incomes for middle- and lower-income households. Wages stagnated with their decoupling from productivity growth and rising inequality; households maintained consumption with falling savings and rising indebtedness. This consumption behaviour can be understood in terms of the emulation of consumption patterns through a relative income effect. A range of authors have argued household debt was central to the global financial crisis. More generally it has been argued that with rising inequality, aggregate demand was only being sustained by rising household indebtedness before the crisis, and since then held back by limited growth in household incomes. Thus, economies are prone to stagnation offset by periodic unsustainable credit booms.

To date, though, specific studies have focused almost exclusively on the US. There are a number of reasons why it may be useful to extend this analysis to European economies, allowing comparative tests of key hypotheses in this field. This chapter provides a comparative analysis across European economies to test the key hypotheses here, examining how far changes in inequality across these economies can explain debt levels and how far aggregate demand was sustained by rising household debt.

Chapter 6, by Hanna Szymborska, reviews policy proposals to reduce economic inequality in the context of the current institutional structures in the financial sector. It focuses on advanced economies, and the USA in particular. The chapter considers the impact the transformation of financial sector operations since the 1980s has had on income and wealth inequality. It provides an account of how this impact has undermined the effectiveness of policy instruments to tackle inequality. Having discussed why economic policy has failed to reduce income and wealth disparities in the USA, the author reviews policy proposals put forward in the inequality literature. These proposals are assessed in light of recent institutional changes in the US economy. The chapter calls for an explicit strategy to address wealth inequality alongside income, and highlights three areas of policy action to achieve sustainable reductions in economic inequality, focusing on wealth taxation, measures shaping the distribution of market wealth, and broader macroeconomic policy.

Hélène de Largentaye and Renaud du Tertre, in Chapter 7, argue that the casting aside in the 1970s and 1980s of economic policies inspired by Keynes's theory highlighting the role played by aggregate demand, in favour of policies inspired by neo-liberal postulates, laid the foundations for a neo-liberal growth regime in France in the 1990s. "Ordo-liberal" economic policies, a European brand of neo-liberalism, were carried out throughout the European monetary integration process (1993–2007).

Financial variables played a key role, replacing wages and job creation, which became adjustment variables. Consequently, employment and output growth were sacrificed. In the last period (2007–16), the same economic policies did not succeed in dealing with the Great Financial Crisis and the subsequent European Sovereign Debt crisis, so that employment and output continued to perform poorly and debt kept increasing. Recovery from this depressed situation would require a major European investment programme which could lay down the foundations for a new "sustainable development regime".

In Chapter 8, Pablo G. Bortz, Gabriel Michelena, and Fernando Toledo argue that starting in the early 1990s, several advanced and developing countries have adopted fiscal rules as their framework for determining their expenditure and tax policy, with the stated objective of securing the long-term solvency of the public debt. The adoption of ever-stricter fiscal rules has not been unchallenged. The authors extend the criticisms by differentiating between conventional and unconventional fiscal rules, and by adding to the discussion the importance of balance-of-payments considerations, particularly relevant for developing countries. Within an open economy Kaleckian model of growth and distribution, they conduct simulations to analyze the impact of changes in external lending when governments have rules constraining their expenditure rates. Results show that, with balance-of-payments dominance, public expenditures tend to be procyclical to changes in external lending, with an overshooting reaction, leading to cyclical dynamic patterns.

In the second part of the book, on post-Keynesian views on monetary policy, authors take a closer look at the nature of monetary and financial policies before and after the crisis.

Nathan Perry and Carlos Schönerwald, in Chapter 9, revisit the horizontalist (accommodationist) and structuralist debates and test the causality for the endogenous money hypothesis in the United States from 1980 to 2017. The authors employ Granger causality tests in order to determine the causality of loans to various bank level variables. The results show evidence for the endogenous money hypothesis. The combination of the results suggests that the demand for loans is the ultimate driver of bank activity, which is consistent with the endogenous money hypothesis.

In Chapter 10, Cristiano Boaventura Duarte explores corporate debt expansion in emerging countries after the 2008 crisis, emphasizing the growth of leverage, net foreign exchange exposure, and the deterioration in firms' debt repayment capacity. Next, the author does a panel regression to identify the main changes in the determinants of emerging market corporate debt expansion before and after the 2008 crisis. The conclusion suggests that the exchange rate was one of the most important determinants through the period 2000–16, and also in the period before 2008. But after 2008, beyond some country level factors (exchange rate, national GDP growth, firms' higher liquidity levels), other factors that have global origins (more accommodative monetary policy stance in USA, lower financial market volatility, higher commodity prices, global GDP growth) have become increasingly important. Duarte identifies a factor not previously emphasized in the literature, which investigates the determinants of corporate debt in emerging economies: the interaction between higher commodity prices and more appreciated exchange rates. Combined with a particularly uncertain international scenario, this rising indebtedness generated many challenges for enterprises in emerging economies: currency mismatch, firms' susceptibility to creditors'/banks'/institutional investors' interests, macroeconomic volatility. In addition, although several lines of defense have been developed by governments at national level, the capacity of these lines to provide the necessary support for private agents is still unclear, raising concerns with financial instability. Those concerns would be better addressed if emerging countries and international institutions took additional initiatives, such as an improvement in regulatory frameworks, as well as coordinated macro and micro-prudential measures. In this sense, an enhancement of the available instruments to face new financial crises would take place, opening space to pursue a better strategy towards sustainable growth in the medium/long-term.

In Chapter 11, Hasan Cömert argues that many economists see the concept of trilemma (where out of an independent monetary policy, free capital movement or a fixed exchange rate regime only two can exist at the same time) as a strong tool to explore the effectiveness of monetary policy during the Bretton Woods (BW) regime and afterwards. However, under this regime, beside capital controls, regulated domestic financial markets and diversity in central bank instruments contributed to the existence of independent monetary policy. After the collapse of the BW system, capital controls were lifted, domestic financial markets were deregulated, existing regulations were not implemented properly, and short-term interest rates became the sole instrument of central banks. Given the size of financial flows and financial markets has reached unprecedented levels, the author argues the effectiveness (either short- or long-term) of a central bank mainly depends on the institutional framework in which the central bank operates. Since there have been very dramatic changes in the institutional structure enabling domestic and international financial markets to be much more decisive in determining asset prices and credit expansion, the ability of central banks in both developed and developing countries has weakened although this is much more apparent in developing countries. This process can be considered a gradual transition from trilemma to dilemma implying that under current conditions exchange rate regimes become irrelevant for the effectiveness of central banks especially in developing countries. The unorthodox policies implemented after the global financial crisis in both advanced and developing countries can be considered partial realization of this dilemma by central banks.

In Chapter 12, Max Nagel and Matthias Thiemann argue that unconventional and highly accommodative monetary policies deployed by central banks after the financial crisis of 2007, reduced pressures on the economy and on financial markets. However, integrated monetary and financial systems transmit loose monetary and financing conditions across the globe, evoking volatile international capital flows and the unsustainable build-up of foreign-denominated debt. The authors trace the discussions in the international expert debate regarding these negative spillover effects, analyzing speeches and texts by the Federal Reserve, the International Monetary Fund (IMF) and the Bank for International Settlements (BIS). International debates among policymakers and experts could neither agree on the size of these negative spillovers nor how to counter them via adjustments of global monetary governance and monetary policy frameworks. However, they find that particularly the adoption of insights from international macro-finance induced a shift in the discourse of IMF and BIS towards the acknowledgment of the need to account for the role of monetary policies in affecting (international) financial stability. They conclude post-Keynesians could make a substantial contribution to this debate as alleys towards reform of global monetary governance and monetary policy frameworks open up.

The third part of the book addresses a topic of increased interest in post-Keynesian and heterodox economics: the dual economy, where two distinct sub-economies develop. On the one hand, there is a dominant economy, and on the other hand, a subservient economy, such as skilled vs unskilled labour, or even profit (or rentier) vs wage (or worker) economies. The fundamental question is whether such economies are sustainable or are they more prone to crises?

In Chapter 13, David Leadbeater offers "notes" on the dual economy, and presents a historical overview of the concept of dualism, before offering a critique of it. In his historical discussion, the author argues that the concept of dualism in labour market first appeared over discussion over race and gender, in the 1960s, along with the decline in unions.

Finally, in Chapter 14, Arpita Bhattacharjee and Gary Dymski begin by asking a number of questions. From their introduction, they ask how will the increasing presence of robots and artificial intelligence (AI) affect production and consumption processes? Do they constitute a threat to the human workers whose roles and tasks they increasingly replace, or a source of liberation from drudgery? Debate over these questions in journals and policy forums the world has exposed contradictory views, and led primarily to still further questions. Do robots create the conditions for a new human renaissance or endanger the rights of humans? And do robots threaten "us" because we don't know precisely what they can do, or what they can do that we can't? The profound uncertainty thus exposed constitutes a key aspect of this area of inquiry.

REFERENCES

Blanchard, O.J. (2018), "On the future of macroeconomic models", *Oxford Review of Economic Policy*, 34 (1–2), pp. 43–54.

Inui, M., N.Sudo and T. Yamada (2017), "The effects of monetary policy shocks on inequality in Japan", BIS No. 642, https://www.bis.org/publ/work642.pdf.

King, J.E. (2012), *The Microfoundations Delusion: Metaphor and Dogma in the History of Macroeconomics*, Cheltenham, UK and Northampton, MA, USA: Edward Elgar.

Krugman, P. (2009a), "How did economists get it so wrong?", *The New York Times Magazine*, September 2, available at www.nytimes.com/2009/09/06/magazine/06 Economic-t.html. Last accessed August 27, 2018.

Krugman, P. (2013), "Microfoundations and the parting of the waters", *New York Times Blogs*, December 20, available at https://krugman.blogs.nytimes.com/2013/12/20/microfoundations-and-the-parting-of-the-waters/. Last accessed August 24, 2018.

Lee, F.S. and M. Lavoie (eds) (2013), *In Defense of Post-Keynesian Economics and Heterodox Economics: Response to their Critics*, London: Routledge.

Lavoie, M. (2018), "Rethinking macroeconomic theory before the next crisis", *Review of Keynesian Economics*, 6 (1), pp. 1–21.

Rochon, L.-P. and S. Rossi (2018), "The state of macro", *Ola Financiera*, forthcoming.

Solow, R. (2008), "The state of macroeconomics", *Journal of Economic Perspectives*, 22 (1), pp. 243–249.

Solow, R. (2010), "Building a science of economics for the real world", House Committee on Science and Technology, Subcommittee on Investigations and Oversight, July 20.

The Economist (2009), "The other-worldly philosophers", July 16, available at https://www.economist.com/briefing/2009/07/16/the-other-worldly-philosophers. Last accessed August 12, 2018.

Vines, D. and S. Wills (2018), "The rebuilding macroeconomic theory project: an analytical assessment", *Oxford Review of Economic Policy*, 34 (1–2), pp. 1–42.

Wren-Lewis, S. (2016), "Unravelling the new classical counter revolution", *Review of Keynesian Economics*, 4 (1), pp. 20–35.

Wren-Lewis, S. (2018), "Ending the microfoundations hegemony", *Oxford Review of Economic Policy*, 34 (1–2), pp. 55–69.

PART 1

Post-Keynesian views on finance and financialization

1. Measuring finance for the economy and finance for finance

Marcello Spanò

INTRODUCTION

This work proposes a new approach to measuring the creation of finance in excess of the quantity needed by the real economy, and to assess how finance is distributed across sectors. The methodology is validated by examining yearly changes that occurred in sectorial balance sheets in 14 founder countries of the European Union from 1995 to 2015.

Measuring the superfluous amount of finance in Europe is relevant for at least three reasons. First, a general reason is that finance is crucial in economic analysis. In modern industrialised economies the economic system is a monetary economy of production, where the production of goods and services cannot take place without the opportune creation and circulation of financial capital. Finance is needed in each period to both reactivate existing real activities and provide funds for new activities (Schumpeter, 1912; Keynes, 1937; Graziani, 2003; Godley and Lavoie, 2007; Keen, 2010).[1] The present study empirically identifies the flows of finance that are inessential to carry out the process of economic production and provides the basis for a discussion on reforms aimed at restoring and safeguarding the crucial role of the financial system.

The second reason is that the role of finance has changed in quality and quantity over the last three decades. This has been investigated by a strand of studies on the financialisation of the economy which has addressed different aspects: single individuals enhancing indebtedness, risk-taking positions and participation in financial markets (Lapavistas, 2011; Martin, 2002); corporate management increasingly targeted at maximising shareholder value (Gallino, 2005; Krippner, 2005); financial assets increasingly used as sources of profitability instead of real production (Epstein, 2005; Erturk et al., 2008; Pollin, 2007; Van Treeck, 2009). The financialisation of the economy has also been associated with income polarisation and inequality (Onaran et al., 2011; Palma, 2009; Stockhammer, 2015), with endogenous financial instability and global imbalances (Crotty, 2008;

Keen, 2011; Kindleberger, 1986; Minsky, 1986; Nersisyan and Wray, 2010), and with the inadequacy of regulation (Lordon, 2011). This study provides new evidence for the analysis of financialisation by detecting how superfluous financial flows grow and how they are allocated, subject to overarching accounting constraints, between sectors which have different functions (purchasing power creators vs users) and between different economic activities (real production vs. wealth appropriation).

The third reason relates specifically to the debate on the advanced European economies, which are still trapped in a low demand and production equilibrium. Different studies of European economies have already underlined how macroeconomic imbalances can be traced back to institutional flaws within the Eurozone, which is characterised by a common currency (and clearing account system), by the separation of monetary and fiscal authorities, and by bank balance sheets and household debt growing in an uncontrolled way (Wray, 2012; De Grauwe, 2013; Storm, 2016; Lavoie, 2015; Mitchell, 2016). Whatever strategy is suggested to resolve the problem, it is generally agreed that downsizing the financial sector and increasing regulation is an essential step to restore stability and growth (Febrero et al., 2018). The present work provides new empirical tools to examine and reinterpret the imbalances in Europe in terms of the creation of excessive finance. What is more, such a phenomenon is not exclusively associated with the set of rules adopted within the Eurozone, but rather with rising financial integration across all European economies, including those that have kept their national currencies.

The financial flows of the 14 countries of the European Union (EU14) examined in this work are divided into three different components: (i) transactions in financial assets that are associated with the process of real economic decisions on production and spending; (ii) transactions in financial assets that are not clearly related to economic transactions; (iii) changes in the market value of existing and newly created financial assets. As the first two components cannot be distinguished from official accounting, two proxies are here proposed as analytical tools to separate them and to provide measures of deliberately created excessive, unnecessary finance.

Financial flows are analysed by separating and quantifying flows that are channelled into the real sectors of the economy and flows that only circulate within the financial sector at the international level. To this end, the institutional sectors of the economies are grouped into two macro sectors on the basis of their ability to create and/or control the allocation of purchasing power. The foreign sector and domestic financial sector are treated as a single macroeconomic sector responsible for creating, distributing and directing financial flows across sectors and countries. The second macro sector aggregates all the domestic sectors that need financial flows to carry out economic production and transactions. It aggregates households, non-financial corporations and the government. The main function of the real domestic sector is to generate most of the value added by using the financial sources available.

The remainder of the chapter is organised as follows: Section 2 describes the accounting framework and defines the proxies and variables used for the empirical analysis; Sections 3 and 4, respectively, report the results of the two proxies, identifying superfluous flows of finance; Section 5 reports the results on volumes of flows generated by transactions (separated into formal and informal assets) in comparison with valuation effects due to market price changes; Section 6 concludes.

ACCOUNTING FRAMEWORK AND METHODOLOGY

The collected dataset provides information on financial flows within the 14 founder countries of the European Union (EU14), on a sector-by-sector basis, over 21 years (1995–2015). Data have been collected from Eurostat, Annual sector accounts (ESA2010).[2] In line with the stock-flow accounting tradition (Godley and Lavoie, 2007), this study builds on a fully integrated dataset reporting economic transactions, financial transactions and revaluation of assets. This approach makes it possible to monitor how financial flows are distributed across all sectors of the economy, how this distribution changes over time, how major changes in investment and saving are related to changes in financial transactions, and to changes in the value of net assets.

Definitions and Aggregation

Table 1.1 reports two examples, referring to the year 2006 for the UK and Spain, of the accounting matrix integrating the transaction flows of sectors and the changes in values of the financial stocks from balance sheets. This includes three sections. The first reports conventional income and expenditure flows, aggregated in the saving and investment. *Saving* (line a) is what is left from disposable income after taking out consumption and adding net capital transfer. *Investment* (line b) refers to real capital and excludes financial assets, therefore it aggregates gross fixed capital formation, changes in inventories, acquisitions less disposals of valuables, acquisition less disposals of non-produced non-financial assets.[3] The balancing item in line A, *Net saving*, is the difference between saving and investment.

Table 1.1 Sectorial accounting: flow-of-funds, proxies and revaluation

	Percent of GDP							
UK. 2006	NFC	GOV	HH	RD	FC	RoW	FF	SUM
a Saving	4.98	−1.69	−0.48	2.81	−0.75	2.33	1.58	4.38
b. Investment	2.46	1.12	0.68	4.27	0.12	0.00	0.12	4.38
A. Surplus (a-b)	**2.51**	**−2.81**	**−1.16**	**−1.46**	**−0.87**	**2.33**	**1.46**	**0.00**
c. Lending (Δ fin. assets)	10.70	0.83	10.92	22.45	92.81	42.88	135.69	158.14
d. Borrowing (Δ fin. liab)	9.10	3.67	11.23	24.00	93.22	40.92	134.14	158.14
Borrowing exceeding investment (d-b)	*6.64*	*2.55*	*10.55*	19.73	*93.11*	*40.92*	*134.02*	
B. Net lending (c-d)	**1.60**	**−2.84**	**−0.31**	**−1.55**	**−0.42**	**1.96**	**1.55**	**0.01**
Excess financial flows	*9.10*	*0.83*	*10.92*		*92.81*	*40.92*		
e. Δ value of assets	9.84	1.06	17.27	28.17	100.14	44.49	144.63	172.80
f. Δ value of liab.	13.37	7.07	11.19	31.63	99.89	41.25	141.14	172.77
C. Valuation effects (e-f)	**−3.54**	**−6.01**	**6.08**	**−3.46**	**0.26**	**3.24**	**3.50**	**0.04**
D. Δ value of net assets (B+C)	**−1.93**	**−8.85**	**5.78**	**−5.01**	**−0.16**	**5.21**	**5.04**	**0.04**
SPAIN. 2006	NFC	GOV	HH	RD	FC	RoW	FF	SUM
a. Saving (Δ net worth)	1.20	4.32	1.32	6.84	1.00	8.46	9.46	16.30
b. Investment	8.72	2.13	5.35	16.20	0.14	−0.04	0.10	16.30
A. Surplus (a-b)	**−7.52**	**2.20**	**−4.03**	**−9.36**	**0.85**	**8.51**	**9.36**	**0.00**
c. Lending (Δ fin. assets)	25.58	3.08	10.58	39.24	52.04	25.91	77.94	117.18
d. Borrowing (Δ fin. liab)	33.98	0.89	13.73	48.60	51.19	17.40	68.59	117.18
Borrowing exceedinginvestment (d-b)	*25.26*	*−1.24*	*8.38*	32.40	*51.04*	*17.44*	*68.48*	
B. Net lending (c-d)	**−8.40**	**2.20**	**−3.16**	**−9.36**	**0.85**	**8.51**	**9.36**	**0.01**
Excess financial flows	25.58	0.89	10.58		*51.19*	*17.40*		
e. Δ value of assets	31.28	3.14	25.21	59.63	51.93	25.03	76.96	136.59
f. Δ value of liab.	30.82	−4.12	8.16	34.86	56.49	5.62	62.11	96.97
C. Valuation effects (e-f)	**0.46**	**7.25**	**17.05**	**24.77**	**−4.56**	**19.41**	**14.85**	**39.61**
D. Δ value of net assets (B+C)	**−7.94**	**9.45**	**13.90**	**15.41**	**−3.71**	**27.92**	**24.21**	**39.61**

The second section reports flows of assets and liabilities arising from financial transactions. *Lending* (line c) refers to net acquisition of financial assets, *Borrowing* (line d) to net incurrence of financial liabilities, both items balancing in line B, *Net lending*. Consistency across flows is assured by the fact that the sum of sectorial deficits and surpluses of an economy must be equal to zero. This must be verified when the balances of both non-financial (line A) and financial (line B) transactions are considered, the difference being due to statistical discrepancy.

The third section reports changes in the values of assets and liabilities that do not arise from financial transactions. These include the revaluation of assets (nominal holding gains(+)/losses(−)) and other changes in volumes. They aggregate the changes in the value of financial stocks (assets in line e, liabilities in line f) that had occurred by the end of the accounting period. Stocks refer to all financial assets (liabilities), whether they are inherited from the previous period or added in the accounting period. Line C, *Valuation effects*, balances changes in the value of assets and liabilities.

The sectors considered are the 5 institutional sectors defined by the ESA accounting agreement: non-financial corporations (NFC), General government (GOV), Households and Non-profit institutions servicing households (HH), Financial corporations (FC) and Rest of the World (RoW). For the purposes of separating and quantifying flows that are channelled to the real sectors of the economy, and flows that only circulate within the financial sector at the international level, throughout this work these institutional sectors are also grouped into two macro sectors: real domestic sector (RD) aggregating NFC, GOV and HH; and foreign and financial sector (FF) aggregating FC and RoW.

This choice of aggregation is likely to generate perplexity in some readers with a background in post-Keynesian thinking. According to the circuitist viewpoint (Rochon, 1999; Keen, 2015) it is incorrect to consider the whole financial sector as a creator of financial flows, as only the banks play this role by issuing new credit, whereas the non-bank financial institutions deal with the portfolio allocation of pre-existing stocks. This study is well aware of the specific role of the banking system in creating credit *ex nihilo*. However, its purpose is to measure excess finance in a context where the financialisation of the economy has increased the complexity of financial instruments. The emphasis is on the ability of the whole international financial sector not only to create new credit, but also to control, direct and allocate the quantity and value of the financial wealth (including the existing assets inherited from the past). Moreover, even from a circuitist viewpoint, non-bank institutions can be interpreted as symbiotic to the banking system in creating a liquid short-term store of wealth that can be considered as near-monies (Michell, 2017). A second perplexity might arise from readers who adopt the viewpoint of the Modern Money Theory (MMT). In their view, the choice of classifying the government as a sector that does not create money can be criticised as the government is the only possible issuer of the net financial assets held by the non-government sector (Wray, 2012; Mitchell, 2016). The definition of government by the MMT, however, considers the treasury and the central bank as a single consolidated sector. While this perspective can be fully endorsed from a theoretical point of view, there are two reasons why it is not adopted in this work. The first is that the central bank represents a supranational institution in 10 countries of the Eurozone, out of the EU14 group; therefore, it would be a difficult task to consider it as part of a single country's consolidated government sector. The second reason is that the MMT view that government finance is substantially unconstrained is not shared by actual practice in the EU, which is driven by the mainstream theory that government spending needs to be funded by either taxes or private saving. The outcome is that national governments often behave as if they were constrained. Moreover, apart from self-imposed rules, as the authors promoting MMT clearly underline, national governments in the Eurozone are truly money users without being money issuers, and their debt is no longer default-free.

Proxies and Variables Under Observation

The value of financial assets or liabilities can change as a result of three components: (i) transactions in financial assets that are a direct counterpart of economic transactions; (ii) transactions in financial assets that are not clearly related to economic transactions; (iii) changes in the market value of existing and newly created financial assets.

Accounting rules alone do not allow us to distinguish between the first and the second components. However, it should be clear that, while a sector's net lending is of the same amount as its surplus, gross lending and borrowing items are virtually unlimited. Asset creation and transactions, generally speaking, are not the simple effect of net saving flows adding to existing stocks. Lending does not need prior saving, it needs the availability of means of payments (typically, a line of bank credit). Borrowing might not be channelled to real expenditure in newly produced goods and services, but to purchasing a stock of assets (either real or financial).

To assess how, each year, transactions in financial flows can be delinked from sectorial real transactions in produced goods and services, two proxies are here defined (and reported in Table 1.1).

The first proxy measures sectorial *Borrowing exceeding investment*. It takes inspiration from the theory of Schumpeter (1912), according to which the fundamental role of newly issued credit is to finance a change in the productive system. The liabilities of a sector exceeding its investment are interpreted as a signal that this sector has increased borrowing to undertake transactions that are not related to new productive capacity. The mirror image of this process is lending exceeding saving, which is identically equal to the exceeding incurrence of liabilities, given the accounting rule that the net lending of a sector is equal to its surplus.

The second proxy defines *Excess financial flows* (EFF) with respect to the sectorial net lending position (line B). This takes inspiration from the idea that the financial sector makes sure that sectors in surplus are final holders of the financial liabilities of sectors in deficit. As sectors in deficit are net borrowers by definition, financial flows in excess arise from the amount of borrowing exceeding their deficit. Given that:

$$\text{Borrowing (d)} - \text{Net borrowing (d} - \text{c)} = \text{Lending (c)},$$

the proxy EFF of a sector in deficit is equal to its (gross) lending. Similarly, as sectors in surplus are net lenders, EFF takes the value from the amount of the sector's (gross) borrowing. To focus on the creation and allocation of additional flows of superflous finance, negative values of EFF are set equal to zero.

Valuation effects are the last element of the chain going from economic transactions to changes in gross and net financial assets, the latter being accounted in the sectorial balance sheets. They will be examined separately from the flows of financial assets arising from transactions. As value changes, roughly speaking, are determined by price movements in financial markets, they are not intrinsically connected with sectorial surplus and deficit positions. It may thus happen that a sector registers a negative change in the overall value of its net financial assets even though it realises a surplus from economic transactions (see NFC in UK in 2006, Table 1.1). Moreover, the sum of the valuation effect of all sectors is not bound to be zero, as it depends on the composition of the asset portfolios.

Throughout the analysis (see below), financial assets are broken down into two quantities, here labelled formal and informal claims. Formal claims are fixed income commitments to other sectors, that is, all claims legally binding on a nominal value determined at the date they are issued: failure to pay the holder implies bankruptcy of the issuer disciplined by law; they include money items, debt securities and loans. Informal claims are the residual, non-fixed income categories (equities, insurance, pensions, financial derivatives and other accounts), plus fixed income claims whose counterpart is from the same sector. By separating formal and informal claims, it is possible to observe items and commitments of different characteristics, in terms of market value exposure.

BORROWING EXCEEDING INVESTMENT

In the examination of the first proxy, borrowing exceeding investment, we focus on aggregate sectors to underline the connection between sectors that collect and create purchasing power (FF) and sectors that use it (RD), as illustrated in Figure 1.1 for some selected countries (the UK, France, Spain, Germany). The figure decomposes total borrowing into investment plus borrowing exceeding investment and (mirror side) total lending into saving plus lending exceeding saving. The continuous line reports the balance of the RD sectors, which is approximately equal to the country's current account (as the FC balance is nearly zero).

We first analyse borrowing exceeding investment for RD sectors in isolation, to quantify the size of financial flows available to the real economy which exceed its investment in productive capacity. Subsequently, we compare the same proxy with that of the FF sectors, to quantify the financial flows that do not even seem to be channelled to the RD sector.

The RD sectors of the economy appear to have increased their borrowing in excess of their investment over the two decades considered, and they did so at a higher intensity in the period 1999–2007, with a median value of around 12% of GDP per year. The trend towards increasing borrowing beyond investment continued even during and after the credit crunch crisis (Spain is the only country where the RD sector deleveraged during the credit crunch period). The distribution of flows within the RD sectors has changed over time: from 1999 to 2002, the years of the bubble in the stock market brought about by the dotcom companies, the rise in assets from transactions was led by non-financial corporations (NFC), which increased excess liabilities by 38.7% (median level) over 4 years. In the following period, culminating in the credit crunch crisis (2003–2007), characterised by credit financing (mainly) housing and consumption levels, the Households sector (HH) also remarkably increased its excess financial positions: excess borrowing increased by 15.2% over 5 years. During the years of the great recession, the rise in excess liabilities of the RD sector as a whole can be mainly attributed to GOV, to facilitate the restoration of the private sector's balance sheets to more sustainable positions in terms of both risk exposure and net worth, whereas NFC remained nearly unchanged and HH slightly decreased.

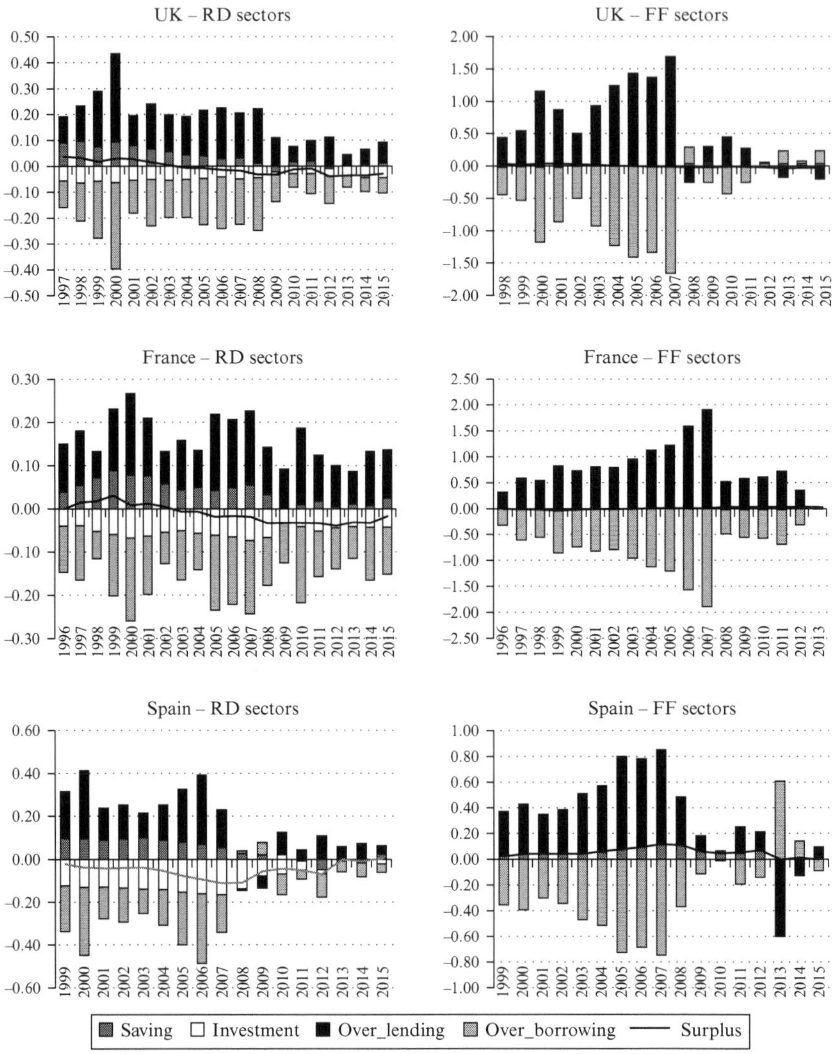

Figure 1.1 Saving and investment vs. lending and borrowing

Comparing the FF and RD sectors, the difference in the size of lending and borrowing is striking. As accounting rules imply that the net lending of RD and FF are perfectly balanced, the systematically higher gross financial flows in the FF sector should be interpreted as flows of funds that are likely to be generated and transacted within the FF sector, thus across domestic and foreign financial organisations, without flowing through the

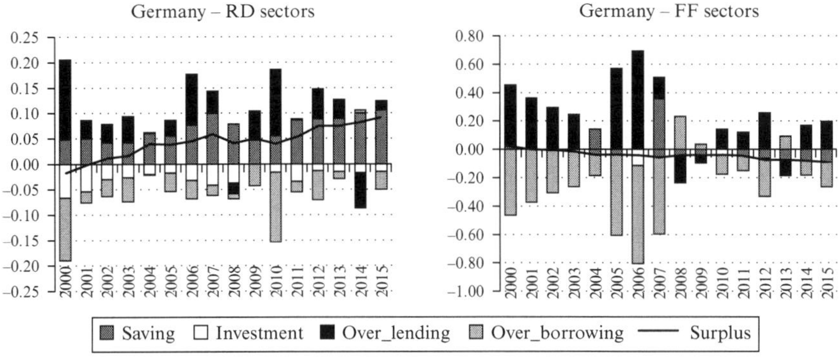

Figure 1.1 (continued)

RD sector. The yearly median value of borrowing exceeding investment was 43% of GDP from 1999 to 2002 (30% higher than RD) and 67% (55% higher than RD) from 2003 to 2007. The crisis and the following years of great recession have hit gross financial flows more dramatically in the FF sectors, where they were disproportionate compared to RD; however, they have not clearly inverted (only restrained) the process of enhancing financial balance sheet items from transactions.

Borrowing exceeding investment can be interpreted, in the light of Schumpeter's analysis, as a measure of the new credit that is not used for its essential purpose, which is, precisely, to finance the new investment (Schumpeter, 1912).[4] The proxy reveals that a large share of the new borrowing is used to purchase existing financial assets, thereby adding 'to society's debt level without increasing its productive capacity' (Keen, 2011, p.339). Borrowing in excess of the productive needs does not enhance the prosperity of the society as a whole, although it can be profitable. Especially in a context of rising stock prices (in both the stock market and housing market), banks may consider a customer wishing to purchase existing wealth as safer and more creditworthy than one planning to transform the productive structure of the economy. Back in 1936 Keynes had already underlined, in his Chapter XII of the General Theory, that the development of the 'organised investment markets' changed the nature of the investment, from the entrepreneurial one – irrevocable and based on genuine knowledge and non-measurable returns – to a portfolio one – revisable and based on conventional knowledge and tentative measurements of risky outcomes (Keynes, 1936, pp.152–3). The observed excess lending (and borrowing) is consistent with this change in perspective and suggests that banks have adapted their conventional assessment of customer creditworthiness to suit a widespread, long term wave of rent-seeking practices (Palma, 2009).

EXCESS FINANCIAL FLOWS

The second proxy isolating the flows of financial transactions that are not clearly related to real economic activities, EFF, is equal to gross lending for a net borrower sector and to gross borrowing for a net lender sector (see Table 1.1). Two observations will be raised in relation to this second proxy: one is theoretical, the other is technical.

The first observation is that EFF is more flexible, in theoretical terms, than the proxy in the previous section, as it is not limited to the view that 'normal' or 'essential' borrowing should be equal to the investment. The idea behind the EFF proxy is that essential financial flows are needed to assist the real economic process by guaranteeing the connection between surpluses and deficits at any stage of the circuit. In a simple scheme of a pure credit economy, initial finance corresponds to a creation of financial funds (deposits) available to the producer. These are immediately transferred to pay wages and constitute households' income (surplus), which is equal to firms' investment (deficit). In the final stage of the circuit, firms collect back (part of) the cash balances from households by either selling goods (for consumption) or by issuing equities (Godley and Lavoie, 2007). This, in principle, should allow the firms to reduce their outstanding loans, even though, in practice, finance is rolled over to restart the circuit (Keynes, 1937; Keen, 2010, 2011). EFF captures the financial flows that are generated in addition to this needed finance, since, at the date of accounting, it measures the amount of borrowing exceeding a sector's deficit or the amount of lending exceeding a sector's surplus.

The second observation is a warning about the way numbers will be interpreted. As the data are non-consolidated, sectorial measures of EFF, by definition, include lending (and borrowing) between subjects aggregated in the same sector (for instance, a non-financial firm holding obligations of another non-financial firm). As intra-sector lending is not automatically interpretable as non-essential, EFF levels might overestimate excess finance. To minimise the intra-sectorial component, the proxy is applied to the five institutional sectors, and not to the RD and FF macro sectors. Given this caveat, we shall consider the proxy as more effective at interpreting excess finance if we focus on dynamics over time and on relative levels rather than on absolute levels.

To provide a different perspective from the last section, the size of a sector's EFF is divided by the GDP of all EU14 countries (not by a single country's GDP). The sum of all countries' sectorial EFF is economically meaningful: it is a proxy for non-essential financial transactions globally associated with the same sector in the whole EU14 economy. Figure 1.2 illustrates the results.

The overall picture emerging with the EFF proxy for financial transactions unrelated to the real economy is similar to and consistent with that described in the last section referring to borrowing exceeding investment. All RD sectors increase the excess financial flows over the period considered: NFC and the HH sectors before and GOV after the crisis. The peak of EFF for the NFC sector is in 2000 (nearly 18% of EU14 GDP) and not in 2006 (nearly 11%) as for the other private sectors (HH, FC, RoW). The EFF of the HH sector fluctuates between 4% and 6% of EU14 GDP before 2008 and then drastically decreases below 2%. The high EFF from 1999 to 2007 can be associated to the massive amount of credit flowing to households to finance housing, consumption and acquisitions of financial assets out of their disposable income allowance. After 2008, credit to households has dropped, as has the EFF. National governments try to cushion the consequence of the crisis by increasing excess borrowing, and thereby EFF, to help other sectors to reduce their liabilities simultaneously. Governments of different countries have broken records in their level of EFF in different years after the credit crunch: the UK in 2008/09 (a faster reaction to the financial crisis and bank bailouts), Germany in 2010, Spain and France in 2012. As a result, RD sectors, by expanding gross items of financial balance sheets, increase the proportion of transactions financed by debt and decrease the proportion financed by disposable income (Bezemer, 2010; Keen, 2015). This enhances the dependency of RD sectors on the liabilities made available by the financial sector (at both the domestic and the international levels).

The continental financial institutions collect or deliberately create financial assets in excess of real economic needs until 2008, thereby establishing a cumulative growth in the volume of financial assets and liabilities in the whole EU14 zone. FC yearly value of EFF (equivalent to 30% of EU14 GDP) is nearly double that of NFC and six times higher than HH in the earlier years (1999–2002), and rises progressively to a level 7 times higher than NFC and 15 times higher than HH in 2007 (equivalent to 70% of EU14 GDP). The EFF of the RoW sector isolates the share of financial transactions that are carried out across countries and is more than half the value of FC before 2008, less than half after 2008. This confirms the high degree of internationalisation of financial markets, but also the restraint in the balance of payments' financial account flows that occurred in the aftermath of the credit crunch across EU countries, especially in the Eurozone.

The crisis and the subsequent economic slowdown have brought about a fall in the creation of excess finance at a continental level, and a partial shift in the debt burden to governments. The extent of the EFF of the

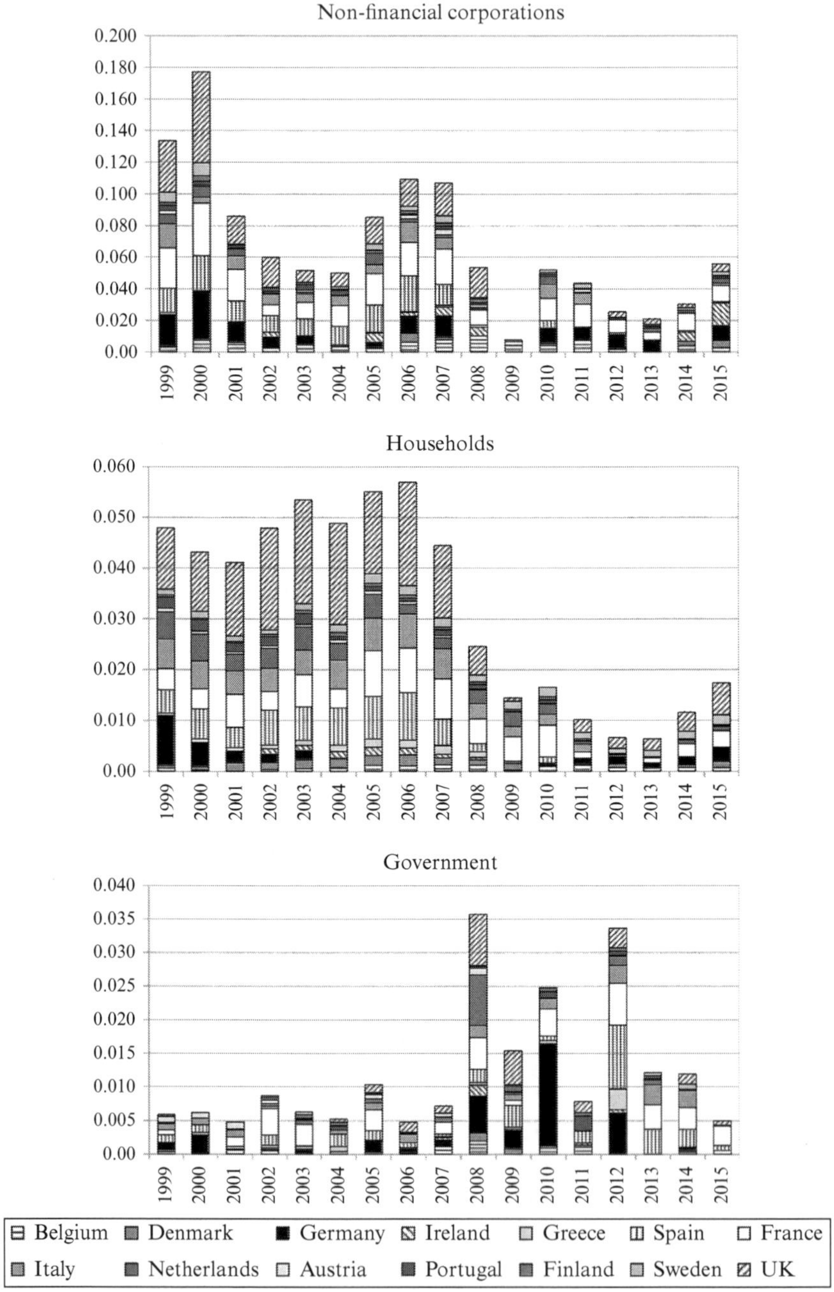

Figure 1.2 Excess financial flows by sector and country

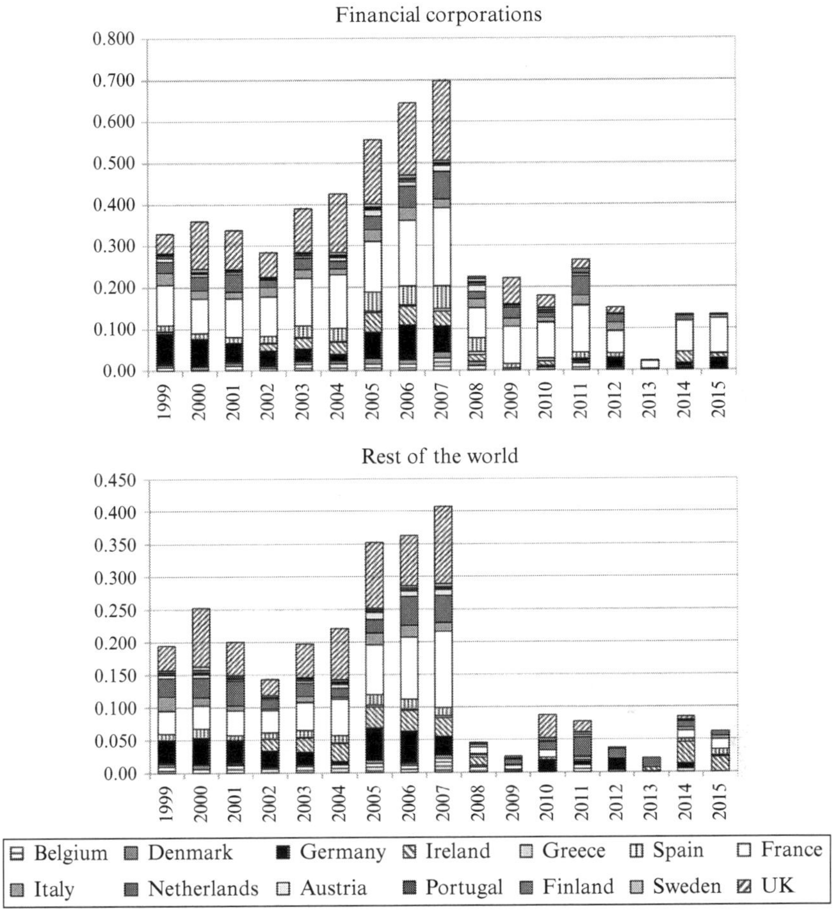

Figure 1.2 (continued)

financial sector has decreased sharply, even in relative terms with respect to RD sectors: in 2015, the EFF is of the order of magnitude of 10% of EU14 GDP for FC, 1% for GOV, 2% for HH and 5% for NFC. It should be remarked, thus, that excess finance has not disappeared. While the yearly flow is definitely lower than that of the pre-crisis period, and although it is still constant, nevertheless it is not zero. Neither in the borrowing exceeding investment proxy (Section 3), nor in the EFF proxy can a clear tendency to reduce the size of the financial stocks to levels comparable with those of the 1990s be envisaged: the proportion of financial balance sheet stocks of the FC sector is still close to the highest levels reached in 2007. This is not necessarily a signal of unchanged danger, as balance sheet items of the central banks rose and many toxic assets have been cleared away from non-banking financial firms. A more detailed assessment of the current stability of the financial sector requires a more thorough analysis of the composition of the financial portfolios, which is outside the scope of this study. What is worth noticing, however, as a potential warning, is the path-dependency of the size of the financial sector, whose level, eight years after the crisis, was as large as it was just before it (Spanò, 2015; Tissot, 2016).

TRANSACTIONS AND VALUATION EFFECTS

Changes in sectorial balance sheets are affected by financial transactions, resulting from deliberate decisions, and from valuation effects, resulting mainly from market price changes. In this section we compare both the sources of changes in the values of assets and liabilities and we underline their relative importance. From the analysis of the data, it is possible to establish that valuation effects are not only strongly associated with changes in the size of financial balance sheets (gross values of assets and liabilities), but they are also heavily associated with changes in the net value. We first focus on gross values and, subsequently, on the net values of financial balance sheets.

Table 1.2 reports the median values to GDP ratios of all EU14 countries resulting from transactions (Panel A) and from valuations (Panel B). Assets are divided into two typologies, labelled formal and informal, as defined in Section 2. Valuation effects due to price changes hit informal more than formal types of assets.

The HH sector increases net lending in informal assets and net borrowing in formal assets from financial transactions. This is consistent with the analysis of excess finance in the previous two sections and suggests that part of the borrowing, especially before 2008, was channelled to financial transactions in informal assets. The change in valuation of informal assets is positive for HH in normal years and negative in the years of financial crisis, i.e. in 2000–2002 and in 2008 (the latter fall being huge: –18% of GDP the median, –21% the mean). The size of the valuation effects of informal assets is of the same order of magnitude as flows from transactions, thereby leading to double the value of flows deliberately generated and boosting the asset side of HH financial balance sheets.

The NFC sector also increases net lending in informal assets and, before 2008, net borrowing in formal assets. The change in valuation of informal liabilities mirrors that observed for HH. The sign reverses in the years of

Table 1.2 Changes in net assets and liabilities; formal vs. informal assets

EU14 sectors' median values. Ratios to GDP

Panel A. Changes arising from transactions

		Assets						Liabilities					
		1995–98	1999–02	2003–07	2008–09	2010–13	2014–15	1995–98	1999–02	2003–07	2008–09	2010–13	2014–15
HH	formal	0.049	0.100	0.187	0.056	0.055	0.004	0.076	0.147	0.307	0.050	0.027	0.006
	informal	0.174	0.227	0.213	0.039	0.072	0.029	0.005	0.018	0.011	0.003	0.001	0.001
NFC	formal	0.077	0.115	0.133	0.033	0.052	0.009	0.101	0.224	0.268	0.086	0.033	−0.007
	informal	0.164	0.333	0.365	0.043	0.107	0.043	0.142	0.235	0.178	0.026	0.087	0.037
GOV	formal	−0.001	0.016	0.020	0.023	0.019	0.001	0.072	0.041	0.080	0.138	0.186	0.039
	informal	0.015	0.024	0.038	0.019	0.020	0.007	0.024	0.028	0.028	0.004	0.009	0.006
RD	formal	**0.095**	**0.311**	**0.313**	**0.128**	**0.130**	**0.015**	**0.178**	**0.239**	**0.483**	**0.186**	**0.225**	**0.031**
	informal	**0.413**	**0.440**	**0.592**	**0.119**	**0.262**	**0.097**	**0.042**	**0.050**	**0.044**	**0.017**	**0.011**	**0.017**
FC	formal	0.314	0.555	1.092	0.178	0.054	0.038	0.176	0.427	0.823	0.142	−0.014	−0.004
	informal	0.331	0.415	0.993	0.186	0.216	−0.004	0.436	0.473	1.137	0.294	0.234	0.020
RoW	formal	0.219	0.454	0.858	0.118	0.062	0.022	0.169	0.379	0.672	0.030	−0.044	0.016
	informal	0.101	0.215	0.264	0.036	0.064	0.041	0.137	0.311	0.399	0.046	0.101	0.052
FF	formal	**0.525**	**1.002**	**1.964**	**0.254**	**0.184**	**0.045**	**0.354**	**0.851**	**1.575**	**0.128**	**−0.008**	**0.045**
	informal	**0.420**	**0.556**	**1.194**	**0.297**	**0.312**	**0.015**	**0.527**	**0.751**	**1.554**	**0.341**	**0.405**	**0.052**

Table 1.2 (continued)

EU14 sectors' median values. Ratios to GDP

Panel B. Changes arising from valuation effects

		Assets						Liabilities					
		1995–98	1999–02	2003–07	2008–09	2010–13	2014–15	1995–98	1999–02	2003–07	2008–09	2010–13	2014–15
HH	formal	−0.004	−0.003	−0.010	−0.001	0.005	0.004	−0.014	0.000	−0.001	0.000	0.001	0.000
	informal	0.190	0.002	0.221	−0.126	0.187	0.051	−0.002	0.000	0.000	0.000	0.000	0.000
NFC	formal	−0.010	−0.006	−0.017	0.001	−0.003	0.004	−0.005	0.020	−0.030	−0.002	0.002	0.004
	informal	0.197	−0.060	0.141	−0.060	0.049	0.006	0.429	0.023	0.420	−0.221	0.176	0.031
GOV	formal	−0.005	0.001	−0.001	0.000	0.007	0.002	0.013	−0.004	−0.021	0.013	0.031	0.055
	informal	0.030	0.014	0.043	−0.008	0.030	0.019	−0.001	0.001	0.002	0.002	0.003	0.001
RD	formal	**−0.005**	**0.007**	**−0.015**	**0.002**	**0.019**	**0.010**	**−0.001**	**−0.008**	**−0.023**	**0.015**	**0.040**	**0.056**
	informal	**0.237**	**0.038**	**0.300**	**−0.126**	**0.221**	**0.045**	**−0.004**	**0.001**	**0.008**	**0.001**	**0.001**	**0.001**
FC	formal	−0.003	0.008	−0.050	0.009	0.059	0.072	0.017	−0.008	−0.043	0.015	0.022	0.029
	informal	0.112	−0.039	0.372	−0.055	0.008	0.095	0.159	−0.048	0.418	−0.129	0.101	0.111
RoW	formal	0.031	0.056	−0.043	0.037	0.011	0.062	0.023	0.008	−0.043	0.013	0.028	0.052
	informal	0.109	−0.042	0.251	−0.102	0.099	0.059	0.053	−0.044	0.101	−0.020	0.138	0.084
FF	formal	**0.047**	**0.075**	**−0.085**	**0.045**	**0.062**	**0.115**	**0.029**	**0.009**	**−0.088**	**0.026**	**0.050**	**0.070**
	informal	**0.273**	**−0.077**	**0.666**	**−0.113**	**0.113**	**0.135**	**0.203**	**−0.091**	**0.550**	**−0.154**	**0.102**	**0.201**

financial crisis, in 2000–2002 and in 2008 (when the median gain from the falling value of informal liabilities is around 32% of GDP). It can also be observed that the median size of valuation effects is generally higher than the median size of flows from transactions, heavily boosting both sides (the liability side slightly more) of the NFC financial balance sheets.

The GOV sector, before 2008, increases formal liabilities more than formal assets and raises net formal debt, but to a much lower extent compared to HH and NFC: GOV median value is generally not higher than 6% per year, whereas NFC and HH together increased formal liabilities by around 10.5% per year from 2000 to 2008. A radically different trend can be observed after 2008, where GOV boosts the flows of formal liabilities (4.5% on average from 2009 to 2015), whereas HH and NFC reduce them (to 1.4% from 2009 to 2015). As already noted in Section 4, this is clearly the result of the tentative policy cushioning the effects of the crisis by replacing assets. Informal transactions in assets and liabilities for GOV play only a small role. The size of valuation effects is increasing after the crisis (progressively increasing the value of GOV formal liabilities in 2011, 2012 and 2014).

The FC increases formal assets more than formal liabilities over all 20 years considered, therefore raising the net formal credit position to RD and RoW. This does not imply that the FC credit position grows in an unbalanced way, as an important part of the fixed-income assets and liabilities are domestic interbank credit and deposits, which are registered as informal asset transactions (see Section 2). What is important to notice is that the overall size of FC transaction flows rises, from above 20% of GDP per year in the second half of the 1990s to 80% in 2007, then falls back to 20% per year. It doubles from 1.3 times the size of all RD sector financial transactions (1995–1998) to 2.3 times (2003–2007) and then it falls after the crisis to reach 0.3 in 2014–2015. The change in valuation of FC informal liabilities is higher than that of informal assets, both in normal years and in the years of financial crisis (2001–2002, 2008). Meanwhile, the valuations of formal assets increase after the crisis, as the mirror side of increasing the valuations of liabilities of GOV.

The RoW increases the flows of assets and liabilities (formal and informal) before 2008 and sharply falls in the following years. The size of financial flows is smaller but comparable to that of FC. Overall, the FF sector flows, summing FC and RoW, are spectacularly higher than RD flows before 2008 (from 2003 to 2007, liabilities grow six times higher, assets 3.5 times higher), and then fall after the 2008 crisis.

Overall, it is possible to establish that the yearly impact of the valuation effects on the size of both sides (assets and liabilities) of the sectorial balance sheet is all but negligible. This is already worthy of notice, as it implies the precarious balance sheets of institutions and individuals holding and controlling the allocation of financial assets. But valuation effect is also heavily associated to the net financial position of sectors. Table 1.3 compares the correlation of the sectorial net financial position, measured from the sectorial balance sheet, to both net saving (resulting from transactions) and the net valuation effect (resulting from market price changes). Correlations refer to single countries as well as to median and average values. The result is unambiguous: net valuation effects are positively and more highly correlated with changes in net financial positions than is net saving. This suggests that sectorial net financial positions are more affected by the decisions on the portfolio allocation of the financial instruments (especially the non-fixed income ones, which are more exposed to price volatility) than by accumulation patterns anchored to real economic activities (saving and investment).

The observed impact of the valuation effects on the sectorial balance sheets is consistent with several studies, inspired by Minsky's financial instability hypothesis, which emphasises how the validation of optimistic expectations (rising asset prices) drives rising bank lending and the deterioration of financial ratios, until the moment where debtors perceive the burden of their debt to be unsustainable and/or the creditors perceive the borrowers to be unreliable, and the crisis is triggered (Minsky, 1982; Taylor and O'Connel, 1985; Ryoo, 2013).

This study has established that the twofold boom in stock and housing markets associated to growing indebtedness, observed in the decade before the crisis (Palma, 2009; Stockhammer and Wildauer, 2016), can be empirically described as a combined effect of deliberate decisions to create new financial flows exceeding real economic transactions (analysed in the last two sections), and price effects that are not directly under the control of individuals or institutions (analysed in this section). Before 2008, excess finance had to increase every year to transact existing assets with increasing value. The fact that, in the years following the crisis, the size of the financial sector and the volume of existing financial wealth has not reversed the sign significantly should lead us to think that: on the one hand, as Seccareccia (2017) argues, monetary policy after the crisis has generally preserved the value of the existing stock of financial assets; and, on the other hand, valuation effects could still be a potential amplifier of a new wave of deliberate change in financial flow transactions.

CONCLUSION

This work has developed a methodology for analysing how superfluous financial flows grow and how they are allocated between sectors with

Table 1.3 Correlation of sectorial net position with valuation effects and with net saving (2001–2015)

	NFC		HH		GOV		FC		RoW	
	val eff	net sav	val eff	net sav	val eff	net sav	val eff	net sav	val eff	net sav
Belgium	0.46	0.09	0.55	−0.01	0.16	−0.13	0.34	−0.43	0.13	−0.39
Denmark	0.35	0.41	0.44	0.11	0.65	0.00	0.55	−0.14	0.70	0.84
Germany	0.77	−0.21	0.77	0.30	0.37	−0.13	0.32	−0.05	0.53	0.66
Ireland	0.33	−0.61	0.70	−0.15	0.67	0.53	0.68	−0.16	0.71	0.05
Greece	0.50	0.38	0.22	−0.71	0.64	0.56	0.87	0.56	0.33	−0.38
Spain	0.14	−0.19	0.68	−0.01	0.75	0.60	0.37	0.49	−0.16	−0.20
France	0.65	0.43	0.69	−0.24	0.42	0.64	0.53	−0.48	−0.10	0.84
Italy	0.19	0.11	0.54	0.66	0.61	0.08	0.14	0.63	−0.09	0.24
Netherlands	0.23	0.78	0.34	0.85	0.42	0.56	0.51	−0.16	0.26	0.78
Austria	−0.17	0.36	0.34	−0.30	−0.05	0.24	0.26	0.71	−0.44	0.20
Portugal	0.21	−0.35	0.39	0.35	0.54	0.34	0.23	0.41	0.33	−0.46
Finland	0.03	−0.37	0.77	0.07	0.75	−0.23	0.78	−0.43	−0.64	−0.83
Sweden	0.61	0.26	0.69	0.48	0.42	0.00	0.43	−0.30	0.50	0.04
United Kingdom	0.63	0.24	0.52	0.44	0.63	0.74	−0.17	0.79	0.68	0.23
average	**0.352**	**0.095**	**0.545**	**0.131**	**0.499**	**0.270**	**0.417**	**0.103**	**0.196**	**0.117**
median	**0.340**	**0.179**	**0.542**	**0.091**	**0.579**	**0.289**	**0.399**	**−0.097**	**0.295**	**0.123**

different functions (purchasing power creators vs. users) and between different economic activities (real production vs. wealth appropriation).

The methodology, based on a stock-flow consistent accounting framework, has been validated by analysing the composition of the yearly changes in financial balance sheets across the sectors of 14 founder countries of the European Union over 20 years. Two proxies have been used to separate financial transaction flows that are connected to the determination of current real income (decisions on production and spending) from transaction flows involving assets only (either pure financial or financial for real). Moreover, by grouping the institutional sectors into two macro sectors, it has been possible to separate and quantify, albeit approximately, flows that are channelled to the real domestic (RD) sector and flows that only circulate within the foreign and financial (FF) sector. Finally, changes in the market value of existing and newly created financial assets have been analysed to assess their incidence in sectorial balance sheets.

The empirical analysis has emphasised that an increasing amount of credit in the EU14 group of countries has involved transactions of assets already in place (housing, stock market) or of newly generated financial assets without contributing to the generation of real income. A prevalent and growing share of the gross excess finance has circulated within the domestic and foreign financial sector only. Investments aimed at purchasing existing wealth appear to have been perceived as a safer line of credit by banks in search of creditworthy customers, compared to investments aimed at transforming the productive structure of the economy.

The RD sector, considered as a single aggregate, increased its gross asset and liability positions in excess of its real economic activities over the entire period. Before the credit crunch crisis in 2008, this was the result of non-financial corporations (NFC) and households (HH) increasing indebtedness and simultaneously purchasing assets. After the 2008 crisis, governments increased excess liabilities to the private sectors, to cushion the effects of the financial crisis by draining the private sector's liabilities (including those of the financial system) accumulated in previous years.

Before the crisis, the Financial and foreign sector (FF) deliberately created purchasing power and increased financial transaction flows to an extent that is highly disproportionate with respect to the RD sector. The flow of finance circulating within the financial sector reached levels equivalent to 70% of all the EU14 group's GDP, 7 times higher than the excess finance of non-financial corporations and 15 times higher than that of households. During the crisis and the following years of great recession, the FF sector reduced gross financial flows more dramatically than the RD sector. While this has certainly contributed to economic recession or stagnation, it has not reduced the size of financial assets and the leverage of the financial sector across the continent.

Price effects are of the same order of magnitude as private sector transaction flows and they do not only affect the gross values of balance sheets, but also the sectorial net financial position. Valuation effects interacted with deliberate decisions on finance creation in a self-propelling process, where rising values of transactions required increasing amounts of borrowing, an endogenous process culminating in balance sheets deterioration being perceived as unsustainable. The subsequent great recession, overall, has preserved the value of the existing financial stock.

NOTES

1. For a review of this approach from a historical perspective, see Bezemer (2010).
2. Non-financial transactions (nasa_10_nf_tr), Financial transactions (nasa_10_f_tr), Financial balance sheets (nasa_10_f_bs).
3. In this accounting framework, real transactions in goods include durables produced in past periods, such as existing houses or second-hand cars. A purchase of a real asset is accounted twice, as an investment for the sector purchasing it and as a negative investment of the equivalent amount for the sector selling it. In national accounting, where all sectorial balances are aggregated, transactions in real assets are netted out and cannot be observed.
4. To be philologically more accurate, Schumpeter did not refer to 'new investments' in quantitative terms, but to investment in new combinations, i.e. innovations introducing new methods of production or new types of commodities.

REFERENCES

Bernanke B.S. (2000), *Essays on the Great Depression*, Princeton: Princeton University Press.

Bezemer, D.J. (2010), Understanding financial crisis through accounting models, *Accounting, Organizations and Society*, 35, 676–688.

Bezemer, D.J. (2011), Causes of financial instability: don't forget finance, *Levy Economics Institute, Working Paper* 665.

Crotty, J. (2008), Structural causes of the global financial crisis: a critical assessment of the 'New Financial Architecture', *University of Massachusetts, Department of Economics, Working Paper 14*.

De Grauwe, P. (2013), The political economy of the euro, *Annual Review of Political Science*, 16, 153–170.

Epstein, J. (2005) (ed.), *Financialization and the World Economy*, Cheltenham, UK and Northampton, MA, USA: Edward Elgar.

Erturk, I., J. Froud, J. Sukhdev, A. Leaver and K. Williams (2008), *Financialization at Work*, Oxford: Routledge.

Febrero, E., J. Uxò and F. Bermejo (2018), The financial crisis in the Euro Zone. A balance of payments crisis with a single currency? *Review of Keynesian Economics*, 6, 221–239.

Gallino, L. (2005), *L'impresa irresponsabile*, Turin: Einaudi.
Godley, W. and M. Lavoie (2007), *Monetary Economics: An Integrated Approach to Credit, Money, Income, Production and Wealth*, London: Palgrave Macmillan.
Graziani, A. (2003), *The Monetary Theory of Production*, Cambridge: Cambridge University Press.
Keen, S. (2010), Solving the paradox of monetary profits, *Economics. Open-Access, Open-Assessment E-Journal*, 4, 1–32.
Keen, S. (2011), *Debunking Economics*, London: Zed Books.
Keen, S. (2015), Post-Keynesian theories of crisis, *American Journal of Economics and Sociology*, 74, 298–324.
Keynes, J.M. (1936), The general theory of employment, interest and money, in *Collected Writings*, 7, London: Macmillan.
Keynes, J.M. (1937), Alternative theories of the rate of interest, in *Collected Writings*, 14, London: Macmillan, 210–215.
Kindleberger, C. (1986), *Manias, Panics, and Crashes: A History of Financial Crises*, New York: Wiley.
Krippner, G. (2005), The financialization of the American economy, *Socio-Economic Review*, 3, 173–208.
Lapavistas, C. (2011), Theorizing financialization, *Work, Employment and Society*, 25, 611–626.
Lavoie, M. (2014), *Post-Keynesian Economics: New Foundations*, Cheltenham, UK and Northampton, MA, USA: Edward Elgar.
Lavoie, M. (2015), The Eurozone: similarities and differencies from Keynes's plan, *International Journal of Political Economy*, 44, 3–17.
Lordon, F. (2011), L'effreyante passivité de la 're-regulation financière', in *Les Economistes Atterrés*, eds., Changer d'économie!, 223–244. Paris: Les Liens qui Libèrent (LLL).
Martin, R. (2002), *Financialization of Daily Life*, Philadelphia, PA: Temple University Press.
Michell J. (2017), Do shadow banks create money? 'Financialisation' and the monetary circuit, *Metroeconomica*, 68, 354–377.
Minsky, H. (1982), *Can 'It' Happen Again? Essays on Instability and Finance*, New York: M.E. Sharpe.
Minsky, H. (1986), *Stabilizing an Unstable Economy*, New York: McGraw-Hill.
Mitchell, W. (2016), *Eurozone Dystopia. Groupthinking and Denial on a Grand Scale*, Cheltenham, UK and Northampton, MA, USA: Edward Elgar.
Nersisyan, Y., and L.R. Wray (2010), The global financial crisis and the shift to shadow banking, *Levy Economics Institute, Working Paper* 587.
Onaran, O., Stockhammer, E., and Graft, L. (2011), Financialization, income distribution and aggregate demand in the USA, *Cambridge Journal of Economics*, 35, 637–61.
Palma, J.G. (2009), The revenge of the market on the rentiers. Why neo-liberal reports of the end of history turned out to be premature, *Cambridge Journal of Economics*, 33, 829–869.
Pollin, R. (2007), The resurrection of the Rentier, *New Left Review*, 46, 140–153.
Rochon L.P. (1999), *Credit, Money and Production. An Alternative Post-Keynesian Approach*, Cheltenham, UK and Northampton, MA, USA: Edward Elgar.
Ryoo. S. (2013), Minsky cycles in Keynesian models of growth and distribution, *Review of Keynesian Economics*, 1(1), 37–60.
Schumpeter, J.A. (1912), *The Theory of Economic Development: An Inquiry into*

Profits, Capital, Credit, Interest, and the Business Cycle, Cambridge, MA: Harvard University Press, 1949.
Seccareccia M. (2017), Which vested interests do central banks really serve? Understanding central bank policy since the global financial crisis, *Journal of Economic Issues*, 51(2), 341–50.
Spanò, M. (2015), Financial assets overhang in Europe, *Journal of Post Keynesian Economics*, 37, 303–527.
Stockhammer, E. (2015), Rising inequality as a cause of the present crisis, *Cambridge Journal of Economics*, 39, 935–958.
Stockhammer E. and R. Wildauer (2016), Debt-driven growth? Wealth, distribution and demand in OECD countries, *Cambridge Journal of Economics*, 40, 1609–1634.
Storm, S. (2016), Rejoinder to Flassbeck and Lapavitsas, *Institute for New Economic Thinking blog*, 28 January, http://ineteconomics.org/ideas-papers/blog/rejoinder-to-flassbeck-and-lapavitsas.
Taylor, L. and S.A. O'Connel (1985), A Minsky's crisis, *The Quarterly Journal of Economics*, 100, 871–885.
Tissot, B. (2016), Development of financial sectoral accounts: new opportunities and challenges for supporting financial stability analysis. *Bank for International Settlements, IFC Working Papers* 15.
Van Treeck, T. (2009), The political economy debate on 'financialization' – a macroeconomic perspective, *Review of International Political Economy*, 16, 907–944.
Wray L.R. (2012), *Modern Money Theory*, London: Palgrave Macmillan.

2. Economic limits of the originate to distribute model of banking

Óscar Dejuán and John S. L. McCombie*

INTRODUCTION

The history of capitalism is filled with episodes of overexpansion of credit leading to a financial crash with serious consequences on the real economy. The Great Depression of 1929 and the Great Recession of 2007 stand as the major examples. Is there something new in the most recent one? This is the question that prompted this chapter.

In our opinion, the distinctive element of the Great Recession is the existence of a new model of finance that we can call ODMB ("originate to distribute model of banking"). In the traditional model of banking ("originate to hold") a mortgage loan stays on the balance sheet of the lender for several decades, until maturity. In the ODMB introduced after 1995, the mortgage loans were sold to the shadow banking system that securitized them and created more liquid financial products – the so-called "mortgage backed securities" (MBS). The 2007–08 crisis resulted from the connivance between the traditional banking system, able to create money out of nothing, and the shadow banking system that transformed mortgage loans into tradable securities and distributed them after concealing the risks with a variety of financial derivatives. Minsky (1982, 1986) warned that credit is debt, and the debt structures deteriorate endogenously leading to the collapse of the financial system. In his opinion, this was a long-run process that might last a couple of decades (Minsky, 1995). Our claim is that the securitization machinery accelerated credit, bringing about an unprecedented burden of debt and asset inflation.

The purpose of this chapter is to analyze the economic limits of credit acceleration, which is a permanent threat to capitalist economies, most of all since the introduction of the ODMB. The chapter is structured in the following way. Section 2 reviews the super-multiplier model, "the most Keynesian of the Keynesian growth models" (Palley, 2018). The key variable is the expected growth of permanent autonomous demand, here identified as residential investment. It "rules the roost" in the sense that other economic variables tend to grow at the same rate. We contend that the multiplier and supermultiplier are stable and stabilizing mechanisms . . . until we introduce the service of debt into the propensity to consume.

Section 3 shows the dynamics of credit, debt service and deposits. We consider a pure credit economy where the banking industry appears as a vertically integrated sector in the Sraffian sense (Sraffa, 1960; Pasinetti, 1973). In the provision of credit for output transactions, banks follow the "endogenous" behavior claimed by the post-Keynesian school (Moore, 1988; Graziani, 2003; Lavoie, 2014; Rochon and Rossi, 2017). Yet, banks also grant loans for non-output transactions that allows an unlimited credit expansion (Werner, 2005, 2014).

Section 4 explains how the ODMB accelerated credit expansion and increased the financial risks despite the ancillary safety nets introduced by the shadow banks. Section 5 contends that a permanent gap between the growth of credit and the growth of nominal GDP transforms a credit-led economy into a credit-burdened economy and a bubble factory. We illustrate these effects with data form the US economy where the ODMB got to its climax after 2002. Section 6 details our theoretical conclusions and policy recommendations. They are aimed at preventing another cycle of a credit boom leading to overindebtedness, a financial crash and an economic recession.

OUTPUT GROWTH IN THE SUPERMULTIPLIER MODEL

In order to focus on specific goals, we consider a closed economy without government services. It contains three vertically integrated sectors (VIS) whose final output consists of goods and services for household consumption (VISC), capital goods for business investment (VISK) and houses for dwelling (VISZ). Intermediate consumption and capital consumption appear as indirect labor and indirect fixed capital. As is the case for the aggregate economy, the value added (wages and profits) of each VIS coincides with its final output (Pasinetti, 1973). To make clear the relationship between distribution and final demand, we adopt the classical expenditure assumption: all wages, and only wages, are consumed.

According to the Keynesian-Kaleckian principle of effective demand, current output is not determined by the available stocks of labor and capital, but by expected demand at normal prices (Keynes, 1936; Kalecki, 1971).[1] Aggregated demand includes final induced consumption of households (C), expansionary investment from productive firms (I), and (proper) autonomous demand (Z), here identified as residential investment by households.[2]

The equilibrium level of output at a given time is explained by the following set of equations:

$$[1] \quad Y = C + I + Z$$
$$[2] \quad C = c \cdot (1 - \tau) \cdot Y = c' \cdot Y$$
$$[3] \quad I = k \cdot \gamma \cdot Y = h \cdot Y$$
$$[4] \quad Z = Z_{(-1)}(1 + \gamma)$$

Induced consumption (C in Equation 2) can be computed as the propensity to consume (c) times the disposable income (Y_d) or the effective propensity to consume (c') times the income. Because of our classical expenditure assumptions, the propensity to consume coincides with the share of wages in income. To obtain the effective propensity to consume (c'), we subtract the tax rate (nil in our private economy) and the compulsory transfers from borrowers (workers) to lenders (banks). The debt service can be presented as a proportion (τ) of wages. This is the first link of our economic model with financial variables. In Section 3 we shall see that it may be the source of instability problems. They are somehow contained because of the existence of a maximum and a minimum rate of compulsory transfers. The maximum rate ($\hat{\tau}$) derives from the subsistence consumption (historically given) (c'). The minimum transfer rate (τ), derives from the minimum dwelling services – workers are supposed to spare a part of their wages in order to pay for the subsistence dwelling ($\underline{z}$).

Expansionary investment (I), i.e. productive investment of firms willing to expand capacity, depends on the expected growth of permanent demand (γ). According to Eatwell (1983) this is the key variable of the Keynesian system.[3] The "accelerator of investment" adjusts capacity to meet efficiently the expected increases in permanent aggregate demand (γ). The result is: $h = I/Y = k \cdot \gamma$.[4] k is the "optimal" capital/output ratio; it implies the normal rate of capacity utilization that we normalize at unity. The actual rate may differ from 1, although in their search for efficiency, firms will try to recover "normality" via investment. Full employment, on the contrary, is not an equilibrium condition either in the short or in the long run.

Autonomous demand (Z) encompasses all the elements of aggregate demand that are different from induced consumption and expansionary investment; namely, autonomous consumption, modernization investment, residential investment, public expenditure and exports. In our private and closed model that explores the dynamics of a construction-driven economy, we will focus on residential investment and assume that it is completely funded by mortgage loans (CR_z). Our model takes as given the level of autonomous demand at the base year (Z_o) and its expected growth in the following years (g_z). If these expectations last long enough, they will affect the growth of aggregate demand. Therefore, we can use γ instead of g_z.

After introducing [4], [3] and [2] into [1], we obtain the equilibrium level of output at a given moment. It can be computed as μ (the multiplier) times broad autonomous demand ($I+Z$) or as *sm* (the supermultiplier) times autonomous demand (Z). Both results coincide if in [5a] we compute investment as the required capital in the previous year, times the expected growth of permanent demand: $I=KR_{(-1)}\cdot\gamma$.

$$[5a] \qquad Y = \frac{I+Z}{1-c(1-\tau)} = \frac{I+Z}{1-c'} = \mu\cdot(I+Z)$$

$$[5b] \qquad Y = \frac{Z}{1-c(1-\tau)-k\cdot\gamma} = \frac{Z}{1-c'-h} = (sm)\cdot Z$$

In the previous equations, Y refers to the long-period equilibrium output in t that corresponds to the expected permanent demand. The actual growth takes into account transitory increases in autonomous demand (A'). They will have an impact on induced consumption captured by the traditional multiplier. It will not accelerate investment since firms do not consider them as permanent demand.

$$[6] \qquad Y'_t = (sm)\cdot Z_t + \mu\cdot A'_t$$

The theoreticians of the supermultiplier[5] have proved that, if properly formulated, it is a stable and stabilizing mechanism. The key message of the model is that the expected growth of permanent autonomous demand is supposed to shape the structure of demand and production until the rates of growth of demand, output and capital coincide: $g_z = g_d = g_k = g_w = \gamma$.[6] The autonomous trend (so to speak) "rules the roost". Banks may accelerate it by relaxing the creditworthiness requirements. A credit-led growth has obvious limits, however. Macroeconomic equilibrium requires that productive investment absorbs the income not spent in consumption type expenditure, $h = k\cdot\gamma = 1\text{-}c'\text{-}z$. The maximum rate of growth becomes $\overset{*}{\gamma} = 1\text{-}\underline{c}'\text{-}\underline{z} = 1\text{-}\underline{c}''$, where $\underline{c}''$ is the minimum consumption type expenditure (historically given). Before reaching this limit, economic expansion may be constrained by the potential market of the goods included in the autonomous demand vector (construction, in our case). When the majority of households own a house, the rate of expansion of construction will stagnate or fall.

Table 2.1 summarizes the relationship between supply, demand, distribution and finance under the simplified assumptions we have introduced.

Table 2.1 Economic flows in an equilibrium path of growth

Production (Y) and demand	Distribution and redistribution of income (VA)	Sources of expenditure
$Y = C + I + Z = sm \cdot Z$	$VA = W + R = W_d + TF + R$	
$C = c' \cdot Y = Y_c$	$W_d = W(1 - \tau)$	Disposable wages
$I = k \cdot \gamma \cdot Y = Y_k$	$R = Y - W$	Retained profits → Equity.
$Z = Z_{(-1)} \cdot (1 + \gamma)$	$TF = \tau \cdot W$	Mortgage loans (CR_z)

Notes: In a long-period equilibrium (given our expenditure assumptions), the cells of each row are equal: $C = W_d; I = R; Z = TF = CR_z$ (Mortgage loans). In the Keynesian system, the production of capital goods and houses generate the "savings" (income not spent in consumption type expenditures) that "may" finance I and Z.

It serves as a conclusion of Section 2 and an introduction of Section 3. Consumption goods are paid with disposable wages. Capital goods, with the retained profits of the investing firms that eventually will become equity. The new houses are bought by workers' households financed by mortgage loans (CR_z). *TF* represents the "debt service", a "compulsory transfer" from borrowers (households) to lenders (banks). As a first approximation, we can represent this transfer as a constant portion of wages (τ). The multiplier would adopt the traditional expression $m = 1/(1-c(1-\tau))$, where the tax rate has been replaced by τ. The problem is that τ represents the debt service ratio (f), a ratio that evolves endogenously and may reduce or increase the multiplier in a cumulative way. The preceding variables are related by the following expression where *ia* is the gross interest rate, the sum of the amortization rate (a) and the interest rate (i); $\beta = [DB]/W$ stands for the share of the stock of debt in wages (the "debt burden", so to speak).[7]

$$[7] \qquad f = (ia) \cdot \beta = (a + i) \cdot \frac{[DB]}{W}$$

CREDIT ACCELERATION: ENDOGENOUS AND AUTONOMOUS FORCES

In our model of vertically integrated sectors (VIS), the bank industry can be considered a sector (VISB) that provides financial services (F) to producers and consumers. In a long-period path of growth, it coincides with the interest payments (*INT*), the sum of the wages and normal profits paid to the factors directly or indirectly employed in VISB: $F = INT = W_b + R_b$. According to our classical expenditure assumptions, W_b will be consumed while R_b will buy the equities issued by the expanding firms. These flows were already accounted for in the C and I of Table 2.1. In the previous section, F was included in Z. In this section, we split the two variables in order to focus on the financial flows.[8] Our goal is to analyze the financial circuit of a pure credit economy from a threefold perspective: banks granting loans, borrowers transferring a part of their income to banks and all agents holding a part of their wealth in liquid assets (deposits). The spectrum of loans and deposits is broadened, although the continuous focus is the same.

Among the multiple varieties of credit, we are especially interested in the distinction between *credit for output-transactions* (CR_y) and *credit for non-output transactions* (CR_x). The first group includes at least three flows. (a) Short-term loans to advance the working capital required at the beginning of a new process of production (CR_o).[9] (b) Medium and long-term loans to small and medium firms that allow them to finance a part of productive investment and to households purchasing durable consumption goods (CR_k). (c) Very long-term loans to households that finance residential investment (CR_z). The second type of credit ($\mathrm{CR_x}$) refers to the loans for non-output transactions that we shall identify with the purchase of land, old houses and equity. Usually, they have a speculative bias.

The post-Keynesian hypothesis of the endogeneity of credit-money focuses on the loans for output transactions granted to firms.[10] The supply of loans is supposed to adapt to the borrowing needs of the firms willing to grow. An autonomous acceleration of this type of credit is bound to fail. No matter the financial facilities offered by banks, firms will not borrow to expand production and/or capacity if demand expectations are gloomy. Banks have more chances to induce borrowing in speculative operations and residential investment. If so, the rate of growth of credit (φ) would surpass the rate of growth of nominal GDP (γ). This may have a positive impact on demand and production: $\Delta\varphi \rightarrow \Delta\gamma$. We have seen, however, that γ has clear limits related to the potential growth of the market and to the minimum consumption rate. On the contrary, the limits of credit expansion are quite flexible, not to say inexistent. This is more evident in boom periods where all the banks expand in parallel.

The dynamics of credit is replicated by the following set of equations, where angular brackets refer to stocks.

[9] $CR = (CR_y) + CR_x = (CR_o + CR_k + CR_z) + CR_x$

[10] $CR = CR_{(-1)}(1 + \varphi)$

[11] $CR_n = CRA - AM$

[12] $[CR] = [CR]_{(-1)} + CR_{n(-1)} = [DB]$

Equations [9] and [10] have been already described. Equation [11] focuses on the net credit (CR_n) that results from subtracting the amortization allowances (AM) from the total flow of credit (CR) in the same period. Net credit feeds the stock of outstanding loans and outstanding debt (this is equation [12]). We should never forget that credit and debt are two sides of the same coin.

Money is created by the very fact of granting a loan, that conveys a deposit in the borrowers account. Credit-money is destroyed when the deposit is devoted to cancel the outstanding debt associated to the outstanding credit. In our pure credit economy, the deposits at a given moment ($[DP]$ a stock) coincides with the outstanding loans ($[CR]$) and with the money supply ($[M^s]$). The determinants of loans and deposits are, however, different. The motives to spare a part of their wealth in deposits of negligible yield are different from the bank's reasons to lend. Keynes (1936, ch. 15) explained "liquidity preference" or "money demand" ($[M^d]$) for the transaction motive, the precautionary motive and the speculative motive.

Equation [13] reminds the different definitions of the stock of deposits and their main determinants, namely, the level of income (Y), the interest rate (i) and the emergence of speculative opportunities ($P^{\#}_x$). The stock of wealth (WE) does also matter, since a part it is hoarded in deposits. Equation [14] organizes deposits according to its origin: $[DP_0]$: outstanding short-term loans to advance wages at the beginning of the production period;[11] $[DP_1]$: outstanding loans to investing firms and to households buying durable consumption goods; $[DP_2]$: outstanding mortgage loans; $[DP_3]$: outstanding loans to buy real and financial assets.

$$[13]\quad [DP] = [CR] = [M^s] = [M^d] = f(Y, i, P^{\#}_x, WE)$$
$$[14]\quad [DP] = [DP_0] + [DP_1] + [DP_2] + [DP_3]$$

From the borrowers' point of view, what matters is the obligation to transfer regularly a part of their current income to the lender (TF in equation [15]). The first part of the debt service corresponds to the amortization allowances: $TF_o = AM = a[DB]$ where a is an inverse measure of the length of the amortization period (equation [16]). The second, to the interest payments: $TF_1 = INT = i \cdot [CR]$. The flow of interests allows banks to pay normal wages and normal profits. Extraordinary profits (R_{bx} in equation [17]) may emerge in special circumstances. The interest rate (i) is a function of the three variables of equation [18]. (a) the official interest rate set by the Central Bank in their loans to banks (i_o). (b) the normal mark-up that allows banks to cover the costs of production (included the normal rate of profit), ψ^*. And (c), a second mark-up covering the special risks associated to overindebtedness, ψ'.

$$[15] \quad TF = TFo + TF_1 = AM + INT$$
$$[16] \quad AM = a \cdot [DB]$$
$$[17) \quad INT = i \cdot [\mathrm{DB}] = W_b + R_b + (R_{bx})$$
$$[18] \quad \mathrm{i} = f(i_o, \psi^*, \psi')$$

The necessary balance between the different credit and debt categories depends on the scenario under consideration. It is convenient to separate amortization allowances from interest payments.

Panel A of Table 2.2 considers a stagnant economy that has accumulated a stock of credit and debt equal to [*DB*].[12] The yearly flow of credit coincides with the cost of production of the new houses. In our simplified model, where credit is identified with mortgage loans, we get:

Table 2.2 Financial flows in equilibrium and disequilibrium paths of growth[(1)]

Output	*Transfers from borrowers to banks*(2)	*Use of CR*	*Flows of CR*
Panel A: Stationary economy ($\varphi = \gamma = 0$, after having accumulated [CR]=[DB])			
$Z=Z_{-1}$	$TF_0 = a[DB] = AM$	CR_0 $CRn=0$	$CR = CRz$
$F=F_{-1}$	$TF_1 = i[DB] = INT = W_b+R_b$		
Panel B: Balanced expansion: ($\varphi = \gamma$)			
$Z=Z_{-1}(1+\gamma)$	$TF_0 = AM$ *outstanding payments,* $[DP_2]$	CR_0 $CRn \rightarrow \Delta\ [CR]$	$CR = CRz$
$F=F_{-1}(1+\varphi)$	$TF_1 = INT = W_b+R_b$		
Panel C: Asymmetric expansion ($\varphi' > \gamma$), after the acceleration of credit [(3)]			
$Z=Z_{-1}(1+\gamma)\cdot$ $(1+\boldsymbol{\Delta Px})$	$TF_0 = AM^+$ *outstanding payments*$^+$, $\Delta\,[DP_2]^+$	CRo^+ CRn^+ $\rightarrow \Delta\,[CR]^+$	$CR^+ =$ $CRz + \boldsymbol{CRx}$
$F=F_{-1}(1+\varphi')$	$TF_1 = INT^+ = W_b + R_b + \boldsymbol{R_{bx}}$		

Notes:

(1) The table can be read from right to left. The cells of each row are supposed to be equal.

(2) Transfers from borrowers to banks include amortization allowances and interest payments. In panel A, amortization allowances coincide with mortgage loans. In panel B, CRz coincides with amortization in t, plus the increase in outstanding deposits that will be used to pay for the outstanding debt (equal to the outstanding credit).

(3) The acceleration of credit brings about asset inflation (ΔPx) and an increase in the indebtedness ratio since credit grows faster than output, income and wages. Sign "+" in panel C reminds us of the absolute and relative increase of financial variables compared to those in panel B. Bold letters highlight qualitative changes: namely, asset inflation ($\boldsymbol{\Delta Px}$) and extra profits of banks ($\boldsymbol{R_{bx}}$).

$CR = CR_y = CR_z = Z$. Each year, the amortization allowances will match it: $AM = CR = Z$.

In panel B we consider an economy where the flow of credit is growing at the same rate of construction, income and wages: $\varphi = \gamma$. If $a = 0.05$, the sum of amortization allowances in the next 20 years (1/0,05=20) will be $\overrightarrow{AM} = CR = Z$. The amortization allowances collected in t are less: $(AM = a \cdot [DB]) < (CR = Z)$. The difference corresponds to the outstanding payments, that is, to the increase in debt ([*DB*]) that borrowers are supposed to return in the following years. Meanwhile they stand as deposits [*DP2*]. In panel C, credit is growing faster than output ($\varphi > \gamma$). Amortization allowances, too. Yet, they continue below the current flow of credit: $(AM^+) < (CR^+)$.

In the three scenarios, interest payments are a fraction (i) of the outstanding debt. In A and B, *INT* is just enough to pay normal wages and profits to the factors directly and indirectly employed in VISB. They represent a transfer of purchasing power from the indebted households to the banks. In principle, aggregate demand will keep constant. The fall of consumption associated to the lower disposable wages everywhere in the economy, will be offset by the consumption of financial workers and the investment derived from financial profits.

Panel 3 introduces some novelties. When $\varphi > \gamma$, the stock of debt grows faster than income. The banking sector becomes a "sinkhole" and has a deflationary impact on aggregate demand. A higher burden of debt implies a higher debt service, a falling multiplier and a lower level of income corresponding to the same level of autonomous demand. The extraction of an additional part of wages brings about extra profits in the banking sector (R_{bx}). Since they are concentrated in few people, we can expect that an important part of it will be devoted to speculative expenditure. An increase in the monopoly power of banks could also result in additional interest payments and profits, draining resources from the real economy.

THE ODMB, A MACHINE TO ACCELERATE CREDIT EXPANSION

So far, we have referred to traditional banks (BT), also known as commercial banks or deposits banks. They are monetary financial institutions that create (destroy) money in the very process of granting (amortizing) loans. According to the traditional banking strategy ("originate to hold"), they grant mortgage loans and retain them until maturity. The non-monetary financial institutions produce and sell financial products. Investment banks, for instance, produce mutual funds by mixing variable and fixed income assets (equity and bonds) to generate a new product (SH, shares), a variable income asset.

The last decade of the 20th century introduced the "originate to distribute model of banking" (ODMB). The main player is the shadow banking system, a variety of investment banks outside the strict financial regulation of monetary authorities.[13] Shadow banks (BS) buy mortgage loans and securitize them. They transform very long-term loans into short-term assets that can be easily exchanged in the capital markets. These mortgage-backed securities (MBS) are sold to other financial institutions and to households looking for more profitable, more liquid and safer products than the typical deposits. For this purpose, BS mix the securitized loans into new financial products. In a further step, they are "structured" in different tranches. The higher the risk of a tranche, the higher the yield received by the investors. A variety of derivatives enhances the safety of the new financial product that we shall call MBS^+.[14] BS are supposed to pay a fixed yield to the owners of the MBS^+, plus a commission to the banks that continue collecting the interest payments, plus a commission to the institutions that issue the derivatives that protect them and to the rating agencies that evaluates them. To solve the temporal mismatches, BS borrow in the "money market mutual funds" (MMF).[15]

Table 2.3 explains the two types of banking activity. The shadowed cells in the bottom panel show the key transformation of $[CR_z]$ into $[MBS^+]$.

In principle, the financial subsystem created by the ODMB is a sustainable one. The general condition of equilibrium is that, in each period, the monetary obligations of the BS are lower than the payments from the securitized mortgage loans. In other words, the cash outflow has to be lower than their cash inflow. The difference would be the value added by BS that allow them to pay wages and profits to the factors directly and indirectly employed there.

$$[19] \quad i' \cdot [MBS^+] < i \cdot [CR_{z2}]$$

i' is assumed to be lower than the interest on mortgage loans (i), because the new financial products are more liquid and safer. At the same time, i' is higher than the interest rate paid on medium term deposits (DP_R) – the main source of demand for the new products. We have seen, however, that $[MBS^+]$ includes a variety of derivatives. The commissions claimed by them may push upwards the actual transfer from BS to households.

BS have the expertise in disguising risks. They cannot eliminate them, however. At least we should consider the following "persistent" risks.

Table 2.3 The traditional and new models of finance reflected in a single balance sheet

Traditional model of finance					
Hh and Firms		BT		BI	
[DP_W]	[CR_o]	[CR_o]	[DP_W]		
[DP_R]	[CR_k]	[CR_k]	[DP_R]		
	[CR_z]	[CR_z]			
[EQ_1]	[EQ]		[NW]	[EQ_2]	
[BD_1]	[BD]			[BD_2]	
[SH]					[SH]
Originate to distribute model of finance (ODMB)					
Hh and Firms		BT		BI and BS	
[DP_W]	[CR_o]	[CR_o]	[DP_W]		
~~[DP_R]~~	[CR_k]	[CR_k]	~~[DP_R]~~		
[MBS^+]	[CR_z]	**[CR_{z1}]**		**[CR_{z2}]**	**[MBS^+]**
[EQ_1]	[EQ]		[NW]	[EQ_2]	
[BD_1]	[BD]			[DD_2]	
[SH]					[SH]

Notes: Angular brackets indicate stocks. Hh: households. BT: traditional banks or banks of deposits. BI: investment banks. BS: shadow banks. CR_o: short term loans to advance working capital. CR_k: long term loans for investment in small and medium firms. CR_z: mortgage loans. EQ: equity. BD: bonds (subscript 1 and 2 refer to the part owned by Hh and BI). SH: shares issued by BI. DP_W: short-term deposits by workers (average of the year). DP_R: medium-term deposits of capitalists and rentiers, usually for speculative purposes. NW: net financial wealth of BT (the difference between assets and liabilities). In the ODMB, BS securitize a part of mortgage loans (CR_{z2}) and sell to households the new product: Mortgage Backed Securities (MBS^+). Hh use their DP_R to purchase the MBS^+.

(a) *Risk of default of the (subprime) borrowers*. The growth of credit involves a relaxation of the creditworthiness criteria. The rapid expansion of loans after 2002 was possible because banks lent to poorer people at a higher interest rate. They are the so-called NINJAs: households with no income, no job, and no assets to be offered as collateral. Note that a pyramid of financial derivatives is sustained by subprime mortgages paying the highest interest rates.

(b) *Risk of default of financial institutions in a recession if they cannot serve their fixed income commitments.* The traditional shares (*SH*) created by investment banks were variable income products. In a recession, the yield of EQ_2 falls but also the payments due to the share's owners. On the contrary, the MBS^* are fixed yield assets.

Shadow banks are supposed to pay their owners the same amount in the boom and in the bust.

(c) *Risk of default of financial institutions if the money market closes.* The variety of short-term commitments involved in the MBS^{+} obliged BS to go to the money market in search of liquidity (*MMF,* money market mutual funds). Probably, a month later they will borrow twice as much in order to cancel the previous loan and to pay the current commitments to the holders of *MBS.* This explains the explosion of very short-term loans among financial institutions, including banks. A lack of trust may close the money market and generate a financial crush. By the way, this was the immediate cause of the default of Lehman Brothers in September 2008 – the trigger of the financial crisis.

(d) *Risk of credit/debt overexpansion.* This is the main point we want to highlight. The overexpansion after 1995 (accelerated after 2002) resulted from the connivance of the traditional banks, who were able to create money out of nothing, just by granting loans, and the shadow banks who were able to sell the new financial products, after disguising their risks. In the traditional model of banking, BT should hold the loans and the inherent risks during the 20 or 30 years of the mortgage term. Now they can sell on Friday the loans granted during the week, transferring the default risk implicit in the subprime loans. In addition to the price received from the transferred mortgage loans, traditional banks benefit from the regular commissions paid by shadow banks in exchange for collecting interest payments.

FROM CREDIT-LED GROWTH TO DEBT-BURDENED GROWTH

Figure 2.1 summarizes the story of a credit boom leading to a financial crash and an economic recession, as we shall illustrate later with data from the US. It represents the technological frontier of growth, which coincides with the frontier of distribution when wages (and only wages) are consumed. The ordinate axis ($c''=c'+z$) shows the share in income of consumption-type expenditure, which do not expand capacity. Residential investment, on which this chapter focuses, belongs to this group. In a fully adjusted path of growth (and a given technology), all the real variables (autonomous demand, aggregate demand, output, labour and capital) grow at the same rate, γ (on the abscissa). γ can be defined as "full capacity rate of growth". Its maximum rate (γ^*) is set by the potential market for

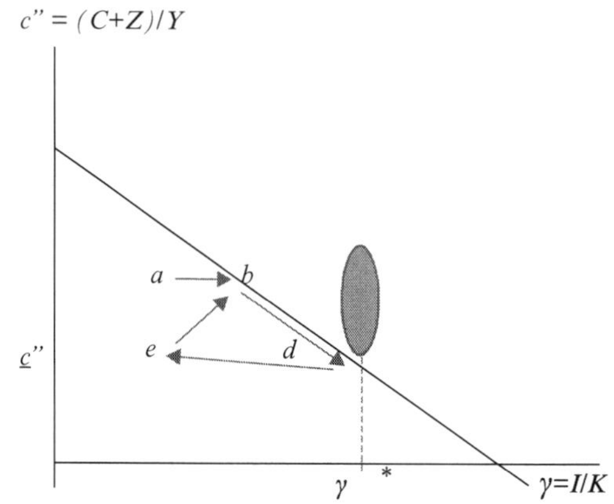

Note: The oval represents an increase in the indebtedness ratio and a bubble in the asset market.

Figure 2.1 Movements around the technological frontier of growth in a financialized economy

dwelling (g_z*) and/or by the warranted rate associated with the subsistence consumption. At point *a,* the economy was out of equilibrium with involuntary unemployment and excess capacity. Banks were able to foster the construction industry by granting cheap mortgage loans to households. Residential investment became the driver of the economy that reached full capacity (not full employment) at point *b*. A second acceleration of credit increased the autonomous trend up to γ*. After this moment, the rate of growth of credit (φ) grew systematically above the rate of growth of nominal GDP, that tops at γ*.

The goal of this section is to analyze the impact of a persistent gap $\varphi > \gamma$. These effects occur in any model of banking but they are particularly quick and disrupting in the ODMB. We shall focus on three effects: asset inflation, overindebtedness and massive default. Post-Keynesian literature is well aware of these phenomena.[16]

Werner (2014) explains asset inflation through the "quantitative theory of credit". Since the supply of non-produced assets is fixed or moves slowly, an acceleration of credit is bound to pump bubbles in the residential and the stock exchange markets.[17, 18] This push is encapsulated in the following equation where ε is a positive parameter.

$$[20] \quad P_x = P_{x(-1)}(1 + \varepsilon(\varphi - \gamma)$$

The second impact of a persistent gap ($\varphi > \gamma$ is the increase of the indebtedness coefficient or the burden of debt ratio ($\beta = [DB]/W$). This ratio evolves according to the following expression derived from the definitions given in equations [15] to [17].

$$[21] \quad \beta = \beta_{(-1)} \cdot \left(1 + \frac{\varphi - \gamma}{[CR]}\right)$$

The debt–service ratio rises with the debt–burden: $f = ia \cdot \beta$, where ia is the gross interest rate. Any increase in f causes a fall in the effective propensity to consume ($\nabla c'$), the multiplier ($\nabla \mu$, ∇sm) and the level of income and wages associated to a given level of autonomous demand. This is the deflationary effect of debt on demand. It may lead to a downward spiral in the economy since lower wages convey a higher debt–burden ratio. The multiplier is the key piece of such cumulative process.

$$(\varphi > \gamma) \rightarrow \Delta\beta \rightarrow \Delta f \rightarrow \nabla c' \rightarrow \nabla(\mu, sm) \rightarrow (Y, W)$$

As the legal debt service (f) approaches the maximum affordable transfer to banks ($\hat{\tau}$), the most fragile portion of debtors will default. After a point, we can expect a massive default that may jeopardize the viability of the banking system and trigger a recession. When signing the mortgage contract, borrowers know the portion of wages they have to spare regularly (τ) and are confident they will honor their future commitments. As time evolves, this portion may increase and surpass the threshold that the majority of borrowers can afford. The main concern here is that the debt–service ratio increases by forces outside the borrower's control. Namely: (i) a rise in the official interest rate; (ii) an economic recession that cuts down employment and wages and (iii) an acceleration of credit that raises the stock of debt faster than output and wages.

To end this section, we will illustrate the implications of Figure 2.1 with data from the US economy where the securitization process led by the ODMB was more prevalent. In Figure 2.2 we see that the share in income of bank credit was stable until 1995, when it was around 125%. From this moment, it escalated steadily up to the 200% registered in 2007. An important explanation of the credit acceleration was the introduction of asset- backed securities (ABS, whose most important element is the MBS). Over 17 years it increased from negligible levels to 13% of GDP. Securitization involved the expansion of the money market to provide instant liquidity (MMF). In the period 1990–95 it represented 6% of GDP and by 2009 it had topped 26%.

Figure 2.3 defines overexpansion of credit by the difference between the growth of credit and the growth of nominal GDP. It conveys the rise

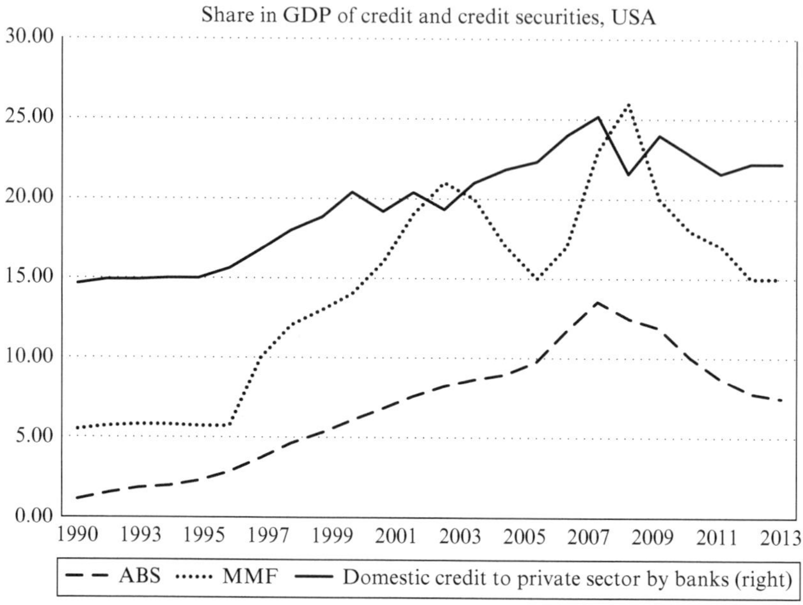

Note: ABS (asset-backed securities). MMF: money market mutual funds.

Source: FRED.

Figure 2.2 Increasing securitization and indebtedness

of loans for non-output transactions and it is supposed to cause asset inflation. A positive gap from 1995 to 2000 created a bubble in the stock exchange market. A second (more pronounced) gap between 2004 and 2008 created twin bubbles – in the stock exchange market and in the residential market.

Over-indebtedness is registered by the solid line in Figure 2.2, since $[CR]/Y = [DB]/Y$. The main concern is that the debt–service ratio may start rising endogenously and, after a moment, it will surpass the threshold that most borrowers can afford. This will cause a massive default. Figure 2.4 shows that the rate of defaults was relatively low and constant until 2005 since a growing economy offsets the rising interest payments. When the real economy decelerated in 2006, the rate of default shifted from 0.8% to 5% in two years.

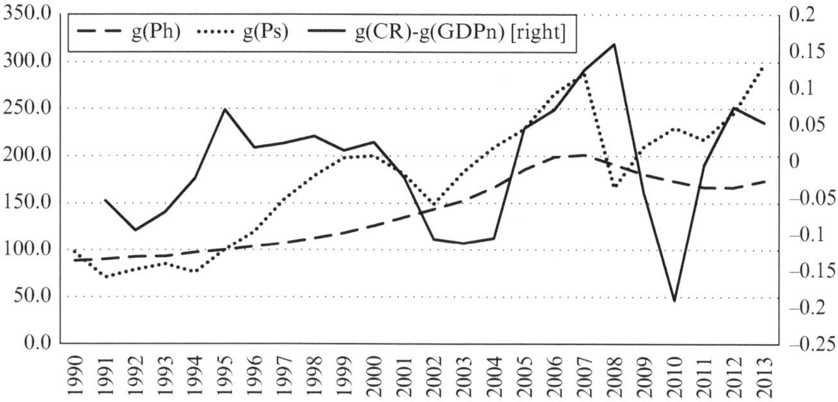

Note: g(Ph): growth of the price index in the residential market; g(Ps): growth in the price index of the stock exchange; g(CR)-g(GDPn) = φ-γ gap between the growth of credit and nominal output.

Source: Own elaboration with data from FRED and NIPA.

Figure 2.3 Credit for non-output transactions and asset bubbles (USA)

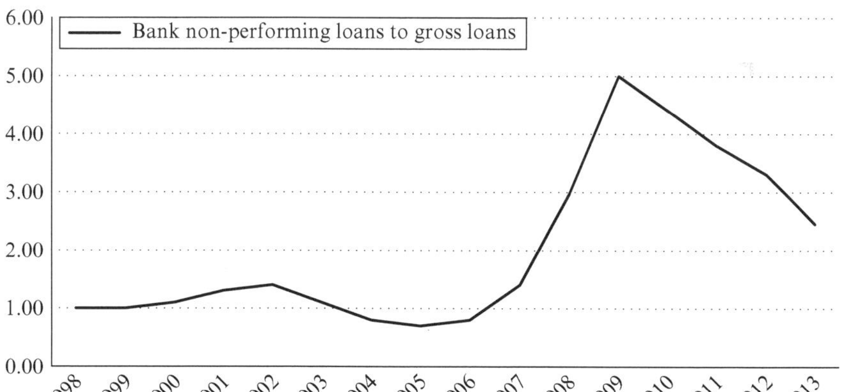

Source: FRED.

Figure 2.4 Default rate

CONCLUSIONS AND POLICY IMPLICATIONS

Several important conclusions and policy implications may be drawn from this analysis. We encapsulate them in the following:

1. Credit explosions leading to asset bubbles and an increasing burden of debt are an endemic disease of advanced capitalism. Eventually the credit-led growth is transformed into a debt-burdened growth. Even the traditional originate-to-hold model of banking is not free from such a virus. Yet, as Minsky himself recognized, a couple of decades are necessary for the virus to propagate. The novelty of the originate-to-distribute model of finance is that it has assembled the machinery to pump debt and asset bubbles in four or five years. The period 2002–06 is the best example.
2. Credit explosions result easily from connivance between the traditional banking system, which is able to create money out of nothing, and the shadow banking system that transforms mortgage loans into tradable securities and distributes them after concealing the inherent risks with a variety of financial derivatives. Traditional banks would not have expanded mortgages loans so fast and so far if they had been obliged to hold them on their balance sheets until maturity. They would not have dared to lend to, no-income, no-job, no-assets households (NINJA) for up to 30–40 years, if shadow banks had not been willing to absorb subprime mortgages. Shadow banks would not have expanded so fast and so far if commercial banks had not absorbed the near-money issued by the shadow banking system in need of liquidity. The low interest rates also helped to divert deposits into mortgage backed securities (MBS) and their complementary derivatives.
3. Arguably, the shadow banks leading the process were not aware of the economic limits of securitization. A shadow bank's lens is only equipped for scrutinizing the matching of the cash-flow associated with any single asset-backed security. Someone with a macroeconomic perspective, the regulator, has to specify the limits derived from the potential rate of growth of output and to keep the expansion of credit below it. And to keep the debt–service ratio (the gross interest rate times the debt burden ratio) below the maximum affordable transfer rate. Otherwise, a massive default leading to a financial crash is unavoidable.
4. Regulation is more necessary in financial services than in any other industry, since banks enjoy formidable economies of scale. The risk that credit expands faster than output for a long time is a major concern. We support, therefore, any measure that makes banks and bankers more prudent and accountable. The shadow banking system

cannot be an exception. Financial institutions may differ in size and specialty, but not in their submission to the law.

5. Our first particular proposal is that the monetary authority introduces checks to credit expansion when it is above the rate of growth of nominal GDP. Basil III agreements that impose on banks stronger capital requirements, weighted by the risk implicit in their asset structure, are most welcome. Monetary authorities should also account for macroeconomic risks, in particular for the gap $\varphi > \gamma$.
6. To avoid a massive default, it may be convenient to delay the repayment obligations in critical times. Our second proposal is to introduce in mortgage contracts the following clause: "The yearly service of mortgages divided by the wage of the borrower, should not surpass the percentage $\hat{\tau}$ agreed in the contract. If the difference is positive (and the borrower agrees), the mortgage period will be extended".
7. Our third proposal is to differentiate credit regulation according to its allocation. Mortgage loans should be checked if they grow faster than the construction of new dwelling and/or the price index of houses is above the CPI. Credit for the purchase of non-reproducible assets should be bluntly forbidden since they pump bubbles that eventually destabilize the economy. Agents willing to invest in land and financial stocks should use their own savings or issue medium-term bonds to capture someone else's savings. This was the genuine role of investment banks. Speculation and bubbles will always be a part of a capitalist economy. The have nothing to do, however, with the size and speed of the bubbles pumped with direct credit after 1996. Keynes' verdict resounds stronger than ever before:

> Speculators may do no harm as bubbles on a steady stream of enterprise. But the position is serious when enterprise becomes a bubble on a whirlpool of speculation. When the capital development of a country becomes a by-product of the activities of a casino, the job is likely to be ill done.
>
> (Keynes, 1936, ch. 12)

NOTES

* Acknowledgements: During the research for this chapter, we received useful comments from Richard Werner (University of Southampton), Gumersindo Ruiz (University of Malaga), Eladio Febrero (University of Castilla – La Mancha) and Daniel Dejuán-Bitriá (Banco de España). Many thanks to all of them. Also, to the people attending the seminar in Centro Sraffa (Università Roma Tre) on 30 May 2018. In the Università of Roma Tre we have the opportunity to present the paper "The supermultiplier-cum-finance" which included a detailed simulation exercise on the impact of credit expansion.

1. Demand expectations are referred to "normal prices" or "prices of production" in the Sraffian sense (Sraffa, 1960). In this chapter, under the assumption that the three VIS share the same technology and real wage, prices of production are equal to one and constant. The nominal wage is assumed to rise when there are tensions in the labour market. Migration has diluted these tensions so we can assume away output-inflation.
2. In our equations, all the variables (in capital letters) should bear the subscript t. When there is not a risk of confusion, we have deleted it. The value of a variable in the previous period is indicated by the subscript "(–1)".
3. In Chapter 3 of *The General Theory*, Keynes refers to the "the long-term state of expectations".
4. Transient demand is met by increasing temporarily the rate of capacity utilization. It includes the once-and-for-all adjustment of capacity after an acceleration of permanent demand.
5. The revival of Harrod's multiplier-accelerator model and Hicks' supermultiplier appeared in Serrano, (1995), Bortis (1997), Cesaratto, Serrano, and Stirati (2003), Dejuán (2005), The proof of its stability (contrary to Harrod's "knife edge" simile) is more recent: White (2009), Allain (2015), Serrano and Freitas (2015), Lavoie (2016) and Dejuán (2016). The introduction of financial variables in the supermultiplier appears in Dejuán (2013), Pariboni (2016), Dejuán and Dejuán-Bitriá (2018). According to Dejuán (2016) the key condition for stability is that expectations refer to "permanent" demand. The "prudence" that is supposed to rule investors ensure this result. Firms adapt to increases of demand by rising the rate of capacity utilization. If the increase in demand persists, firms will expand capacity via investment. If the overutilization of capacity continues despite investment, firms will revise their growth expectation upwards.
6. g_w stands for the "warranted" or "potential" rate of growth. $g_w = \frac{1-c'-z}{k} = \frac{\sigma}{k} = \frac{h}{k} = \gamma$. The warranted rate adapts, via h, to changes in the expected permanent growth of demand.
7. [*DB*] is the stock of mortgage debt that, by definition, equals the stock of outstanding mortgage loans ([*CR*]). To obtain a ratio, this stock is usually divided by the flow of current income. In our model, where credits are mortgage loans to workers' households, it seems sensible to divide by current wages (W).
8. In the new presentation, financial services would be part of autonomous demand. $Y = sm \cdot (Z+F)$.
9. This corresponds to Graziani's "initial finance" (Graziani, 2003). He contrasts it to "final finance" that supports final demand, bridging the gap between agents in a net lending and a net borrowing position.
10. We follow, with some provisos, the post-Keynesian hypothesis of money endogeneity as it appears in Moore (1988), Lavoie (2014), Rochon and Rossi (2017).
11. These loans disappear at the end of the year but we can compute the average stock of firms' short-term deposits.
12. The model also applies to an economy where debt is cancelled in one year ($a=1$).
13. McCulley (2009) coined the term "shadow banking system", the key piece of the ODMB. Botta, Caverzasi, and Tori (2015) explain how to introduce the new financial innovation into the "circuit". Lysandrou (2014) criticizes the usefulness of circuit models for such endeavor. See also Claessens and Ratnovski (2014), Pozsar, Adrian, Ashcraft and Boesky (2010), Taub (2013). Gorton and Metriick (2012) explains the importance of money market instruments to provide liquidity to the ODMB.
14. The typical product of the structure finance is called CDO (*Collateral Debt Obligation*). The typical derivative based on it is the CDS (*Credit Default Swaps*).
15. Repurchase Agreements (REPOS) are the typical instrument in the money market.
16. Most of the post-Keynesian literature on financial crises derives from Minsky's "financial instability hypothesis" (Minsky, 1986, 1994 (1992)). Adaptations of this hypothesis to the modern financial system appear in these books: Keen (2001) Chapter 11, Epstein (2005), Wolfson and Epstein (2013), Palley, (2013), Hein, Detzer, and Dodig (2016). See also these: Badhuri, Laski, and Riese (2006), Blankenburg and Palma (2013), Hein

and Treeck (2010), Badhuri (2011), Arestis, Sobreira, and Oreiro (2011), Lang (2015), Dejuán and Dejuán-Bitriá (2018). In this section, we will complete the Minskyan hypothesis with Werner's quantitative theory of credit applied to non-output transactions (Werner, 2014).

17. The Post-Keynesian model explains output inflation through the Phillips curve. The globalization of the economy (international migration, in particular) explains why nominal wages do not rise with employment and output. In our chapter, we assume that the consumption price index (P_y) is 1 and constant.
18. Asset inflation has dangerous pro-cyclical effects on the economy. In the boom, it stimulates aggregate demand for both produced goods and non-produced assets. In the bust, the wealth effects become negative. The burst of the bubble may cause a deep financial crash. Many banks can be bankrupted when the value of their assets fall abruptly.

REFERENCES

Allain, O. (2015). Tackling the instability of growth: a Kaleckian-Harrodian model with an autonomous expenditure component. *Cambridge Journal of Economics*, *39*(5), 1351–1371.

Arestis, P., Sobreira, R., and Oreiro, J. L. (2011). *The Financial Crisis: Origins and Implications*. London: Palgrave Macmillan.

Badhuri, A. (2011). A contribution to the theory of financial fragility and crisis. *Cambridge Journal of Economics*, *35*, 995–1014. DOI: 10.1093/cje/ber011.

Badhuri, A., Laski, K., and Riese, M. (2006). A model of interaction between the virtual and the real economy. *Metroeconomica*, *57*, 412–427.

Blankenburg, S., and Palma, G. (2009). The global financial crisis. *Cambridge Journal of Economics*, *33*(4), (semimonographic), xx–xxx.

Bortis, H. (1997). *Institutions, Behaviour and Economic Theory: A Contributioln to Classical–Keynesian Political Economy*. Cambridge: Cambridge University Press.

Botta, A., Caverzasi, E., and Tori, D. (2015). Financial-real side interactions in an extended monetary circuit with shadow banking: loving or dangerous hugs. *International Journal of Political Economy*, *44*(3), 196–227.

Cesaratto, S., Serrano, F., and Stirati, A. (2003). Technical change, effective demand and employment. *Review of Political Economy*, *XV*(1), 19.

Claessens, S., and Ratnovski, L. (2014). What is shadow banking? *IMF Working Paper, 14/25*, 1–8.

Dejuán, O. (2005). Paths of accumulation and growth: towards a Keynesian long-period theory of output. *Review of Political Economy*, *17*(2), 231–252.

Dejuán, Ó. (2013). The debt trap. In Ó. Dejuán, E. Febrero, and J. Uxó (eds), *Post-Keynesian Views of the Economic Crisis and its Remedies* (pp. 87–107). London and New York: Routledge.

Dejuán, Ó. (2016). Hidden links in the warranted rate of growth. The supermultiplier way out. *European Journal of the History of Economic Thought*, *24*(4), 369–394.

Dejuán, Ó., and Dejuán, D. (2018). A predator–prey model in financial-driven economies. *Review of Keynesian Economics*, *6*(2), 159–179. DOI: 10.4337/roke.2018.02.01.

Eatwell, J. (1983). The long-period theory of unemployment. *Cambridge Journal of Economics*, *7*(3), 269–285.

Epstein, G. A. (2005). *Financialization and the World Economy*. Cheltenham: Edward Elgar.
Gorton, G. B., and Metriick, A. (2012). Securitized banking and the run on REPO. *Journal of Financial Economics*, *104*(3), 425–451.
Graziani, A. (2003). *The Monetary Theory of Production*. Cambridge: Cambridge University Press.
Hein, E., and Treeck, T. (2010). "Financialisation" in Post-Keynesian Models of Distribution and Growth – A Systematic Review. In M. M. Setterfield (ed.), *Handbook of Alternative Theories of Economic Growth*. Cheltenham: Edward Elgar.
Hein, E., Detzer, D., and Dodig, N. (2016). *Financializatiuon and the Financial and Economic Crises. Country Studies*. Cheltenham: Edward Elgar.
Kalecki, M. (1971). *Selected Essays in the Dynamics of the Capitalist Economy (1933–1970)*. Cambridge: Cambridge University Press.
Keen, S. (2001). *Debunking Economics: The Naked Emperor of the Social Sciences*. Sydney: Pluto Press.
Keynes, J.M. (1936). *The General Theory of Employment, Interest and Money*. London: Macmillan.
Lang, D. (2015). Financialisation, income distribution and crisis. *Cambridge Journal of Economics*, *39*(3), (monographic), 867–986.
Lavoie, M. (2014). *Post-Keynesian Economics. New Foundations*. Cheltenham: Edward Elgar.
Lavoie, M. (2016). Convergence towards the normal rate of capacity utilization in Kaleckian models: the role of non-capacity creating autonomous expenditures. *Metroeconomica*, *67*(1), 172–201.
Lysandrou, P. (2014). Financialisation and the Limits of Circuit Theory. *SOAS 24th Annual Workshop*, 1–21.
McCulley, P. (2009). The shadow banking system and Hyman Minsky's economic journey. *PIMCO – Global Central Banks Focus, May*, 1–12.
Minsky, H. P. (1982). *Can it Happen Again?* Armonk (NY): M.E. Sharpe.
Minsky, H. P. (1986). *Stabilizing an Unstable Economy*. New Haven: Yale University Press.
Minsky, H. P. (1994 (1992)). The financial instability hypothesis. In P. Arestis and M. Sawyer (eds), *Handbook of Radical Political Economy* (pp. 147–157). Cheltenham: Edward Elgar.
Minsky, H. P. (1995). Longer waves in financial relations: financial factors in the more severe depressions ii. *Journal of Economic Issues*, *29*(1), 83–96.
Moore, B. J. (1988). *Horizontalists and Verticalists: the Macroeconomics of Credit Money*. Cambridge: Cambridge University Press.
Palley, T. I. (2013). *Financialization: The Economics of Finance Capital Domination*. New York: Palgrave Macmillan.
Palley, T. (2018). The economics of the super-multiplier: a comprehensive treatment with labor markets. *Unpublished Paper*.
Pariboni, R. (2016). Household consumer debt, endogenous money and growth: a supermultiplier-based analysis. *PSL Quaterly Review*, *69*(278), 211–233.
Pasinetti, L. (1973). The notion of vertical integration in economic analysis. *Metroeconomica*, *XXV*, 1–29.
Pozsar, S., Adrian, T., Ashcraft, A. B., and Boesky, H. (2010). Shadow banking. *Federal Reserve Board of New York*, *458* (July).
Rochon, L. P., and Rossi, S. (2017). *Advances in Endogenous Money Analysis*. Cheltenham: Edward Elgar.

Serrano, F. (1995). Long period effective demand and the Sraffian supermultiplier. *Contributions to Political Economy*, *14*, 67–90.

Serrano, F., and Freitas, F. (2015). Growth rate and level effects: the adjustment of capacity to demand and the Sraffian supermultiplier. *Review of Political Economy*, *27*(3), 258–281.

Sraffa, P. (1960). *Production of Commodities by Means of Commodities. Prelude to a Critique of Economic Theory*. Cambridge: Cambridge University Press.

Taub, J. S. (2013). What we don't talk about when talk about banking. In M. H. Wolfson and G. A. Epstein (eds), *The Political Economy of Financial Crisis* (pp. 447–466). New York: Oxford University Press.

Werner, R. A. (2005). *The New Paradigm in Macroeconomics*. Basingstoke: Palgrave Macmillan.

Werner, R. A. (2014). The Quantity Theory of Credit and some of its policy implications. In B. Winkler, A. v. Riet, and Bull, P. (eds), *A Flow-of-Funds Perspective on the Financial Crisis* (Vol. 1, pp. 22–45). Basingstoke: Palgrave Macmillan.

White, G. (2009). Demand-led growth in a multi-commodity model with learning: some preliminary results. *The University of Sydney. Economics Working Paper Series*, *2009*(1), 1–35.

Wolfson, M. H., and Epstein, G. A. (2013). *The Handbook of the Political Economy of Financial Crises*. New York: Oxford University Press.

3. Private pension funds in emerging economies: from broken promises to financialisation

Bruno Bonizzi and Diego Guevara

INTRODUCTION

In recent decades, private pension funds have emerged as important players in financial markets across many emerging economies. While being promoted by virtue of their alleged economic and financial benefits, pension funds have in many respects failed to deliver on their promise of reduced fiscal pressures, increasing saving for national development and raising the coverage rate. Furthermore, while often mentioned as an important aspect of financialisation, they have remained nevertheless under-analysed in the context of developing and emerging economies. Financialisation is not a uniform process, and despite the limited development and sophistication of capital markets, pension funds have been key in shaping financialisation in these countries.

In this chapter, we will focus on the development of private pension funds and their relationship with financialisation in emerging economies. Firstly, we will show how in the last decades (since the 1990s) in developing countries private pension funds have been imposed on public pay-as-you-go (PAYGO) pension systems under the neoclassical argument of saving causing investment in order to have financial deepening. Secondly, we will expose how private pension funds promises in emerging economies have not been actually delivered in terms of coverage, low pension values, replacement rates, decrease of fiscal pressures and national saving rates. Finally, we analyse how private pension funds can be framed as financialisation promoters in emerging economies, by increasing risk and dependency in local economies.

FROM THE PAY-AS-YOU-GO SYSTEM TO PRIVATE PENSION FUNDS

Pension arrangements have been at the core of policymakers discussions since the early 1990s. Traditional 'Pay As You Go' (PAYGO) systems were based on a social solidarity principle using a collective fund against risk and with public sector support, to finance non-contributory pensions. In many cases the State guaranteed a minimum pension for minimum wage contributors and other social protection programmes. However, some elements of the PAYGO system came under fire, as critics put forward the idea of an impending crisis due to the aging of the population and the impact that this could have on the fiscal sustainability of pension systems (World Bank, 1994). As the baby boomer generation aged and started to retire, it was argued, the PAYGO would become unsustainable. As Palley (1998, p.93) states: 'the key element in the retirement crisis hypothesis is the claim that an increased number of retirees will pose an insupportably large burden on the future working age population'. Against this looming crisis, the introduction pre-funded private schemes were seen as a sustainable alternative.

However, this argument forgets how in the last few decades, with the help of technological progress, labour productivity has increased, and with it the capacity to produce enough income for a larger population. Crucially to sustain retirement income, productivity growth should be associated with increases in wages, out which pensions can be paid. Therefore, key to reduce the burden of a rising retired population are the issues of productivity growth and income distribution. In this order of ideas Palley (1998, p.97) states that:

> The issue of income distribution is central to the problem of supporting a growing population of elderly. Not only must total productivity be growing, so that society has enough total income to provide for the elderly, but the income must get into workers' hands. That is, the income must first get into the hands of those paying for the retirement system, and then get transferred to retirees. If the system is financed through payroll taxes, then wages must also grow. Absent this, the burden on workers of supporting the elderly will grow. Avoiding wage stagnation is therefore central to successfully reducing the burden of public pensions financed by payroll taxes.

In other words, the growing literature testifying the evidence of economic inequality needs to be introduced in the PAYGO system sustainability debate. The point is clear, if the distribution of income favours wage-earners, the traditional public system will not necessarily result in fiscal pressures.

While the arguments in favour of the capitalisation and privatisation of pensions are mainly associated with the reduction of fiscal burden for the state, they also are connected to the standard neoclassical growth theories, which highlight the connections between saving and investment. In this sense Cesaratto (2002, p.160) affirms that:

> The causal link that runs from the 'foresight motive' for saving to capital accumulation may lead those who argue along conventional lines to the conclusion that the mere existence of Capitalisation System (CS) . . . is necessarily associated with a higher share of saving in income.

Private pension funds are seen to promote investment, through their role as enhancers of financial deepening: by accumulating saving, private schemes would mobilise a greater amount of 'funds' available to be lent out to support real investment, thus favouring economic growth. Holzmann and Hinz (2005) argue that significant long-term saving in the CS supports innovative securities markets that can deliver growth of private fixed-capital investment. In sum, 'a higher rate of saving would lead to more finance available for the private sector to carry out real investment' (Trigg and Lowe, 2011, p.1253).

Such an argument, however, forgets that saving is not a constraint on lending and actually what is important is that financial constraints 'reflect congestion in financial markets that arises because of insufficient liquidity or an excessive degree of liquidity preference. Thus, banks and financial intermediaries may be short of liquidity as a result of a monetary tightening imposed by the central bank, or they may be unwilling to lend because of excessive risk aversion' (Palley, 1998, p.100). By implication, increasing saving, may not necessarily increase lending, let alone investment.

Other arguments focus on the increased efficiency of markets, as the introduction of a private system can reduce payroll taxes, thus eliminating market distortions and enhancing the flexibility between working, lifelong education, and retirement (Trigg and Lowe, 2011). As we will show in the second section, however, private pension systems in emerging economies have not promoted less taxes.

Beyond the neoclassical arguments in favour of an individual capitalisation system for retirement, the emergence of this new retirement structure raises warning concerns regarding risk, transactions costs and fairness. In terms of risks there is as a main factor associated to the market unpredictability and the variability of individual investment returns; inadequate saving or poor financial returns increases the risk of poverty of retirees (Palley, 1998). And 20 years after the introduction of private pension funds in Latin America, this discussion resonates as nowadays the benefits that pensioners are receiving in some countries under more than two decades of CS are lower than in the PAYGO system, as evidenced in countries such as Colombia or Peru, which maintain alternative private and public system.

Despite the different arguments against private pension funds, a wave of pension reforms were introduced in the 1980s and 1990s across several emerging economies, aimed at changing the public PAYGO pension system with a private pension fund system. The new systems were based on the principle of an individual account for the insured worker.[1] Basically, private pension funds (known as AFP [*Administradoras de Fondos de Pensión*] in Latin America) can be understood as an individual saving plan for retirement, which is managed with financial criteria by fund managers, rather than intergenerational solidarity and state support as in the PAYGO system.

The privatisation of pension systems in developing countries occurs in the context of structural reforms that took place in the 1980s and 1990s, and were part of a broader privatisation package. Thus, the pension system went from a public model of defined benefits, to one of defined contributions, individual accounts and private managers.

Latin America, Eastern Europe and Central Asia undertook reforms of their pension systems and introduced a substitute, mixed or parallel model based on individual accounts (Mesa Lago, 2014). The first country to implement the privatisation of the pension system was Chile in 1981 followed by Peru in 1993, Argentina and Colombia in 1994, Mexico in 1997. Other countries of the region like Nicaragua, Costa Rica and Ecuador implemented their reforms after the year 2000. A similar pattern was followed in Eastern Europe and Central Asia, where under the worldwide neoliberal wave individual private accounts for pensions were introduced for Hungary in 1998, Poland in 1999, Latvia and Kazakhstan in 2001, Bulgaria, Croatia and Estonia in 2002, Lithuania in 2004, Slovakia in 2005 and Romania in 2008. In many countries in Latin America, private systems with individual accounts were introduced, but in some cases, such as Colombia and Peru, a public PAYGO system remained as a parallel alternative for workers. Cohabitation of both systems was not part of the original plan from the multilateral entities which supported the reform, however public pressure and political cost on this sensitive issue helped to maintain the possibility to choose alternative retirement options.

Despite the private system with individual capitalisation being introduced in more than 20 emerging countries, after 2008 some of them, such as Argentina (2008), Bolivia (Plurinational State of) (2011), Hungary (2011), Kazakhstan (2013), Poland (2011/2014) and the Czech Republic (2014) have reversed the previous reforms and recovered or strengthened their public and PAYGO system. Other countries, such as Slovakia (2012), Estonia (2009), Latvia (2009) and Lithuania (2009), drastically reduced the size of their individual accounts regimes, decreasing contribution rates and redirecting funding towards public pension systems (ILO, 2017).

PRIVATE PENSION FUNDS: BROKEN PROMISES

The private funded system (AFP) was originally presented as a virtuous system that would bring multiple benefits, including economic growth through greater savings, as was explained in the previous section. They would support capital markets deepening and at the same time would ensure sustainability. They had also promised, as an element in favour of the private pension system, an increase in coverage rates, benefit levels and even replacement rates.

Such benefits have however, to a very large extent, failed to materialise. The ILO (1995) had already warned in recent times of the CS regimes that the substitution of social security by individual savings schemes would lead to an unacceptably high risk for workers and pensioners, and it also would increase the cost of protection for adults and the transition would place a heavy burden on the generation of current workers. Many of these warnings were not taken into account and the promises of social policy makers in the 1990s were not fulfilled.

In terms of coverage in almost all countries that established private pension systems with individual accounts, rates fell and benefit levels stagnated or decreased. For example, in Argentina, after the implementation of a private system, the coverage rate fell by 10% between 1992 and 2004, while in Bolivia the coverage stagnated at 12% (ILO, 2017). In other countries such as Hungary, Kazakhstan and Poland, coverage rates also did not meet ambitious expectations and stagnated or even suffered a slight drop compared to pre-reform levels (ILO, 2017). For 18 Latin American countries[2] in aggregate terms, average coverage rate fell from 42% before the reforms to 32% in 2002 when the reforms have been implemented and developed in the region and then recovered to 37% for 2010 (Rofman and Oliveri, 2012). This small increase was largely due to the sustained output and employment growth rates in several emerging economics during the 2000s. Nevertheless, it is important to argue that despite the recovery for 2010, still the level is lower than in in the early 1990s. Such low levels of coverage are to a large extent the product of the labour market structure typical of emerging economies, with many employed in informal sectors, and therefore unable to be contribute to the private pension system. This is a large contributor to inequalities among the elderly in Latin America (Arza, 2008).

In terms of management fees in private pension systems, the increase has been significant and usually above the management fees in the PAYGO system. The main explanations for the high cost of CS are associated with two points: first, high management fees and expensive premiums to finance disabilities insurance and pensions for relatives' survivors. The consequences of this high fees scheme are reflected in a significant reduction in the net rate of return for contributors, which in turn affects the net value of the return on investments. According to ILO (2017) in El Salvador, the management fees of the public system before the reform (expressed as a percentage of the workers' salary) amounted to 0.5% and increased to 2.98% in 2003, after privatisation; in the case of Chile, the total administrative costs increased from 2.44% of the salaries in the contributory schemes in 1981 to 3.6% in 1984, and only decreased to 2.26% in 2003. Meanwhile, in Poland until the year 2004, the commissions fees was not regulated and the pension fund managers charged up to 10% of the value of the contribution. The highest management fees were recorded in Mexico and Argentina, where they represented 38% and 32% of the contributions, respectively. According to Mesa Lago (2004), the average of the management costs of 11 countries in Latin America, expressed as a percentage of contributions, was 26% in 2003.

Another unfulfilled promise relates to the limited capacity to generate adequate retirement incomes. This is particularly clear when examining the replacement rate, i.e. the ratio between pension entitlements and pre-retirement income. For example in Chile, between 1990 and 2000, replacement rates dropped, as the minimum pension decreased, which is received by 50% of the affiliates to the AFP (Crabbe, 2005). Borzutzky and Hyde (2015) also indicate that replacement rates were especially low in the case of women, due to the low level of female enrolment in the pension system. Overall pension performance in Chile was poor, which is translated into inadequate pensions. In 2015, the Chilean Government established a special commission – *Comisión Asesora Presidencial sobre el Sistema de Pensiones* (CAPSP) – to undertake a comprehensive analysis of the adequacy of the pension system. The commission found that 79% of the pensions in Chile were under the minimum wage (CAPSP, 2015). Cichon et al (2004) also concludes that the average of the amounts of pensions tends to fall to the minimum levels and according to Crabbe (2005), There is general agreement that a large of the population will not meet the requirements established to receive the minimum pension (Cichon et al, 2004; Crabbe, 2005). The CAPSP (2015) suggest reforms to the pension system that recognise the importance of a public and solidarity pillar for low income workers.

Another controversial point is that in most of the cases, the introduction of private pension systems has not resulted in significant cost reduction. As discussed, one of the main motivations for introducing private pension systems was the fiscal pressure generated by public systems, due to the existence of financial deficits and/or the accumulation long-term pension liabilities. It was assumed that the privatisation reforms would reduce the fiscal expenditure that social protection implied for the state. However, when CS systems were implemented, there were high transition costs that generated further deficit problems and indebtedness in the PAYGO system, which required more fiscal expenditure. According to the ILO (2017), for example, in Bolivia the transition costs after the reforms were 2.5 times higher than before the reform. Another example is Argentina, where the PAYGO system had a deficit that in the year 2000 represented 3.3% of GDP, while the contributions diverted to the private system amounted to about 1.5%, in Hungary, the transition cost of the reform imposed a fiscal burden on the government that increased from 0.3% of GDP in 1998 to 1.2% in 2010 (ILO, 2017).

Finally, it is important to highlight that saving levels in emerging economies have by and large not increased and fell in the years following the introduction of private pensions. As Figure 3.1 shows, emerging economies in Europe and Latin America, where the pension privatisation was most intense, present substantially lower saving rates than developing economies in Asia, and present figures similar to the least developed countries in Sub-Saharan Africa.[3] Even if one accepts the problematic

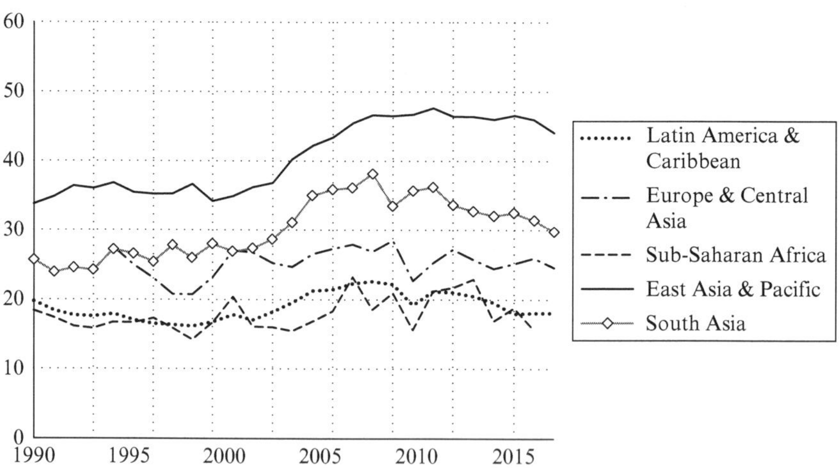

Note: Country groupings exclude high-income countries.

Source: Authors' elaboration based on World Bank – World Development Indicators.

Figure 3.1 Saving rates, % GNI

view that saving generates investment and growth, pension funds do not seem to substantially contribute to this.

Three decades since the push for pension privatisation, it is clear that many promises have remained unfulfilled. Private pensions have failed to significantly increase saving, raise finance for investment, and have had worsened old-age welfare and increased inequalities. As mentioned, many countries have reversed the private pension funds reforms for all the arguments and failed promises that we have described in this section. However, in other countries, despite these failures financial actors have managed to remain in the game, under political pressure and lobby, while they keep looking for new sources of sustainability and profitability in foreign financial markets that create financialisation scenarios for emerging economies, as we will show in the next section.

PRIVATE PENSION FUNDS AND FINANCIALISATION

While the capitalisation system (CS) has not provided the benefits promised, it has helped shape the process of financialisation in emerging economies. The most common idea, financialisation, is associated with Epstein (2005, p.1), who defines the phenomenon as 'the increasing importance of financial markets, financial motives, financial institutions, and financial elites in the operation of the economy and its governing institutions, both at the national and international levels'. However, this definition still is introductory as there are different approaches to financialisation; as Sawyer (2013) argues, 'the term . . . is not limited to a specific period or place, though it would be anticipated that the pace and form of financialisation varies across time and space' (p.6). Existing accounts of financialisation however remain largely focused on national experiences, and in particular the experiences of developed countries. However, recent works, such as Bonizzi (2013), Karwowski and Stockhammer (2017) and Bortz and Kaltenbrunner (2018), have started to show how some empirical regularities associated with financialisation in developed countries are also replicated in some developing countries. In addition to these common regularities, there are also specific phenomena that can be associated with the financialisation in emerging economies, particularly microfinance (Bateman, 2010; Aitken, 2013) and the recurring vulnerability to external capital inflows and financial Dutch disease (Bortz and Kaltenbrunner, 2018; Botta et al, 2016). Even in the small – but expanding – literature on financialisation in developing countries, little attention is given to pension funds from the financialisation approach.

Pension funds can contribute to the process of financialisation. By institutionalising the process of saving, a 'wall of money' (Fernandez and Aalbers, 2016) is generated in search for profitable financial assets, as pension funds need to generate sufficient returns to meet their future commitments. In advanced countries these needs were largely made by the secular expansion and inflation of capital markets (Engelen, 2003; Toporowski, 2000). In the current context, low yields on bonds constitute a barrier in the search of their financial targets, pushing pension funds actors to search for higher yielding assets (Fernandez and Aalbers, 2016; Bonizzi and Churchill, 2017; Bonizzi and Kaltenbrunner, 2017; Bonizzi et al, 2018). Thus, the dimension of financialisation associated with the growth and innovation of the financial markets, is driven by the urgent need of the pension funds to generate profits. With this, possible scenarios of instability can appear, as was seen with derivatives associated with mortgages and hedge funds (Lysandrou and Nesvetailova, 2015).

Such a process can also occur, in a particular form, in emerging economies. In some of these countries pension funds have grown substantially, even though they remain small in absolute terms compared to developed countries. Figure 3.2 shows how pension fund assets to GDP are quite large, especially in Latin America.

In their search for profitable investment returns, they have also started to extend their reach to a wider range of asset classes and promoted financial innovation, while pushing for reforms to remove their investment constraints. A good example of this can be seen in Colombia and Peru. For these two countries, the portfolio configuration in pension funds has changed over the last 15 years towards greater diversification and at the same time a greater risk in investments. A first key trend has been the substantial increase in the proportion of foreign assets, which have taken advantage of the liberalisation and deregulation that allows them to have more investment in foreign securities. This possibility did not exist at the beginning of the century in Colombia and Peru, but as liberalisation proceeded, foreign assets increased their share in AFP's portfolios to 13% and 9% respectively in 2006, and 33% and 40% in 2015 (FIAP, 2016). The other important point has been how in portfolio allocations fixed-income has lost prominence while equity has gained considerable shares. Equities allocations were zero in Colombia's portfolios in 2001, while in Peru the figure stood at 30%. By 2015 they had increased to 48% and 55% respectively. The shares of government bonds have fallen in Colombia, but still represent the most significant asset with 35% in 2016, while in Peru they rose from 13% to 18% (FIAP, 2016). Importantly, pension funds have also been key purchasers of new asset classes, sparking the development of private equity markets and foreign exchange swaps, to hedge their international investments (Bonizzi et al, 2018).

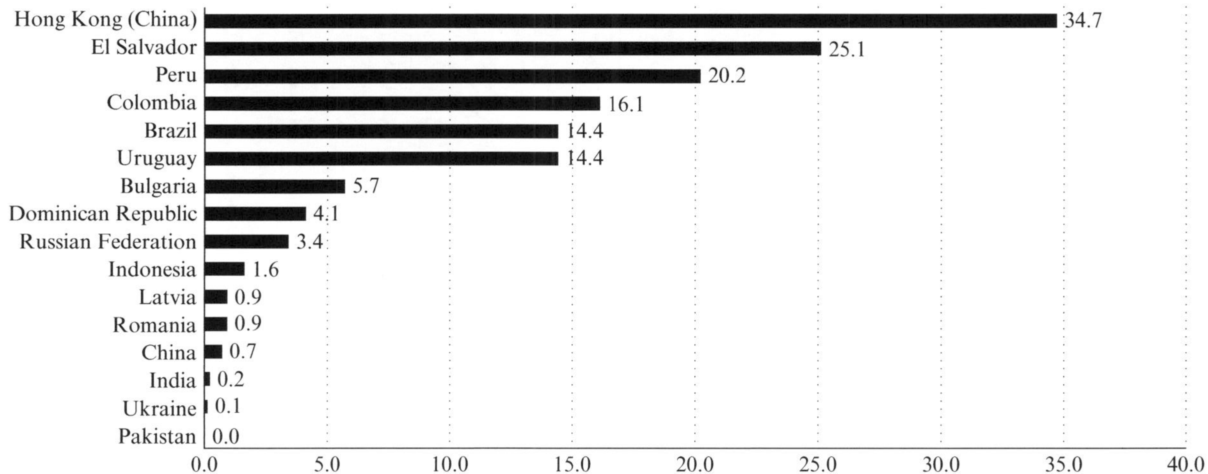

Source: OCDE Pension reports (2010).

Figure 3.2 Importance of pension funds relative to the size of the economy in selected non-OECD countries, 2010

Pension funds and their asset demand are highly important in shaping financialisation in these countries. Domestic capital markets remain peripheral to private and public borrowers in these countries, a situation that pension funds have not managed to substantially affect (Didier and Schumkler, 2013). Furthermore, they receive large sums of foreign capital inflows, with foreign investors and lenders becoming key but volatile players in financial markets, a key feature showing the subordinate character of emerging economies' financial integration (Andrade and Prates, 2013; Powell, 2013; Levy-Orlik and Ortiz, 2016; Bonizzi, 2017; Bortz and Kaltenbrunner, 2018; Kaltenbrunner and Painceira, 2018). Faced with this situation, pension funds have looked beyond domestic capital markets to find avenues for their investments. This has strengthened the pressures for financial innovation and deregulation, and as such is a primary force behind financialisation in these countries. These new investments can however generate more risks, and it is not entirely clear to what extent they will foster economic and social development, at a time where export-led growth is in crisis.

CONCLUSIONS

Private pension funds are at the core of the latest stage of capitalism in emerging economies. The main arguments behind the policy pressures leading to their rise has been based on the fiscal pressures that are generated by the aging crisis, as well as the promise of increased saving, based on the (neoclassical) argument that this will be causing investment. However, that saving is not a constraint on lending and actually what is important is that financial constraints reflect congestion in financial markets. Fiscal pressure would ease if distribution of income in favour of wage earners improves, as productivity growth continues. Despite these arguments, since the early 1990s private pension funds based on individual accounts started to replace the PAYGO solidarity system in many emerging countries around the world. After more than two decades, many of their promises have not been fulfilled: the coverage rate for retirement has not improved, the replacement rate has fallen, saving rates have not significantly increased, and fiscal pressures still exist, driven by the high costs of transition from the solidarity system to the individual system. Finally, we have shown how the private pension AFP have emerged as an important characteristic of the financialisation in developing countries. AFP have allocated growing financial shares to foreign assets and sparked the development of new asset classes and practices, in a context of high capital inflows that affects the local assets supply.

The balance of evidence overall does not seem to be particularly positive for the privatised pension system in emerging economies. Indeed, the discontent in some countries has been so widespread that they have re-nationalised their systems. A wider rethinking about pension policy is therefore needed, to protect the wellbeing of the elderly, as well as ensuring the financial system is fit to promote economic development.

NOTES

1. As Mesa Lago (2014) stated, private pensions systems normally lack endogenous social solidarity.
2. Argentina, Bolivia, Chile, Colombia, Costa Rica, El Salvador, Mexico, Peru, Uruguay, Honduras, Nicaragua, Guyana, Dominican Republic, Venezuela, Mexico, Paraguay, Ecuador and Brazil.
3. See Grigoli et al (2015) for further details on Latin America's saving rates.

REFERENCES

Aitken, R. (2013). The financialisation of micro-credit. *Development and Change*, 44(3), 473–499.

Andrade, R. P. and Prates, D. M. (2013). Exchange rate dynamics in a peripheral monetary economy. *Journal of Post Keynesian Economics*, 35, 399–416.

Arza, C. (2008). Pension reform in Latin America: distributional principles, inequalities and alternative policy options. *Journal of Latin American Studies*, 40(1), 1–28.

Bateman, M. (2010). *Why Doesn't Microfinance Work?: The Destructive Rise of Local Neoliberalism*. London: Zed Books.

Bonizzi, B. (2013). Financialisation in developing and emerging countries: a survey. *International Journal of Political Economy*, 42(4), 83–107.

Bonizzi, B. (2017). An alternative post-Keynesian framework for understanding capital flows to emerging markets. *Journal of Economic Issues*, 51, 137–162.

Bonizzi, B. and Churchill, J. (2017). Pension funds and financialisation in the European Union. *Revista de economía mundial*, 46, 71–90.

Bonizzi, B. and Kaltenbrunner, A. (2017). *Liability Driven Investment and Pension Fund Exposure to Emerging Markets: A Minskyan Analysis*. Mimeo.

Bonizzi, B., Churchill, J. and Guevara, D. (2018). *Variegated Financialisation and Pension Fund Asset Demand: The Case of Colombia and Peru*. Mimeo.

Bortz, P. G. and Kaltenbrunner, A. (2018). The international dimension of financialisation in developing and emerging economies. *Development and Change*, 49(2), 375–393.

Botta, A., Godin, A. and Missaglia, M. (2016). Finance, foreign (direct) investment and Dutch disease: the case of Colombia. *Economia Politica*, 33(2), 265–289.

Borzutzky, S. and Hyde, M. (2015). Chile's Social Welfare System: the socio-economic impact of pension privatisation and health reform, in Aspalter, C. (ed.), *Ashgate Research Companion on Welfare State Systems*. Aldershot: Ashgate.

CAPSP-Comisión Asesora Presidencial sobre el Sistema de Pensiones (2015). Informe Final. Presidencia de Chile. ISBN: 978-956-358-961-0

Cichon, M., Scholz, W., Van de Meerendonk, A., Hagemejer, K., Bertranou, F. and Plamondon, P. (2004). *Financing Social Protection* (Vol. 5). Geneva: International Labour Organization.

Crabbe, C. A. (2005). *A Quarter Century of Pension Reform in Latin America and the Caribbean: Lessons Learned and Next Steps*. Washington, DC: IDB.

Didier, T. and Schmukler, S. (2013). The financing and growth of firms in China and India: evidence from capital markets. *Journal of International Money and Finance, Elsevier*, 39(C), 111–137.

Engelen, E. (2003). The logic of funding European pension restructuring and the dangers of financialisation. *Environment and Planning A*, 35(8), 1357–1372.

Epstein, G. A. (ed.). (2005). *Financialisation and the World Economy*. Cheltenham: Edward Elgar Publishing.

Fernandez, R. and Aalbers, M. (2016). Financialisation and housing: between globalisation and varieties of capitalism. *Competition and Change*, 20(2), 71–88.

FIAP (2016). *Opportunities and Challenges in the Investment of Pension Funds and Voluntary Pension Savings Funds*. International Federation of Pension Funds Administrators.

Grigoli, F., Herman, A. and Schmidt-Hebbel, K. (2015). Saving in Latin America and the Caribbean: Performance and Policies (No. 15–108). *International Monetary Fund.*

Holzmann, R. and Hinz, R. (2005). Old-Age Income Support in the 21st Century. An International Perspective on Pension Systems and Reform, *Policy Report.* Washington: World Bank.

ILO (2017). *World Social Protection Report 2017–19: Universal Social Protection to Achieve the Sustainable Development Goals*. Geneva: International Labour Organization.

Kaltenbrunner, A. and Painceira, J. P. (2018). Subordinated financial integration and financialisation in emerging capitalist economies: the Brazilian experience. *New Political Economy*, 23, 290–313.

Karwowski, E. and Stockhammer, E. (2017). Financialisation in emerging economies: a systematic overview and comparison with Anglo-Saxon economies. *Economic and Political Studies*, 5(1), 60–86.

Levy-Orlik, N. and Ortiz, E. (2016). *The Financialisation Response to Economic Disequilibria: European and Latin American Experiences*. Cheltenham: Edward Elgar Publishing.

Lysandrou, P. and Nesvetailova, A. (2015). The role of shadow banking entities in the financial crisis: a disaggregated view. *Review of International Political Economy*, 22, 257–279.

Mesa-Lago, C. (2004). Las reformas de pensiones en América Latina y su impacto en los principios de la Seguridad Social. Serie Documentos de Trabajo sobre Financiamiento del Desarrollo CEPAL, No. 144.

Mesa-Lago, C. (2014). *Reversing Pension Privatisation: The Experience of Argentina, Bolivia, Chile and Hungary* (No. 994848943402676). International Labour Organization.

Palley, T. I. (1998). The economics of social security: an old Keynesian perspective. *Journal of Post Keynesian Economics*, 21(1), 93–110.

Powell, J. (2013). *Subordinate Financialisation: A Study of Mexico and Its Non-Financial Corporations*. PhD, SOAS, University of London.

Rofman, R. and Oliveri, M. L. (2012). Pension coverage in Latin America: Trends and determinants. Social Protection and Labour Discussion Paper No. 1217.
Sawyer, M. (2013). What is financialisation? *International Journal of Political Economy*, 42(4), 5–18.
Toporowski, J. (2000). *The End of Finance: Capital Market Inflation, Financial Derivatives and Pension Fund Capitalism*. London: Routledge.
Trigg, A. B. and Lowe, J. T. (2011). Comparing pension systems in the circular flow of income. *American Journal of Economics and Sociology*, 70(5), 1248–1281.
World Bank (1994). *Averting the Old Age Crisis: Policies to Protect the Old and Promote Growth*. Washington, DC: World Bank.

4. Financialization and bancarization of Argentina, Brazil and Mexico: financial services transformations from the post-crisis period

Alicia Girón and Marcia Solorza

INTRODUCTION

For countries such as Argentina, Brazil and Mexico, financialization developed within conceptual changes the International Monetary Fund (IMF) started more than two decades ago to rename many of the developing countries as emerging markets. This was a precise concept because of the close and unbreakable relationship between national and international financial circuits, precedents of which are not only the capital transfers, but the opening to the reception of capital that allowed the main consortiums and financial corporations to absorb the national financial circuits.

> *These are countries that [in the last decades of the 20th century and the first ones of the 21st century] have entered into a growth and modernization process that makes them susceptible to the interest of financial investors. [For this reason], the heterogeneous concept includes countries with vigorous economic growth, but with lack of strength on their current account and banking system. In addition, some are producers of raw materials and base products; others have focused their development on the production of manufactured articles; and the rest has specialized in the provision of services* (Guillén, 2010, p. 8).

At the same time, the gradual insertion of the national financial circuits (of Argentina, Brazil and Mexico) to the international ones sided with the economic cycle of instability of the economic system at an international level. According to Kregel (2008), channelling Minsky (1992), the instability in the economic system is endogenous (the stability in the economic system itself generates behaviours that produce instability), and the increasing fragility makes the economic system more inclined to unstable responses and to changes in the financial conditions that are important for the profits of investment projects. Minsky expressed this idea highlighting that these events are unavoidable because of the fact that sustained periods of economic stability produce increasing financial fragility due to the euphoria or bubble type obsession that arises (Minsky, 1992).

In order to avoid the fragility of banking and financial institutions, as well as the instability in the economic system structures caused by them, new financial architectures were built, and reforms or regulations to the operational, supervisory and regulatory practices of financial institutions and markets in developed and developing economies were implemented.[1] Such is the case of the New Deal that operated 'successfully' after the 1929 crisis and promoted the creation of the international monetary and financial system (active until the 1970s) of Bretton Woods. Nowadays, in the post-crisis period, *financialization* as a process encompasses all sectors and deepens great inequalities; it is constructed and reconstructed based on the financial and banking indicators that we will develop below.

THE FINANCIALIZATION PROCESS

After the breach of the Bretton Woods Agreements, the collapse of the dollar convertibility in 1971 and of the fixed exchange rates in 1973, the flexibility of the exchange rates promoted a bigger opening of the economies and an increasing interdependence of the national economies within the global system. The establishment of the Washington Consensus was emblematic: it promoted the opening up of economies, the free mobility of international capital flows and the financial adjustment of the capital account of the balance of payments. This way, financial instability became a feature of financial markets, in both developed and developing countries, which caused recurring currency, banking and financial crises over the last four decades.

The transformation of globalized financial circuits led the way for the increase of financial capital over productive capital, that is, it redefined the behaviour of development financing. Particularly in Latin American countries, this transformation modified the objectives of banking and financial institutions, promoted financial innovation and created a stream of new institutional participants in the financial markets, generating and strengthening a process of *financialization* of the economies.

This capitalist process involves moving the centre of gravity of the economic activity from real production and services to the financial sector: so, the financial sector became a driving force of capital accumulation, and speculative finances were transformed into a kind of secondary engine of growth due to the weakness of productive investment (Foster and Magdoff, 2009). And it is from the process of insertion of the financial circuits of countries like Argentina, Brazil and Mexico into the international financial circuits, that these became a central axis for institutional investors and also for the necessary profitability of international financial agents.

The term *financialization* has been addressed from different theoretical perspectives, especially those that belong to the post-Keynesian and Marxian approaches. Here we pick up on the conceptualization presented by some economists. According to Epstein (2005), it refers to the increased role of financial motives, financial markets, financial actors, financial institutions and financial elites in the operation of the national and international economy. Stockhammer (2012) makes it clear that this process has deeply transformed the developed (and developing) economies, and that the term encompasses a set of changes in the relationship between the 'real' sector and the 'financial' sector, giving more importance to the financial motives or actors. Palley (2007) defines it as the transformation of the operation of economic systems at macro and microeconomic levels. For Lapavitsas (2011), it is the result of the systematic transformation of the capitalist economy, which revolves around the financial system and involves the creation of new sources of profit. On the other hand, Greta Krippner (2005) emphasizes that it is an accumulation pattern where obtaining profits is achieved through financial channels instead of trade or goods production; while Arrighi (1999) identifies the long waves of economic development in global capitalism, which involves geographical and economic changes, highlighting that in the phases of economic slowdown there is a process of *financialization* characterized by the power that had initially established a competitive advantage in terms of production, but when that model of growth is exhausted, it provokes a series of changes or movements towards financial activities with new actors participation.

This is how *financialization* shows characteristics *sui generis* in countries recently inserted into the international financial circuits, where institutional investors, mutual funds, hedge funds, insurances, bank funds, investment companies and others, emerge in the developing countries with specific characteristics, which have implied structural transformations of national financial systems, limited by their links with developed countries. According to Costas Lapavitsas (2013), a return to formal imperialism has not been aroused, but *financialization* in developing countries has been subordinated to the hierarchical and exploitative nature of the interactions in the global market.

ECONOMIC AND FINANCIAL OPENING

The *financialization* process in the developing countries begins, as in the developed countries, during the financial liberalization wave of the 1970s.

However, they maintained an integrated development strategy until the late 1980s when the International Monetary Fund (IMF) and the World Bank (WB) imposed the Washington Consensus, forcing developing countries to open their economies and modify their economic-financial systems. From then on, in the 1990s, especially in the first decades of the 21st century, *financialization* took shape and laid its foundations, where one of the priorities is financial opening. This can be seen with the behaviour of the index made by Chinn-Ito (2015) that measures restrictions degree of external transactions[2] with values between −1.8 and 2.6, where, the closer the value is to 2.6, the bigger the opening of a country's capital account. In the Latin American countries analyzed, this condition accelerated since the 2008 crisis; however, Mexico, since the beginning of this century, has maintained its index stable (1.082403) showing that it is an economy 'with an intermediate level of opening'.

Another of the essential components of the Washington Consensus and the *financialization* progress indicator is that the reception of net international capital flows,[3] with the argument that development is being promoted, comes from developed or emerging countries, which have shown an erratic tendency in the period of 1995–2016 (see Figure 4.1). In some years,

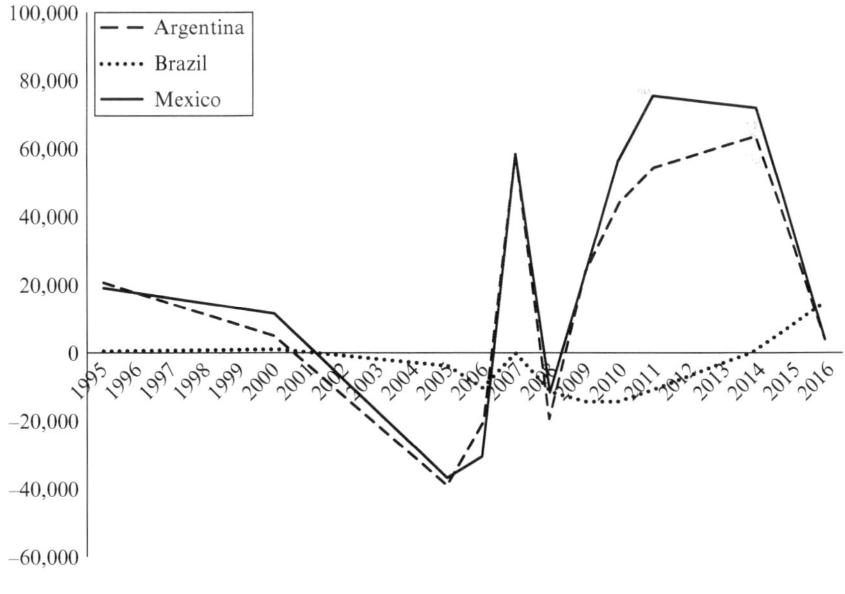

Note: Adapted from CEPAL (2004–2017). Preliminary balance sheet of the Economies of Latin America and the Caribbean, Santiago de Chile.

Figure 4.1 Net transfer of resources, 1995–2016 (million dollars)

this indicator was negative due to the high transfer of resources abroad by the countries studied. It is important to mention that the accumulation of international reserves, to which the countries have also been forced by the IMF and the WB, through the *self-insurance* policy[4] and through intervention in the Forex markets during strong capital flows moments, is used in case of a sudden stop of these markets, to protect from possible outflows of private capital, that is, it is considered a countercyclical response to the instability of international capital flows (Akyüz, 2008).

However, we found that, when applying the *self-insurance* policy, the countries receiving the capital flows have financed the capital exporting countries, mainly the United States of America (the issuer of the world money) and have paid an informal tribute (seigniorage), at the expense of quitting policies that support development, reducing social spending and making the inequalities and poverty indicators deeper. Inflation control also demands the accumulation of international reserves due to the relative link of the exchange rate with a world currency, the dollar, which completes the partially integral formalization of *subordinated financialization*.

Financialization in Latin American countries as Argentina, Brazil and Mexico impacted with results below expectations in terms of productive investment, efficiency and growth. This is despite the fact that the economic-financial systems have supported their growth in the banking system (bank-based) and promoted the development of capital markets (market-based) and banking institutions through private financial mechanisms that act completely freely in these larger economies.[5]

Argentina, Brazil and Mexico, although in different degrees, face significant limiting aspects in their structures (labour, educational, corporate-business and so on), which prevents them from moving forward in terms of productive, commercial and financial diversification. This is easy to identify by means of commercial relationships, which are limited to a few countries (as it is with the United States of America, in the case of Mexico), despite having multiple trade agreements with different countries. However, their financial systems have been gradually segmented and transferred to foreign hands, adapting them to national and international macro and microeconomic conditions, reason why the activities in capital markets have increased, although limitedly, particularly the bond market.

FINANCIAL SERVICES EXPANSION

In the financial field, the international demands for the restructuring of the institutional framework and architecture have contributed to the transformation of the behaviour of financial corporations, highlighting the importance of the banks' participation in the securities market. For this reason, the Washington Consensus not only promoted the opening of the capital account of the balance of payments, but also the commercial flows and the entry of foreign banks, justification for which was declaring that they would provide efficiency and effectiveness to the sector and increase short-term loans for small and medium-sized enterprises.

The incursion of foreign banks in Latin American countries began in the 1980s, with the exception of Chile, where the privatization of numerous banking assets started in the 1970s. The entry of foreign banks into Latin American countries such as Argentina and Brazil has been significant in recent years (2000–2016), representing 23% and 11% respectively of the total assets of their banking systems; 65.9% when it comes to the Mexican case, a very important proportion. Nevertheless, the accelerated growth of Grupo Financiero Banorte-IXE-Interacciones, a national consortium, has inclined to counteract the tendency to transfer this sector to foreign ownership.

Reversing this characteristic trajectory of *financialization* has become one of the challenges of the institutions in charge of supervising and regulating banking entities, as well as promoting an adequate development and operation of the financial system. Mexico is moving towards that goal, Argentina seeks to close the constant depredation of vulture funds while some national banks increase their presence in other Latin American countries and Brazil extends significantly the participation of its banking firms in other countries of the world and the region.

The incorporation of foreign banks in financial systems has broadened the size, scope, inclusion and demographic penetration of the transmission channels of the financial system services, according to Table 4.1, making its operation more complex in order to maximize the benefit, and accelerating it to: (1) strategically segment their commercial activity; (2) record high levels of concentration; (3) show little orientation towards productive activities; (4) increase the volume of credit cards; (5) increase mortgage loans; (6) substantially increase personal loans and (7) try to reverse the low and different levels of banking and financial deepening and inclusion (see Table 4.1).

The Federation of Latin American Banks (FELABAN, 2008) defines banking segmentation as a management and control mechanism to have specialized knowledge of the market based on the grouping of clients by market niche. This allows knowing the needs of services and the transactions characteristic to be carried out. Correspondingly, the segmentation of the banking market is defined geographically, demographically, psychographically (concerning behaviours and consumption habits) and, more decisively, based on the behaviour corresponding to the expected benefits,

Table 4.1 Number of bank companies, branches and cash dispensers (ATM), 2011–2015

Branches and cash dispensers for every 100,000 inhabitants

	2011			2013			2015		
Country	No. Banks	Branches	ATM	No. Banks	Branches	ATM	No. Banks	Branches	ATM
Argentina	80	10.1	35.6	81	10.6	43.4	n.d	n.d	n.d
Brazil	160	11.1	134.6	155	11.4	82.6	141.3	10.1	90
Mexico	42	10.1	31.3	47	10.6	34.3	82	15.4	35
Latin America*	n.d	n.d	n.d	32.3	11.9	31.5	n.d	n.d	n.d

Figures for Latin America in the year 2013 are averages. In Brazil, the decrease of the number of cash dispensers from the year 2011 to 2013 owes to changes in the Legislation of the Banco Central do Brasil.

Note: Adapted from FELABAN (2014). Financial indicators Authorized for Latin America.

that is, the level of income and the activity performed by the clients, the latter being public institutions, companies or individuals.

The banking market has been divided to know and differentiate the client sectors to which the activities and services offered by commercial banks will be directed, even when they operate as a multipurpose or universal bank. Following Stanton, Etzel and Walker (2007), the banking services division is based on the consideration that the groups of individuals to be reached have similarities depending on the factors contributing to the demand; therefore, their response to the marketing strategies will be similar. The effectiveness of this practice is evident as it can be measured, and because the segments are large and accessible.

Both the segmentation of the financial market and the introduction of new technologies, such as ATMs, favour the concentration of banking assets and the credit portfolio in a few firms, national or foreign. The ratio of deposits to Gross Domestic Product (GDP) and of total credit to GDP (conceptual indicators of financial deepening and development, and of the financial deepening that measures the relative size of credit of the financial system with respect to the size of the economy) in Argentina, Mexico and Brazil has risen in recent years, but they are still relatively low and diverse compared to the levels of financial deepening in developed countries and, in the case of Mexico, regarding the size of its economy (see Table 4.2).

Mexico shows one of the highest rates of financial deepening. It is the economy with the highest rate of internationalization of its financial system, making it clear that the credit restriction to the productive sector

Table 4.2 Deposits and total credit to GDP (percentages)

	Total Deposits/GDP		Total Credit/GDP	
Country	2011	2013	2011	2013
Argentina	24.3	27.3	13.2	16.4
Brazil	63.1	64.2	49.1	56.1
Mexico	19.1	19.8	15.7	17.9
Latin America*	n.d	40.1	n.d	33.0

Figures for Latin America in the year 2013 are averages.

Note: Adapted from FELABAN (2014). Financial indicators Authorized for Latin America.

and the low levels of income is completely inflexible, as well as that in this country the entry of foreign banks and international capital flows give priority to the appropriation of high rates of profitability, generating high volatility and instability in the structure of the financial system.

Domestic banks have also been attracted to the obtaining of large profits, directing their actions, together with those of foreign banks, into the acceleration of the *financialization* of personal income, by producing a sustained growth of household debts and encouraging the increased use of credit cards, debit cards and electronic payments, granting personal and mortgage loans, in a few words, *banking*[6] the population, or increasing financial inclusion with the entry of the poor sectors of the population to financial services.

Likewise, the figures in Table 4.3 confirm the upward trend of loan money in the three largest economies in the Latin American region and, at the same time, presume the possibility of a bigger financial instability. The innovation of methods of payment creates uncertainty about the fraud possibility; it is required therefore to manage it, but banks delegate this battle to the users, focusing the suppression (partial or total) strategies on client's self-management.

Innovations are a driving force of profit maximization, the goal of every company, which is magnified in periods of *financialization* of economies, becoming a purpose itself for multinational corporations such as banking firms.

Competition is no longer limited to a national financial space; the opening and financial deregulation promoted the acquisition of existing banking firms in the countries in the last three decades of the twentieth century, and now, in the twenty first century, the newly formed (multi-Latin) multinational financial corporations are expanded and strengthened. These operate at the same time in several countries of the world, the region

Table 4.3 *Possession of credit and debit cards and index of demand of electronic payments, 2012–2015, for every 100,000 inhabitants*

Country	2012				2014				2015			
	Total cards	Debit cards	Credit cards	Electronic payment demand index	Total cards	Debit cards	Credit cards	Electronic payment demand index	Total cards	Debit cards	Credit cards	Electronic payment demand index
Argentina	n.d	n.d	n.d	n.d	n.d	n.d	n.d	n.d	n.d	n.d	n.d	n.d
Brazil	70.4	53.0	58.9	66.3	70.8	53.6	60.1	69.4	n.d	150	80	n.d
Mexico	39.6	26.6	29.4	37.4	39.7	29.0	30.5	37.0	n.d	110	22.2	n.d

In the year 2014 there was a setback in the bancarización and financial incorporation.

Note: Adapted from Afi-Tecnocom (2015). Trends in Means of Payments.

and Latin American sub-regions, contributing to create a new wave of mergers and acquisitions and extending their hierarchical control over the countries and a large proportion of their economic activities (Schneider, 2009) (see Table 4.4).

These conditions have boosted the benefits of commercial banking, not only of assets profitability (Return On Assets), but of Return On Equity (ROE), in the three countries studied (see Figure 4.2).

Meanwhile, two important factors in the performance analysis of the financial system: leverage and costs of operation, did not concur harmonically to elevate the profits of the commercial bank. The fall in leverage and its cost (the interest rate), understood as the ratio between assets and equity, and the reduction in the ratio between costs or operating expenses and operating margin,[7] were not substantial in any financial system. However, the financial systems of Mexico and Argentina recorded, within two years (2011–2013), a drop in the ratio between operating expense and operating margin from 78.6% to 76.5% and from 59.3% to 52.1%, respectively. While in Brazil it increased considerably (almost 4%) from 96.5% to 110.1%. It can be stated that in the first two countries the leverage of the banks can be low and/or easy to handle, the banks are efficient and the new regulations based on Basel III are adequate for the banking business to be profitable and flourishing; while Brazilian banks, mostly state-owned, can be highly leveraged and show considerable degrees of inefficiency.

SOME REGULATORY ELEMENTS

The great crisis of 2008, still without being completely and globally overcome, and with serious consequences in Europe, showed the laxity of the institutional regulations of the international financial systems. Argentina, Brazil and Mexico, in the decade of the 1990s and in the first decade of the 2000s, had restructured their banking regulatory systems and applied the Basel I and II Agreements on financial risk management systems: credit, liquidity, market and operability. Consequently, they delivered statistical reports to the regulatory bodies of each country.

In recent years, 2010–2015, these Latin American countries once again adapted the rules and supervision of banking activity to the momentary needs of controlling financial instability. Now, Mexico as a member of the Organisation for Economic Co-operation and Development (OECD) is committed to follow the rules of Basel III, a global regulatory standard for capital requirements that involves applying stress tests to crisis situations, market risks, credit and liquidity. And, without belonging to said

Table 4.4 Trans-Latin or multi-Latin banks, 2017

Name	Country of Origin	Country of Operation		Representative Offices	Agencies	Correspondent Banks	Strategic Alliances
Banco de la Nación Argentina	Argentina	Argentina USA United Kingdom Japan France Brazil Spain	Panama China Bolivia Chile Paraguay Uruguay Cayman Islands	Venezuela China Brazil			
Bank of Galicia and Buenos Aires	Argentina	Argentina Uruguay		Brazil Chile			
Bank of Brazil	Brazil	Brazil Argentina Chile Bolivia USA Mexico Colombia Spain Uruguay	Paraguay Venezuela Ecuador Peru Panama Costa Rica Guatemala Morocco Japan	Russia	Netherlands El Salvador Monaco Bahamas Cayman Islands Luxembourg Belgium China Australia India	South Africa United Kingdom France	

Table 4.4 (continued)

Name	Country of Origin	Country of Operation		Representative Offices	Agencies	Correspondent Banks	Strategic Alliances
Itau Unibanco Investor Relations	Brazil	Brazil Luxembourg Argentina Chile Colombia Paraguay Uruguay Venezuela Japan	Mexico USA Panama Bolivia United Arab Emirates France Portugal Spain Switzerland	South Korea United Kingdom	Cayman Islands Bahamas South Korea United Kingdom Morocco		
Bradesco	Brazil	Brazil Mexico Japan Spain Portugal Argentina	Peru Paraguay Uruguay Luxembourg Australia		Ecuador Venezuela Bolivia Costa Rica Panama Bahamas Cayman Islands Belgium France Morocco	Ecuador China Germany United Kingdom South Africa United Arab Emirtes	Chile
Banorte	Mexico	Mexico					Spain Japan
Banco Azteca	Mexico	Costa Rica El Salvador Panama Guatemala Honduras	Nicaragua Colombia Ecuador Peru				
Compartamos Banco	Mexico	Mexico Guatemala Peru					

Note: Personal collection.

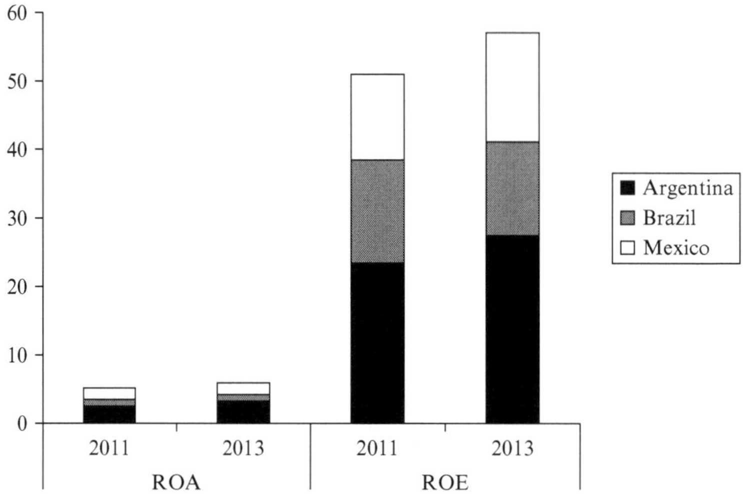

Note: Adapted from FELABAN (2014). Financial indicators Authorized for Latin America.

Figure 4.2 Profitability on average assets and profitability on heritage, 2011–2013, percentages

organization, Argentina and Brazil have also joined to comply with the new bank capital requirements established by said rules.

Basel III requires banks to have a *Tier 1* of minimum 6% of capital,[8] a financial cushion of 2.5% extra of capital, and 2.5% more as a prudent measure for credit growth. In addition, there are very strict liquidity rules for very large banks (too big to fail), in order to avoid bankruptcy. This way, Basel III imposes measures so that the banks' capital is placed in instruments subject to rigorous criteria of liquidity, timing and losses absorption. This has stipulated that banks must comply in agreement with the new criteria of solvency and risk management (risk weighting) within a certain time horizon, which is why the central banks of Argentina, Brazil and Mexico, their supervisory bodies and the Federation of Latin American Banks (FELABAN) have approved the measurement of financial indicators of quality and soundness of the national banking systems. The technical rules of Basel III, particularly those related to portfolio valuation, credit risks and liquidity, require sophisticated programming development that will not only require high mathematical and software knowledge, but will also incur costs to the banks.

Here we are focusing on studying the behaviour of the provisions and total credits ratio[9] as well as the regulatory capital and risk-weighted assets and contingencies ratio,[10] which represent statistical information that brings us closer to noticing how the national banking systems foresee losses and if they would have enough capital to absorb them. Briefly, from 2011–2013, the banking systems of Argentina and Mexico raised their quality index to 2.0% and 4.97%, respectively, while Brazil showed a drop from 5.66% to 4.97%. Paradoxically, the solvency degree of banks in Argentina and Mexico decreased from 16.6% to 14.2% and from 15.7% to 15.5% and, in Brazil, it increased from 16.3% to 16.6% in the same period. This gap between quality indexes and banking solvency underlines that it is not enough to know the *ex ante* risk of losses; it is necessary to apply regulatory policies aimed at controlling financial investment by banking institutions, especially if the intention is to avoid central bank assistance. Fact that is actually possible in Brazil, where the state ownership of assets in the banking system predominates.

All these new characteristics of the *subordinated financialization* of Latin American countries have led to the 'growth' of national financial markets, particularly public bond markets.

DEEPENING OF FINANCIAL MARKETS

The *subordinated financialization* of the countries has led them to focus their attention on monetary policy, the acquisition of international reserves by their central banks (see Table 4.5) and the implementation of sterilization mechanisms to avoid the risk of an inflation rate increase above the fixed targets. But, the obligations issued by the countries to perform the sterilization imply paying domestic interest rates, which are considerably higher than the interest rates paid for the foreign public assets acquired in turn by the central banks of the Latin American countries. The spread between domestic interest rates and foreign interest rates has a cost for the States of Argentina, Brazil and Mexico, which must be paid by the society.

This monetary environment has promoted the heterogeneous growth of national financial markets in larger economies. The markets of public bonds (public debt) have expanded diametrically in Brazil and Mexico, facilitating their acquisition by pension funds and national banks, which have turned their investments towards transactions in open financial markets. The emission of public bonds in Argentina has been much smaller because the country had not reached a negotiation with the vulture funds (De la Torre, Ize and Shmukler 2012).

This is a guide or reference to set the prices for the emission of domestic private fixed income securities and to evaluate portfolios, a condition that hypothetically can contribute to the development of derivatives markets,

Table 4.5 International reserves, 2010–2016, millions of dollars

Country	2010	2011	2012	2013	2014	2015	2016
Argentina	52,145	46,376	43,290	30,599	31,443	25,563	37,772
Brazil	288,575	352,012	373,147	358,808	363,551	356,464	365,016
Mexico	120,587	149,209	167,050	180,200	195,682	117,597	178,025
Latin America	655,672	773,910	835,905	830,207	857,618	811,907	830,440

Note: Adapted from CEPAL (2015 and 2017). Economic study of Latin America and the Caribbean.

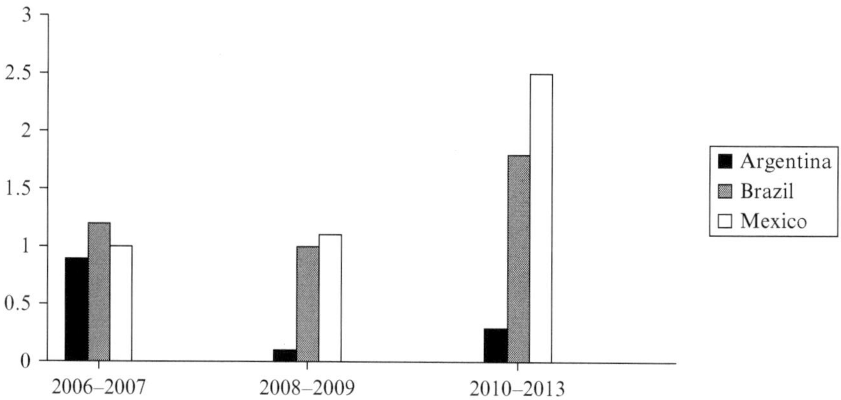

Note: Adapted from CEPAL (2016). Economic study of Latin America and the Caribbean.

Figure 4.3 International bond issues, 2006–2013, (percentage of GDP)

which has not occurred in the countries of Latin America. The emission of corporate bonds that regularly follows the emission of public bonds has maintained a higher capitalization than its reference indexes in Brazil and Mexico, and, in the latter, the market for these securities is strong and attractive for institutional investors.

The issuance of public bonds and bank and corporate bonds linked to foreign currency (dollars) have increased in recent years. Mexico has seen them grow up to 55 billion dollars in 2012 (see Figure 4.3).

While the bond markets have grown, access to equity markets has remained relatively limited in Latin American countries; besides they are highly concentrated in some companies, basically large multinational or multi-Latin conglomerates (consortiums) arising from the domestic field, where the organized market (stock exchange) is located. The list of registered companies is relatively small and shows a clear tendency to decrease, so the stock funding is restricted and concentrated in few emissions, causing a low volume of transactions. The behaviour of the indexes of the stock exchanges proves this, mainly in Brazil and Mexico. However, in Argentina, the Merval index showed important increases in the 2013–2015 period caused by the expectations of the ruling party's victory in the presidential elections.

This behaviour is typical of countries with *subordinated financialization*. As the concentration of capital is exacerbated, it destroys small and medium business owners and opens up their economies to competition between national and international conglomerates in different sectors.

Additionally, alternative product markets that include non-traditional forms of financing: derivatives, factoring, exchange-trade-funds (ETFs), securitization, credit cooperatives and commercial chain financing, have developed in a non-significant way in Latin American countries. The exchange rate derivative negotiations: swaps, options and forwards, have increased in dollars, but not significantly as a percentage of the Gross Domestic Product (GDP). The financing type that has been relatively expanded in Mexico is the financing by commercial chains and by the traditional and on-line factoring markets, which approached 2% of GDP in 2007.

Among the alternative products, we find the ETFs (exchange-trade-funds) or portfolios composed of stocks, commodities and bonds, which have the objective of diversifying the portfolio risk with low transaction costs. The securitized instruments of assets, such as loans for automobiles, credits on credit cards, consumer loans and mortgages, have expanded in Mexico, placing it as the Latin American country where these instruments have increased the most, without reaching relevant levels compared to their negotiation in developed countries, or in the off shore or over the counter (OTC) markets.

Finally, as an important part of the *financialization* of developed countries is the participation of the new financial actors: institutional investors and investment funds. The actions of institutional investors in Latin America have not been important because they have not contributed significantly to the development of markets. Its activity has been centred on the purchase of fixed income financial instruments: public bonds and deposits. And its participation has been restricted to the bond and stock corporate markets. In Mexico, for example, there have been investments in government securities.

The investment funds have had a behaviour similar to that described for institutional investors. An important part of their portfolios include government bonds and money market instruments, although they have recently migrated to investments in equity assets.

FINAL REFLECTIONS

The insertion of Argentina, Brazil and Mexico, in the last four decades, into the process of globalization and deregulation of the world markets turned them into countries with a significant degree of financial opening, especially Mexico. This demanding condition of structural and financial reforms have led to a progressive *financialization* of their economies.

The costs of *financialization* in Latin American countries have been very high. We have seen that, in order to maintain the attraction of international capital flows, their short-term interest rates (set by their central banks) have been raised, so that their differential with respect to the foreign interest rates are attractive to financial investors. Similarly, monetary sterilization (comprising open market operations, OMO, the purchase and sale of currencies and public bonds followed by the central banks) in the studied countries has meant paying a tribute to developed countries, particularly to the United States of America, the hegemonic issuer of the dollar (world currency), because they must comply with the self-insurance policy or the accumulation of international reserves to protect themselves from possible outflows of private capital. In other words, given the growing financial instability fuelled by *financialization*, it is necessary to have the possibility of giving a countercyclical response to a crisis or recession phase.

While international capital flows have influenced the *financialization* of Latin American countries such as Argentina, Brazil and Mexico; this in turn has driven the growth of domestic financial markets without having to displace the financial system based on the credit efficiency of the banks (bank-based financial system). Thus, the entry of foreign banks has exacerbated the *subordinated financialization* by applying banking practices oriented towards personal incomes as a source of financial profits, and by adding the same business logic to domestic banks.

The banking system, foreign or domestic, as some foreign-domestic mergers, has formed multinational financial corporations, operating in various countries of the Latin American region, has made its operations more complex in order to maximize its benefit and has segmented its commercial activities, raising its level of assets concentration by increasing the volume of credit cards, mortgage loans and personal loans at the expense of limiting the credits directed to productive activities, which has caused an increasing individual indebtedness and a greater absorption of personal income by banks.

From the post-crisis period, the banking entities and the positioning of Latin American financial entities and groups in the international region have been blurred, unlike the period prior to the bankruptcy of Lehman Brothers. This does not imply a guarantee, nor does it represent a triumph for the national financial groups and monopolies of the region, neither does it mean a change in the prevailing economic model or a change in the economic policy that would cause social spending by Latin American governments, as during the first decade of the present century. On the contrary, the regime called 'finance-led capitalism', as pointed out by Guttmann (2016), has had its setbacks, and this has influenced the apparent breakdown and gradual withdrawal of some investments of foreign banks in Argentina, Brazil and Mexico (McKinsey Global Institute, 2017). Even the fall in commodities prices, the main withholdings source and the channel for the resources transfer from these countries to the international financial markets, has weakened the possibility of a deeper recovery. To all of this, we can add the economic sanctions, the strict Basel III regulations and those from central banks against shady and irregular operations such as financing terrorism and money laundering (*The Economist*, 2017). Thus, the characterization of the financial circuits in countries such as Argentina, Brazil and Mexico and the rest of Latin America lays on the table the discussion of several lines of research such as those indicated above.

NOTES

1. According to Kregel (1993), who follows Minsky, financial fragility originates from changes due to bankers' and businessmen's preference for liquidity; it is expressed in the changes to the safety margins required for the creation of liquidity, when the transformation of maturity periods is carried out. Therefore, fragility cannot be prevented with different financial structures, it could rather be said that these structures represent different behaviours of fragility.
2. The variables considered by Chinn-Ito (2015) measure the presence of multiple exchange rates, restrictions affecting the capital account and the current account, as well as restrictions on the free mobility of foreign exchange that proceeds from exports.
3. Following the IMF methodology (2009), the net capital flows include net foreign direct investment (FDI), net portfolio investment and other long- and short-term public and private investment flows.
4. The IMF and the WB monitor reserve levels with respect to exports and domestic monetary growth and have established three rules to determine the appropriate level to maintain: (i) the relation between reserves and imports must be enough to face an unexpected deterioration of the balance of payments, (ii) reserves must reach an adequate amount to cover the short-term external debt (short-term understood as up to 12 months) and (iii) the relation between reserves and money supply (M2 monetary aggregate) must replace the flows of capital that suddenly leave the country (Aizenman and Lee, 2005).

5. This conceptualization was based on the premise of Lapavitsas (2013), but the responsibility is of its own.
6. Banking refers to the widespread use the population gives to the services provided by the formal financial system, financial and economic transactions that are currently not constrained to traditional savings and credit operations, but also include transfers of resources, payments through the global banking network and all the regulated financial operations.
7. This ratio is an efficiency indicator that shows the income portion that proceeds from the financial intermediation business, which is absorbed by the operational expenses (in personnel, directory, services received from third parties, taxes, contributions and amortization) (FELABAN, 2014).
8. *Tier 1* calculates what each bank has in capital, plus reserves, undistributed profits and perpetual preferred shares to deal with risk assets (loans granted, shares and other investments). The higher the percentage of capital, the greater the solvency; therefore, this coefficient measures the solvency of banks.
9. This ratio is a quality indicator, it includes the expected loss and the *ex ante* risk assumed by the financial institution (FELABAN, 2014).
10. This ratio is a solvency indicator, it measures the adequacy of capital and the capacity of the financial system institutions to absorb losses (FELABAN, 2014).

BIBLIOGRAPHY

Afi-Tecnocom (2015). Tendencias en Medios de Pagos. 2014–2017. May 15, 2017. Retrieved from http://bit.ly/2n85SKa; http://bit.ly/2vRbevz.

Aizenman, J. and Lee, J. (2005). International Reserves: Precautionary vs. Mercantilist Views, Theory and Evidence. IMF Working Paper. Research Department. WP/05/198. June 28, 2017. Retrieved from http://bit.ly/2rECHmF.

Akyüz, Y. (2008). Managing Financial Instability in Emerging Markets: A Keynesian Perspective. *TWN Global Economy Series*, 12. July 19, 2017. Retrieved from http://bit.ly/2GbiA2B.

Arrighi, G. (1999). *El largo siglo XX*. Madrid: Akal.

CEPAL (2015). Estudio Económico de América Latina y el Caribe. May 12, 2017. Retrieved from http://bit.ly/2DCWgkP.

CEPAL (2016). Estudio Económico de América Latina y el Caribe. May 12, 2017. Retrieved from http://bit.ly/2DCWgkP.

CEPAL (2017a). Balance Preliminar de las Economías de América Latina y El Caribe 2004–2017. Santiago de Chile: CEPAL – ONU.

CEPAL (2017b). Estudio Económico de América Latina y el Caribe. May 12, 2017. Retrieved from http://bit.ly/2DCWgk.

Chinn-Ito (2015). Financial Openness Index. May 12, 2017. Retrieved from http://bit.ly/2DwF8ZM.

De la Torre, A., Ize, A. and Shmukler, S.L. (2012). El Desarrollo Financiero en América Latina y el Caribe. July 30, 2017. Retrieved from http://bit.ly/2E7bYBH.

Epstein, G. (2005). Introduction: Financialization and the World Economy, in Epstein, G. (ed.) *Financialization and the World Economy*, (pp. 3–16). Cheltenham, UK and Northampton, USA: Edward Elgar.

FELABAN (2008). Indicadores Financieros Homologados para Latinoamérica. June 10, 2017. Retrieved from http://bit.ly/2n7h4Wz.

FELABAN (2014). Indicadores Financieros Homologados para Latinoamérica. June 10, 2017. Retrieved from http://bit.ly/2n7h4Wz.

Foster, J. and Magdoff, F. (2009). La gran crisis financiera. Causas y consecuencias. Mexico: Fondo de Cultura Económica.
Galindo, A., Izquierdo, A. and Rojas-Suárez, L. (2010). Integración en Centroamérica. Nuevos Desafíos en el Contexto de la Crisis Internacional. Documento de Trabajo del BID, 153. Washington DC: BID.
Guillén, R. (2010). Dos gigantes emergentes. Pasado y presente de la India y China. August 20, 2017. Retrieved from http://bit.ly/2BrgS9u.
Guttmann, R. (2016). *Finance-Led Capitalism: Shadow Banking, Re-Regulation, and the Future of Global Markets*. Basingstoke: Palgrave Macmillan.
IMF (2009). World Economic Outlook. May 19, 2017. Retrieved from http://bit.ly/2DEXbAb.
Kregel, J. (1993). Financial Fragility and the Structure of Financial Markets. April 18, 2017. Retrieved from http://bit.ly/2E52jve.
Kregel, J. (2008). Usando el 'Minsky's Cushions of Safety' para Analizar la Crisis del Mercado Hipotecario en Estados Unidos. *Ola Financiera*, 1, Sept–Dec. 64–98. April 18, 2017. Retrieved from http://bit.ly/1RhiMPZ.
Krippner, G. (2005). The Financialization of the American Economy. *Socio-Economic Review*, 3(2), 173–208.
Lapavitsas, C. (2011). El capitalismo financiarizado. Crisis y expropiación financiera, in Lapavitsas, C. and Morera, C. (eds). *La Crisis de la Financiarización* (pp. 33–90). Mexico City: IIEc-CLACSO-UNAM.
Lapvitsas, C. (2013). *Profiting Without Producing. How Finance Exploits Us All*. London and New York: Verso.
McKinsey Global Institute (2017). The New Dynamics of Financial Globalization. September 28. Retrieved from http://bit.ly/2fZW57Z.
Minsky, H. (1992). The Financial Instability Hypothesis. *Working Paper*. The Jerome Levy Economics Institute of Bard College, 74.
Palley, T. (2007). Financialization: What It Is and Why It Matters. *Working Paper*, 525, 1–31. New York: The Levy Economics Institute of Bard College.
Schneider, B. (2009). Hierarchical Market Economies and Varieties of Capitalism in Latin America. *J. Lat. Amer. Stud.*, 41, 553–575. April 30, 2017. Retrieved from http://bit.ly/2E7jBYL.
Stanton, W., Etzel, M. and Walker, B. (2007). *Fundamentos de Marketing*. Mexico City: McGraw Hill.
Stockhammer, E. (2012). Financialization, Income Distribution and the Crisis. *Investigación Económica*, 279, 39–70.
The Economist (2017). The Shape of Global Banking Has Turned Upside Down. August 26. Retrieved from http://econ.st/2xprwNs.

PART 2

Post-Keynesian views on distribution and growth

5. Macroeconomic implications of inequality and household debt: European evidence

Jonathan Perraton

INTRODUCTION

Recently a number of accounts have claimed that the 2007–08 global financial crisis (GFC) had its origins in rising inequality across developed economies. Specifically, in response to stagnant or declining real wages households maintained their desired consumption levels by reducing net savings and increasing their debt levels. Increasing levels of household debt made them vulnerable to even a relatively small worsening of conditions and, crucially, this had severe macroeconomic consequences. Under certain conditions this will lead to unsustainable debt cycles. Wages stagnated with their decoupling from productivity growth and rising inequality; aggregate demand was only sustained as households maintained consumption through falling savings and rising indebtedness. Since the GFC the trends have reversed and expansion has been held back as households have consolidated their finances.

Versions of this hypothesis have been proposed, but much of the discussion has been in general terms with specific evidence largely drawn from the US experience. Although broadly similar trends can be observed elsewhere, there are particular features of the US experience that mark it out and important variations between European economies in these trends.[1] To date, though, there has been little specific examination of the European experience.

Section two sets out the main hypotheses advanced here and notes evidence for the US case. Section three examines European experience in the light of the core hypotheses, particularly those recently advanced in the post-Keynesian literature. Section four concludes.

INEQUALITY–CONSUMPTION–DEBT HYPOTHESIS

A number of authors have hypothesised that inequality has led to higher household debt and ultimately financial crisis, although there are differences between versions and their underlying models and much of this discussion has been couched in terms of the US experience. Former IMF chief economist Raghuram Rajan, who warned of these developments in the mid-2000s, has maintained a version of this hypothesis (Rajan, 2010, esp. ch. 1). Mian and Sufi (2015) find a clear household debt dynamic over the same period in the US: mortgage credit was extended to increasingly marginal households and fuelled house price rises. This in turn led to increased borrowing out of house equity. The fall in US house prices from 2006 that precipitated the GFC led to a sharp fall in consumption as indebted households facing falling house prices deleveraged. Kumhof and Rancière (2015) model an increase in income inequality leading to increased purchase of financial assets by the wealthy based on loans to workers; working households are thereby able to maintain consumption levels. However, this leads to financial fragility and potential crisis. Iacoviello (2008) found that inequality was a key driver of falling US household savings, although explains this in terms of increased idiosyncratic income shocks. Alichi, Kantenga and Solé, (2016) estimated that growing inequality in the US has reduced the propensity to consume leading to a fall in real consumption of around 3.5 per cent – most of this fall has occurred since 2007 and is comparable in magnitude to the post-GFC stimulus package. The notion that rising inequality may have adverse consequences for aggregate demand has gained wider currency; even the 2012 Economic Report to the President noted the unequal growth of incomes from the 1980s and evidence of the potential impact of this on aggregate demand.

These works mark a shift away from the baseline mainstream macro model of a representative household agent with full access to capital markets. Such models of the consumption function have well known and longstanding problems with empirical applications. Estimates of the resulting Euler equation fail to provide consistent results for the intertemporal elasticity of substitution and consumption appears to track income to a degree inconsistent with consumption smoothing. There have been some attempts to modify the baseline consumption function variously incorporating habit persistence, ‘hand-to-mouth’ households and credit constraints, but testing of these hypotheses is weak (e.g. Carroll, 2001; Canzoneri *et al.*, 2007). Muellbauer (2010), amongst others, has argued the representative agent consumption function was central to the failure of mainstream macro models in the context of the GFC.[2] In some interpretations this reflects developments with greater dispersion of transitory income from increased income volatility; if this did not reflect increased inequality in permanent income then increased use of credit could be a rational response by households. This appears inconsistent with wider evidence in the US case and beyond; the current 'gilded age' is associated with relatively low social mobility (OECD, 2018) – it is difficult to reconcile this with notions that increased inequality reflects changes in transitory income.

Although these analyses raise useful points, they have a number of specific and generic limitations (cf. Palley, 2015). Accounts in terms of credit expansion to marginal households can effectively be seen as situating the GFC in terms of inappropriate lending policies (or government policies that promoted them). To the extent that these accounts acknowledge that inequality could potentially lead to insufficient aggregate demand this is effectively in terms of possible problems from the zero lower bound. Although these models make some modifications of standard mainstream consumption functions, the broader implications of inequality for aggregate demand are downplayed or ignored. They still remain limited as accounts for the fall in US household savings from the 1980s; changes in standard consumption function variables – changes in wealth and expected future income, demographic shifts, reduced levels of precautionary with financial innovation increasing credit availability – leave much of the fall in savings unexplained (Barba and Pivetti, 2009; Brown, 2008). These explanations effectively deny that economies could face structural features that prevent the generation of effective demand over an extended period, outside of the special case of the zero lower bound. Related to this, they retain standard new Keynesian assumptions that economies can be stabilised through interest rate adjustment. By contrast, post-Keynesian models provide grounds for predicting systematic differences in propensities to consume between rich and poor, wage earners and capitalists and between net debtors and net creditors (Palley, 2010). These appear broadly consistent with available evidence.

A range of recent contributions have set out post-Keynesian models of inequality, consumer debt and aggregate demand. Setterfield (2013) argues that as growth in potential supply is approximately equal to the growth of labour productivity then if real wage growth keeps pace with this (and thus the labour income share remains constant over time) steady growth with a stable level of unemployment will be maintained. Whereas this was approximately the case during the post-war 'Golden Age', during the 'Great Moderation' period a situation of 'latent fragility' developed with aggregate demand maintained in the face of stagnating household incomes amongst swathes of the workforce through lower savings and increased debt. As Setterfield notes, this is not a case of the wisdom in hindsight and these dangers were highlighted before the GFC (cf. Brown, 2008; Cynamon and Fazzari, 2013; Drennan, 2015; Palley, 2002). A shift in the functional distribution of income from labour to capital, a pronounced rise in inequality and stagnation of household incomes would all ordinarily be expected to depress consumption through a shift in income from groups with relatively high propensities to consume to those with relatively low propensities. In the period before the GFC household consumption was maintained through falling savings and rising indebtedness. Further, increased concentration of income and wealth led to increased demand for new financial products based on growth of loans to worker households (cf. Ivanova, 2016; Kumhof and Rancière, 2015; Wisman, 2013).

Rising inequality and stagnant incomes for lower and middle income households in the US led to falling household savings and greater leverage as such households sought to maintain consumption levels in the context of rising house prices. The decline in US savings can be traced to rising inequality. Subsequent evidence points to effects consistent with the post-Keynesian account set out here. Whilst savings rates remained stable for the highest income households, there was a sharp fall in savings by middle income households and dissaving by the lowest income households (Bunting, 2009). Thus, the evidence of higher debt-income ratios in poorer and middle income households is not consistent with borrowing rising amongst higher net worth individuals and households, as standard consumption functions and some sanguine accounts indicate, but is consistent with the post-Keynesian account noted here.

It is not simply the empirical weaknesses of standard models of the consumption function. Rather than modelling households as intertemporal optimising, post-Keynesian accounts stress the pervasive uncertainty faced by households and the role of rules of thumb and inertia in their decision making (Stanley, 2000, ch. 6). Attempts to maintain consumption levels in the face of stagnant earnings may partly reflect this. Further, consumption here is conceived in social terms (Barba and Pivetti, 2009; Brown, 2008, ch. 2; Cynamon and Fazzari, 2013); household consumption takes social reference points, households are concerned with relative as well as absolute consumption levels. This consumption behaviour can be modelled in terms of emulation of consumption patterns through a relative income effect in the context of the development of the US housing market. Rising inequality might then be expected to raise consumption through emulation effects. Note that there are two effects here: households attempting to maintain consumption relative to historic norms in the face of stagnant or falling incomes; the effect of emulative consumption in the context of rising inequality so that households attempt to emulate consumption of household groups increasingly further away from them in real income terms. Before the GFC growth was dependent on debt-led consumption; since then recovery has been held back by limited growth in household incomes and such recovery as has been achieved has been generated by renewed rises in household debt (Cynamon and Fazzari, 2016). This is in contrast to earlier downturns, when private consumption played a more stabilising role. Whereas standard theories of the consumption function explicitly model it as smoothing consumption, here the reverse applies for large groups of households – it was only the richest households that appeared able to operate consumption smoothing. By contrast much of the household sector saw rising consumption–income ratios from debt before the GFC, whilst expansion since has been held back as they have sharply cut back consumption and attempted to consolidate debts (Cynamon and Fazzari, 2016; Dynan, 2012). Consumption by the richest households has been insufficient to maintain overall demand; this is despite historically low interest rates that might be expected to redistribute income from saver to debtor households. Storm (2017) expounds this for the longer term; the squeezing of incomes leads to lower demand, but in turn this through Verdoorn effects leads to lower productivity growth.

Kim (2013; 2016) found evidence of developments in the spirit of Minsky since the period of growth of debt with availability of credit from the 1980s. Before then, in the post-war period, when real wage growth approximately tracked productivity growth, there was no evidence of negative effects of household debt on output; subsequently there is evidence that higher household debt levels have negative long run effects on output, with some evidence that new household borrowing boosts output in the short run. Thus, the evidence for the US in the period of falling savings is broadly consistent with destabilising debt-led cycles of activity from the 1980s, i.e. the period of household income stagnation in the face of rising inequality. Kim *et al.* (2014) and Setterfield *et al.* (2016) set out in detail the conditions under which unsustainable debt accumulation followed by 'sudden stops' in household consumption.

EUROPEAN EVIDENCE

Although these hypotheses have been set out in general terms, the specific evidence advanced is overwhelmingly from the US. Key trends appear most pronounced for the US, with longstanding stagnation of wages for swathes of lower and middle income households, a shift in the functional income distribution from labour to capital, rising inequality and rising household debt. There are a number of reasons why it may be useful to analyse

European economies more generally. A number of studies highlight similar patterns of household debt-fuelled consumption in the United Kingdom (Coutts and Gudgin, 2015; Crouch, 2009; Hay, 2009; Hay and Smith, 2013). Glick and Lansing (2010) found evidence of similar developments in other industrialised economies with falling savings rates associated with house price booms followed by deleveraging since the GFC, but they did not directly consider inequality or wage developments. Kumhof and Rancière (2015) found that inequality is associated with weaker current account positions across industrialised countries, consistent with greater inequality leading to greater debt-led consumption (cf. Behringer and van Treeck, 2015). Bofinger and Scheuermeyer (2016) find evidence of a U-shaped relationship between inequality and savings rates. Rocher and Stierle (2015) found no significant effect on inequality on household savings rates across EU countries; whilst conventional consumption function variables had some explanatory power, much of the variation in savings rates across countries could not be explained by these variables.

There is clear cross-country evidence linking credit booms and associated consumption-led growth with subsequent crises (Kharroubi and Kohlscheen, 2017; Jorda *et al.*, 2012; Mian *et al.*, 2017). Consumption-led expansion episodes tend to distort economic activity, channelling resources to low productivity sectors such as construction. Lombardi *et al.* (2017) found similar evidence of household debt effects to the US for a sample of 54 countries since 1990 – increases in household debt-to-GDP levels appear to raise growth in the short run but have a negative effect over the long run with a threshold level around 80 per cent.

However, the specific evidence linking inequality to crisis through credit booms is less clear cut. Critics of this hypothesis, such as Roberts (2016: 85–89), have noted that post-GFC recessions in the Eurozone were longer and more severe than in the US and UK but inequality is clearly lower. Bordo and Meissner (2012), though, found no evidence that changes in top income shares led to credit booms for a sample of 14 developed economies; credit booms did raise the probability of crisis but these could be explained by standard variables without inequality trends. There are limitations to this study and more recent work does find evidence of a long run relationship between inequality and crises for developed economies (Gu and Huang, 2014; Malinen, 2016).

There are a number of issues with a direct cross-country comparison. The US case has particular features which do not necessarily apply elsewhere. The dynamics of debt and consumption partly reflect the costs of health care and college education for many US households (cf. Mason and Jayadev, 2014; 2015). More subtly if consumption is conceived in social terms then it should be noted that cultural attitudes to credit and emulative consumption differ between the US and Europe (as also exemplified in apparent differences in income–leisure trade-offs). There have been clear differences in both the development of credit industries within countries and the emergent social and cultural attitudes to personal debt (Trentmann, 2016). Financial systems and housing markets differ, as will be explored further. The relations here are more complex than simply predicting higher income inequality leading to greater credit booms and crises.

The wage share has typically fallen across European economies, in common with much of the world (e.g. ILO, 2015). The timing and degree of this shift varies across European economies, but in general there is clear evidence of a regime change from the 1980s with real wages becoming decoupled from productivity growth, reflecting declines in unionisation and the impact of globalisation, but this was still partially mediated through national institutions (Carter, 2007; Judzik and Sala, 2013).[3] Pasimeni (2018) finds a divergence of productivity growth and real wages amongst European economies from the 1990s, although with significant variation between countries.

In post-Keynesian models such a shift in functional income distribution would be expected to affect aggregate demand assuming a lower propensity to consume amongst the capitalist class. Following Piketty (2014), it is evident that the capitalist class as such is small in the sense of those who derive the majority of their income from capital. A key development amongst top income earners in recent decades has been the increased importance of labour income for them (although capital income has become more important in this century for top earners). Nikiforos (2016) proposes an approach that can move beyond a simple focus on functional income distribution – if the richest have a relatively low and stable propensity to consume,[4] the demand can only be maintained in the face of rising inequality through rising consumption by poorer households, however this is achieved.

In general wage inequality appears to have risen in developed countries since the 1980s with much lower increases in consumption inequality, particularly amongst the bottom 50 per cent (Krueger *et al.* 2010). Fitoussi and Saraceno (2010) note the general rise in income inequality across developed economies, including for major European countries, and that consumption inequality has not risen commensurately. They also argue that increased concentration of income had raised demand for high return assets with resulting asset bubbles. Central banks responded to the incipient shortage of aggregate demand by maintaining loose monetary policy, fuelling the credit boom and bubbles. Real interest rates fell through the 1990s and 2000s, with particularly pronounced falls in some eurozone countries as a result of the formation of the Economic and Monetary Union (EMU) eliminating exchange rate risk. Hay (2009) argues that the monetary policy framework of the period in the UK and the eurozone played a key role here: the general framework of inflation targeting led to a singular focus on headline inflation that downplayed developments in asset prices in general and house prices in particular. This is particularly the case in the EU where the Harmonised Index of Consumer Prices (HICP) is used by both the ECB and, from 2003, by the Bank of England – a measure that excludes mortgage repayments.[5]

In the US case, a falling wage share as wages become decoupled from productivity was clearly associated with rising household inequality and stagnant real incomes for middle and lower income households. The US is an extreme case here. The first key difference is that the stagnation of median incomes is much less evident outside the US. A disconnect between median incomes since 1980 can be observed widely across developed economies, but this disconnect was greater for the US which also had an exceptionally low growth in median incomes over this period (Bailey *et al.*, 2011; Nolan *et al.*, 2016). Further, whilst increasing inequality was a significant contributory factor in the US case elsewhere this was less prevalent, only affecting particular countries over certain period. Other factors – differentials between GDP deflators, changes in household size – also account for the some of the observed disconnect.

Changes in key inequality measures show certain cross-country patterns – the rise in the share of top incomes amongst the top 1 and 10 per cent since the 1980s has been stronger amongst Anglo-Saxon economies than amongst continental European economies; correspondingly the fall in the share of the bottom 50 per cent has been more muted in major European economies apart from the UK (World Inequality Report 2018, ch. 2). The rise in the income shares of the very richest highlighted by Piketty (2014) is most pronounced in the English-speaking world. The impact on overall inequality reflects this with strongest rises in Gini coefficients amongst Anglo-Saxon economies and also amongst Nordic economies, albeit from relatively low initial levels in the latter case (OECD, 2015).

At first sight these developments appear somewhat paradoxical. The link between a shift in functional income distribution and changes in household inequality is not necessarily straightforward, but a fall in the wage share would be expected to lead to greater household inequality under current European conditions of concentration in capital ownership (Atkinson, 2009; Bengtsson and Waldenström, 2015; Milanovic, 2017; Molero-Simarro, 2016). The impact on headline Gini coefficients is mediated through various factors and changes in inequality and the course of median household incomes cannot simply be read off directly from changes in functional distribution. Although the falling wage share in European economies is well attested, the disconnect between GDP per capita growth and median household incomes is less pronounced than in the US. This is of course simply for median household incomes and obscures wage inequality developments. Furthermore, the periodisation is important here.

In contrast to the US case, there was no general stagnation of household incomes over the 1980s and 1990s, with considerable variation between European countries in the growth of median incomes. There has widespread stagnation in household incomes has been observed across Europe since the mid-2000s (McKinsey Global Institute, 2016). Whilst this is clearly affected by the GFC, in key cases the trend pre-dates the crisis – and has persisted even with recoveries in European economies. The timing of stagnation of household incomes and disconnect from productivity growth occurred later in European economies than in the US, but has become widespread over the past decade. Within this there have been clear rises in inequality with the exceptions of Belgium, France and the Netherlands (OECD, 2015).

Overall developments are broadly consistent with the core hypothesis here. Household savings rates have fallen across European economies from the 1980s with the key exceptions of France and Germany. In the former case, although there was a clear shift in functional distribution to capital overall income inequality fell or stabilised from the 1980s. Median incomes have become detached from productivity growth and stagnated in these two economies in the current century. Falls in savings rates were also muted in Austria and Belgium and essentially only fell with the GFC.

The effects of this shift in consumption behaviour across Europe has led to the expected cyclical trends. Consumption trends before the crisis saw a relatively high contribution of consumption to GDP growth in the decade before the financial crisis. There is clear evidence of house price bubbles over this period (Engsted, *et al*., 2016). Developments in the eurozone are strongly consistent with the core hypothesis here, as Figure 5.1 illustrates. In the context of the double-dip recession following the GFC, consumer expenditure fell sharply and subsequent recovery has been muted relative to previous downturns. This is also in clear contrast to mainstream consumption function models, which would predict consumption smoothing behaviour.

Within the eurozone the average propensity to consume systematically varies across income groups as expected (ECB, 2016, ch. 6). There is relatively little variation in the propensity by housing status, with the highest for outright home owners and the lowest for mortgage holders (this suggests relatively muted borrowing against property for the latter group, in some contrast to the US case). Thus, overall there is clear evidence of systematic differences in propensities to consume, a relatively strong

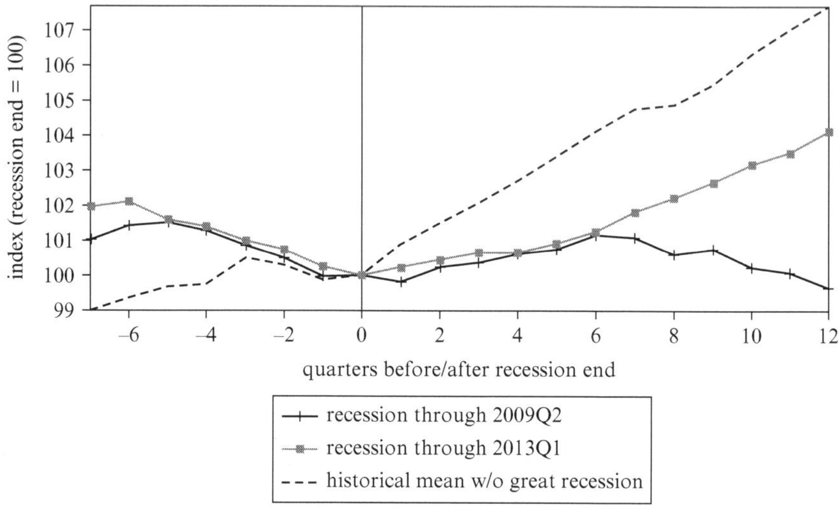

Source: ECB.[6]

Figure 5.1 Consumption recovery in the Euro area after recession trough

growth in consumption before the crisis and strong household consolidation thereafter. There are important differences between countries in terms of household debt developments, examined in more detail below, but in general European countries saw a clear rise in household debt–household income ratios in the years before the GFC (Isaksen *et al.*, 2011). Despite consolidation since the GFC, there have only been limited falls in household debt ratios from their peaks (McKinsey Global Institute, 2015).

Beyond the eurozone, other European economies exhibited similar developments. In particular, developments in the United Kingdom were strikingly consistent with the central hypothesis here. The UK saw a pronounced rise in inequality during the 1980s and early 1990s, an extended period which also saw stagnating incomes for lower income groups during the 1980s, a phase of rising inequality. Past phases of rising inequality also saw significant mortgage equity withdrawal to sustain consumption levels (Froud *et al.*, 2011). From the late 1990s there were general rises in household incomes across income groups during a period when overall inequality was roughly stable; from around 2000 inequality rose again (Burkhauser *et al.*, 2016). As noted, the share of the richest rose in this period. However, across most household income groups income growth stalled and then fell with the GFC. Initially this led to a sharp fall in consumer expenditure. The limited recovery since the GFC has been almost entirely driven by private consumption as initial rises in household savings have been reversed. Households initially consolidated, but then resumed borrowing with household debt–income ratios approaching their pre-crisis peaks. Further, official projections expect these trends to continue – expansion driven by falling household savings and rising household debt. This is not a simple case of decoupling of wages from productivity in the period since the GFC, since UK productivity stagnated, but can be seen in terms of a low wage/low productivity economy with roots before the GFC but clear developments since. The weak economic recovery has thus been based on a resumption of the 'privatised' or 'house-price' Keynesian model. The distributional patterns of this are again consistent with the core hypothesis here; as net savings by UK households have fallen to historic lows since the GFC, this has been driven by middle and lower income groups; the bottom 60 per cent now have zero net savings.

More generally across Europe, variations in developments reflect an interaction between historic growth models and financialisation developments. Baccaro and Pontusson (2016) note the contrast between the UK model and export-led growth in Germany. The German case was exceptional with relatively limited home ownership and a fall in house prices before the GFC. A fall in the wage share and flat-lining household incomes through the 2000s underpinned export-led growth through effective internal devaluation. This has particular effects within the eurozone given the impossibility of nominal exchange rate changes. Nevertheless, the German case here is somewhat exceptional; by 2007 in all eurozone countries except Germany the majority of households were owner-occupiers (ECB, 2009), although household access to credit still varied significantly. Rising home ownership and credit availability partly cut across existing growth models (cf. Baccaro and Pontusson, 2016; Schwartz and Seabrooke, 2008). Elsewhere developments fall into distinct groups. The second group that broadly fits the hypothesis here are the countries that were hit by the eurozone crisis. Greece is clearly an extreme case, but Spain, Portugal and Ireland display patterns consistent with the broad hypothesis – the Irish case has features in common with both Southern European countries and with other Anglo-Saxon economies. Swings in household borrowing were central to the boom-to-crisis developments amongst peripheral members of the eurozone (Martin and Phillippon, 2014). The Spanish case fits the core hypothesis of rising inequality and household debt accumulation before the crisis (Pardo and Santos, 2014).[7] Italy is an exception amongst this group, and did not see a pre-crisis consumption boom; instead the Italian economy stagnated being unable to sustain either export-led growth or, in the absence of credit expansion to households, a consumption boom (Baccaro and Pontusson, 2016).

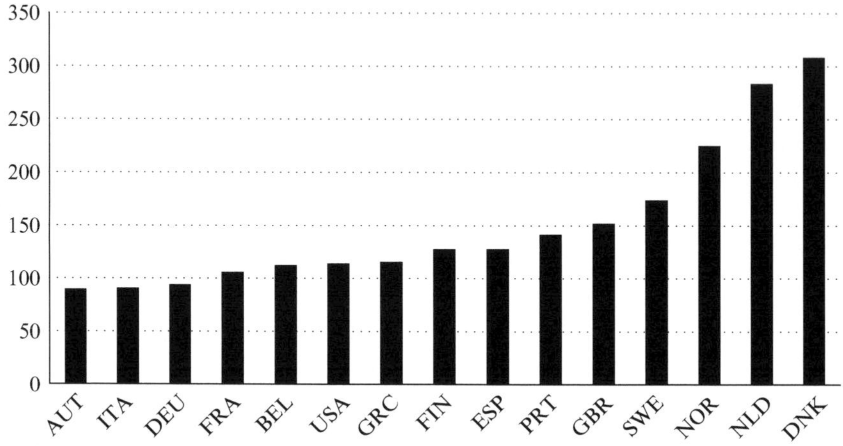

Figure 5.2 Household debt/income (% of GDP)

The final group consists of the Nordics and the Netherlands. It is this group that has seen the highest rises in household debt and currently the highest levels amongst developed economies. This third group thus partially fits the hypothesis of consumption sustained through increased household borrowing against property. It also shows the complexity of the interaction between existing growth models and rising home ownership and credit availability. These economies continue to have relatively co-ordinated wage bargaining systems based on settlements in the exposed sector to ensure external competitiveness.

This group thus has some features in common with export-led growth economies, but has also seen a higher contribution of consumption to growth than economies such as Germany. There are key features of this group that distinguish it from the core hypothesis here. Rising household indebtedness has also been accompanied by rising wealth with house price booms (Isaksen *et al.*, 2011). Borrowing and indebtedness has not been clearly linked to poorer income groups; this is not a case of poorer households and/or those with stagnating incomes attempting to maintain consumption levels.

CONCLUSIONS

A growing body of work argues that the US in particular only maintained aggregate demand before the GFC through an unsustainable credit boom as households borrowed to maintain consumption levels in the face of stagnant incomes. Such episodes may promote short run growth but typically lead to crisis and weaker growth over the long term. The US experience of rising inequality and stagnant incomes for swathes of households is exceptional; European economies have mostly experienced a disconnect between productivity and wage growth from the 1990s, but smaller rises in inequality – reflecting different labour market institutions and more redistributive tax and welfare systems – and not the sustained stagnation in household incomes. There is still evidence of these effects across Europe. The Anglo-Saxon economies of the UK and (possibly to a lesser degree) Ireland still appear to have a growth model based on periodic debt-fuelled consumption booms in the context of relatively high inequality. The relationships between inequality, credit growth and crisis are complex and require further exploration. Although this has been related to the secular decline in the wage share, there is no simple relationship between this and changes in household inequality. Growth of household inequality has been more pronounced in the US and the stagnation of household incomes has also been more distinct and longer lasting. Trends in wages and household incomes have been more variable across Europe since the 1980s. This has interacted with developments in housing markets to produce a range of developments. The major economies where household borrowing did not substitute for income stagnation were France, where inequality saw relatively little change, and Germany where financial conditions made such developments less likely. Elsewhere there were developments broadly consistent with the hypothesis of stagnating incomes leading to households relying on debt-fuelled consumption. This can be seen in Anglo-Saxon economies and in Southern European economies. A parallel development has seen household debt rise to unprecedented levels in the Nordic economies and the Netherlands; thus far, sustained house price levels have meant that this group has not seen household consolidation seen elsewhere.

The sustainability of this remains unclear, given its basis in sustaining house price levels, as does its longer-term effects on income, wealth and consumption. In particular, there are major generational effects; the timing of house price booms has led to rising household wealth for older households and a profound shift in generational patterns of wealth.

NOTES

1. Europe here refers to Western Europe. There have been interesting parallel developments amongst Central and East European economies, but for reasons of space these are not considered here.
2. http://voxeu.org/article/why-central-bank-models-failed-and-how-repair-them.
3. Judzik and Sala (2013) are unable to reject the hypothesis of a long run unit elasticity

between real wages and productivity for developed economies from 1960 to 2010, but find that this has been affected by globalisation and falling union density; Carter (2007) finds evidence of a structural break in this relationship around 1979.

4. Even this assumption may be questionable; Bakker and Felman (2014) found that much of the fluctuation in consumption in the US before and since the GFC was due to changes in consumption by rich households.
5. Sweden's Riksbank does target CPI, but also notes developments in CPIX, which excludes mortgage repayments. There is some evidence that the Riksbank has both monitored and responded to house price developments.
6. http://www.ecb.europa.eu/pub/economic-research/resbull/2016/html/rb161028.en.html.
7. Even here, though, there was a key role for rising debt of non-financial corporations (Caldentey and Vernengo, 2015).

REFERENCES

Alichi, A., Kantenga, K. and Solé, J. (2016). Income polarization in the United States, International Monetary Fund Working Paper No. 16/121.

Atkinson, A. B. (2009). Factor shares: the principal problem of political economy?, *Oxford Review of Economic Policy*, 25(1), 3–16.

Baccaro, L. and Pontusson, J. (2016). Rethinking comparative political economy: the growth model perspective, *Politics and Society*, 44(2), 175–207.

Bakker, B. and Felman, J. (2014). The Rich and the Great Recession, International Monetary Fund Working Paper No. 14/225.

Bailey, J., Coward, J. and Whittaker, M. (2011). *Painful Separation: An International Study of the Weakening Relationship Between Economic Growth and the Pay of Ordinary Workers*, London: Resolution Foundation.

Barba, A. and Pivetti, M. (2009). Rising household debt: its causes and macroeconomic implications – a long-period analysis, *Cambridge Journal of Economics*, 33(1), 113–37.

Behringer, J. and van Treeck, T. (2015). Income Distribution and the Current Account: A Sectoral Perspective, Society for the Study of Inequality Working Paper No. 379.

Bengtsson, E. and Waldenström, D. (2015). Capital shares and income inequality: evidence from the long run, IZA Discussion Paper No. 9581.

Bofinger, P. and Scheuermeyer, P. (2016). Income Distribution and Aggregate Saving: A Non-Monotonic Relationship, CEPR Discussion Paper No. 11435.

Bordo, M. and Meissner, C. (2012). Does inequality lead to a financial crisis?, *Journal of International Money and Finance*, 31, 2147–61.

Brown, C. (2008). *Inequality, Consumer Debt and the Saving Puzzle*, Cheltenham: Edward Elgar.

Bunting, D. (2009). The saving decline: macro-facts, micro behavior, *Journal of Economic Behavior and Organization*, 70, 282–95.

Burkhauser, R., Hérault, N., Jenkins, S. and Wilkins, R. (2016). What has Been Happening to UK Income Inequality Since the Mid-1990s?, NBER Working Paper No. 21991.

Caldentey, E. P. and Vernengo, M. (2015). Integration, Spurious Convergence, and Financial Fragility: A Post-Keynesian Interpretation of the Spanish Crisis. Jerome Levy Institute Working Paper No. 847.

Canzoneri, M., Cumby, R. and Diba, B. (2007). Euler equations and money

market interest rates: a challenge for monetary policy models, *Journal of Monetary Economics*, 54(7), 1863–81.
Carroll, C. (2001). A theory of the consumption function, with and without liquidity constraints, *Journal of Economic Perspectives*, 5(1), 129–43.
Carter, S. (2007). Real wage productivity elasticity across advanced economies, 1963–1996, *Journal of Post Keynesian Economics*, 29(4), 573–600.
Council of Economic Advisers (2012). Economic Report of the President, Washington DC, United States Government Printing Office.
Coutts, K. and Gudgin, G. (2015). The Macroeconomic Impact of Liberal Economic Policies in the UK, Centre for Business Research Report, University of Cambridge.
Crouch, C. (2009). Privatised Keynesianism: an unacknowledged policy regime, *British Journal of Politics and International Relations*, 11, 382–99.
Cynamon, B. Z. and Fazzari, S. M. (2013). The end of the consumer age, in Cynamon B. Z., Fazzari S. M. and Setterfield M. (eds), *After the Great Recession: The Struggle for Economic Recovery and Growth*, Cambridge: Cambridge University Press, 129–57.
Cynamon, B. Z. and Fazzari, S. M. (2016). Inequality, the Great Recession and slow recovery, *Cambridge Journal of Economics*, 40(2), 373–99.
Drennan, M. P. (2015). *Income Inequality: Why It Matters and Why Most Economists Didn't Notice*, New Haven: Yale University Press.
Dynan, K. (2012). Is a Household Debt Overhang Holding Back Consumption? *Brookings Papers on Economic Activity*, 1, 299–362.
ECB (2009). Housing Finance in the Euro Area, European Central Bank Occasional Paper 101.
ECB (2016). The Household Finance and Consumption Survey: results from the second wave, Household Finance and Consumption Network Statistics Paper Series 18.
Engsted, T., Hviid, S. and Pedersen, T. (2016). Explosive bubbles in house prices? Evidence from the OECD countries, *Journal of International Financial Markets, Institutions and Money*, 40, 14–25.
Fitoussi, J.-P. and Saraceno, F. (2010). Inequality and Macroeconomic Performance, OFCE Working Paper No. 2010–13.
Froud, J., Johal, S., Law, J., Leaver, A. and Williams, K. (2011). Rebalancing the Economy, CRESC Working Paper No. 87.
Frowen, S. and Karakitsos, E. (1996). Monetary and fiscal policy under conditions of globalised money and capital markets: lessons for the UK personal sector, *Public Finance*, 51(3), 305–24.
Glick, R. and Lansing, K. (2010). Global Household Leverage, House Prices, and Consumption, FRBSF Economic Letter 2010–11.
Gu, X. and Huang, B. (2014). Does inequality lead to a financial crisis? Revisited, *Review of Development Economics*, 18(3), 502–16.
Hay, C. (2009), Good inflation, bad inflation: the housing boom, economic growth and the disaggregation of inflationary preferences in the UK and Ireland, *British Journal of Politics and International Relations*, 11(3), 461–78.
Hay, C. and Smith, N. (2013). The story of a North Sea bubble: the strange demise of the anglo-liberal growth model in the United Kingdom and Ireland, *European Political Science Review*, 5, 401–30.
Iacoviello, M. (2008). Household debt and income inequality, 1963–2003, *Journal of Money, Credit and Banking*, 40, 929–65.

ILO (2015). *Global Wage Report 2014/15: Wages and Income Inequality*, Geneva: International Labour Office.
Isaksen, J., Kramp, P. L., Sørensen, L. F. and Sørensen, S. V. (2011). Household balance sheets and debt – an international country study, *Danmarks Nationalbank Monetary Review*, 4th Quarter, 47–58.
Ivanova, M. (2016). Profit growth in boom and bust: the Great Recession and the Great Depression in comparative perspective, *Industrial and Corporate Change*.
Jordà, O., Schularick, M. and Taylor, A.M. (2011). Financial crises, credit booms, and external imbalances: 140 years of lessons, *IMF Economic Review*, 59(2), 340–78.
Judzik, D. and Sala, H. (2013). Productivity, deunionization and trade: wage effects and labour share implications, *International Labour Review*, 152(2), 205–36.
Kharroubi, E. and Kohlscheen, E. (2017). Consumption-led expansions, *BIS Quarterly Review*, March, 25–37.
Kim, Y. K. (2013). Household debt, financialization, and macroeconomic performance in the United States, 1951–2009, *Journal of Post Keynesian Economics*, 35(4), 675–94.
Kim, Y. K. (2016). Macroeconomic effects of household debt: an empirical analysis, *Review of Keynesian Economics*, 4(2), 127–50.
Kim, Y. K., Setterfield, M. and Mei, Y. (2014). A theory of aggregate consumption, *European Journal of Economics and Economic Policies: Intervention*, 11(1), 31–49.
Kim, Y. K., Setterfield, M. and Mei, Y. (2015). Aggregate consumption and debt accumulation: an empirical examination of US household behaviour, *Cambridge Journal of Economics*, 39, 93–112.
Krueger, D., Perri, F., Pistaferri, L. and Violante, G. (2010). Cross-sectional facts for macroeconomists, *Review of Economic Dynamics*, 13(1), 1–14.
Kumhof, M. and Rancière, R. (2015). Inequality, leverage and the crisis, *American Economic Review*, 105(3), 1217–45.
Kumhof, M., Lebarz, C., Rancière, R., Richter, A. and Throckmorton, N. (2012). Income Inequality and Current Account Imbalances, IMF Working Paper No. 12/8.
Lombardi, M., Mohanty, M. and Shim, I. (2017). The real effects of household debt in the short and long run, Bank for International Settlements Working Paper No. 607.
Malinen, T. (2016). Does income inequality contribute to credit cycles?, *Journal of Economic Inequality*, 14, 309–25.
Martin, P. and Phillippon, T. (2014). Inspecting the Mechanism: Leverage and the Great Recession in the Eurozone, National Bureau of Economic Research Working Paper No. 20572.
Mason, J. W. and Jayadev, A. (2014). Fisher dynamics in household debt: the case of the United States, 1929–2011, *American Economic Journal: Macroeconomics*.
Mason, J. W. and Jayadev, A. (2015). The post-1980 debt disinflation: an exercise in historical accounting, *Review of Keynesian Economics*, 3(3), 314–35.
McKinsey Global Institute (2015). Debt and (Not Much) Deleveraging.
McKinsey Global Institute (2016). Poorer than Their Parents? Flat or Falling Incomes in Advanced Economies.
Mian, A. and Sufi, A. (2015). *House of Debt*, Chicago: University of Chicago Press.
Mian, A., Sufi, A. and Verner, E. (2017). Household debt and business cycles worldwide, *Quarterly Journal of Economics*, 132(4), 1755–817.

Milanovic, B. (2017). Increasing capital income share and its effect on personal income inequality, in Boushey, H., de Long, B. and Steinbaum, M. (eds), *After Piketty: The Agenda for Economics and Inequality*, Cambridge, MA: Harvard University Press, 235–59.
Molero-Simarro, R. (2016). Growth and inequality revisited: the role of primary distribution of income. A new approach for understanding today's economic and social crises, *Cambridge Journal of Economics*, 41(2), 367–90.
Muellbauer, J. (2010). Household Decisions, Credit Markets and the Macroeconomy, Bank for International Settlements Discussion Paper No. 306.
Nikiforos, M. (2016). A nonbehavioral theory of saving, *Journal of Post Keynesian Economics*, 39(4), 562–92.
Nolan, B., Roser, M. and Thewissen, S. (2016). GDP per capita versus median household income: what gives rise to divergence over time?, INET Oxford Working Paper.
OECD (2015). *In It Together: Why Less Inequality Benefits All*, Paris: OECD Publishing.
OECD (2018). *A Broken Social Elevator: How to Promote Social Mobility*, Paris: OECD Publishing.
Offer, A. (2017). The market turn: from social democracy to market liberalism, *Economic History Review*, 70(4), 1051–71.
Palley, T. (2002). Economic contradictions coming home to roost? Does the U.S. economy face a long-term aggregate demand generation problem?, *Journal of Post Keynesian Economics*, 25(1), 9–32.
Palley, T. (2010). The relative permanent income theory of consumption: a synthetic Keynes–Duesenberry–Friedman model, *Review of Political Economy*, 22(1), 41–56.
Palley, T. (2012). *From Financial Crisis to Stagnation: The Destruction of Shared Prosperity and the Role of Economics*, Cambridge: Cambridge University Press.
Palley, T. (2015). Inequality, the financial crisis and stagnation: competing stories and why they matter, IMF Working Paper No. 151.
Pardo, G. P. and Santos, J. M. S. (2014). Household debt and consumption inequality: the Spanish case, *Economies*, (2), 147–70.
Pasimeni, P. (2018). The Relation Between Productivity and Compensation in Europe, European Economy Discussion Paper No. 079.
Piketty, T. (2014). *Capital in the Twenty-First Century*, Cambridge, MA: Harvard University Press.
Rajan, R. G. (2010). *Fault Lines: How Hidden Fractures Still Threaten the World Economy*, Princeton: Princeton University Press.
Roberts, M. (2016). *The Long Depression*, Chicago: Haymarket Books.
Rocher, S. and Stierle, M. (2015). Household Savings Rates in the EU: Why Do They Differ So Much?, European Economy Discussion Paper No. 005.
Schwartz, H. and Seabrooke, L. (2008). Varieties of residential capitalism in the international political economy: old welfare states and the new politics of housing, *Comparative European Politics*, 6, 237–61.
Setterfield, M. (2013). Wages, demand, and U.S. macroeconomic travails: diagnosis and prognosis, in Cynamon, B. Z., Fazzari, S. M. and Setterfield, M. (eds), *After the Great Recession: The Struggle for Economic Recovery and Growth*, Cambridge: Cambridge University Press, 158–84.
Setterfield, M., Kim, Y. K. and Rees, J. (2016). Inequality, debt servicing and sustainability of steady state growth, *Review of Political Economy*, 28(1), 45–63.

Stanley, T. D. (2000). *Challenging Time Series: Limits to Knowledge, Inertia and Caprice*, Cheltenham: Edward Elgar.
Storm, S. (2017). The new normal: demand, secular stagnation, and the vanishing middle class, *International Journal of Political Economy*, 46(4), 169–210.
Trentmann, F. (2016). *Empire of Things: How We Became a World of Consumers, from the Fifteenth Century to the Twenty-first*, London: Allen Lane.
Wisman, J. (2013). Wage stagnation, rising inequality and the financial crisis of 2008, *Cambridge Journal of Economics*, 37(4), 921–45.
World Inequality Report (2018).

6. How can policy tackle inequality in the 21st century?

Hanna K. Szymborska[1]

INTRODUCTION

Recent developments in the inequality literature indicate that differences in wealth (Piketty 2014) and household balance sheet structures have become a significant determinant of economic inequality in advanced capitalist economies (Ampudia *et al.* 2014; Austen *et al.* 2014; Wolff 2014; Lindner 2015; Szymborska 2017; Williams 2016). In the USA, the rise in wealth inequality has been particularly acute since the 1980s, with the Gini index for wealth increasing from 0.79 in 1989 to 0.850 in 2013, and the Gini index of income rising from 0.54 to 0.574 in the period (source: U.S. Survey of Consumer Finances). This was paralleled by privatisation of public services, liberalisation of labour market regulations, and large-scale financial deregulation leading to the development of structured finance based on subprime lending expansion (Barba/Pivetti 2009; Dos Santos 2009; Dymski 2009; Dymski *et al.* 2013; Goda/Lysandrou 2014). These institutional changes shaped household balance sheet structures and influenced wealth accumulation across the distribution by generating disparities in rates of return available to different households and in leverage (Szymborska 2017). Households at the top of the distribution were able to accumulate more diverse and more profitable assets like financial securities, business equity, and property other than main residence. This allowed them to earn larger returns on their wealth and enjoy greater income increases than households relying on primary residence and low-yielding financial assets as their main source of wealth (*ibid.*).

The impact of disparities in balance sheet composition on wealth inequality was exposed by the Great Recession. Unlike income inequality, which decreased during the 2007 crisis, wealth inequality continued to rise. The Gini index for income declined from 0.574 to 0.549 over 2007 and 2010, while the Gini index for wealth increased from 0.816 in 2007 and 0.846 in 2010 (source: U.S. Survey of Consumer Finances). In the aftermath of the Great Recession, the ability to accumulate wealth among low- and middle-income households, as well as among women, people of colour, and the young, was undermined by the volatility of house prices and became tied to financial market performance (cf. Young 2010). Together with low valuation of their assets, this was linked to stagnating income growth for the bottom 90% of the income distribution, which was associated with labour market liberalisation and privatisation measures in the USA since the 1980s (Bivens *et al.* 2014). Low-to-middle income households suffered from higher leverage in terms of the ratio of debt to assets and debt payments to income than households at the top, even though the latter group held the highest amounts of debt. Simultaneously, the richest 10% experienced rapid income growth in the period (particularly when employed as financial sector executives), supported by government bank bailouts during the 2007 crisis, and greater diversification of more profitable assets, which led to overall smaller losses due to the Great Recession (Philippon/Reshef 2012; Arestis *et al.* 2013; Wolff 2014).

Financial deregulation and development of structured finance, coupled with liberalisation and privatisation policies in the USA since the 1980s, changed the landscape of household finances. More low-income households became wealth owners, albeit at the cost of unsustainable indebtedness, while wealth holdings of the rich became increasingly complex. In light of this growing heterogeneity of household wealth, what is the role of policy to alleviate rising inequality? To answer this question, the chapter first reviews policy measures implemented in the USA to date, providing an institutional context to their failure to curb inequality. It then discusses relevant policy proposals put forward in the literature, evaluating their effectiveness in light of the increased heterogeneity of household balance sheets. The chapter then proposes alternative measures to tackle high inequality in the USA.

WHY DOESN'T CURRENT POLICY WORK?

Most of the existing policy measures to reduce inequality have been concentrated on income rather than wealth, through direct income taxation, provision of cash transfers and income subsidies, and indirect taxation of consumption (Schneider *et al.* 2016:141). According to this approach, income is a sufficient tool to alleviate wealth inequality since parallel increases in savings would boost wealth accumulation. However, these measures have failed to rein in rising wealth inequality. Redistribution of income by itself cannot promote a more equal wealth accumulation through saving when income is directed to maintain consumption in light of rising costs of living. While increasing income flows of those worse off would enable them to fund immediate expenses, it would not allow for a sustained accumulation of savings to finance education, healthcare, and other investments. Lower income households are documented to save a lower portion of their income that the rich, so income policy is less likely to promote wealth accumulation among the poorest. In fact, the personal saving rate in the USA has declined from 13.3% in 1971 to just 2.6% in 2005, stabilising at around 5% since 2014 (BEA 2017). Moreover, taxation of income only affects returns earned from wealth but not its stock, which continues to earn large returns (Piketty 2014). Thus, income taxes alone do not dampen the economic power of the rich associated with their large wealth holdings (McCain 2017:83). Furthermore, indirect taxation of consumption puts a greater tax burden on small savers and households towards the middle and the bottom of the distribution, particularly in the context of the rising costs of privatised public services (cf. ITEP 2004).

The main reason why policy measures to date have failed to counteract rising wealth and income inequality is their inappropriate design given changing institutional conditions in the US economy. Firstly, the chosen approach to promoting wealth accumulation through private markets has led to predatory inclusion of wealth poor households into the housing and financial markets, leading to unsustainable accumulation of debt. Secondly, the existing tax code and bankruptcy laws have failed to reach wealth poor households, placing an increasing tax burden on low-to-middle income households while favouring those with existing wealth holdings. Thirdly, broader macroeconomic policy measures implemented in the USA in recent years have had knock-on effects on the patterns of household wealth accumulation across the distribution.

These flaws arise from the fact that policy has not caught up with the growing heterogeneity of household wealth across the distribution. This has been a direct consequence of wealth accumulation being outsourced to the private sector since the 1980s. The availability and quality of social housing was reduced, and the private housing market was booming in the early 2000s. The housing boom was fuelled by the development of structured finance, which pooled and transformed mortgages of varying risk into securitised instruments purchased by wealthy financial investors. While government agencies Fannie Mae and Freddie Mac were involved in this process, the bulk of securitisation was based on predatory lending to low-income and vulnerable households and was conducted by unregulated private institutions. This was enabled by financial deregulation measures like the 1999 Gramm-Leach-Bliley Act which permitted commercial banks to engage in financial investment activities (Pollin/Heintz 2013). Moreover, rising costs of education and healthcare together with stagnating wages and declining employment security made home ownership an attractive tool for households to extract additional equity to finance necessary purchases.

Subprime lending expansion increased home ownership among low-to-middle income households, boosting their wealth between the 1990s and 2000s. The home ownership rate among the poorest 20% of households jumped by nearly 23% between 1989 and 2007, from 33% to 41.6% (U.S. Survey of Consumer Finances, 1989–2013). By comparison, the overall home ownership rate rose by 8% in that period. Sustained by growing house prices, median net wealth of the poorest 20% skyrocketed, increasing by 188% between 1989 and 2007. But this has been underpinned by accumulation of unsustainable debt owing to harsh lending conditions faced by subprime borrowers. Highly leveraged homeowners in the bottom and middle of the distribution saw their wealth gains practically erode in the aftermath of the Great Recession. The poorest 20% of households experienced the largest declines in their median net wealth after the crisis, which fell by nearly 40% between 2010 and 2013 compared to a 10% decrease for the richest 10%. Consequently, privatisation of housing generated predatory inclusion and deepened structural inequalities between the rich owners of diversified asset portfolios and low-to-middle income households relying on leveraged home ownership or not being able to accumulate any valuable assets at all.

While the US policy has been focused on targeting asset accumulation through private markets, it has not paid sufficient attention to indebtedness. The 2000s housing boom has been accompanied by ballooning household debt levels. While the ratio of household debt to GDP had been rising steadily since the mid 1980s, it took off in the second quarter of 2001, with an average annual growth rate of 5% until the second quarter of 2008 (source: own calculations based on Federal Reserve Economic Data, St Louis Fed). But the increase has not been even across the distribution. The conditional median value of debt-to-income ratio of the poorest 20% expanded at the fastest rate between 1989 and 2007, more than doubling from 32% to 75% (U.S. Survey of Consumer Finances, 1989–2013). Similarly, the median ratio of debt to asset holdings for households owning debt increased substantially for this group in the period, rising from 9% to 13.5%. A parallel rapid increase in the debt-to-asset ratio occurred for middle-income households between the 20th and 90th percentile of income distribution. This leverage measure was the highest for this group, rising from 15.6% to 23% between 1989 and 2007. By comparison, the conditional median debt-to-income ratio of the richest 10% of households increased from 62% to 98% in the same period, while the debt-to-asset ratio actually decreased from 8.4% to 8.3%. The rise in household leverage at the bottom of the distribution was fuelled by the mortgage lending expansion described above. The proportion of households among the poorest 20%

who owned mortgages secured by their main residence increased by more than twofold from 7.5% to 16% between 1989 and 2004. A parallel increase is observed for the proportion of households among the poorest 20% owning credit card debt, which rose from 15% to 30% in the same period.

Crucially, although the ratio of overall household debt to US GDP declined from 98% to 79% between mid 2008 and the end of 2016, the Great Recession did not provide a check on the indebtedness of the poor. Leverage of the poorest 20% of households continued to rise in the aftermath of the crisis. The debt-to-income ratio of this group increased from 75% to 85.6% between 2007 and 2013, while the debt-to-asset ratio rose from 13.5% to 18.6% in this period. This was paralleled by a rising share of households filing for bankruptcy since 2010 (Scott/Pressman 2015). Several factors can explain insufficient deleveraging of the poor. The "originate-to-distribute" banking model, which underpinned the securitisation process, generated an unequal hierarchy of monetary claims across households, favouring the interests of investors into securities markets at the expense of the original borrowers whose loans formed the basis of the securitised instruments (Szymborska 2016). This greatly hindered possibilities of debt renegotiations or forgiveness for leveraged borrowers in times of distress. This uneven monetary hierarchy was reinforced by the bankruptcy law reform implemented in 2005, which guaranteed financial income in case one party of a security transaction defaulted, but which did not allow for discharge of education debt (Stiglitz 2012). This treatment directly disadvantaged low-income households, whose debt holdings are composed primarily of unsecured debt (U.S. Survey of Consumer Finances, 1989–2013). Because poorer households have not deleveraged properly after the Great Recession, they have not experienced increases in consumption and saving necessary for reductions in overall income and wealth inequality.

Rising wealth ownership at the bottom of the distribution also became a challenge to the US tax structure, rendering it an active contributor rather than a counteraction to inequality. In the USA, wealth taxation is limited to property and inheritance (estate) taxes. Since the property tax is imposed on the gross value of property wealth, it ignores the issue of leverage (Pressman 2016:141). Consequently, the greatest tax burden is placed on households in the middle of the distribution, whose balance sheets rely on property wealth, and whose leverage levels are comparatively the highest.

Moreover, the US estate tax is levied on the donor, creating incentives for exploitation of existing tax reliefs and passing on wealth tax free throughout the lifetime (Boadway *et al.* 2010). The current law only taxes the net value of inheritable wealth (IRS 2017). Rich households can thus accumulate mortgage debt to reduce the taxable value of their real estate, which does not affect their financial stability as their leverage is kept low due to high-yielding asset holdings and high incomes. Consequently, in its current form, the inheritance tax may fall disproportionately on households in the middle of the distribution whose wealth is tied up in housing.

Furthermore, income tax cuts implemented by the US government in 1986 and 2017 in the name of boosting incentives for saving have benefitted those at the top of the income distribution. This is because much of the income of the US rich is earned from stocks, bonds, and real estate, which are all tax-exempt (Pressman 2016:146). Since a large part of income of households at the top is composed of investment and capital income from wealth ownership, income taxation alone is not enough to effectively reduce income inequality. Furthermore, recent research indicates that the present structure of the tax relief programmes is highly regressive – in 2013 the bottom 60% of families received only 12% of funds accruing to these programmes, while the top 1% obtained over a quarter of the support (Levin *et al.* 2014:6).

Another channel through which US policy exacerbated inequality is related to valuation dynamics of macroeconomic policies implemented since the 1980s. Expansion of US public debt from around 30% of GDP in early 1980s to over 100% since 2013 has important distributive implications (source: Federal Reserve Economic Data, St Louis Fed). Since the majority of government bonds created through the issuance of public debt are owned by the rich, increasing public deficit perpetuates wealth inequality by driving up asset prices (Piketty 2014). Moreover, monetary policy has been particularly relevant for wealth inequality after the Great Recession (Claeys *et al.* 2015; Montecino/Epstein 2015; Domanski *et al.* 2016). Unconventional low-interest rates and quantitative easing (QE) policies adopted after the 2007 crisis by the Federal Reserve have alleviated some of the negative consequences of the recession by restoring confidence in the economy and boosting demand (Ennis/Wolman 2015). But by selling government bonds QE drove up asset prices. This benefited asset owners, who are highly concentrated at the top of the distribution. Furthermore, low interest rates encouraged highly-indebted households to borrow even more. Not only did it weigh negatively on their net wealth, but it also inflated house prices by keeping borrowing costs low and boosting the availability of credit. While rising house prices have increased the wealth of homeowners, home ownership has become unaffordable for those not on the housing ladder, forcing these groups to rent at increasing costs.

Overall, changes in the US economic policy over the past few decades have contributed to increasing wealth and income inequality. Financial deregulation, privatisation of public services, liberalisation of labour markets, and tax reforms have favoured the rich, pushing low-to-middle income households into unsustainable wealth accumulation underpinned by rising indebtedness. Immediately after the Great Recession, policy prioritised the banking sector by directing resources towards bailouts rather than social programmes to support vulnerable households suffering from unemployment and excessive leverage. While the key mechanisms of increasing inequality are attributable to private financial markets through predatory financial inclusion of low-income households and uneven access to wealth accumulation opportunities, policy was a facilitating rather than a hindering factor for this expansion. There is a need for a major overhaul of current policies to counteract increasing wealth and income inequality and improve financial wellbeing of the poor.

WHAT SOLUTIONS HAVE BEEN PUT FORWARD?

Standard recommendation to reduce inequality among mainstream economists is investment in human capital through education (Murphy/Topel 2016). According to permanent income hypothesis (Friedman 1957), inequality arises due to differences in skills and marginal productivities across households. However, empirical evidence suggests that recently observed decreases in human capital inequality have not been accompanied by falling income and wealth inequality (Castelló-Climent/Doménech 2014). Promoting education may not be as relevant for reducing inequality in the context of today's corporate structure in the USA as traditionally envisaged in the literature. This is because income inequality arises primarily due to high salaries paid in highly innovative winner-take-all markets, which are restricted to a small number of employees (Galbraith 2016:142). Consequently, unless provided publicly at all levels, higher education is bound to exacerbate inequality rather than alleviate it.

Recent inequality literature has proposed numerous measures to reduce wealth inequality in advanced capitalist economies like the USA. Piketty (2014) has been the main proponent of introducing wealth taxation to directly reduce the amount of wealth, decrease its growth rate relative to income, and curb inequality. He advocates a progressive global wealth tax alongside progressive income taxes, which would be imposed annually on the value of all assets exceeding $1.35 million, less the value of debt. Such wealth tax must be implemented globally in order to escape revenue losses due to tax evasion[2] associated with the mobility of wealth.

Wealth taxation is also a part of Atkinson's (2015) policy programme to combat rising inequality in high-income countries. He puts forward 15 comprehensive policy proposals and 5 further ideas to pursue to reduce income and wealth inequality.[3] Proposals 5 to 7 explicitly focus on policies affecting the distribution of wealth. Highlighting that there are differences in the rates of return on wealth across households, Atkinson postulates the establishment of a national savings bonds programme with maximum holdings per person, which would guarantee a positive rate of return on savings for small savers, thus equalising to a certain extent the return on wealth across households (Atkinson 2015:167–168). To improve the ability to accumulate wealth among households at the bottom of the distribution, Atkinson proposes payment of a capital endowment on reaching adulthood.[4] This would be equivalent to a minimum inheritance, aiming to equalise the distribution of bequests, although Atkinson does not specify how much should be paid out or whether the use of such capital endowment should be subjected to any restrictions (e.g. financing of education). To improve the intergenerational wealth distribution, Atkinson emphasises the importance of building up of net worth by the state through accumulating state assets. He thus urges to see beyond national debt towards public assets as a part of the economic legacy passed down to the future generations.

To fund the national savings bonds programme, payments of capital endowment, and acquisition of state assets, Atkinson suggests various progressive income and wealth tax reforms in proposals 8 to 11. He postulates to increase the marginal tax rates on personal income up to 65% for the top earners. Moreover, he proposes to extend the Earned Income Tax Credit-type measures, which exclude wage income from taxes until a certain threshold, to a larger base of low-income families. In terms of taxing wealth, Atkinson is in favour of replacing the inheritance tax with a progressive lifetime capital receipts tax (Atkinson 2015:194). He argues that this would increase revenue coming from this form of taxation, which has stood at only around 0.2% of national income in the USA since the 1990s (Boadway *et al.* 2010). Importantly, he advocates switching from the present taxation of inheritance upon giving to taxing wealth receipts, which would provide greater incentives for spreading wealth more equally. The final form of wealth taxation put forward by Atkinson is a progressive property tax linked to the ability to pay.

While not explicitly proposed, Atkinson ponders the possibility of introducing an annual wealth tax *à la* Piketty. He is optimistic about its success for two reasons. Firstly, the increasing levels of wealth inequality make the need for a general wealth tax more pressing (Weale 2010:834). Secondly, the accumulation of household wealth has not been a result of rising savings but rather of increasing asset prices (Atkinson 2015:200). For this reason, the introduction of a wealth tax would not directly impede savings among the rich as these have not contributed to the observed wealth increases.

A different distinction between the various areas of policy action to reduce inequality is undertaken by Galbraith (2016). He distinguishes between three levels of policy responses to inequality, albeit focusing on income – changing the structure of market incomes, redistribution through taxes and transfers, and affecting the costs of living through public goods provision or taxing sales and consumption. Unionisation, minimum wage policies, national wage bargaining, and the Earned Income Tax Credit are some of the more effective measures improving the distribution of market incomes.

Galbraith argues that progressive income taxation is a more powerful tool for alleviating inequality than sales taxes or social insurance policies because it takes into account final household welfare. The latter are deemed problematic as they are highly regressive. For instance, non-wage income and incomes above a certain threshold are excluded from contributions to Social Security and Medicaid. In addition, they may inflate inequality measures while simultaneously creating low-income high-wealth households. Furthermore, the disproportionate impact of sales taxes on the lower income households is hidden from the conventional income inequality measures, which exclude final consumption.

Galbraith is sceptical about Piketty's annual wealth tax proposition for two reasons. Firstly, problems of valuation make it difficult to adequately assess the value of wealth on an annual basis, creating incentives for tax avoidance (for instance by shifting towards tax exempt forms of wealth before the valuation date) and generating high costs of detailed record keeping required to adequately redistribute wealth (*ibid.*:156). Secondly, partial liquidation of non-money financial assets needed to pay the tax would lower the price of these assets, thus reducing the tax revenue.

An alternative form of wealth taxation proposed by Galbraith is taxation of land. He argues that given the unproductive nature of land, its taxation would have a less damaging effect on incentives and could thus face comparatively less opposition than the annual wealth tax (*ibid.*:159). Moreover, the fixed locality of land would make this tax more effective in capturing rents. Similar benefits accrue to the estate and gift taxes, which provide a check on today's outcomes and future opportunities, improving the intergenerational distribution of income. Moreover, Galbraith considers a financial transaction tax as a means of reducing inequality, but he argues that it would have little impact on the structure of market incomes (*ibid.*:139). However, we argue that financial transaction tax could contribute to reining in *wealth* concentration at the global level. This is because it could reduce the amount of wealth accumulated in the financial sector, thus lowering returns to high-yielding financial assets.

Using taxation and financial sector regulation to reduce inequality has also been considered by Stiglitz (2012). His policy proposals are mainly concerned with reducing income inequality through improving market competition and reducing market imperfections which allow for rent seeking. Nevertheless, some of his proposals on financial sector reform, bankruptcy laws, public investment, taxation, and corporate policy carry positive implications for alleviating wealth inequality. Firstly, increasing banking transparency, restricting leverage and excessive risk taking, reducing interconnectedness across financial institutions, and regulating predatory lending practices are important in curbing the excessive wealth concentration and reducing financial fragility of low-to-middle income households. Secondly, reforming bankruptcy laws to make them more debtor-friendly has the capacity not only to discourage lax lending practices by banks, but also to alleviate high debt burden of highly leveraged households. Similar benefit accrues to increasing public investment in education, healthcare, social protection programmes, and subsidised savings to the poor, which would reduce the need for debt accumulation among the low-income households. Moreover, Stiglitz advocates increasing inheritance taxes to alleviate intergenerational wealth inequality, as well as enforcing more progressive income and corporate taxes to discourage rent seeking. He argues that by reducing government subsidies to corporations, returns on business equity would be lowered, which would decrease market power of individual firms.

Like Galbraith, Stiglitz (2014) is also sceptical of Piketty's global wealth tax proposal. He argues that it is politically unfeasible and discourages incentives for productive activities. Instead, he proposes improving the existing income and corporate taxation to promote competition and economic efficiency, which would reduce the size and the availability of rents in the economy which are captured by the rich. He advocates a gradual phasing out of tax subsidies such as mortgage deductions, as these narrow the tax base, favour rich homeowners, and encourage excessive borrowing and housing consumption, which drives up house prices and enables rent seeking. This can have another positive impact for alleviating wealth inequality by reducing the possibility of tax avoidance by the rich through accumulating mortgage debt against property wealth.

Overall, the above works represent some of the most comprehensive views on the role of economic policy in reducing wealth and income inequality. Piketty's global wealth tax proposal seems to be received rather sceptically by other scholars in the field. In the remainder of this chapter, we assess these criticisms as well as the rest of the proposed policies to redistribute wealth and influence its market distribution. This evaluation is conducted along two lines of argument. Firstly, we support Piketty's call for the necessity to explicitly address the distribution of wealth to combat rising economic inequality. Secondly, in line with Galbraith and Stiglitz, we argue that taxation is not enough to achieve this goal and needs to be complemented by policies affecting the distribution of market wealth as well as measures reducing the debt burden of households towards the bottom of the distribution.

WHAT CAN BE DONE?

To successfully tackle inequality in the context of the current institutional structures of the US economy, policy needs to explicitly address wealth disparities. This requires a more proactive role of the state. Based on the above literature, policy could focus on three areas: wealth taxation, affecting the distribution of market wealth, and macroeconomic policy.

Wealth Taxation

As mentioned in the literature progressive taxation of earnings with marginal tax rates increasing with income has great potential to redistribute wage income more equally. But given wealth heterogeneity among households, it would do not adequately target incomes of the rich. An alternative way to reduce wealth inequality through income taxation is by raising corporate income tax as corporate stock ownership is concentrated at the top of the distribution. But while corporate taxation is enforced at the national level, modern corporations operate as multi-national entities (Pressman 2016:133). The ability to shift revenues overseas provides strong incentives for a race-to-the-bottom in terms of lowering of corporate tax rates across countries. A potential solution is to base the tax on wage payments and sales in a given country rather than on corporate revenues (Piketty 2014:561). Such corporate tax reform has the potential to influence not only the distribution of income but also wealth. This is because it would decrease the future after-tax profits of firms, thus reducing the stock valuation and directly affecting wealth holdings of the rich (Pressman 2016:135).

Apart from reducing the economic power and returns to wealth of the richest, taxation of wealth holdings suggested by Piketty (2014) would allow the concentration of wealth to be reined in by providing incentives to sell assets. Greater mobility of wealth across the distribution induced by asset sales is argued to increase economic efficiency (Pressman 2016:147) and could also reduce the returns on assets, provided that there is enough supply to avoid an asset bubble.

Nevertheless, there are challenges to the implementation of taxes on wealth holdings. In addition to the political and logistical obstacles highlighted by Stiglitz (2014) and Galbraith (2016), we support Piketty's concern that taxation of wealth holdings generates incentives for tax avoidance and evasion associated with the mobility of wealth. These are particularly likely in the case of financial wealth owned by the richest households, which is highly liquid. The ability to shift wealth overseas or to other types of holdings highlights the need for a comprehensive design of wealth taxation, which would capture the diversity of forms which are taken by wealth ownership and its associated capital income flows. Consequently, wealth tax on holdings could be more effective in reducing wealth inequality if complemented by other types of taxes. An additional advantage of such a comprehensive taxation reform is that many of these alternative forms of taxation are already in place, and their reform would be more feasible to implement in the short run than Piketty's proposition.

The first alternative form of wealth taxation to be considered is the inclusion of capital gains in taxable income. This would prevent large growth of wealth at the top and would provide greater financial stability to households in the middle of the distribution, who leverage up in the process of home equity withdrawal (IMF 2017). Since at present capital gains are only taxed once sold, wealth accumulates tax free (Weale 2010:833–34). For this reason, a progressive capital gains tax has potential to immediately redistribute wealth more equally.

Secondly, progressive taxation of wealth transfers (gifts and bequests) could effectively target intergenerational inequality. We support Atkinson's (2015) call for this type of taxation to be collected on receipt, because it would provide incentives for asset sales, which under conditions mentioned earlier could result in a more equal distribution. Moreover, to curb tax avoidance, taxation of wealth transfers could be extended to incorporate transfers among corporations. The financial transactions tax proposed by Galbraith (2016) could be particularly powerful in harnessing the large wealth holdings accumulated in the financial sector and in reducing the rate of return earned on securities and other financial investment assets. Moreover, Atkinson's (2015) idea of the lifetime capital receipts tax could be seriously considered by policymakers. Not only would it diminish the possibilities of spreading wealth transfers throughout lifetime to avoid the inheritance tax, but it could also boost the currently small revenues from this type of wealth transfer taxation.

In addition, the comprehensive tax reform could include designing more progressive tax breaks. In contrast to Stiglitz (2012) who advocates their abandonment, we see the potential of mortgage deduction schemes to effectively reduce wealth inequality by alleviating the debt burden of the lower income borrowers.

McCain (2017) puts forward a similar proposition of complementing taxation of wealth holdings with an additional tax on flows. He proposes that the annual wealth tax be accompanied by a tax on net revenue of large businesses, corporations, multinationals, and multi-state organisations. The net revenue tax would be imposed on corporate profits net of input costs as well as wages and salaries paid within the taxing jurisdiction, but including bonuses paid above a certain threshold, transfer payments, and payments for intellectual property rights. It would thus replace the corporate income tax and the sales taxes. The major advantage of introducing such net revenue tax alongside the tax on wealth holdings is that documented wealth tax payments by a company would be deducted from its net revenue, thus reducing the overall tax liability on the transaction tax. As such, the combination of the wealth tax on holdings and the net revenue tax would discourage tax evasion and avoidance by including capital income earned on business equity held by the rich, and providing incentives for tax payments by businesses and high net worth individuals, who will "*want* to report the transaction to save [themselves] taxes" (Higgins 1968:531; Kaldor 1956b; McCain 2017:78).

While the comprehensive wealth tax reform has great potential to tackle wealth inequality by better targeting, we appreciate that taxation of wealth is problematic and there is a historical record of failed attempts at wealth tax implementation (Pressman 2016:140–1). In the absence of global cooperation, there are strong incentives for wealth holders to relocate their assets to whichever country offers the lowest tax rates, resulting in the estimated $200bn losses in tax revenue around the world (Zucman 2016). This problem may persist even after introducing a more comprehensive wealth transaction tax if costs of moving funds abroad remain low. Thus, a coordinated global effort focused on a worldwide system of redistribution may be necessary to rein in the perverse incentives to evade taxes, and to alleviate losses in national wealth associated with the shift of individual and corporate wealth to tax havens (*ibid.*). Such global coordination should address the problem of wealth arbitrage, when asset ownership is separated from return (e.g. through establishing a trust, where a part of wealth is sold in exchange for regular interest payments). This is because it prevents identification of the actual owners of wealth, so that taxes cannot be effectively levied (Pressman 2016:144).

Furthermore, as highlighted by Galbraith (2016) taxation of wealth faces substantial valuation issues. While more frequently traded financial assets and property are evaluated more regularly and thus rigorously, the value of consumer durables, pension funds, and family trusts is more difficult to assess because they are either sold infrequently or it is complex to identify the actual asset owner (Pressman 2016:142). Moreover, most contemporary wealth taxes around the world rely on self-declared wealth values, which are likely to be underreported (*ibid.*:145). Furthermore, wealth tax in the form proposed by Piketty faces liquidity problems for wealth owners with little income flow, such as pensioners, or owners of illiquid assets for whom property is the major source of collateral, thus disproportionately affecting low-to-middle-income households (*ibid.*:143). In this situation, in order to pay the tax on wealth, an individual may be forced to borrow even more against her wealth, which further perpetuates inequality by increasing household leverage.

Affecting Distribution of Market Wealth

Overall, one of the greatest challenges to the design and implementation of an effective wealth tax is ensuring that it accurately targets the owners of the highest fortunes. Hence, taxation alone may not achieve sustainable reductions in wealth inequality. We support Galbraith's (2012) and Atkinson's (2015) proposals to develop policy strategies directly affecting the distribution of market wealth. These measures necessitate dedication of public spending and a coherent government-led strategy which would become the pinnacle of improving the *ex ante* distribution of wealth. Such policies could be focused in a number of areas – affecting the rates of return earned on various assets, direct wealth transfers to low-income households, and asset-building programmes, e.g. subsidised saving.

Measures influencing rates of return earned on the different types of wealth have potential to reduce wealth inequality by boosting returns for small savers and reigning in high returns earned on business equity and high-yielding financial assets at the top. Atkinson's (2015) proposal 5 is focused on ensuring a guaranteed positive return on savings for small savers and lower-income households through the national savings bonds programme. This is desirable given that returns earned by small savers towards the bottom of the distribution have been kept below the average rates of return on wealth, partially due to low-interest rate policy. Since the wedge between these two rates constitutes an income for the financial sector, the national savings bonds programme could counteract the incentive among financial intermediaries to keep the rate of return for small savers low (Atkinson 2015:167). Moreover, policy could affect rates of return by limiting the charges imposed by the wealth management funds (*ibid*:164). In addition to these measures, increased financial regulation and supervision of financial sector operations could rein in high returns earned by households at the top of the distribution, who have been the main beneficiaries of financial deregulation and innovation since the 1980s. Furthermore, it would act to disassociate the fate of highly leveraged wealth owners from the whimsies of financial markets, as was the case in the 2007 crash.

Furthermore, government can provide direct wealth payments to individuals subject to certain conditions, as put forward by Atkinson (2015) in his proposal 6 of the capital endowment payments and proposal 7 of a public Investment Authority running a sovereign fund raising the net worth of the state. In addition, creating an inclusive social security programme is vital to providing a sustainable safety net for households at the bottom of the distribution (Atkinson 2015), with potential to improve gender and intergenerational inequalities. These policies are important in promoting the equality of opportunity in the accumulation of wealth. This is because inclusive social security, accumulation of public net worth, and the establishment of capital endowment payments to the young have capacity to improve wealth accumulation possibilities for everyone in the society. Consequently, such policies constitute more long term solutions to wealth inequality. This means that the initial reduction in inequality may be rather small compared to other policy measures which explicitly address the excessive concentration of wealth at the top or target low wealth households.

Ex ante policy can also promote asset holdings among the poor, for example through social housing. This has been the objective of savings subsidies proposed and partially implemented in the USA such as the Individual Development Accounts (IDAs), the Children's Savings Accounts (CSAs), and the Universal Savings Accounts (USAs). IDAs were implemented at the federal and the state level in 1996 as savings accounts drawn from the household earned income, which match savings of low-income households with public and privately raised funds. In turn, CSAs are federal and state matched savings accounts encouraging investment in education by low-income families (Cramer/Newville 2009). After the completion of a college degree, any remaining funds on the CSA can be spent on the accumulation of other assets, e.g. housing. Finally, USAs are proposed tax-free savings accounts aimed at small savers, which would be available to adult citizens and permanent residents (US Congress 2017a). Contributions to the USAs would resemble the Individual Retirement Accounts (IRAs) with the difference that funds could be withdrawn at any time (versus after retirement under IRAs) and may not exceed $5,500 a year. USAs were first introduced to the Senate Committee on Finance in November 2015, but the proposal has not been developed since (US Congress 2017a and 2017b). The advantage of such measures is that in addition to providing resources to satisfy household financial needs and generate opportunities for investment in human and tangible capital, they offer a more sustained way out of poverty, allowing households to achieve a degree of long term economic security (Sherraden 1991).

Promoting asset ownership among low-income households is important in providing a more level playing field for wealth accumulation in the society, and should be conducted by the state. Due to the systemic role of finance described in the earlier sections, private provision of asset-based welfare policies is likely to increase inequality through valuation dynamics. Such policies may lead to an unsustainable accumulation of debt among low-income households as the increased demand following the promotion of a particular type of asset ownership may drive up its prices. This is supported by the example of the UK, where the push for home ownership under the Help to Buy and the Buy to Let policy has contributed to rising house prices, and made home ownership unaffordable for first-time buyers (Montgomerie/Buedenbender 2015). This example is particularly important to consider in the US context given the changing structure of the housing market after the Great Recession, which increased the number of households renting their residence (JCHS 2015).

Moreover, similar pitfalls can be attributed to asset-based welfare policies focused on promoting financial literacy and inclusion. This is because they shift the responsibility for the adverse consequences of unsustainable wealth accumulation towards the individual rather than acknowledging the role of financial institutions in increasing wealth inequality. With rates of return determined in the financial markets (as evidenced by the case of housing in the recent bubble), these measures threaten to increase inequality even more. Moreover, given the rising costs of private education, expansion of CSAs may not be enough to boost the educational attainment of the youth from low-income families. To even out the educational opportunities more effectively, we echo Galbraith's call for the provision of public education at all levels.

Consequently, asset-based welfare policies should be closely supervised by the government. This is to avoid the build-up of leverage among low-income households who may become priced out of the asset markets. This reveals that to effectively reduce wealth inequality it is necessary to consider the other side of net wealth and leverage – debt.

As suggested by Stiglitz (2012), measures reducing debt burden of households can be focused on debt forgiveness and restructuring for low-income borrowers, as well as on regulation of lending practices to discourage predatory lending. Moreover, in the long run the increased provision of public goods and raising wages would act to reduce the necessity to take on debt.

Current debt reduction initiatives in the USA are rather limited and more often applied to businesses and banks. One reason for such insufficient consideration of personal debt relief is a fall in the overall levels of household debt relative to GDP after the Great Recession (cf. Bricker *et al.* 2011, 2014). However, as mentioned earlier not all households have deleveraged sufficiently. Furthermore, while the problem of subprime mortgages may have been reduced after the 2007 crisis (albeit at the cost of millions of households facing foreclosures, cf. Newman/Schafran 2013), house prices are on the rise again and are close to their pre-recessionary levels (S&P Dow Jones Indices LLC 2017). This has a twofold implication for wealth inequality. On the one hand, it provides incentives for refinancing through home equity withdrawal for the existing homeowners and can increase household leverage. On the other hand, rising house prices increase the wealth gap between homeowners and the growing group of renters, making access to housing a decisive factor in perpetuating wealth inequality in the future. Moreover, there has been a rise in the unsustainable patterns of borrowing reminiscing the pre-crisis subprime mortgage lending after the 2007 crisis, however this time they are focused on other forms of borrowing, such as auto loans (U.S. Survey of Consumer Finances, 1989–2013). Unsecured debt, particularly student loans and vehicle loans, remains problematic and is on the rise particularly among low-income households. Consequently, addressing the problem of overindebtedness remains important after the Great Recession and is necessary to combat growing wealth inequality.

As a part of the debt relief initiatives after the 2007 crisis, the 2010 Dodd Frank Act established the Consumer Financial Protection Bureau (CFPB) in order to supervise bank and non-bank institutions, as well as credit reporting and debt collection agencies in order to make lending conditions more transparent (USA.gov 2017). In light of the growing holdings of unsecured debt among low-income households, the authority of CFPB could be strengthened to focus on regulating lending conditions in consumer credit markets.

Macroeconomic Policy

In order to be effective, wealth taxation and policies affecting the distribution of market wealth require an active role of the state. Both fiscal and monetary policy have a role in ensuring adequate targeting of high wealth individuals to benefit wealth poor and highly leveraged households.

Dedicated public spending programmes focused on affordable housing, public provision of education, and improving public services have the potential to inspire the common goal of social justice, which could lead to more sustainable reductions in wealth inequality. Moreover, they could reduce the pressures on household expenditures, enabling low-income households to use a greater portion of their income to save or purchase assets. For this reason, government policy oriented towards supporting working rights, raising minimum wages, improving the social safety net, and boosting employment has great potential to contribute to alleviating wealth inequality by increasing incomes at the bottom of the distribution.

Central bank's response to growing inequality could be focused in three areas. Firstly, it could be through a closer supervision of financial activity. In this way, the Fed could monitor how the extra liquidity is invested by banks, prioritising investment in productivity-enhancing activities and discouraging speculative investment in real estate and financial products. Secondly, through financial supervision the Fed could also liaise with CFPB to regulate lending conditions – particularly unsecured lending and lending to low-income borrowers. This could contain the rising leverage and financial instability faced by these households. Moreover, the Fed could cooperate with the government to move towards a broader fiscal approach to economic policy. This is to ensure that the positive implications of monetary policy for household wealth through asset price increases are shared more equally. In addition, such coordinated monetary-fiscal policy could serve to reduce macroeconomic volatility (Romer/Romer 2017).

An important challenge to the proposed policies is government's ability to raise sufficient tax revenue so as not to expand public debt to levels which would induce asset price inflation and increase inequality. There is a danger of political opposition to higher taxation as the society tends to perceive inequality to be lower than it actually is, and can thus underestimate the degree of taxation necessary to redistribute wealth (Norton/Ariely 2011). Measures improving the quality of public services and investment in research informing about the causes and consequences of inequality can generate a sense of shared participation in the benefits of taxation policy. With such tangible benefits and knowledge, taxpayers may be more willing to pay their taxes and participate in a more egalitarian economic development.

It is crucial, however, that commitment to equality and justice is shared at the global level. Atkinson proposes to establish an international progressive wealth and income tax authority, which would offer personal tax payers the opportunity to opt out of the national tax regimes by entering the global system (Atkinson 2015:201). He ponders the possibility of introducing a minimum net worth required to be a part of the global tax regime. He argues that this could create prestige equivalent to the Forbes 400 list, thus providing incentives for the rich to pay their taxes under a unified global scheme. Such initiative seems to be a feasible tool for international efforts against tax evasion.

CONCLUSION

This chapter analysed the role of economic policy in rising wealth and income inequality in the USA since the 1980s. We showed that current policy promoted asset ownership in a way that was not sustainable to vulnerable households, because it induced rising indebtedness and linked household wealth accumulation to financial market performance. Deregulation of financial markets and banks fuelled the development of structured finance based on subprime lending expansion, and generated incentives for predatory inclusion of low-income households into financial services. Liberalisation of labour market legislation, tax reform, and privatisation of public services put a strain on household finances, creating the need for debt accumulation and home equity withdrawal to compensate for stagnant incomes. This made household wealth holdings across the distribution more complex, with high increases in home ownership at the bottom of the distribution, and new sources of financial wealth for rich investors.

Based on the recent inequality literature we advocated the need for explicit wealth policy. This is because measures focusing only on income disparities were shown to insufficiently curb economic inequality in the context of the profit-oriented financial sector and heterogeneity of household wealth. To effectively alleviate inequality, we argued for a more holistic approach to policy based on wealth taxation, measures affecting the distribution of market wealth, and coordinated fiscal-monetary policies. A comprehensive wealth tax reform including taxes on holdings and transfers of wealth was argued to more adequately target the owners of the highest wealth in the US economy. Such reform could be based on progressive taxes collected as a proportion of wealth holdings above a certain tax-free threshold with increasing marginal rates, as well as on increases in wealth through a progressive capital gains tax and transaction taxes. Such approach would have an additional advantage of being able to dampen revenue losses from tax evasion and avoidance. This is because transactions have locality attached to them. Consequently, taxing wealth transfers between individuals as well as financial and non-financial businesses would ensure that redistribution takes place in a given tax jurisdiction, so that tax avoidance becomes costly, and high returns on financial assets held by households at the top of the distribution are limited. Such tax reform should be complemented by coordinated fiscal and monetary policies focused on debt relief and increasing government support through social security, subsidised savings, and the provision of affordable home ownership and public services.

The chapter argued that in order to overcome the political obstacles to increased wealth taxation and public spending, commitment to achieving greater equality should be shared within the society and globally. Global cooperation and proactive government strategy focused on improving the quality and access to public services and on promoting research on the causes and consequences of high inequality were argued to be capable of bringing the US society closer to that goal.

NOTES

1. I am grateful to Prof Gary Dymski, Prof Giuseppe Fontana, and Dr Peter Phelps for their comments on an earlier draft of this chapter.
2. It is important to distinguish between tax evasion and tax avoidance. While both practices pose problems to effective redistribution, only tax evasion is illegal (cf. Pressman 2016). In contrast, tax avoidance is a practice of using the legal system to switch to non-taxable forms of income/wealth to reduce tax burden.
3. Proposals 1 to 4 are aimed at the distribution of income through employability-enhancing innovation, improving workers' bargaining power, guaranteed public employment at minimum wage, and a national pay programme. Proposals 12 to 15 concentrate on improving social security systems and international cooperation on development issues.
4. See also: Sandford 1969; Atkinson 1972; Ackerman/Alstott 1999; LeGrand/Nissan 2000.

REFERENCES

Ackerman, B. and Alstott, A. (1999) *The Stake-Holder Society*, New Haven: Yale University Press.

Ampudia, M., van Vlokhoven, H. and Zochowski, D. (2014) "Financial fragility of euro area households," Working Paper No. 1737, European Central Bank.

Arestis, P., Charles, A. and Fontana, G. (2013) "Financialization, the Great Recession, and the stratification of the US Labor Market," *Feminist Economics*, 19(3), 152–80.

Atkinson, A.B. (1972) *Unequal Shares*, London: Allen Lane.

Atkinson, A.B. (2015) *Inequality. What Can Be Done?* London: Harvard University Press.

Austen, S., Jefferson, T. and Ong, R. (2014) "The gender gap in financial security: what we know and don't know about Australian households," *Feminist Economics*, 20(3), 25–52.

Barba, A. and Pivetti, M. (2009) "Rising household debt: its causes and macroeconomic implications – a long-period analysis," *Cambridge Journal of Economics*, 33, 113–37.

Bivens, J., Gould, E., Mishel, L. and Shierholz, H. (2014) "Raising America's Pay. Why It's Our Central Economic Challenge," Economic Policy Institute Briefing Paper No. 378.

Boadway, R., Chamberlain, E. and Emmerson, C. (2010) "Taxation of wealth and wealth transfers." In: Adam, S., Besley, T., Blundell, R., Bond, S., Chote, R., Gammie, M., Johnson, P., Myles, G. and Poterba, J. (eds) *Dimensions of Tax Design*, Oxford: Oxford University Press.

Bricker, J., Bucks, B., Kennickell, A., Mach, T. and Moore, K.B. (2011) "Surveying the Aftermath of the Storm: Changes in Family Finances from 2007 to 2009," Finance and Economics Discussion Series 2011–17, Divisions of Research and Statistics and Monetary Affairs, Federal Reserve Board, Washington, D.C.

Bricker, J., Dettling, L.J., Henriques, A., Hsu, J.W., Moore, K.B., Sabelhaus, J., Thompson, J., Windle, R.A., Devlin-Foltz, S. and Krimmel, J. (2014) "Changes in U.S. family finances from 2010 to 2013: evidence from the Survey of Consumer Finances," *Federal Reserve Bulletin*, 100(4), 1–41.

Castelló-Climent, A. and Doménech, R. (2014) "Human Capital and Income Inequality: Some Facts and Some Puzzles," BBVA Research Working Paper No. 12/28.

Claeys, G., Darvas, Z., Leandro, A. and Walsh, T. (2015) "The Effects of Ultra-Loose Monetary Policies on Inequality," Bruegel Policy Contribution Issue 2015/09.

Cramer, R. and Newville, D. (2009) "Children's Savings Accounts. The Case for Creating a Lifelong Savings Platform at Birth as a Foundation for a 'Save-and-Invest' Economy," New America Foundation Report.

Domanski, D., Scatigna, M. and Zabai, A. (2016) "Wealth inequality and monetary policy," *BIS Quarterly Review*, March 2016.

Dos Santos, P.L. (2009) "At the Heart of the Matter: Household Debt in Contemporary Banking and the International Crisis," Research on Money and Finance Discussion Paper No. 11.

Dymski, G.A. (2009) "Racial exclusion and the political economy of the subprime crisis," *Historical Materialism*, 17, 149–79.

Dymski, G.A., Hernandez, J. and Mohanty, L. (2013) "Race, gender, power, and the US subprime mortgage and foreclosure crisis: a Meso analysis," *Feminist Economics*, 19(3), 124–51.

Ennis, H.M. and Wolman, A.L. (2015) "Large excess reserves in the United States: a view from the cross-section of banks," *International Journal of Central Banking*, 11(1), 251–89.

Federal Reserve Economic Data St. Louis Fed. Available at: https://fred.stlouisfed.org.

Friedman, M. (1957) *A Theory of the Consumption Function*, Princeton: Princeton University Press.

Galbraith, J.K. (2016) *Inequality. What Everyone Needs to Know*, Oxford: Oxford University Press.

Goda, T. and Lysandrou, P. (2014) "The contribution of wealth concentration to the subprime crisis: a quantitative estimation," *Cambridge Journal of Economics*, 38(2), 301–27.

Higgins, B. (1968) *Economic Development*, revised edition, New York: Norton.

Institute on Taxation and Economic Policy (ITEP) (2004) "The Effects of Replacing Most Federal Taxes with a National Sales Tax: A State-by-State Distributional Analysis," Report, September 2004. Available at: https://itep.org/wp-content/uploads/sale0904.pdf.

Internal Revenue Service (2017) "Estate and Gift Taxes" webpage. Available at: https://www.irs.gov/businesses/small-businesses-self-employed/estate-tax [Accessed: 04/06/2017].

International Monetary Fund (2017) "Fiscal Monitor October 2017. Tackling Inequality," *World Economic and Financial Surveys*.

Kaldor, N. (1956) *Indian Tax Reform*, Delhi: Ministry of Finance.

LeGrand, J. and Nissan, D. (2000) *A Capital Idea: Start-Up Grants for Young People*, London: Fabian Society.

Levin, E., Greer, J. and Rademacher, I. (2014) "From Upside Down to Right-Side Up. Redeploying $540 billion in federal spending to help all families save, invest, and build wealth," Corporation for Enterprise and Development Report.

Lindner, P. (2015) "Factor decomposition of the wealth distribution in the euro area," *Empirica*, 42(2), 291–322.

McCain, R. (2017) *Approaching Equality*, Cheltenham: Edward Elgar.

Montecino, J.A. and Epstein, G. (2015) "Did Quantitative Easing Increase Income Inequality?," INET Working Paper No. 28.

Montgomerie, J. and Buedenbender M. (2015) "Round the houses: homeownership and failures of asset-based welfare in the United Kingdom," *New Political Economy*, 20(3), 386–405.

Murphy, K.M. and Topel, R.H. (2016) "Human Capital Investment, Inequality and Economic Growth," NBER Working Paper No. 21841.

Newman, K. and Schafran, A. (2013) "Assessing the foreclosure crisis from the ground up," *Housing Policy Debate*, 23(1), 1–4.

Norton, M.I. and Ariely, D. (2011) "Building a better America – one wealth quintile at a time," *Perspectives on Psychological Science*, 6(1), 9–12.

Philippon, T. and Reshef, A. (2012) "Wages and human capital in the U.S. finance industry: 1909–2006," *The Quarterly Journal of Economics*, 127(4), 1551–609.

Piketty, T. (2014) *Capital in the Twenty First Century*, Harvard: Harvard University Press.

Pollin, R. and Heintz, J, (2013) "Study of U.S. Financial System," FESSUD Studies in Financial Systems No. 10.

Pressman, S. (2016) *Understanding Piketty's Capital in the Twenty First Century*, Abingdon: Routledge.

Romer, C.D. and Romer, D.H. (2017) "Why Some Times Are Different: Macroeconomic Policy and the Aftermath of Financial Crises," University of California Berkeley Working Paper.

S&P Dow Jones Indices LLC (2017) Available at: https://us.spindices.com.

Sandford, C. (1969) *Economics of Public Finance*, Oxford: Pergamon Press.

Schneider, M., Pottenger, M. and King, J. (2016) *The Distribution of Wealth – Growing Inequality?*, Cheltenham: Edward Elgar.

Scott, R. and Pressman, S. (2015) "Inadequate household deleveraging: income, debt and social provisioning," *Journal of Economic Issues*, 49(2), 483–92.

Sherraden, M. (1991) *Assets and the Poor: A New American Welfare Policy*, M.E. Sharpe Inc.

Stiglitz, J.E. (2012) *The Price of Inequality*, London: Penguin Books Ltd.

Stiglitz, J.E. (2014) "Phony Capitalism," *Harper's Magazine*, September 2014 issue.

Szymborska, H.K. (2016) "Financial sector transformation and income inequality – an empirical analysis," *E-Finance Financial Internet Quarterly*, 12(2), 36–48.

Szymborska, H.K. (2017) *Financial sector and household balance sheet dynamics: Rethinking the determinants of income and wealth inequality in the USA since the 1980s.* PhD thesis, University of Leeds.

USA.gov (2017) Consumer Financial Protection Bureau. Available at: https://www.usa.gov/federal-agencies/consumer-financial-protection-bureau [Accessed: 20/06/2017].

U.S. Bureau of Economic Analysis. Available at: https://www.bea.gov [Accessed: 14/06/2017].

U.S. Congress (2017a) Online legislation directory of the 114th Congress. Available at: https://www.congress.gov/bill/114th-congress/senate-bill/2320?q=%7B%22sea

rch%22%3A%5B%22universal+savings+accounts%22%5D%7D&r=5 [Accessed: 19/06/2017].

U.S. Congress (2017b) Online legislation directory of the 115th Congress. Available at: https://www.congress.gov/bill/115th-congress/senate-bill/323?q=%7B%22search%22%3A%5B%22universal+savings+accounts%22%5D%7D&r=2 [Accessed: 19/06/2017].

U.S. Survey of Consumer Finances, 1989–2013, Federal Reserve. Available at: http://www.federalreserve.gov/econresdata/scf/scfindex.htm.

Weale, M. (2010) "Commentary." In: Adam, S., Besley, T., Blundell, R., Bond, S., Chote, R., Gammie, M., Johnson, P., Myles, G. and Poterba, J. (eds) *Dimensions of Tax Design*, Oxford: Oxford University Press.

Williams, R.B. (2016) *The Privileges of Wealth: Rising Inequality and the Growing Racial Divide*, Abingdon: Routledge.

Wolff, E.N. (2014) "Household wealth trends in the United States, 1983–2010," *Oxford Review of Economic Policy*, 30(1), 21–43.

Young, B. (2010) "The gendered dimension of money, finance and the subprime crisis." In: Bauhardt, C. and Caglar, G. (eds) *Gender and Economics. Feministische Kritik der politischen Oekonomie*, Wiesbaden: VS Verlag für Sozialwissenschaften.

Zucman, G. (2016) *The Hidden Wealth of Nations: The Scourge of Tax Havens*, Chicago: University of Chicago Press.

7. Economic policies and growth regimes in France (1974–2016)

Hélène de Largentaye and Renaud du Tertre

INTRODUCTION

Looking at the evolution of the French economy since World War II, we find a striking contrast between the remarkable performance of the real economy during the first three decades and their gradual deterioration during the last four decades.

The purpose of this chapter is to highlight the interactions between economic policy choices and socio-economic structures that we believe explain France's long-term growth regime. On the one hand, public action is constrained by the institutional framework in which it operates, and on the other, this framework changes markedly as a result of a reorientation of strategic choices in economic policy.

We will show that the abandonment in the mid-1970s of Keynesian guidelines of economic policies that prevailed in France during the "Fordist" growth regime (1954–1973) led to a long transitional phase, characterised by a succession of ruptures and by the emergence of new socio-economic institutions (1974–1992). These transformations in turn ushered in a "neo-liberal" growth regime (1992–2007), which the Great Financial Crisis (2008–2009) destabilised dramatically.

In this perspective, the theoretical framework of this chapter is twofold. It is first based on J.M. Keynes's *The General Theory* according to which aggregate demand plays the key role in determining economic results (i.e. national income, employment, etc.). Secondly, it refers to the French Regulation School, which analyses structural features of growth regimes (Aglietta, 1976; Boyer, 2015). Keynes's *General Theory* is a short-term theory showing how finance influences the expected yield of the investment and hence effective demand, whereas the second theory is a long-term one, highlighting the changes that may occur in the relation between the financial sphere and the real sphere, hence the importance of the financial constraint on investment and on economic activity. Both theories are necessary when studying policies and appraising economic performance over several decades – in the case of our subject, the decades overlapping the 20th and 21st centuries in France.

The 42-year period (1974–2016) that we have chosen to analyse starts after the immediate post-war reconstruction and catching-up period (1945–1953) which was followed by the "Fordist" growth regime (from 1954 to 1973), as dubbed by the French regulation school. This 30-year period was characterised by strong state intervention which we will recall briefly.

Indeed, throughout this period, public policies targeting full employment (as stated in the preamble of the 1946 Constitution of the Fourth Republic) did away with the deflationary economic policies of the 1930s and laid down new structures which made it possible for the "Fordist" growth regime to prosper.

To regulate economic activity and thus control market mechanisms, the state took action in different directions. It set up a welfare state providing health insurance, family allowances, pension systems, unemployment benefits. It took over industrial policy and installed a collective bargaining framework. The state took strong control over credit: on the domestic side, the Bank of France and the country's five largest banks were nationalised and on the external side, the franc–dollar exchange rate was fixed (although revisable by government decision) and capital flows were controlled (in accordance with the 1944 Bretton Woods agreement) so that monetary policy could be domestically monitored. State-owned firms dominated key sectors including energy, transport, telecommunications, shipbuilding, aeronautics, and the Renault car industry. Lastly, the *Commissariat général du Plan* brought together "social partners" (employers and trade unions) to define production targets announced in five-year plans and which on the whole were met.

In 1957, France, as well as five other European countries, signed the Treaty of Rome, establishing the European Common Market. Exports to European markets replaced those to former protectorates (Tunisia, Vietnam, Morocco . . .), which had become independent in the post-war period.

In this "Fordist" growth regime featuring high growth rates and full employment, the relationship between the rise in real wages and the labour productivity gains – whereby the former was greater than the latter – played a decisive role. This owed to collective bargaining seeking a compromise at the "macro-social" level. This tight linkage formed a virtuous circle between mass consumption and mass production. Consequently, domestic demand was the real engine driving domestic production.

However, towards the end of the 1960s, demand for durable consumer goods gradually became saturated and prices began to soar (by over 6% in

1969) after the 1968 student crisis and workers' strikes which were followed by substantial wage raises.

In August 1971, President Nixon suspended the gold convertibility of the dollar. This major unilateral decision ushered in a period of international instability. A flexible exchange rate system replaced the previous fixed exchange rate system and the Bretton Woods international monetary system was abandoned altogether in January 1976 (Jamaica Agreements). The first oil shock in September 1973 aggravated this instability, introducing a "period of ruptures" which did away with the previous era of quasi full-employment.

1974–1992: THE "PERIOD OF RUPTURES" AND THE END OF FULL EMPLOYMENT

Figure 7.1 shows how the unemployment rate rose from under 2% in 1960 to 10% in 2014. Over this same long period, growth rates slackened from an average 5% in the 1950s–1960s to below 1% in 2014.

The 61-year period (1954–2015) can be divided into three sub-periods which include two growth regimes separated by a period during which the structures of the first growth regime disappeared and the foundations of the second growth regime were laid.

The "period of ruptures" which we will now analyse, started with the 1973 oil shock and ended with the European Monetary System crisis (1992–1993).

This 18-year period (1974–1992) was not a homogenous one in terms of the social, economic and institutional conditions underpinning growth. The only uniform trend was the rise of unemployment (from 2.1% in 1973 to 9% in 1992) – an indication of a major failure of the economy.

In a first sub-section we will examine economic policy decisions taken by the different governments and which changed the structures of the Fordist growth regime. In a second sub-section we will see how these decisions brought about a long-lasting change in the way wages were settled and in the global income distribution between wages and profits – a distribution which, in the long run, has an impact on growth.

New Economic Policies

Three types of economic policies marked this 18-year period (1974–1992).

Inflation control

The combination of domestic factors and external shocks – the latter having an aggravating impact on the former – that jeopardised the Fordist

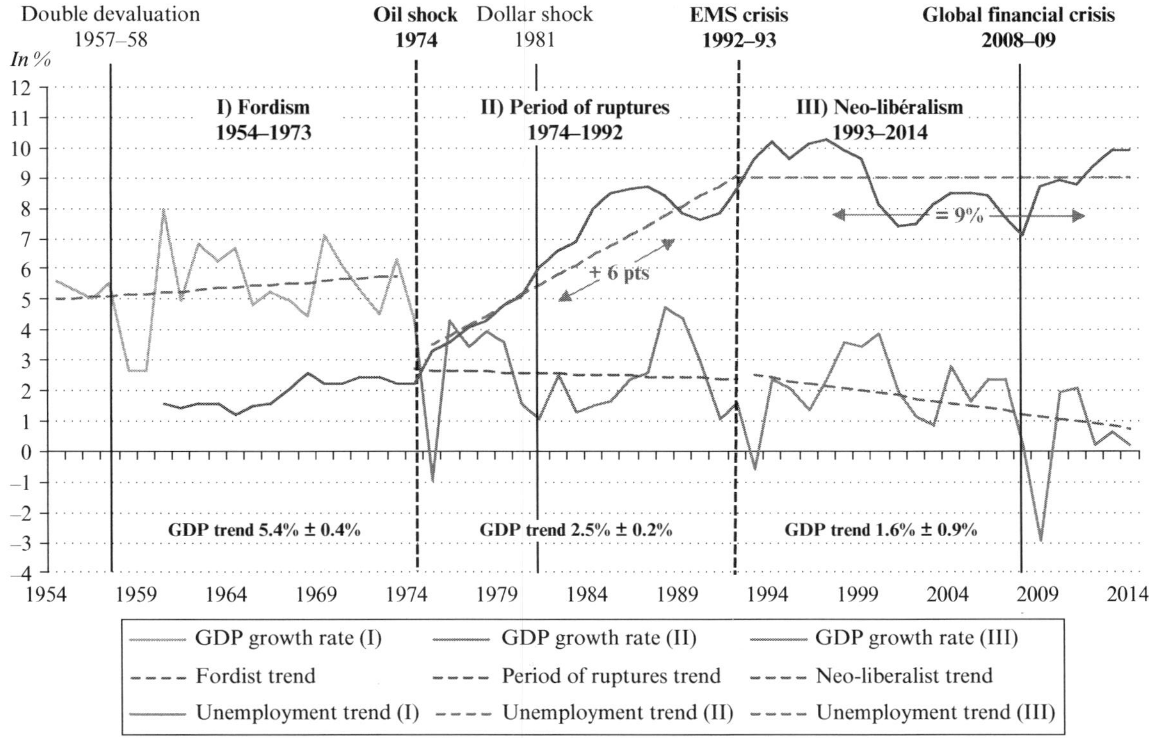

Source: du Tertre (2017), Insee, OECD, Ameco database.[1]

Figure 7.1 GDP growth and unemployment rates in France (1954–2014)

growth regime in the early 1970s, as we have seen, led to stagflation, allying stagnation and inflation which were hitherto considered antithetical.

Starting from 1974, the average annual GDP growth rate was halved, falling from 5.4% over the 1954–1973 period, to 2.5% over the 1974–1992 period. At the same time, the inflation rate which was 5.2%, on average during the first period, accelerated after 1973 and reached 11.4% on average from 1974 to 1982.

Faced with these circumstances, Raymond Barre's[2] economic policy from 1976 to 1981 gave absolute priority to price stability which, according to the mainstream view, implied in particular a stringent wage policy and constraints on public expenditure.

The international competitiveness of French firms improved due to this "disinflation" policy which also aimed at defending a "strong franc" on currency markets. Most large firms focussed their activities on profitable sectors. This specialisation led to massive lay-offs in the abandoned sectors, particularly in the northern, eastern and central regions of France.

An exchange stability zone within the European Economic Community

The choices made by the Barre government can be explained by the fact that President Valéry Giscard d'Estaing and Chancellor Helmut Schmidt both sought to promote a closer Franco-German relationship, which ushered in a new stage in the two countries' cooperation and deepened European integration. Setting up the European Monetary System (EMS) from March 1979 to July 1992 was the most important innovation of this new phase. The objective of the EMS was to create a zone of fixed exchange rates within the European Community.

The French government's purpose was to peg its inflation rate to the German rate (reinforcing the case for a strong domestic inflation control policy) and also to bring about a fall in short- and long-term nominal interest rates, which were in fact much higher in France than in Germany. Consequently, the French government expected a stimulating impact on French exports and domestic investment, which would have triggered economic growth.

This expectation was partly satisfied – but only partly. In fact and more importantly, the EMS established the hegemony of the deutsche mark on the EMS member countries' currencies. It led to a strict harnessing of French monetary policy. Employment was again sacrificed.

The March 1983 economic policy u-turn following the dollar shock

March 1983 is a crucial turning point for economic policy in France. President François Mitterrand then decided to put an end to the global demand-led reflation policy that he himself had implemented just after his election in May 1981, together with a series of nationalisations of large corporations and prominent banks. Turning his back on his political platform, Mitterrand decided to commit himself to a policy of wage stringency mainly aimed at maintaining the franc within the EMS. The old post-war rule of pegging wages to prices (*indexation des salaires sur les prix*) was abandoned in 1982.

The change in France's economic policy in March 1983 cannot be understood without mentioning the dramatic rise in the dollar exchange rate in 1981, which caused a major international shock. This sudden rise followed a ten-year period of erratic fluctuations (*vis-à-vis* all European currencies), both upwards and downwards.[3] The rise was due to a fundamental reorientation of the United States' monetary policy, decided by Paul Volcker in 1979 subsequent to his appointment as President of the Federal Reserve Bank. The policy aimed to raise nominal interest rates well above the inflation rate in order to restore positive real interest rates. As a result, capital was attracted towards assets priced in dollars, first in the banking sector and afterwards in all financial markets.

Against this backdrop, the "strong franc" policy not only sought to stabilise the franc on currency markets in order to reduce inflation. It also had a corollary – a set of legal measures to liberalise financial markets and modernise the French stock exchange. In view of this, public authorities adopted the 1984 banking law that ended state control over short and long- term interest rates. They fostered the development of financial markets through measures taken in 1985 and 1986 by the Fabius and Chirac governments (under President Mitterrand's first mandate) to increase competition between banks. In addition, they gradually lifted exchange controls, which favoured international capital flows.

Hence, the two socialist governments (Mauroy, Fabius) and the moderate right-wing one (Chirac) laid the foundations for the advent of a new growth regime that gave a predominant role to financial markets.

The Disconnect Between Real Wages and Labour Productivity Gains

There is a striking contrast between two fractions of the 18 year "period of ruptures" (1974–1992). The first (1974–1982) is characterised by a succession of external shocks which had not yet brought about domestic responses. The second (1983–1992) is characterised by the sharp deceleration of inflation causing changes in the social, economic and financial structures of the economy which ushered in a new growth regime.

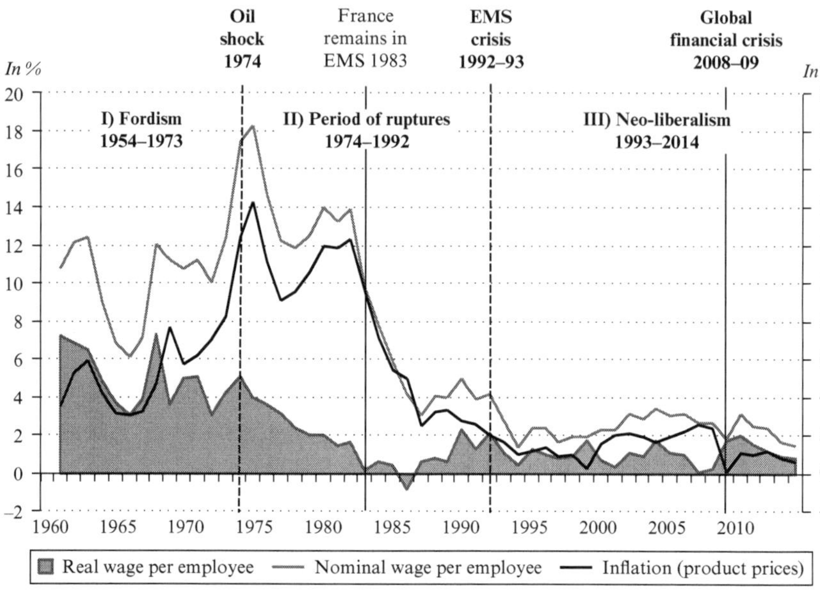

Source: du Tertre (2017), OECD, Ameco database.

Figure 7.2 Inflation rate, nominal and real wage growth rates in France (1960–2014)

These evolutions are illustrated by Figure 7.2 (Inflation and wage growth rates) and by Figure 7.3 (The wage share).

Deceleration of nominal wages and inflation

During this first sub-period (1974–1983), both inflation and nominal annual wage growth rates remained high, above 10% but both started decelerating markedly. However, the inflation rate decelerated less than the nominal wage growth so that the real wage growth rate started declining and became almost nil in 1983, the year after the abandonment of the post-war rule whereby wages were pegged to prices. From 1986 onwards, inflation remained under 4%, nominal wage growth rates were slightly higher and real wage growth stagnated at rates lower than 2%.

Decline of the wage share in domestic income

During the first part (1974–1982) of this "period of ruptures," wage earners' share of national income rose, due to the fact that increases in the workers' nominal wages were indexed to price rises. Their share of GDP

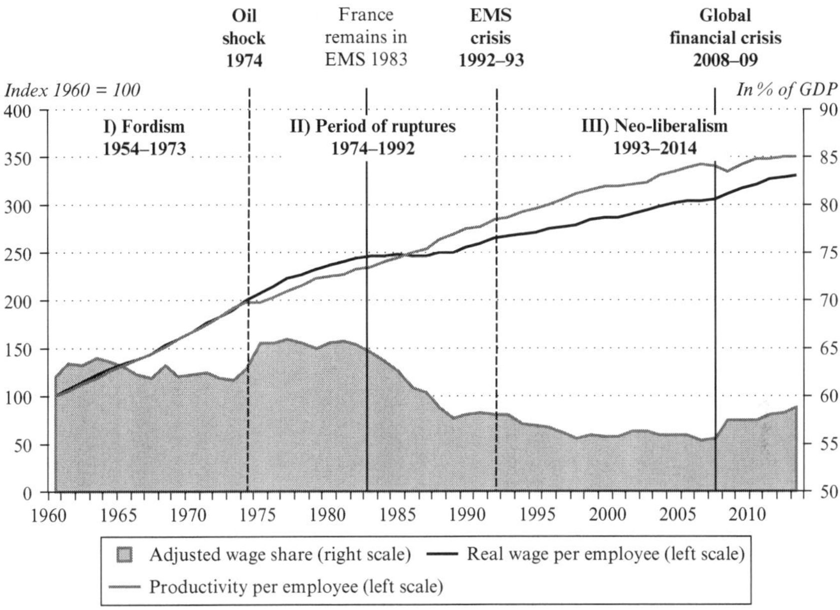

Source: Husson (2012, p. 238), du Tertre (2017), OECD, Ameco database.

Figure 7.3 Real wage and labour productivity growth: the wage share in France (1960–2014)

gained 2.5 points, increasing from an average 62.7% (1962–1973) to 65.2% (1974–1982). Indeed, after the first oil shock in 1974 and until the dollar shock in 1981, real wages grew faster than productivity gains, so that the wage share increased and, conversely, the corporate profit share decreased. But from 1983 onwards, the opposite occurred.

At the beginning of the 1990s, the wage share reached, in a sustained way, a lower level than the level it had attained during the "Fordist" period.

In other words, the lasting decline in the wage share since the early 1990s and, conversely, the lasting increase in the corporate profit share should be interpreted as a significant reversal in the balance of power between wage earners and capital owners in favour of the latter. And as we shall now see, the new income distribution must be understood as a key characteristic of the neo-liberal growth regime that became established in France at the beginning of the 1990s.

1993–2007: THE TRIUMPH OF NEO-LIBERALISM

The foundations of the neo-liberal growth regime were gradually laid down throughout the "period of ruptures" which ended at the beginning of the 1990s.

We will show in this section that, after that, France almost continuously implemented economic policies of a neo-liberal type which reinforced the structural features of this growth regime.

In the first two sub-sections, we will examine two worldwide trends, i.e. financialisation and globalisation, which gained ground in France. In a second sub-section we will recall the economic policies stemming from European integration that replaced domestic demand management policies. In a third sub-section we will see how these trends and policy choices brought about sustained changes in the socio-economic structures at play.

The Increasing Role of the Financial Sector in the French Economy

Following the deregulation movement which started in the United Kingdom and in the USA in the 1980s under respectively Prime Minister Margaret Thatcher and President Ronald Reagan, several laws were voted under the French socialist and conservative governments in office during the second half of the 1980s (see p. 139). They transformed the institutional framework for the financial sector which by 2001 was almost completely privatised.

These policies were based on the "efficiency of financial markets" creed, which assumes that financial markets are able to ensure the optimal allocation of capital within the economy.

The financial component of the banking profession developed rapidly (e.g. asset management departments were created in deposit banks) – contrary to the former legal separation of bank activities between credit allocation and custody of deposits on the one hand and investment banking on the other. Secondly, financial innovations such as derivatives, securitisation of bank credits, etc. developed at an accelerated rhythm due in particular to new information technologies. Lastly, institutional investors (pension funds, OPCVMs[4]. . .) became major actors on the financial market.

Globalisation

The second trend – globalisation – was closely intermingled with the first one, insofar as world-wide deregulation also concerned currency markets (with the end of exchange controls) and foreign investment, making it easier for multinational companies to operate and for national firms to relocate. Both these factors led to greater international competition.

Members of the European Union expanded from 12 in the 1980s to 28 in 2013 (including Austria, Sweden, Finland, several East European countries, Cyprus, Malta and Croatia), meaning that barriers on movements of goods, people, services and capital were removed.

The growing participation of emergent countries (Brazil, China, India, etc.) entering the world economy in the late 1990s amplified this phenomenon.

The openness ratio[5] gained eight percentage points from 1993 (20%) to 2007 (28%). This ratio, a very gross indicator of the way globalisation gained ground in the French economy, does not account for the expansion of foreign corporate capital in the French economy, nor, vice versa, for the growth of French multinational firms abroad, primarily in Europe but also in the major emerging countries in the late 1990s.

Economic Policies

With the exception of the five-year mandate of Prime Minister Lionel Jospin (1997–2002) which clearly gave priority to the fight against unemployment, economic policies aimed to increase French competitiveness in a context of growing European integration – a major political choice.

We shall now examine the three stages of this process leading to the adoption of the euro subject to major concessions made to German "ordo-liberalism."

First of all, the "single market," one of Jacques Delors's major contributions to the shaping of 21st-century Europe, was supposed to be completed by 1992, according to the "Single Act" signed in 1986, which committed the 12 member states to implementing the four freedoms stated in the Treaty of Rome (free movement of goods, people, services and capital). Approximately 250 directives or regulations had to be adopted by European institutions and then transposed into national legislations in order to bring the single market into being.

Secondly, the Maastricht Treaty, the founding treaty of the European Union (replacing the EC), which includes the Economic and Monetary Union (EMU), was signed in 1992.[6] The treaty provided for strict coordination of fiscal policies, including caps on public debt (60% of GDP) and budget deficits (3% of GDP) for all member countries that agreed to give up their national currencies in favour of the euro in 1999 (which was neither the case for Denmark, Sweden or the UK).[7] This is an example of "ordo-liberalism," the concept prevailing in Germany, centred on "free markets, free and undistorted competition, no public bail-outs, an independent central bank, and balanced public budgets"[8] (Bibow, 2017).

Why did France accept these drastic conditions? Germany was reluctant to agree to the single currency because it was unwilling to sacrifice the stability of the DM or its monetary policy or more generally its "ordo-liberal" principles. But she needed France's approval for the re-unification of West and East Germany after the fall of the Berlin Wall (1989).[9] France, on her side, ceded ground so that only a fraction of the initial European integration project was kept, namely the monetary union, while the two other parts (budgetary and social) were excluded so that only the monetary part of the initial Economic and Monetary Union (EMU) project was salvaged, while the economic (mainly budgetary) part was jettisoned. EMU thus turned out to be a "one-legged beast," as Jacques Delors put it.

Finally, in 1997, the Growth and Stability Pact (GSP) was signed by EU members (under President Chirac for France), obliging them to strengthen monitoring and coordination of national fiscal and economic policies and to respect the deficit and debt caps set by the Maastricht Treaty.

In 1993, the EMS crisis which lasted for 10 months (September 1992–July 1993) triggered the severest recession that France had experienced since the first oil shock in September 1973. Output contracted in 1993 and growth remained under 2% in the subsequent years; unemployment reached 10%.

In 1997, following the social unrest in France caused by restrictive budgetary measures, legislative elections were called and, in May, the left-wing coalition led by socialist Prime Minister Lionel Jospin was voted in. During Jospin's five-year mandate (1997–2002), the economic situation recovered: growth picked up and unemployment fell to under 8%, despite the fact that the euro had replaced the franc; inflation did not accelerate and public debt decreased.

The ambitious youth employment programme implemented at the beginning of Jospin's mandate and the enforcement of the Aubry laws on the 35-hour week in 1999 – which according to most experts had created 350 000 jobs – both explain part of this success.

Structural Changes Characterising France's Neo-liberal Growth Regime[10]

France's social and economic structures were modified during the previous "period of ruptures" as we have seen in pp. 136–141. Changes in the same market-friendly direction resulted from anti-Keynesian economic policies carried out during the 1993–2007 period (with the exception of the five-year mandate of Prime Minister Lionel Jospin from 1997 to 2002). As a result, the key variables determining the neo-liberal rationale changed radically compared to the demand-led Fordist growth model of the 1954–1973 period. This is what we shall now highlight.

A shortfall in aggregate demand related to a greater profit share

As we have seen in Figure 7.2, the wage share in income distribution decreased after 1986 and conversely, the profit share increased. However, the investment rate, i.e. the share of investment expenditure in aggregate demand, did not follow this increase. When we compare the 1993–2007 period with the 1954–1973 one, we find that the profit share was higher (32.5% compared to 30%) but that the corporate investment rate was lower (21% compared to 24.5%). Hence, the gap between the corporate profit share and the corporate investment rate increased and exerted a deflationary pressure on aggregate demand (du Tertre and de Largentaye, 2017, p. 13).

Moreover, the rise in the profit share – and its corollary, the decline in the share of wages – aggravated inequalities in income distribution and thus exerted a deflationary pressure on consumption – a major component of aggregate demand – through the increase of the propensity to save which is associated with greater inequality.

A shareholder model of corporate governance

Corporate governance moved towards a shareholder type, which gives decisive power to shareholders in defining the company's strategy (Lazonick and O'Sullivan, 2000). Companies no longer seek to increase their activity (thereby increasing the wage bill as well as profits) as in the Fordist period but aim to create shareholder value for the sole benefit of shareholders.

The supremacy of market finance over bank finance

The analyses of nominal and real long-term interest rates and of stock-market prices in France over the 1960–2015 period shows the marked change that took place during the 1980s and 1990s: nominal and real interest rates fell dramatically (Figure 7.4), while stock-market prices soared (Figure 7.5). When we compare these trends with the fluctuations of the rate of investment starting from the early 1990s, it seems quite clear that market share prices are the variables that determine companies' investment decisions and thus the level of economic activity, with the result that wages and employment became adjustment variables (du Tertre and de Largentaye, 2017, pp. 19–21).

Stronger international competition

Throughout this era of globalisation, various indicators show the decline of the competitiveness of the French economy as a whole.

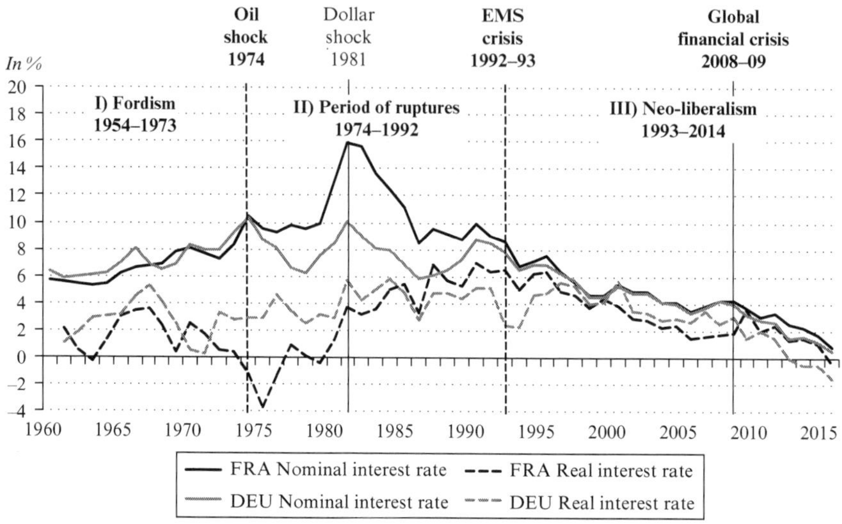

Source: du Tertre (2017), OECD, Ameco data base.

Figure 7.4 Nominal and real long-term interest rates in France and Germany (1960–2015)

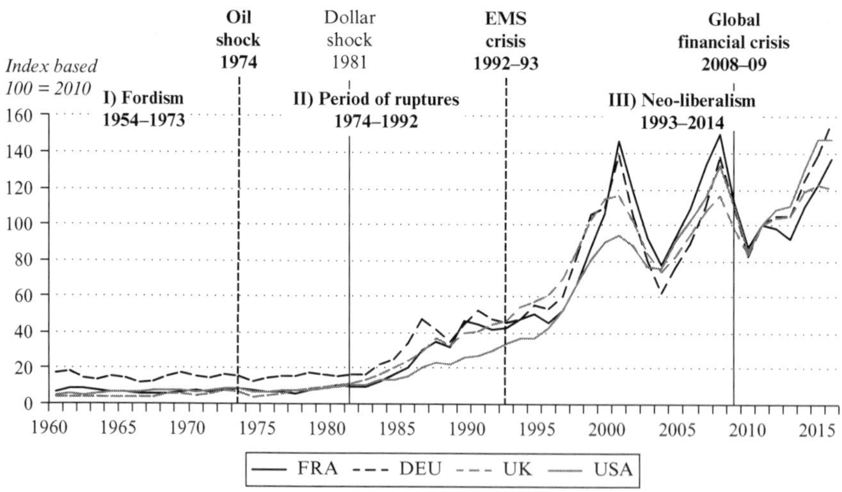

Source: du Tertre (2017), OECD, Share prices (indicators).

Figure 7.5 Evolution of stock market prices in France, Germany, the United Kingdom and the United States (1960–2015)

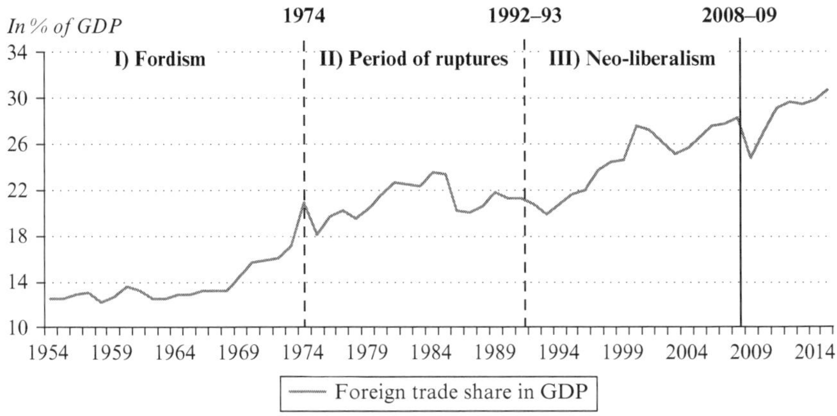

Source: du Tertre (2017), Insee, Comptabilité nationale, 2010 basis.

Figure 7.6 French economy's openness ratio to the world economy (1954–2015)

Figure 7.6 shows that the openness ratio[11] gained eight percentage points from 1993 (20%) to 2007 (28%). The external surplus for manufactured goods diminished regularly after 1996, causing the overall foreign trade balance to fall into deficit after 2005.

French companies exporting from the national territory suffered from a lack of "non-cost competitiveness," particularly in relation to Germany. The adoption of the euro in 1999 amplified this asymmetry since French companies were handicapped by an overvalued currency.

Thus, France's greater international exposure coupled with a weak competitiveness aggravated the deflationary pressure on aggregate demand: none of the latter's four components – exports, consumption, investment expenditure nor public expenditure (since public deficits were capped by the Maastricht Treaty, see p. 143) – were able to stimulate domestic economic activity and employment.

Two major international financial crises, the Great Financial Crisis in 2007–2008 and the European sovereign debt crisis in 2010–2011 added a new burden – external debt – weighing on the French economy as we shall now see.

FINANCIAL CRISES (2008–2016)[12]

The two major financial crises, the Great Financial Crisis (2007–2008) and the European Sovereign Debt crisis (2010–2011) were handled in a way which aggravated deflationary pressures on economic activity during this last period.

Economic policies implemented under the mandates of Presidents Sarkozy and Hollande (respectively 2007–2012 and 2012–2017) will be presented in a first sub-section. The greater indebtedness which resulted from these policies, and which created an extra burden for the future of the French economy, will be examined in a second sub-section.

Austerity Policies and the Risk of a Deflationary Deadlock (2008–2015)

Notwithstanding political differences between the two Presidents (Sarkozy heading the right-wing party and Hollande the socialist one), there were many similarities in their economic policies as they both favoured supply-side reform and neglected aggregate demand stimulus.

President Sarkozy began his mandate by cutting taxes for the rich and partially dismantling the 35-hour working week. As a result, inequality between capital revenues and wages deepened. It was in this context that the 2008 subprime crisis hit Europe. Public expenditure was then reduced, supposedly in order to reduce the public budget deficit and thus comply with the criteria of the "Stability and Growth Pact" (1997). However, the French public debt increased instead, due to the slowdown in economic activity.

In 2012, France signed the Treaty on Stability, Coordination and Governance (TSCG), another illustration of "ordo-liberalism" which mirrored the budget balancing principle enshrined in the German Constitution.

François Hollande, elected in 2012 and who had pledged during his campaign to bring unemployment down significantly and had declared his hostility towards finance ("the enemy"), tried to restore public finance balances which he thought were a prerequisite for setting the economy back on a growth track before reflating the economy and creating jobs. The aim was to tackle four types of deficits: competitiveness, employment, aggregate demand and debt but only the first was dealt with through specific measures. Thus, two programmes (*Crédit d'impôt pour la compétitivité et l'emploi – CICE and Pacte de responsabilité et de solidarité – PRS*) granting huge tax and social contribution deductions to companies were implemented in 2014 and 2015. The implicit deal was that firms were to create employment thanks to these cuts.

Underpinning this major bonus to firms stemmed from "supply-side" rationale. Cheaper labour costs were intended to increase the firms' "margin of manoeuvre," thus improving competitiveness through investment, research and innovation. These cuts to fiscal and social contribution levies were also intended as an incentive to increase employment. However, the demand side failed to materialise, as this "fiscal gift" to firms was financed by heavier taxes (an increased VAT rate and heavier taxes on households), while wages and social transfers stagnated.

The French government's ordo-liberal policy aiming at redressing its public accounts before reflating the country's economy after the Great Financial Crisis was based on a wrong diagnosis according to Keynesian theory. Indeed, public expenditure reduction in a recessionary context aggravates the recession since aggregate demand and tax revenues fall in parallel with expenditure cuts. Likewise, to seek to reduce wage costs in order to improve the economy's international competitiveness in a context where all Eurozone members facing the same difficulties are adopting the same economic policies, not only fails to have any positive result on the external position, but continues to deteriorate domestic demand and hence economic activity. "It is the replica 80 years on of what had already happened in the 1930s" (Muet, 2015).

At the end of this period, the unemployment rate rose to 10%. President Hollande's pledge was not honoured.

Debt Without Deleverage

Corporate and household private debt increased markedly in France as in other developed countries from 2000 to 2007 as we can see in Figure 7.7. This was caused by bank's excessive granting of credit during the boom

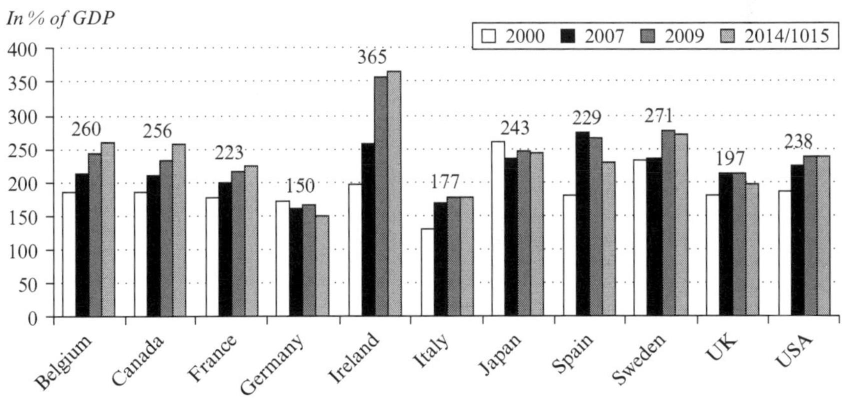

Source: Aglietta and Coudert (2016, pp. 40–41), du Tertre (2017), OECD, National Accounts, Financial Indicators.

Figure 7.7 Debt of the non-financial private sector in the main developed countries (2000–2014)

preceding the Great Financial Crisis and which had sustained growth (Aglietta and Coudert, 2016). But after the crisis broke out, the non-financial private sector did not deleverage in France (nor in most of other OECD countries) so that in 2015, the level of its indebtedness was higher than in 2007.

Moreover, total debt increased over the same period in France; both public sector debt – despite efforts to reduce it – and the private sector debt increased.

Hence, serious concerns weighed on finance at the end of this period and still do. The time bomb is still with us and France, like several other European countries, is mired down in what looks like long-lasting stagnation.

CONCLUSION

Slow growth and high unemployment characterise the French neo-liberal growth regime, contrasting with the successes of the "Fordist" regime in France from the 1950s until the first oil shock. It is difficult not to associate these poor performances with the casting aside of Keynesian policies and with the structural changes (analysed by the French Regulation School) resulting from economic policy choices made by governments in specific socio-institutional contexts and, in particular, France's choice to enter the Eurozone.

What are the solutions?

Most French citizens are reluctant to give up the euro, which replaced the franc in 2000. So the question is: can France achieve full employment while remaining in the Eurozone, which has so far been harnessed to rules at odds with Keynesian policies? And can policies in favour of employment be put in place in an international context subject to financial instability?

We believe it is possible under two conditions.

First of all, there must be greater coordination of national economic policies at the Eurozone level aimed at a full employment "policy mix." This would imply further changes in the European monetary institutions and practices and in particular the completion of the banking and financial reforms. It would also be necessary to set up a new European institution in charge of coordinating member states' public finances (taxation, budgets, public debt) geared to employment targets at the Eurozone level, not only at national levels.

Moreover, we would need a "European New Deal" inspired by Keynesian ideas – i.e. a large-scale investment programme (Aglietta and Brand, 2013).

The "Juncker plan" – a four-year investment programme (2015–2019) – which aims to fill the 15% gap in Europe's investment (compared to its 2008 level) is a first step in this direction.

Projects aimed at "decarbonising" Europe and developing renewable energies could be integrated into the initial programme on the lines set out by the Paris Climate Conference in December 2015. In addition to private finance and Eurobonds, innovations in finance such as "green money" could provide ways of funding these projects and bring about a major breakthrough in credit and finance.

Solving the climate change problem at the European level could indeed be the solution to the economic and social problems of France and Europe. These new European policies could perhaps usher in a "sustainable development" growth regime for the upcoming decades of the 21st century.

NOTES

1. Main source: INSEE:
   - Annual growth rate (GDP, volume) Comptabilité Nationale, 2010 base.
   - Unemployment rate (ILO definition), annual average, 1975–2014 series.

   Additional source: OECD, Annual Macro-Economic, European Commission (Ameco) database.
   - Unemployment rate (Eurostat definition), annual average, 1960–1974 series.
2. Raymond Barre was Prime Minister (1976–1981) under Valéry Giscard d'Estaing's presidency (1974–1981), following Jacques Chirac (1974–1976).
3. The dollar exchange rate vis-à-vis the French franc fell by 20% during the 1970s, then suddenly rose by 133% between 1980 (FF 4.5) and 1985 (FF 10.5).
4. "*OPCVM, Organismes de placement collectif en valeurs mobilières*": undertakings collecting investment in securities.
5. The openness ratio is equal to half the sum of exports and imports divided by GDP.
6. In France, the referendum was approved by a tiny 51% majority.
7. The other three "convergence criteria" dealt with inflation rates, interest rates and exchange rates. Inflation was not supposed to be higher than 1.5% compared to the average inflation rate of the three member states with the lowest inflation rates; long-term interest rates were not supposed to be 2% over the average interest rate of the three member states with the lowest interest rates; and the margins of fluctuation of national currencies compared to pivot rates specific to each member state had to be respected (before 2000).
8. The "Golden rule" requiring that non-investment expenditure in the public budget should be in equilibrium was enshrined in the German Constitution in 2009; it was enacted in 2016 at the federal level and is to be so in 2020 at the regional level.
9. The fall of the Berlin Wall in 1989 called for an expansionary budget at a European level, not simply at the German level. Yet, in the early 1990s, France continued enforcing restrictive policies, holding interest rates high and cutting public expenditure so as to keep the franc pegged to the DM.
10. A detailed version of this section can be found in du Tertre and de Largentaye (2017).
11. The openness ratio is equal to half the sum of exports and imports divided by GDP.
12. A more extended version of this section can be found in du Tertre and de Largentaye (2017).

BIBLIOGRAPHY

Aglietta, Michel (1976), *Régulation et Crises du Capitalisme*, Paris: Calmann-Lévy; (1997) nouvelle édition augmentée d'une postface, Paris: Odile Jacob, Coll. Opus.

Aglietta, Michel, and Coudert, Virginie (2016), "Interrogations sur le système dollar," in CEPII, *L'économie Mondiale 2017*, Paris: La Découverte, Coll. Repères, 2016.

Aglietta, Michel, and Leron, Nicolas (2017), *La Double Démocratie*, Seuil.

Aglietta, Michel, and Rebérioux Antoine (2005), *Corporate Governance Adrift, A Critique of Shareholder Value*, Cheltenham, UK and Northampton, MA, USA: Edward Elgar.

Andreff, Wladimir, and Tertre du, Renaud (2013), "Des firmes multinationales à la mondialisation: l'apport de Charles-Albert Michalet," in Wladimir Anfreff (ed.), *La Mondialisation, Stade Suprême du Capitalisme? En Hommage à Charles-Albert Michalet*, Presses Universitaires de Paris Ouest, pp. 23–58.

Bibow, Jörg (2017), "How Germany's Anti-Keynesianism Has Brought Europe to Its Knees," *Levy Economic Institute of Bard College*, http://www.levyinstitute.org/pubs/wp_886.pdf.

Boyer, Robert (2013), "Les crises financières comme conflit de temporalités," *Vingtième Siècle. Revue d'histoire*, 117, pp. 69–88.

Boyer, Robert (2015), *Économie Politique des Capitalismes. Théorie de la Régulation et des Crises*, Paris: La Découverte, Coll. Grand Repère Manuel.

Galbraith, John Kenneth (1967), *The New Industrial State*, Boston: Houghton Mifflin, republished, Princeton: Princeton University Press, 2007.

Husson, Michel (2012), "France: Baisse de régime. Les salaires en France sur longue période," *La Revue de l'IRES*, spécial, "30 ans de salaire, d'une crise à l'autre," 73, pp. 237–69.

Keynes, John Maynard (1936), *The General Theory of Employment, Interest and Money*, UK: Palgrave Macmillan, 2007 Edition.

Lazonick, William, and O'Sullivan, Mary (2000), "Maximizing shareholder value: a new ideology for corporate governance," *Economy and Society*, vol. 29, 2, pp. 13–35.

Mazier, Jacques and Petit, Pascal (2013), "In search of sustainable paths for the Euro zone in the troubled post-2008 world," *Cambridge Journal of Economics*, vol. 37, 3, pp. 513–32.

Minsky, Hyman P. (1975), *John Maynard Keynes*, new edition 2008, Introduction: D. Papadimitiou and L. R. Wray, New York: McGraw Hill.

Muet, Pierre-Alain (2015), "La grande récession des années 2012–2014: les socialistes européens à l'épreuve des égoïsmes nationaux", http://www.pierrealainmuet.fr/années-parlementaires-2007-2017/action-nationale/item/730-la-grande-récession-des-années-2012-2014-les-socialistes-européens-à-l'épreuve-des-égoïsmes-nationaux.

Tertre du, Renaud, and Largentaye de, Hélène (2017), "When, why and how France gave up Keynesian policies," paper from the communication at Keynes Conference, King's College, "Maynard Keynes in King's College and The General Theory of Employment, Interest and Money (1936)," 8 October 2016, www.kings.cam.ac.uk/members-friends/keynes-conference.

8. Non-conventional fiscal rules in a Kaleckian model of growth and income distribution with external debt

Pablo G. Bortz, Gabriel Michelena and Fernando Toledo

INTRODUCTION

Starting in the early 1990s, several advanced and developing countries have adopted fiscal rules as their framework for determining their expenditure and tax policy, with the stated objective of securing the long-term solvency of the public debt. The adoption of fiscal rules as a policy framework would help to avoid the *time inconsistency problem*, as argued in the Political Economy Models literature. A large list of current fiscal rules can be found in the updated database of Schaechter et al. (2012).

The adoption of ever stricter fiscal rules has not been unchallenged (see a summary of objections in Vera (2009) and Costantini (2015)). This chapter extends the criticisms by differentiating between conventional and unconventional fiscal rules, and by adding to the discussion the importance of balance-of-payments considerations (Ocampo, 2013), particularly relevant for developing countries. We analyse the implications of the concept of "balance-of-payments" dominance through a Kaleckian model of growth and income distribution with external private and public debt, itself an extended version of Bortz et al. (2018a, 2018b). These contributions focus their attention on the effects of external indebtedness on economic growth and income distribution in the context of a conflicting-claims inflation theory, together with specific policy proposals. In one case (Bortz et al. 2018a), we examine the adoption of Tax-based Income Policies (TIPs) to help address the distributive struggle and improve price competitiveness. In turn, in Bortz (2018b) we study the effect of capital control measures, particularly a tax on external borrowing, on the evolution of economic activity and the distributive conflict.

We propose here a third extension on the basic model. We include two unconventional fiscal rules, and we conduct simulations in order to analyse their impact on economic growth, external indebtedness and income distribution. These show that changes in global risk perception can have a substantial impact on the performance of public finances, which tend to overreact to relaxing and tightening conditions of external lending, allowing for cycles of borrowing and lending, though the magnitude depends on the parameters of the model. However, government expenditure still manages to retain a stabilizing role, reducing fluctuations in aggregate demand and accumulation rates.

The structure of the chapter is as follows. Section 2 presents a brief review of the literature on conventional and unconventional fiscal rules. Section 3 describes how we formally add these two types of rules to the model of Bortz et al. (2018a, 2018b), while Section 4 describes the simulations and their results. Section 5 draws some conclusions.

CONVENTIONAL AND UNCONVENTIONAL FISCAL RULES

The concern over the intertemporal sustainability of public debt and the subsidiary role of fiscal policy as stabilizing instrument in the New Macroeconomic Consensus (NMC) has provided the theoretical background[1] for the adoption of conventional fiscal rules by different countries. This institutional framework limits the scope of policy-makers, restricting their tool-box according to certain pre-established criteria (Kumhof and Laxton, 2009). The arguments supporting the usefulness of conventional fiscal rules are justified by the so-called Political Economy approach (Persson and Tabellini, 1990; Drazen, 2004; Wijsman and Crombez, 2017; Bonfatti and Forni, 2017; Halac and Yared, 2017). In this approach, rules are necessary in order to counteract the deficit bias of policy-makers with an electorate that does not fully understand its implications or that is outright indifferent to the assumed intertemporal budget constraint of the public sector (Buchanan and Wagner, 1977). Fiscal rules reduce or remove the tools to profit from short-term political gain that leads to the deficit bias, particularly in electoral periods, without much concern for long-term social welfare (Cukierman and Meltzer, 1986). Fiscal rules impose a stricter discipline on policy makers in the booming phase of the cycle or during electoral periods.[2]

There are different types of conventional fiscal rules (Kopits, 2001). While some Anglo-Saxon countries (Australia, Canada, New Zealand and the United Kingdom) have prioritized "transparency" rules, continental

Europe (with the Stability and Growth Pact, and the Swiss Debt Brake) and some emerging economies (Brazil, Chile, Colombia, India and Peru) have implemented numerical targets for the performance of certain fiscal indicators.

In fact, conventional fiscal rules started with numerical criteria in a Maastricht Treaty style, to restrain fiscal discretion in accordance with some "sound finance" indicators. These fiscal rules, known as "first generation rules" (from the early 1990s to the global financial crisis in 2008), actually induced pro-cyclical behaviour, so that second-generation rules (starting around the 2008 crisis, Eyraud et al., 2018) were designed, centred about the "structural fiscal balance" (i.e. cleaning out cyclical effects). International financial institutions have been sponsoring the adoption of these new types of rules (for instance, see BID, 2018; Caselli et al., 2018).

Among the most well-known rules, we can list the following:[3]

1. *Balanced budget rules:* They can imply (i) equilibrium between total revenues and total expenditure (which entails no public borrowing) or limits on the deficit to GDP ratio; (ii) structural or cyclically adjusted equilibrium or limits on the structural deficit to GDP ratio; or (iii) equilibrium between current revenues and current expenditure (which allows public borrowing only to fund capital expenditures, the so-called "golden rule" of fiscal policy).[4]
2. *Rules on borrowing sources*: Prohibition of borrowing in domestic sources, with the central banks, or limits on borrowing as a proportion of past tax revenues and/or expenditure.
3. *Rules on the debt stock or reserves*: Limits on the stock of gross (or net) debt as percentage of GDP; a target for the stock of extra-budgetary stocks with the establishment of a sovereign fund.
4. *Cash-balance rule*: Current tax revenues fund the expansion of capital outlays.
5. *Permanent-balance rule*: Demands a constant debt to GDP ratio, and allows funding public investment through borrowing as long as that "solvency" condition is fulfilled.

Summing up, first and second generation conventional fiscal rules act like permanent constraints on fiscal policy, by referring to targets of specific indicators, such as the budget deficit, the dynamics of public debt or some other variable expresses in terms of GDP (Kopits and Symansky, 1998). In the NMC governments must explicitly guarantee the intertemporal solvency of their balance sheet, with a restricted margin for an anti-cyclical use of fiscal tools. However, some critics have argued that conventional fiscal rules can also induce non-transparent tinkering and unnecessary bureaucratic proceedings.[5]

The performance of fiscal indicators is affected, particularly in Emerging and Developing Economies (EDEs), by external shocks. Their tax revenues are heavily dependent on exports receipt; they have higher degrees of exchange-rate pass-through (Jasova et al. 2013),[6] with subsequent effects on domestic consumption; and the cost of external (and to some extent, domestic) borrowing depends on global risk perceptions.[7] ECLAC (2016) and IMF (2017) have warned of the fiscal dangers that the region faces in case of an increase in the US interest rate.

There are different varieties of non-conventional fiscal rules, not all of them dealing with external determinants. Drumond and Silva de Jesus (2016) consider a pseudo-Taylor rule for fiscal policy, which adjust (given certain structural components of fiscal deficit) to the gap between the prevailing degree of capacity utilization and a target degree set by the government. Godley and Lavoie (2007) examine alternative reaction functions for public expenditure according to their impact on inflation and employment. Dafermos (2017) deploys a Godley–Minsky stock-flow consistent model with two types of fiscal rules: A Maastricht-type rule, with a debt-to-GDP target, and an unconventional rule, that links public expenditure with private sector indebtedness, in order to examine the link between fiscal performance and financial fragility. Hannsgen (2012) includes non-conventional expenditure rules (which aim to stabilize capacity utilization) in a Kaleckian model with non-linearities *à la* Goodwin and Minskyan financial crises. Finally, Ribeiro and Lima (2017) analyse the detrimental impact that government expenditure ceilings have on the sustainability of the public debt to GDP ratio.

This chapter moves forward in this regard, by including the impact of external sector performance in the design of non-conventional fiscal rules. We do so by extending the Kaleckian model of Bortz et al. (2018a, 2018b). The next section presents some formalization of fiscal rules in a Kaleckian model with external indebtedness.

FISCAL RULES IN A KALECKIAN MODEL

A Brief Description of the Model

Before describing the two unconventional fiscal rules developed in this chapter, we present here the main characteristics of the model, which is fully developed in Bortz et al. (2018a, 2018b). The model is comprised of five sectors (household workers, firms, central banks, government and the rest of the world). Firms produce one good fit for consumption, investment and exports, with a Leontief-type production function, using labour, capital and imported inputs.

There are three endogenous variables of the model.

The first refers to external debt (the only type of debt), which can be either public or private. It is determined by pull (capacity utilization) and push factors (interest rate differentials and global risk perceptions), and it is the determinant of the exchange rate (financial inflows appreciate the exchange rate, outflows depreciate it). So rising debt can mean both higher volume of foreign indebtedness and a more appreciated exchange rate.

The second variable is the wage share, which is endogenously determined in a conflicting-claims model with wage-setting/price-setting behaviour. On top of the relative bargaining power of firms and workers, the main influence on income distribution is the level of private debt. Firms translate their debt servicing costs onto prices. However, rising debt may imply (through an appreciating exchange rate) that the costs in domestic currency may fall, bringing down margins and rising the real wage.

The third endogenous variable is capacity utilization. It adjusts to the discrepancies between savings plans (by households, firms and the government), private investment and the current account balance. Investment is determined by capacity utilization, the profit share, and debt servicing (influenced in turn by the mentioned debt volume and the exchange rate). Public budget reflects the discrepancies between tax revenues, public expenditure (growing, in the baseline model, at an exogenous rate) and interest payments, while the current account balance depends on domestic and foreign demand, debt servicing and price competitiveness (through a Marshall–Lerner condition).

Table 8.1 sums up the signs of the partial differentials that compose the Jacobian matrix. d represents the level of external debt (normalized by the capital stock), ψ is the wage share and u is the capacity utilization rate. It is assumed that the sign of the 9th cell is negative for stability purposes, which implies the validity of the traditional Keynesian stability condition, with savings reacting stronger than investment to changes in capacity utilization. The sign of cells 4, 7 and 8 is a priori undetermined, with two possible "regimes" for each of the cells. These are summed up in Table 8.2.

The difference in the impact of foreign indebtedness on the wage share and capacity utilization is due to the counteracting implications (in terms of domestic-currency debt costs) of rising debt volume, and an appreciating exchange rate. If the latter prevails, rising debt may lead to an exchange-rate driven distribution regime, and a debt-led demand regime. Though those regimes may have some empirical validity in the short-run, we are however of the idea that in the medium run the burden of interest

Table 8.1 Signs of the Jacobian matrix

		Sign			Sign			Sign
1)	$\frac{\partial \hat{d}}{\partial d}$	−	4)	$\frac{\partial \hat{\psi}}{\partial d}$	?	7)	$\frac{\partial \hat{u}}{\partial d}$	?
2)	$\frac{\partial \hat{d}}{\partial \psi}$	0	5)	$\frac{\partial \hat{\psi}}{\partial \psi}$	−	8)	$\frac{\partial \hat{u}}{\partial \psi}$	?
3)	$\frac{\partial \hat{d}}{\partial u}$	+	6)	$\frac{\partial \hat{\psi}}{\partial u}$	0	9)	$\frac{\partial \hat{u}}{\partial u}$	−

Table 8.2 Distributive and demand regimes

Derivative	**Regime**	**Mathematical Expression**	**Meaning**
$\frac{\partial \hat{\psi}}{\partial d}$	*Exchange-rate driven*	$\frac{\partial \hat{\psi}}{\partial d} > 0$	Wage share reacts positively to increments in foreign indebtedness.
	Debt-service driven	$\frac{\partial \hat{\psi}}{\partial d} < 0$	Wage share reacts negatively to increments in foreign indebtedness.
$\frac{\partial \hat{u}}{\partial d}$	*Debt-led*	$\frac{\partial \hat{u}}{\partial d} > 0$	Economic activity reacts positively to increments in foreign indebtedness.
	Debt-burdened	$\frac{\partial \hat{u}}{\partial d} < 0$	Economic activity reacts negatively to increments in foreign indebtedness.
$\frac{\partial \hat{u}}{\partial \psi}$	*Wage-led*	$\frac{\partial \hat{u}}{\partial \psi} > 0$	Economic activity reacts positively to increments in the wage share.
	Profit-led	$\frac{\partial \hat{u}}{\partial \psi} < 0$	Economic activity reacts negatively to increments in the wage share.

payments and overall financial deregulation weights heavily on economic activity.

Finally, the stability analysis shows that there are three combinations of regimes that lead to stability. What we call a "normal" regime consists of a debt-service driven distribution regime and a debt-burdened demand regime. The "puzzling" scenario consists of an exchange-rate driven and a debt-led regime. The third combination, which we called a "conciliating debt" regime, features an exchange-rate distribution demand (in which an appreciating exchange rate lowers profit margins and raises the real wage) and a debt-burdened demand regime, because of its negative impact on competitiveness and the current account balance. All three regimes are compatible with either profit-led or wage-led aggregate demand, though the equilibrium values of capacity utilization differs in each case.

With this description in mind, it is time to present the two alternative, non-conventional fiscal rules that will be simulated in the next section.

A Cyclically Balanced Rule

Traditional cyclically adjusted fiscal rules depend on the estimation of potential output and the structural balance, a procedure not devoid of flaws (Costantini, 2015). In our setting, non-conventional fiscal rule type I implies that government adjusts the level of public expenditure (relative to the capital stock) (γ^*) according to the difference between private investment (g_f) and the exogenous growth rate of labor productivity, times some arbitrary factor ($\beta\widehat{a_0}$). This is shown in equations (1)–(3):

$$\gamma^* = G/K \tag{1}$$

$$\Delta\gamma^* = \Xi(g_f - \beta\widehat{a_0}) \tag{2}$$

A Balance-of-payments Dominated Fiscal Rule

Godley and Cripps (1983) emphasized the constraint imposed by the performance of foreign trade on the ability to use fiscal policy to sustain incomes and output growth in an open economy. Ocampo (2013) defines the "balance of payments dominance" as a "macroeconomic regime in which the short-term macroeconomic dynamics is essentially determined by external shocks, positive or negative," a recurrent situation in emerging economies, particularly in those with high degree of currency substitution (Calvo and Végh, 1994; Agénor and Khan, 1996). In this scenario, a persistently positive current account balance is associated with greater fiscal space. The formulation of this non-conventional fiscal rule type II is similar to the previous one, but it is guided by a different consideration. The government lowers the level of public expenditure (relative to the capital stock) whenever the current account balance falls below the debt servicing requirements of public debt:

$$\gamma^* = G/K \tag{3}$$

$$\Delta\gamma^* = \Theta\,(\Omega - 1) \tag{4}$$

With:

$$\Omega = \frac{b}{e((1 + i^* + \rho)\,((1 - d_1)\,d)} \tag{5}$$

In this setting, b is the current account balance, e is the real exchange rate, i^* is the international interest rate, ρ is the sovereign risk premium, and $(1-d_1)$ is the share of public debt on total external debt.

SIMULATIONS

In order to get a baseline for simulating the impact of different shocks, we first drew randomly and iteratively values for the parameters of the model until all the equilibrium values of the endogenous variables fulfilled the stability conditions in all the extractions. The procedure is described in more detail in Bortz et al. (2018b), together with the values of the parameters and the variables in each of the feasible regimes.

In the first simulation, at period 50 we double the saving propensities of workers, and increase firms' saving propensity by 30%. Figure 8.1 shows the impact in the "normal" case, for a wage-led regime; Figure 8.2 shows the same impact in a profit-led regime; and Figure 8.3 shows the impact for the "puzzling" case wage-led regime. In all three cases, both the capacity utilization and the accumulation rate take a hit, and the current account improves from the baseline scenario, but as government expenditure starts to increase, all of them return to their initial levels. There is a paradox of thrift in this model, but it is nullified (or at the very least attenuated) in the long run. Interestingly, government savings do not explode, but converge to a new steady-state level, certainly lower than the initial. The also noticeable feature of this experiment when comparing the wage and profit-led regimes in the normal case is that the capacity utilization rate is lower, and the government saving rate is higher, in the profit-led than in the wage-led regime. The opposite happens in the "puzzling" case.

When it comes to modelling the effects of non-conventional fiscal rule type II, at period 50 we relax global risk perceptions. In particular, we double the external debt levels (relatively to the capital stock) tolerated by foreign investors, so that they are willing to lend more to the country. There is an increase in foreign lending to firms and government. What happens then?

Figure 8.4 sums up the result for the "normal" case, with a wage-led regime. Higher foreign lending means that the denominator of the

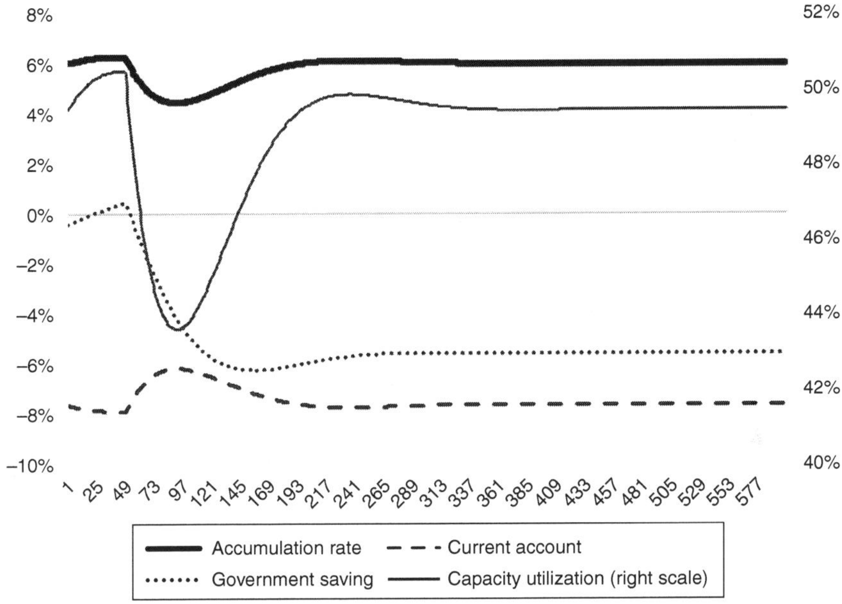

Figure 8.1 Impact of higher savings propensity in the "normal" wage-led scenario

omega parameter in Equation 5 increases, which relax the borrowing constraint. The government increases its expenditure, but at some point, the rule becomes binding and it is forced to reduce its expenditure, but still the levels after the shock are above the initial values. Therefore, the accumulation rate increases due to higher capacity utilization rates, which compensate the burden of increased interest payments.

Government saving stabilizes at a slightly lower levels, with a small fiscal deficit, and the current account deficit also increases. However, one can question whether a sustained (and enlarged) current account deficit, nominated in a foreign currency, will be tolerated for long by investors. It is reasonable to expect that the relaxed terms of lending will not last forever. So what happens when there is an external financial aid reversal? That is pictured in Figure 8.5. As before, we relax global risk perception at period 50, but 200 periods afterward (in period 250) we tighten the external debt levels tolerated by investors, which return to their original levels. There are a couple of features worth highlighting.

First, there is an overshooting in both directions, each overshooting after each shock, in terms of government spending. It increases initially after the first shock, but then the external constraint rule becomes binding

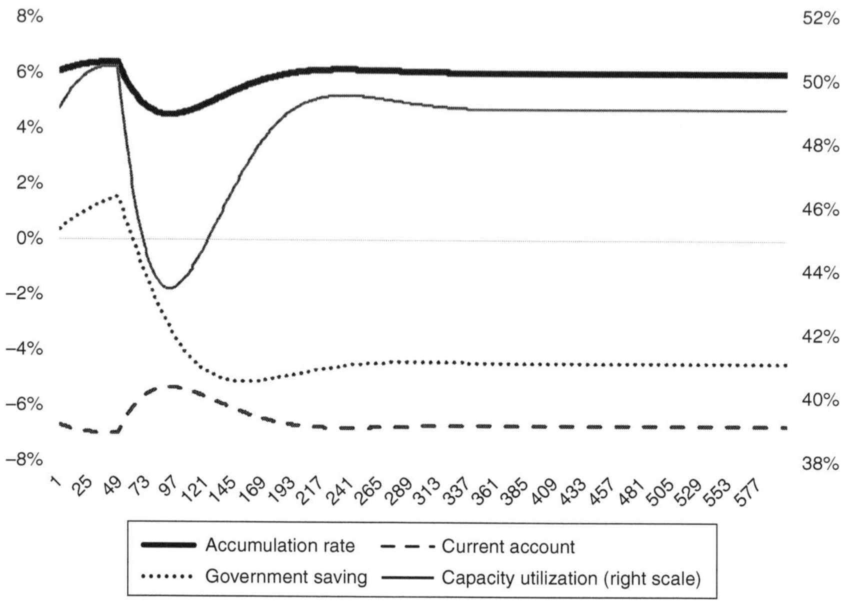

Figure 8.2 *Impact of higher savings propensity in the "normal" profit-led scenario*

and government reduces its expenditures, from a peak of 27.2% (of the capital stock) to as low as 24.7%, right before the second shock. There is an external constraint to government expenditure, which has an impact as well on the accumulation rate. Obviously, after the second shock public expenditure falls to depths of 14.2%, even below the initial levels. By then, the current account has reversed its direction and improved from –12.0% (relatively to the capital stock) to –7.5% in period 324, and will continue to do so for another 35 periods, even though government spending is already recovering from its lows.

The second interesting point to notice, in our view, is the slightly cyclical pattern followed by the variables. Even though they converge to stable values, they do so in an oscillatory fashion, and one can say that the values presented here in period 449 (the last of our simulation) is not the final resting place of the variables, though fluctuations are very nuanced. This is due to the feedback between indebtedness, worsening current account and margins for government spending embedded in the rule type two, reflecting balance-of-payments dominance.

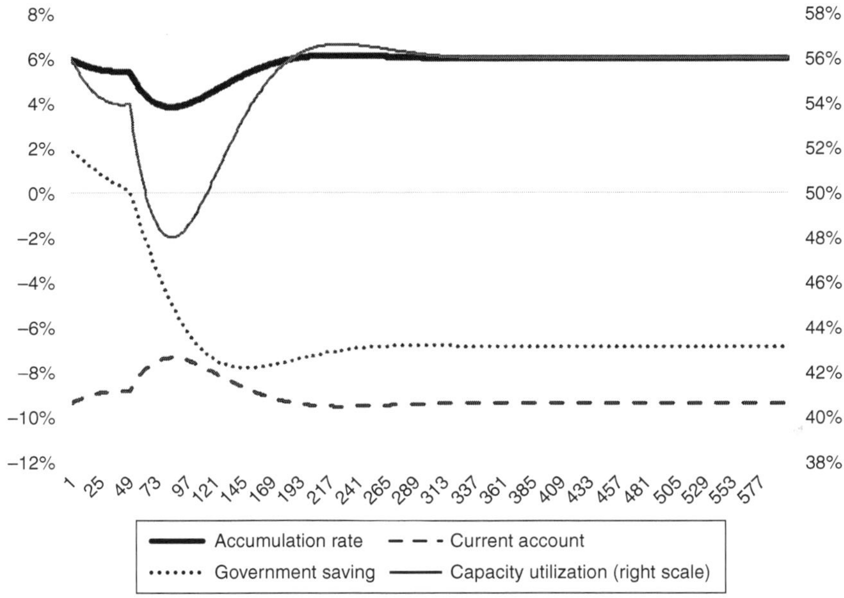

Figure 8.3 Impact of higher savings propensity in the "puzzling" wage-led scenario

FINAL REMARKS

The chapter addresses the relationship among economic growth, income distribution and external debt in a Kaleckian open macroeconomic model that allows for two different non-conventional fiscal rules. Non-conventional fiscal rule type I restricts public expenditure according to the behaviour of accumulation rate and labour productivity, in a similar way to arguments in favour of cyclically adjusted balanced public savings. Non-conventional fiscal rule type II, in turn, restricts the policy space for expanding fiscal expenditure according to the borrowing "tolerance" of foreign investors. We simulate the reaction of the endogenous variables to domestic shocks (in particular, changes in saving propensities) and external shocks (changes in global risk perceptions).

These internal and external shocks on both types of fiscal rules provide interesting results on interaction among capacity utilization, functional income distribution and external debt. Wage and profit-led regimes interacts with these fiscal rules, affecting the overall impact of domestic and external shocks, though not the direction of the reaction. Overall, one can say that the model reflects the validity of the paradox of thrift,

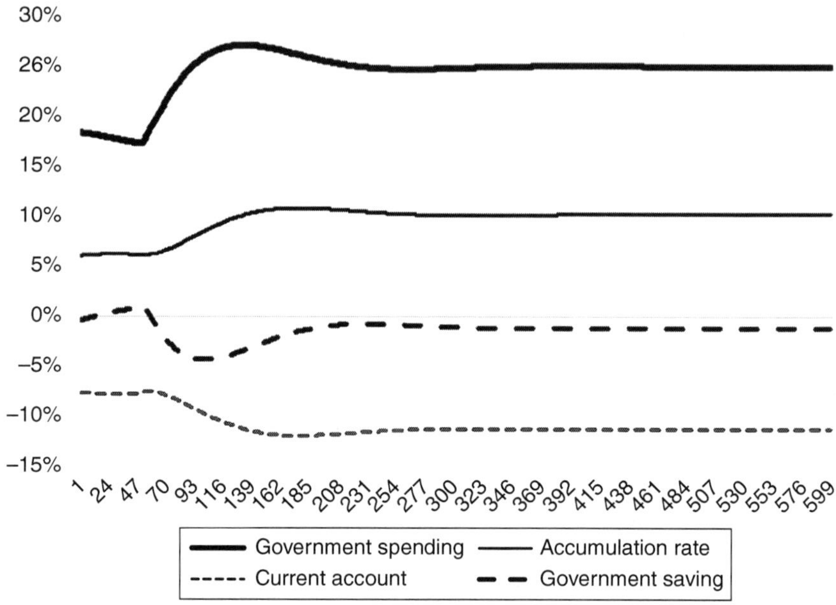

Figure 8.4 Impact of more lax global risk perceptions in the "normal" wage-led scenario

but its impact is mitigated by rising government expenditure, when it acts counter-cyclically.

With regard to changes in lending attitudes of foreign investors, laxer terms of credit entice government expenditure, but come back with a vengeance. Overshooting in the reaction implies that when the tide is reversed and investors are reluctant to fund current account deficits, governments adjust in excess of what balance-of-payments considerations would require, ceteris paribus. The overshooting and ulterior corrections constitute a cyclical dynamic pattern, though with nuanced fluctuations.

Balance of payments dominance emerges as a critical factor that could restrict countercyclical behaviour of public expenditure. Policy-makers should pay attention to avoid vicious cyclical patters in capacity utilization, income distribution, and external debt associated with the adoption of non-conventional fiscal rule type II in the context of foreign constraints and external financial spillovers.

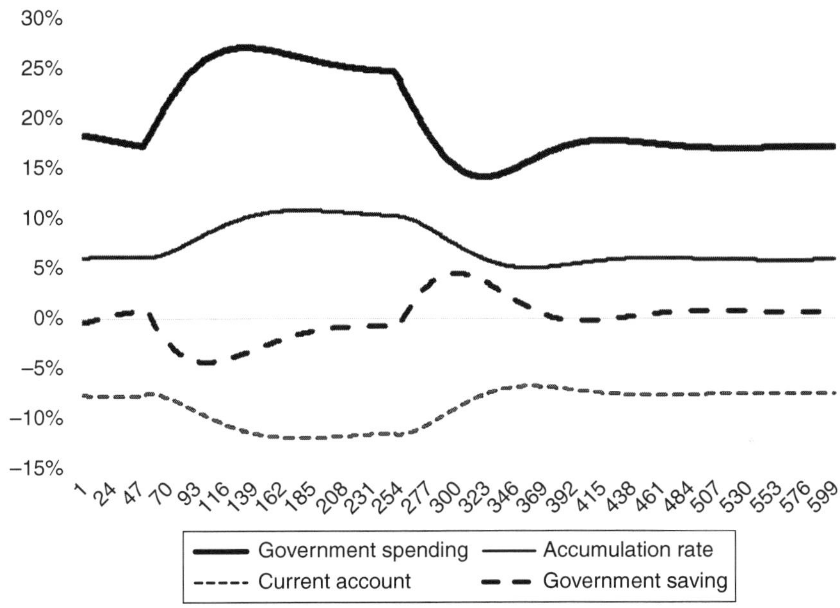

Figure 8.5 Impact of more lax and reversed global risk perceptions in the "normal" wage-led scenario

NOTES

1. On the time consistency debate, see among others Kydland and Prescott (1977), Solow (2005), Leith and Wren-Lewis (2005), Auerbach et al. (2010).
2. Supporters of conventional fiscal rules usually propose the creation of Independent Fiscal Committees, with "qualified technicians," who would determine the magnitude of budget deficit, leaving up to Parliaments the decision on how to allocate public expenditure (Wyploz, 2005). It is claimed that this institutional setting would increase the credibility of fiscal sustainability.
3. This list is by no means exhaustive. For further details, see Kopits and Symansky (1998), Schaechter et al. (2012), Bova et al. (2015) and Caselli et al. (2018).
4. The "golden-rule of fiscal policy" requires a balanced (or surplus) current budget throughout the cycle, in an attempt to use automatic stabilizers that do not jeopardize long-term fiscal "sustainability." Public investment still has a role in this setting, while it is stated that expansionary fiscal policy during recessions is not incompatible with "fiscal discipline" throughout the cycle (Martner, 2003).
5. See Truger and Will (2013) for the case of the German debt-brake.
6. Though the exchange-rate pass-through in EMEs has fallen since the 2008 crisis, several authors have found strong non-linearities in its behaviour (Aron et al. 2014; Caselli and Roitman, 2016; Jasova et al. 2016).
7. Bacha (1992), Bresser-Pereira (1990) and Damill et al. (2005) are classic examples of the argument that net financial flows have been the main determinant of fiscal performance in Latin American countries during the 1980s.

REFERENCES

Agénor, P. and Khan, S. (1996) Foreign currency deposits and the demand for monies in developing countries, *Journal of Development Economics* 50(1): 101–18.

Aron, J., McDonald, R. and Muellbauer, J. (2014) Exchange rate pass-through in developing and emerging markets: A survey of conceptual, methodological and policy issues, and selected empirical findings, *Journal of Development Studies* 50(1): 101–43.

Auerbach, A., Gale, W. and Harris, B. (2010) Activist fiscal policy, *Journal of Economic Perspectives* 24(4): 141–64.

Bacha, E. (1992) External debt, net transfers, and growth in developing countries, *World Development* 20(8): 1183–92.

BID (2018) La Hora del Crecimiento. Informe Macroeconómico de América Latina y el Caribe. Banco Interamericano de Desarrollo. Washington, D.C.

Bonfatti, A. and Forni, L. (2017) Fiscal rules to tame the political budget cycle: Evidence from Italian municipalities, IMF Working Paper 17/6, International Monetary Fund.

Bortz, P., Michelena, G. and Toledo, F. (2018a) Foreign debt, conflicting claims and income policies in a Kaleckian model of growth and distribution, *Journal of Globalization and Development* 9(1): 1–22.

Bortz, P., Michelena, G. and Toledo, F. (2018b) The Global Financial Cycle: Its impact on growth and distribution in emerging economies, mimeo.

Bova, E., Kinda, T., Muthoora, P. and Toscani, F. (2015) Fiscal rules at a glance, International Monetary Fund.

Buchanan, J. and Wagner, R. (1977) *Democracy in Deficit*, Harcourt Brace Jovanovic.

Calvo, G. and Végh, C. (1994) Credibility and the dynamics of stabilization policy: A basic framework, in C. Sims (ed.), *Advances in Econometrics: Sixth World Congress*, Volume II. Cambridge University Press.

Caselli, F. and Roitman, A. (2016) Non-linear exchange rate pass-through in emerging markets, IMF Working Paper 16/1, International Monetary Fund.

Caselli, F., Eyraud, L., Hodge, A., Diaz Kalan, F., Kim, Y., Lledó, V., Mbaye, S., Popescu, A., Reuter, W.H., Reynaud, J., Ture, E. and Wingender, P. (2018) Second generation fiscal rules, IMF Staff Discussion Notes 18/04, International Monetary Fund.

Costantini, O. (2015) The cyclically adjusted budget: History and exegesis of a fateful estimate, Working Paper No. 24, Institute for New Economic Thinking.

Cukierman, A. and Meltzer, A. (1986) A positive theory of discretionary policy, the cost of democratic government and the benefits of a Constitution, *Economic Inquiry* 24(3): 367–88.

Dafermos, Y. (2017) Debt cycles, instability and fiscal rules: A Godley–Minsky synthesis, *Cambridge Journal of Economics*, doi:10.1093/cje/bex046.

Damill, M., Frenkel, R. and y Rapetti, M. (2005) La Deuda Argentina: Historia, Default y Reestructuración, Documento de Trabajo, CEDES, Buenos Aires, Argentina.

Drazen, A. (2004) *Political Economy in Macro Economics*, Princeton University Press.

Drumond, C. and Silva de Jesus, C. (2016) Monetary and fiscal policy interactions

in a post Keynesian open-economy model, *Journal of Post Keynesian Economics*, 39(2): 172–86.
ECLAC (2016) Fiscal Panorama of Latin America and the Caribbean 2016. Public finances and the challenge of reconciling austerity with growth and equality, ECLAC-Cooperación Española, printed in Santiago.
Eyraud, L., Debrun, X., Hodge, A., Lledó, V. and Pattillo, C. (2018) Second-generation fiscal rules: Balancing simplicity, flexibility and enforceability, IMF Staff Discussion Note 18/04, International Monetary Fund.
Godley, W. and Cripps, F. (1983) *Macroeconomics*, Oxford University Press.
Godley, W. and Lavoie, M. (2007) *Monetary Economics: An Integrated Approach to Credit, Money, Income, Production and Wealth*, Palgrave Macmillan.
Halac, M. and Yared, P. (2017) Fiscal rules and discretion under self-enforcement, NBER Working Paper No. 23919, National Bureau of Economic Research.
Hanngsen, G. (2012) Fiscal Policy, Unemployment Insurance, and Financial Crises in a Model of Growth and Distribution, Working Paper No. 723, Levy Economics Institute of Bard College.
IMF (2017) Fiscal Rules Dataset 1985–2015, IMF Fiscal Affairs Department, March, 2017.
Jasova, M., Moessner, R. and Takats, E. (2016) Exchange rate pass-through: What has changed since the crisis?, BIS Working Paper No. 583, Bank for International Settlements.
Kopits, G. (2001) Fiscal rules: Useful policy framework or unnecessary ornament?, IMF Working Paper 01/145, International Monetary Fund.
Kopits, G. and Symansky, S. (1998) Fiscal policy rules, Occasional Paper No. 162, International Monetary Fund.
Kumhof, M. and Laxton, D. (2009) Simple, implementable fiscal policy rules, IMF Working Paper 09/76, International Monetary Fund.
Kydland, F. and Prescott, E. (1977) Rules rather than discretion: The inconsistency of optimal plans, *Journal of Political Economy* 85(3): 473–91.
Leith, C. and Wren-Lewis, S. (2005) Fiscal stabilization policy and fiscal institutions, *Oxford Review of Economic Policy* 21(4): 584–97.
Martner, R. (2003) Presentación: Lecciones de las Experiencias Recientes en el Diseño de Reglas Macrofiscales, Reglas macrofiscales, sostenibilidad y procedimientos presupuestarios, Documentos presentados en el XV Seminario Regional de Política Fiscal Santiago de Chile, 27 al 30 de enero de 2003, ILPES–CEPAL, Santiago de Chile.
Ocampo, J. A. (2013) Balance of payments dominance: Its implications for macroeconomic policy, Initiative for Policy Dialogue Working Paper Series.
Persson, T. and Tabellini, G. (1990) *Macroeconomic Policy Credibility and Politics*, Harwood Academia Publishers: Chur, Switzerland.
Ribeiro, R. and Lima, G.T. (2017) Government expenditure ceiling and public-debt dynamics in a demand-led macromodel, Working Paper No. 2017–35, Department of Economics, University of São Paulo.
Schaechter, A., Kinda, T., Budina, N. and Weber, A. (2012) Fiscal rules in response to the crisis – Towards the "next generation" rules. A dataset, IMF Working Paper 12/187, International Monetary Fund.
Solow, R. (2005) Rethinking fiscal policy, *Oxford Review of Economic Policy* 21(4): 509–14.
Truger, A. and Will, H. (2013) The German "debt-brake": A shining example of European fiscal policy?, *Revue de la OFCE* 2013/1 (127): 153–88.

Vera, L. (2009) Reassessing fiscal policy: Perspective from developing countries, *Development and Change* 40(4): 611–43.

Wijsman, S. and Crombez, C. (2017) The political economy of enforcing fiscal rules, FEB Research Report MSI 1701, KU Leuven.

Wyplosz, C. (2005) Fiscal policy: Institutions versus rules, *National Institute Economic Review* 191(1): 64–78.

PART 3

Post-Keynesian views on monetary policy

9. The transmission of monetary policy in the US: testing the credit channel and the role of endogenous money

Nathan Perry and Carlos Schönerwald

INTRODUCTION

Post-Keynesian economics supports the notion that the money supply is endogenous. Endogenous money creation is the idea that money supply is a function of the demand for bank credit. Within the post-Keynesian tradition lie two primary strands of thought: the first is the accommodationist view, which argues that a demand for loans is met with banks borrowing from the Federal Reserve. The structuralist viewpoint argues that when entities demand loans, banks supply the loans and create funds by using liability management to respond to loan demand. In both views, the demand for loans is the ultimate constraint on bank lending, not excess reserves or deposits. The causality goes from demand for loans to excess reserves, or innovative liability management techniques, not from deposits/reserves to loans as the conventional literature dictates.

The post-Keynesian view contrasts with the exogenous multiplier approach. The money multiplier approach states that the central banks buy short-term debt instruments from banks, increasing excess reserves in the banking system. Banks lend out their excess reserves, only holding required reserves, thereby increasing the total number of loans and hence bank and economic activity. The directional causality goes from a change in open market operations, to a change in excess reserves, to a change in loans. This money multiplier approach is listed in some version in virtually all macroeconomics and money and banking textbooks and is taught as the primary mechanism by which the Federal Reserve conducts monetary policy. The money multiplier approach works in the same way for deposits. Savers deposit money into a bank, the bank lends out the deposit money that is not required reserves, this money makes its way back to the banking system, and the multiple deposit creation approach continues.

The objective of this chapter is to empirically test the endogenous money hypothesis in the US from 1980 to 2017. Granger causality tests are used to determine which way causality runs. The results show evidence for the endogenous money approach. Ultimately, the authors believe that the evidence is more in favor of endogenous money because of the role of the demand for loans.

LITERATURE REVIEW

Within post-Keynesian literature, accommodationist view argues that the Federal Reserve sets a target interest rate, and supplies reserves as needed for banks to meet loan demand. The interest rate in this scenario is perfectly elastic and set by the central bank, with the central bank manipulating excess reserves to keep the interest rate at the desired level. Banks then mark up loans from this interest rate to meet the demand for bank loans, and when loans are taken out, deposits are created.

From the accommodationist perspective, the Federal Reserve has complete control over interest rates through its setting of the discount rate and open market operations. Other rates then move in accordance with these short term rates (Kaldor 1982). Lavoie (2007) points out that several central banks and banking systems in general work the way the accommodationists theorize, including the Bank of Canada, which requires no reserves, and banks may borrow freely from the Bank of Canada, making the Canadian system a fully accommodative system. Pollin (1991) points out three important tenets of accommodative endogeneity. The first tenet is the proportionality in the relative movements of loans and reserves. If the proportionality of loans to reserves stays the same, then there is strong evidence for full accommodationism from the central bank. The second tenet is the substitutability between borrowed and non-borrowed reserves, which implies that borrowed and non-borrowed reserves are equal to a bank, even accounting for "frown costs." The third tenet is that the Federal Reserve sets short term interest rates.

The structuralist view, see Pollin (1991) and Palley (1994), argues that the central bank only partially accommodates a bank's demand for reserves. Instead, in order for banks to meet loan demand, they must pursue liability management to raise funds instead of relying solely on borrowed reserves. Pollin (1991) explains that structural endogeneity does not accept the view that discount window borrowing is a close substitute for non-borrowed reserves, even adjusting for "frown costs." In the structuralist framework, banks do not fully accommodate bank demand for reserves, which forces banks to find other sources of liabilities. The end of regulation Q and the innovative creation of different liability management tools in the 1960s and 1970s made liability management the primary tool by which banks respond to loan demand. Since it is generally frowned upon by financial markets to seek discount loans, these loans are sought only as a last resort. Banks use existing deposits and liability management in response to loan demand, and then seek Federal Funds loans from other banks to meet reserve requirements, and take out discount loans only in emergencies. The Federal Reserve accommodates through open market operations and some discount loans but is not fully accommodating. Pollin (1991, p. 375) notes that liability management creates a "lend first, find reserves later" practice for banks, and allows banks to avoid strict reserve requirement restrictions that an increase in deposits would bring. Liability management practices allow banks to expand the total value of loans offered despite the central bank potentially manipulating the total level of reserves.

In an endogenous money system the Federal Reserve in some form (whether the full accommodationist view or the structuralist view) supplies reserves in response to both the issuance of credit and the demand for money. In the post-Keynesian system the ultimate constraint is not the supply of credit, which is the traditional approach, but the demand for loans, the credit worthiness of banks and bank customers, and the expectation of the overall macroeconomy. The micro-uncertainty constraint refers to the credit worthiness of banks and the willingness of the lender to supply loans based on the probability of default. Borrowers must either show they can produce more income to cover the debt payments or have enough collateral to ensure low default risk (Lavoie 1996). The macro-uncertainty is the uncertainty that all firms face related to the business cycle (Rochon 2006). Micro-uncertainty exists regardless of the business cycle, as firms are still capable of failing even if effective demand is relatively high. Part of the macro-uncertainty is the volatility of interest rates. A rise in interest rates can easily put a poorly hedged bank or business over the tipping point of breaking even to large losses.

As Lavoie (1984), Rochon (2006), and Moore (1988) point out, when macro-uncertainty becomes too great, banks increase the credit requirements for loans. As the business cycle weakens, banks become strict with loans in order to ensure repayment of debts. As the business cycle improves, banks, following their animal spirits, lower loan requirements, becoming less strict with lending and lowering the markup costs of loans. Keynes is more succinct in explaining that "during a boom the popular estimation of the magnitude of lenders risk is apt to become unusually and imprudently low" (Keynes 1936, p. 145). Rochon (2006) explains a credit crunch quite succinctly: "A credit crunch, in a post-Keynesian world, is therefore not explained by a decrease in central bank reserves and a corresponding leftward shift in the supply of bank credit. This implies a scarcity of available funds, and hence the need to ration supply in light of greater demand. For post-Keynesians, credit is constrained not because demand is greater than supply, but because banks become very pessimistic and they *choose* not to lend to certain borrowers" (Rochon 2006, p. 182; italics in original). Minsky (1982) also covers the "credit crunch" phenomenon and argues that a credit crunch can occur when money markets do not generate the necessary reserve supply, at which point loans will be called in and assets will be sold to create the necessary reserves. At this point liability management ceases to be an unlimited source of funds based on the demand for borrowing, and the source of funds in liability management becomes constrained endogenously.

In order to empirically test the endogenous money hypothesis, Granger causality tests are generally employed. Both Vera (2001) and Shanmugam et al. (2003) use Granger causality tests to determine causality for Spain and Malaysia respectively. Each find reasonable evidence that causality runs from loans to other variables, primarily different measures of money supply including M2 and the monetary base. Carpenter and Demiralp (2010) employ two primary procedures to test the money multiplier approach. The first is using bank level data and Granger causality tests. The authors test the standard multiplier approach against the liability management approach (or what we consider closest to the endogenous money story). The authors show no evidence for the money multiplier approach, and strong evidence for the liability management approach. The second procedure employed is a VAR using a methodology similar to Bernanke and Blinder (1992). The findings again showed little evidence for the traditional money multiplier approach after 1990. The empirical section for this chapter will build upon Vera (2001), Shanmugam et al. (2003), Moore (1988), and Carpenter and Demiralp (2010) in an attempt to empirically determine causality for endogenous money vs. exogenous money.

DATA AND METHODOLOGY

Data was collected from the Federal Reserve and is in monthly format. The data stretches from 1980 to 2017.[1] The year 1980 was chosen as the start year for two reasons: (1) Regulation Q was passed which changed the nature of liability management and hence the reliance of banks on reserves and deposits; (2) Bank liability data only goes back to 1978. Each variable was tested for stationarity using the Augmented Dickey Fuller (ADF) test. When unit roots were found, the first difference of the variable was used. All variables are in log form. The optimal lag length for the ADF test was chosen using the Elliott-Rothenberg-Stock (1996) method. The optimal lag length for the Granger causality tests was chosen based on the AIC criterion. The variable definitions are as follows:

LER = ln of required reserves
LM2 = ln of M2
LL = ln of loans
LBL = ln of bank liabilities
LD = ln of deposits

The Granger causality tests are listed in Table 9.2. The goal is to test the causality between bank level variables and loans. If loans are shown to Granger cause reserves, M2, liability management, or deposits, then there is evidence for the endogenous money hypothesis. In an endogenous money world, credit creation creates deposits, which means there should be a strong causality from loans to deposits.

The results of the Granger causality tests indicate evidence for both the money multiplier story and the endogenous money story. However, there is more evidence for the endogenous money story. Using the AIC criterion, 6 lags was determined to be the optimal lag length, so this section will focus on the results of the causality tests with 6 lags. The traditional money multiplier story shows that 2 of the 4 causalities tested are statistically significant, including Δ Deposits → Δ Bank Loans and Δ Liability Management → Δ Bank Loans. The causalities that are not significant at the 90% level are Δ Excess Reserves → Δ Bank Loans and Δ M2 → Δ Bank loans. Regarding the result that an increase in deposits Granger causes an increase in bank loans, there may be an endogenous effect for deposits though because both deposits and loan demand surge as the economy approaches the top of the business cycle.

Three of the 4 endogenous money causalities were significant at least at the 90% level. The Granger causalities that are statistically significant include Δ Loans → Δ Deposits, Δ Loans → Δ Excess Reserves, and Δ Loans → Δ Liability Management. The results show that loans granger cause liability management practices at the 90% level, while the causality from loans to reserves is significant at the 99% threshold. Loans to deposits is 95% significant. The results show a dual causality for liability management and loans, as for both the exogenous and endogenous money story it is significant at the 90% level. Because this is monthly data, and because liability management is conducted very quickly when loan demand is

Table 9.1 Unit root tests

Variables	t-value/(# of lags by AIC)			Critical Values		
	level	1st diff.	2nd diff.	1%	5%	10%
LM2						
with drift	−0.356 (16)	−2.967 (15) **		−3.445	−2.867	−2.570
with drift and trend	−2.417 (16)	−2.961 (15)	−9.542 (14) **	−3.979	−3.420	−3.132
without drift and trend	2.551 (16)	−1.336 (15)	−9.557 (14) **	−2.570	−1.941	−1.616
LL						
with drift	−1.766 (6)	−3.614 (5) **		−3.448	−2.869	−2.570
with drift and trend	−2.561 (6)	−3.868 (5)*		−3.984	−3.422	−3.134
without drift and trend	2.670 (6)	−2.261 (5) *		−2.571	−1.941	−1.616
LBL						
with drift	−2.023 (2)	−4.242 (15) **		−3.444	−2.867	−2.570
with drift and trend	−1.744 (16)	−12.233 (1) **		−3.979	−3.420	−3.132
without drift and trend	3.571 (16)	−2.045 (15) *		−2.570	−1.941	−1.616
LD						
with drift	−0.454 (3)	−4.706 (8) **		−3.445	−2.868	−2.570
with drift and trend	−1.124 (3)	−4.699 (8) **		−3.978	−3.420	−3.133
without drift and trend	7.946 (3)	−1.357 (17)	−9.379 (16) **	−2.570	−1.942	−1.616
LER						
with drift	−0.275 (1)	−24.334 (0) **		−3.445	−2.868	−2.570
with drift and trend	−1.566 (1)	−24.333 (0) **		−3.978	−3.420	−3.132
without drift and trend	1.397 (1)	−24.240 (0) **		−2.570	−1.941	−1.616

* indicates that the null hypothesis $H_0: \gamma = 0$ can be rejected at the 5% significance level, but cannot be rejected at the 1% level.
** indicates that the null hypothesis $H_0: \gamma = 0$ is rejected at the 1% significance level.
Augmented Dickey Fuller (ADF) Tests (lags selected using AIC criterion) (1980 to 2017).

Table 9.2 1980–2017 Granger causality tests

Traditional Story	18 lags	12 lags	6 lags
Δ Deposits → Δ Bank Loans	2.306 ***	3.128 ***	4.650 ***
	(.002)	(0.000)	(0.000)
Δ Excess Reserves → Δ Bank Loans	2.920 ***	2.235 ***	0.217
	(.000)	(0.000)	(0.971)
Δ M2 → Δ Bank loans	1.615 *	1.707 *	0.749
	(0.053)	(0.062)	(0.609)
Δ Liability Management → Δ Bank Loans	7.535***	9.490 ***	1.810 *
	(0.00)	(0.000)	(0.0955)
Endogenous Money Story			
Δ Loans → Δ Deposits	1.942 **	2.216 ***	2.565 **
	(0.011)	(0.010)	(0.018)
Δ Loans → Δ Excess Reserves	3.173 **	3.462***	5.037 ***
	(0.000)	(0.009)	(0.000)
Δ Loans → Δ M2	8.790 ***	11.890***	0.33175
	(0.000)	(0.000)	(0.920)
Δ Loans → Δ Liability Management	2.339	1.000	1.966 *
	(0.001)	(0.447)	(0.069)

*** indicates that the null hypothesis cannot be reject at the 1% level.
** indicates that the null hypothesis can be rejected at the 1% significance level but cannot be rejected at the 5% level.
* indicates that the null hypothesis can be rejected at the 5% significance level but cannot be rejected at the 10% level.

being met, it is difficult to capture the causality unless using more narrow data. One central tenet of accommodationism is that the Federal Reserve fully accommodates bank lending with reserves. It follows that if there is an increase in loans, there should be an increase in reserves. The results confirm this theory at the 99% level. An interesting point to make is that loans are not affected by changes in M2 in either story. M2 is much more important to the exogenous money story than it is the endogenous money story. As the lag structure increases, the exogenous money story seems to hold more weight.

CONCLUSION

There is more evidence for endogenous money when tested against the traditional money multiplier approach. Three of the 4 hypothesis tested showed causality from loans to deposits, reserves, and liability management. Two of the 4 hypotheses for the traditional story were statistically significant, including deposits to loans and liability management to loans. Both accommodationist and structuralist views are confirmed, as loans to liability management and loans to reserves are both statistically significant.

The most recent financial and banking crisis followed by the sub-prime crisis has raised questions about the role of banks in the monetary system. In the aftermath of the banking crisis, central banks injected excess reserves into the banking system, which led many to wonder why lending was not higher. Those who were confused only understand banking through the textbook exogenous money multiplier view, where the Federal Reserve actions cause banks to lend. However, we live in an endogenous money world, where the demand for loans determines lending, and central banks accommodate banks' need for reserves. The Federal Reserve can control the price of overnight lending but cannot control business and consumer demand for loans. It is this demand for loans that causes bank lending, and hence the change in liability management and excess reserves. This chapter has empirically demonstrated this point with econometric results support the post-Keynesian endogenous money hypothesis.

NOTE

1. Results were also found using weekly data and were similar.

BIBLIOGRAPHY

Bellini, T. (2016). *Stress Testing and Risk Integration in Banks: A Statistical Framework and Practical Software Guide (in Matlab and R)*. Elsevier.

Bernanke, B. and Blinder, A. (1992). The Federal Funds rate and the channels of monetary transmission. *American Economic Review*, 82 (4), 901–21.

Carpenter, S. and Demiralp, S. (2010). Money, reserves, and the transmission of monetary policy: Does the money multiplier exist? Federal Reserve Board discussion series, 2010–2041.

Elliot, G., Tothenberg, T. and Stock, J. (1996). Efficient tests for an autoregressive unit root. *Econometrica*, 64 (4), 813–36.

Kaldor, N. (1982). *The Scourge of Monetarism*. New York: Oxford University Press.

Keynes, J.M. (1936). *The General Theory of Employment, Interest and Money*. New York: Harcourt, Brace and World.

Lavoie, M. (2007). Endogenous money: accommodationist, in Arestis, P. and Sawyer, M. (eds), *A Handbook of Alternative Monetary Economics*, Chapter 2. Cheltenham: Edward Elgar Publishing.

Minsky, H. (1982). *Can 'It' Happen Again? Essays on Instability and Finance*. Armonk, NY: M.E. Sharpe.

Moore, B. (1988). *Horizontalists and Verticalists: The Macroeconomics of Credit Money*. New York: Cambridge University Press.
Palley, T. (1994). Competing views of the money supply process: Theory and evidence. *Metroeconomica*, 45 (1), 67–88.
Palley, T. (1996). Accommodationism versus structuralism: time for an accommodation. *Journal of Post Keynesian Economics*, 18 (4), 585–94.
Pollin, Robert (1991). Two theories of money supply endogeneity: some empirical evidence. *Journal of Post Keynesian Economics*, 13 (3), 366–96.
Rochon, L. (2006) Endogenous money, central banks and the banking system: Basil Moore and the supply of credit, in Setterfield, M. (ed), *Complexity, Endogenous Money and Macroeconomic Theory*, Chapter 9. Cheltenham: Edward Elgar Publishing.
Shanmugam, B., Mahendhiran, N. and Ong, L. (2003). The endogenous money hypothesis: empirical evidence from Malaysia (1985–2000). *Journal of Post Keynesian Economics*, 25 (4), 599–611.
Vera, Alfonso Palacio (2001). The endogenous money hypothesis: some evidence from Spain (1987–1998). *Journal of Post Keynesian Economics*, 23 (3), 509–26.

10. Corporate debt expansion in emerging countries after 2008: profile, determinants and policy implications

Cristiano Boaventura Duarte

INTRODUCTION

Private debt ratios, especially of non-financial firms, have grown considerably since the 2000s, in advanced (AEs) and emerging economies (EMEs). However, the 2008 global financial crisis marked a tipping point for both groups of countries. In advanced economies, corporate debt levels generally peaked in 2008. In the post-2008 period, after a limited downward adjustment, corporate debt ratios continued at high levels, and in some countries actually increased, according to OECD (2017). Conversely, emerging economies corporate debt levels increased since the 2000s from lower levels than AEs. Yet,the 2008 crisis did not interrupt this trend, with EMEs corporate debt levels continuing to increase up to 2016. The post-2008 crisis period was marked by a development of international debt markets, with bond issuance growth, coupled with an unprecedented monetary expansion in advanced economies, that eased international financial conditions, lowered risk spreads and increased search for yield, in particular for bonds of emerging countries.

However, this expansion in EMEs' corporate debt started to be challenged by recurrent episodes of volatility in international debt markets: in 2013, the "taper tantrum" in the USA; in 2014, the fall in commodity prices (especially oil/minerals); in 2015, uncertainties in China's foreign exchange/stock markets; in 2016, after the election of the new US president. Hence, the increase in EMEs' corporate debt size (even after the 2008 crisis), the changes in its profile/determinants and the financial stability concerns associated to it raised attention to this issue, which deserves a deeper analysis.

Therefore, this study main objective is to discuss the increase in corporate debt in emerging countries after 2008, aiming to understand the changes in its profile, its determinants, and its economic policy implications. The chapter is structured as follows. After this introduction, the second section presents the main features related to the amount/profile of corporate debt expansion in emerging economies. Some of the main features of this expansion in EMEs' corporate debt were the increase in leverage, net foreign exchange exposure, later leading to a deterioration of debt repayment capacity in a significant share of firms.

In the third section, we do a literature review on theoretical approaches that underpin debt expansion in corporations and its features, including agents' procyclical behavior. We observe that those approaches have been well described both in the mainstream and heterodox literature, related to concepts such as the risk-taking channel of monetary policy, herd behavior, animal spirits, Keynesian "beauty contest" and financial instability hypothesis. We also undertake a literature review on empirical articles that seek to understand the determinants of corporate debt in emerging economies.

In the fourth section, our own panel analysis is presented to explain the main determinants that were behind this debt expansion. Our contributions to this literature are to investigate the determinants of EMEs corporate debt expansion by using a dataset which goes from 2000 Q1 up to a recent period (2016 Q4), and with subsamples before and after the 2008 crisis, so we identify the main changes in the factors that explain EMEs corporate debt expansion before and after this event. Most importantly, we identify a factor which was not previously used in the literature for that purpose: the interaction between higher commodity prices and more appreciated exchange rates. Our findings suggest that the exchange rate has been one of the most important determinants that explain EMEs companies' debt expansion through the period 2000–2016, and also in the period before the 2008 crisis. But after 2008, beyond some country-level factors (exchange rate, national GDP growth, firms' higher liquidity levels), other factors that have global origins (more accommodative monetary policy stance in the USA, lower financial market volatility, global GDP growth, higher commodity prices and its interaction with the exchange rate appreciation) have become increasingly important to explain emerging market corporate debt expansion.

The fifth section discusses the economic policy implications of this debt increase. First, we present additional challenges faced by emerging economies' firms: currency mismatch, firms' susceptibility to creditors'/banks'/institutional investors' interests, macroeconomic volatility, that raise financial stability concerns. Next, we argue that those concerns would be better addressed if developing countries and international institutions took additional measures, enhancing regulatory frameworks, as well as implementing macro- and micro-prudential measures (preferably in a coordinated way), in order to improve instruments to face new financial crises. The sixth section closes the study with final considerations and conclusions.

FEATURES OF CORPORATE DEBT IN EMERGING COUNTRIES

This section presents the main features of the evolution of corporate debt in emerging economies in the recent period, with a special focus on non-financial companies.

Regarding the evolution of non-financial corporate debt in emerging countries, its amount rose from US$9 trillion in March 2008 to US$25.7 trillion in December 2016, according to BIS data (2017). Considering these values as percentages of countries' GDPs, growth between March 2008 and December 2016 was on average 41 percentage points (pp), from 61% to 102% of GDP. In geographical terms, this increase occurred in all major regions that group emerging countries: Asia, Latin America, Emerging Europe, Middle East, and Africa – EMEA. However, this expansion did not occur homogeneously: in Hong Kong and China, the increase in non-financial corporate debt in the period was 82 pp and 69 pp respectively, to levels above 166% of GDP. Chile, Turkey, and Singapore also had significant increases of 38, 34 and 31 pp, respectively. In other emerging markets, the increase in non-financial corporate debt in the period was less than 30 pp, to levels generally below 100% of GDP, as can be seen in Figure 10.1.

In terms of economic sectors, the ones that experienced higher debt growth were construction, real estate and mining (especially the oil and gas sub-sector), according to the IMF (2015).

Concerning leverage, its degree can be measured using various indexes. Two indicators commonly used are: (i) total liabilities to total equity; (ii) total liabilities to earnings before taxes (EBT). Using a compilation of data from EMEs companies, both indicators had a significant expansion between 2007 and 2013: the first, by 88 pp, and the second by 28 pp, according to the IMF (2015).

Regarding emerging companies' foreign debt, an alternative measure of foreign exchange exposure has been estimated by the IMF (2015), which calculates net values excluding financial and operational hedging mechanisms. The study concluded that, with the exception of China, there was a significant expansion of net foreign exchange exposure of emerging companies in the period. The increase in net foreign exchange exposure level in EMEA was from 45% to 50% (5 pp). In Latin America, it has increased from about 40% to 60% (20 pp). In general, non-tradable sectors have higher net foreign exchange exposure, because non-tradables

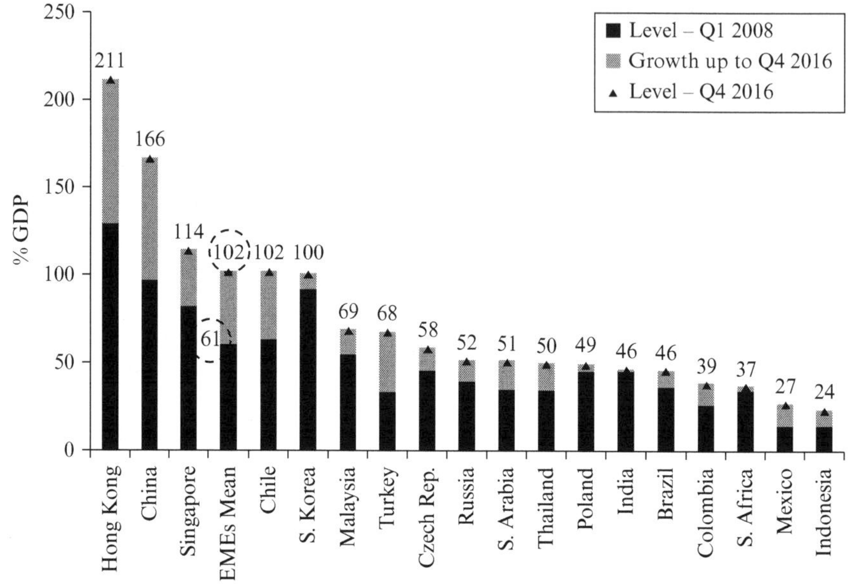

Source: Author own elaboration, based on BIS (2017) data.

Figure 10.1 Credit to non-financial corporations – Q1/2008 to Q4/2016 (% GDP)

cannot rely on the alternative of operational hedging (available for tradable sectors). Still, this operational hedging might not be enough to protect balance sheets of tradable sectors, as they are also negatively affected in occasions when commodity prices fall and exports volumes decline, with a slowdown in international trade.

Regarding the profile of non-financial corporate debt in emerging countries, there was also a significant change in its composition in the post-2008 crisis period. Although most of the debt remained being funded by bank loans, an increasing share of EMEs firms' debt has been funded by bonds issued in capital markets (from 9% in 2007 to 17% in 2014, according to the IMF 2015). In absolute terms, the amount of annual non-financial corporate debt issuance jumped from about US$586 billion in 2007 to US$3.025 trillion in 2014. In many countries, there was an increase in the concentration of debt issuance by major companies. In terms of sectors, the most relevant issuers were construction and oil/gas. Regarding the currency of issuance of these securities, domestic ones accounted for a larger share. However, there was an increase in the foreign share of non-financial corporate debt issuance in EMEs (excluding China), from about 40%

between 2003 and 2007 to 45% between 2010 and 2014. The most used foreign currency was the dollar (usually over 80%), with the euro, yen and other currencies comprising a smaller share.

It is worth mentioning that using bonds as a source of funding has advantages and disadvantages for firms. The advantages are: (i) better financing conditions when compared to bank loans, such as lower costs and longer maturities; and (ii) using capital markets as an alternative source of funding, even when banks are more restrictive. Among the disadvantages, it can be mentioned: (i) the increasing reliance on funding from more volatile sources (i.e. institutional investors); and (ii) market investors are less stringent in monitoring firms' balance sheets than banks, which may encourage excessive risk-taking by firms.

Regarding the allocation of funds raised by companies through bonds, there is no consensus about their destination. The increased availability of resources for funding would have decreased entrepreneurs' minimum expected rate of return. This fact would have removed constraints for the implementation of several new investment projects, including ones with lower profitability. In other words, the availability of funding would have allowed an increase in the volume of investments, but also the implementation of less profitable projects. Then, even with more favorable financing conditions, the growth in debt amounts and the fall in investments profitability led to a deterioration of EMEs firms debt repayment capacity. A study published by the IMF (2016) showed that the percentage of EMEs companies whose earnings were lower than interest expenses (interest coverage ratio below 1, a critical situation) was around 11%, corresponding to US$430 billion of "debt at risk."

Furthermore, several other studies indicated that bond issuance resources were less used for new investments, and more destined towards refinancing debt or buying short-term financial assets. According to the IMF (2015), the allocation of funds raised by firms through bonds was higher for refinancing than for new investments. Moreover, Chui et al (2014) mentioned that high interest rate differentials from domestic to international levels stimulated an intensification in carry trade activities by firms, which suggested the allocation of these resources for speculative purposes. A sign of those activities was the increase in companies' assets held as cash or bank deposits, which has grown significantly since 2009. The fact that this trend has not reversed after the crisis shows that the accumulation of financial resources by firms was not only a precautionary behavior immediately after the 2008 episode. Conversely, it was a strategy to increase financial returns, raising funds abroad with low interest rates and depositing in local banks or buying high-yield assets from institutional investors.

Another factor associated with this process was the expansion of bond issuance through offshore subsidiaries, benefiting from jurisdictions that offer tax and regulatory advantages. The headquarters of these subsidiaries were located mainly in the following countries: China, Brazil, Russia, India, and South Africa. McCauley et al (2015a) estimated that in the second quarter of 2015, these offshore subsidiaries held a volume of bonds of US$558 billion. With the funds obtained abroad, an offshore subsidiary of a non-financial company can transfer funds to their home country through three channels: (i) making a direct loan for its headquarters (within-company flows); (ii) providing credit to other non-financial companies (between-company flows); or (iii) making a cross-border deposit in a bank (corporate deposit flows). Based on an analysis of emerging countries' balance of payments data performed by Avdjiev et al (2014), it was noted that capital flows to EMEs associated with all three mentioned channels grew considerably in the period between 2009 and 2014. As most of these flows were allocated for financial, rather than real activities, evidence suggests that offshore subsidiaries of emerging companies have acted in this period also as financial intermediaries, obtaining funds from global investors through bond issuance and remitting these resources to their home countries through those three different channels. Nonetheless, it is important to point out that the increase in bond issuance abroad by EMEs firms was not only due to their own strategy to enlarge their investor base and raise funds with better conditions, but it was also a consequence of the interests/demands of international investors, seeking higher yields.

Overall, the features of corporate debt presented in this section showed that non-financial companies in emerging countries expanded their presence considerably in financial markets, searching for higher profits and often acting as financial intermediaries. They increased their degree of leverage and net foreign exchange exposure, especially in the post-2008 crisis period, and a significant share of them later presented deterioration in debt repayment capacity.

LITERATURE REVIEW

Theoretical Approaches for Corporate Debt Expansion

The features of corporate debt described in the previous section (increase in leverage and net foreign exchange exposure, with later deterioration in debt repayment capacity) would have as a common point *agents' procyclical behavior*, being in accordance with theoretical approaches that have been well described both in the mainstream and heterodox literature.

In the mainstream literature, Bruno and Shin (2015) highlighted the "risk-taking channel of monetary policy," and its impact on financial and real variables through bank leverage. Feyen et al (2015) argued that the risk-taking channel mechanism would also apply for corporate foreign bond issuance. More specifically, when domestic currency appreciates, local companies' balance sheets strengthen. With stronger balance sheets, local companies increase their external borrowing capacity, fostering higher cross-border inflows into EMEs by international investors who are willing to take on more risk. Conversely, tighter international financial conditions would lead to an appreciation of the US dollar and cross border capital outflows from EMEs, with depreciation of domestic currencies, reducing companies' external borrowing capacity and weakening their balance sheets.

In the heterodox literature, descriptions of agents' procyclical behavior date back to Keynes General Theory (1936). Assuming fundamental uncertainty and adaptive expectations, Keynes argued that each individual has the incentive to imitate other agents' average behavior (conventional behavior or Keynesian "beauty contest"). As long-term expectations are formed under a fragile basis, those expectations would be subject to sudden shifts, due to changes in entrepreneurs "animal spirits" that would influence their actions. This change in entrepreneurs' views could spread through the market (herd behavior), triggering a "self-fulfilling prophecy": entrepreneurs' pessimism leads them to invest less, and thus the economy enters a downward trajectory, "confirming" the initial pessimism. A more in-depth analysis of firms' procyclical behavior was made by Hyman Minsky (1978) with his "Financial Instability Hypothesis." This concept was based on two central propositions: the first is that there are stable funding models and unstable ones; the second is that in prolonged periods of economic growth, stable financial relations may become unstable. Under this view, after an expansionary period with an increase in liquidity and credit, firms would take more speculative and Ponzi postures, deteriorating their "safety margins" (i.e. debt repayment capacity) and weakening their balance sheet positions. In this context, Minsky argued that procyclical behavior and the generation of instability and crises are features intrinsic or endogenous to capitalist dynamics. Hence, he believed that a financial crisis of great magnitude did not need to be necessarily triggered by a huge adverse (external or exogenous) shock. Conversely, a reversal of expectations caused by a one-off episode would be sufficient to modify refinancing conditions and, consequently, to push firms that were already with weak balance sheet conditions to a situation of illiquidity/insolvency.

Empirical Literature Review on the Determinants of Corporate Debt in Emerging Countries

Articles which try to deal specifically with the issue of the determinants of corporate debt in emerging economies in a global sense (not from a single country or region, as a consequence of a local/regional crisis) became more frequent only recently, especially after 2013, when macroeconomic conditions in EMEs in general deteriorated, and institutions such as the IMF and BIS started to highlight in their reports concerns related to the growth of corporate debt in those countries. Among them, we can mention McCauley et al (2015b), Feyen et al (2015), Serena and Moreno (2016), IMF (2015).

In particular, the study presented by the IMF (2015) uses private databases of more than 1 million non-financial firms for 24 emerging market economies, during the period 2004–2013. They run a panel regression model in which their dependent variable is the change in leverage (change of total liabilities/book equity), and their main explanatory variables are grouped into three categories: Firm Indicators (e.g. measures of size, profitability and asset tangibility), Country Macro Indicators (i.e. International Country Risk Guide – ICRG) and Global Indicators (price of oil, US shadow interest rate, VIX, Global GDP). Their main result is that a decrease in the US shadow rate is associated with faster leverage growth, with a more intense impact on the subsample 2010–2013.

DETERMINANTS OF CORPORATE DEBT EXPANSION IN EMERGING COUNTRIES

The objective of this section is to explain the factors that were behind the expansion of corporate debt observed in emerging countries' companies during the period 2000–2016. We undertake a panel analysis in which we present a number of factors, with domestic and global origins, in order to check whether they were significant to explain corporate debt growth in EMEs corporations. In particular, we aim to identify the main changes in the explanatory factors of EMEs corporate debt expansion before and after the 2008 crisis.

Data

Our dataset gathers 15 emerging countries: Brazil, Chile, Czech Republic, China, Hungary, India, Indonesia, Malaysia, Mexico, Poland, Russia, South Africa, South Korea, Thailand, Turkey. All those countries are emerging markets according to the BIS definition, and are listed on the

MSCI EME index, which provides aggregate indicators for firms in each of those countries. Their geographical distribution is the following: Latin America (3 – Brazil, Chile, Mexico); Emerging Europe, Middle East, and Africa (6 – Czech Republic, Hungary, Poland, Russia, South Africa, Turkey); Emerging Asia (6 – China, India, Indonesia, South Korea, Malaysia, Thailand).

The time period analyzed is 2000 Q1–2016 Q4, with quarterly data. We also compare subsamples for periods before the 2008 financial crisis (2000 Q1–2007 Q4), and after the financial crisis (2009 Q1–2016 Q4). In our model, the dependent variable for corporate debt expansion – *Leverage* – is measured as companies' *Debt to Equity ratio* in each of the countries, obtained from MSCI country indexes. According to MSCI index methodology, their country-level measure of debt to equity ratio is obtained by dividing the total debt of firms listed in MSCI index of each country by the shareholder equity of those firms. Both debt and equity are on book value terms.

The explanatory variables are divided into two big groups: *Country* and *Global* factors. "Country Factors" represent factors that are linked with individual features in each country, whether microeconomic (firms' fundamentals) or macroeconomic (aggregate economic indicators).

"Microeconomic Factors" are balance sheet indicators, based on reports from publicly traded companies, which are compiled by MSCI to compose indexes for each indicator in its respective country. They measure companies' main accounting aspects:

(i) Profitability: return on assets (ROA).
(ii) Solvency ratio: free cash flow per share/short- and long-term debt.
(iii) Liquidity: current ratio (current assets/current liabilities).
(iv) Asset quality: tangible assets per share.

"Macroeconomic Factors" are main country indicators supposed to be relevant to companies' leverage.

(i) Real GDP growth (% YoY). Our source for this data was the IMF International Financial Statistics (IFS) database.
(ii) Monetary Policy Rate (% YoY), obtained on the BIS statistics database.
(iii) Real Effective Exchange Rate (REER). Our source was the BIS statistics database.

Some of the country factors are both related to local and international components (i.e. REER). Still, they are classified as "country factors" because the international components reflect on each jurisdiction in a particular way, according to its local components, so that each nation will have its own country factor.

"Global Factors" include elements that have global implications, or are common for the world economy as a whole. They do not vary according to the jurisdiction, as country factors.

(i) Monetary policy rate of four major central banks (Fed, ECB, BOE, BOJ). Measured through the "Shadow Short Rate (SSR)," based on the short-term policy interest rate, but accounting the stance and direction of monetary policy (level and slope), including the use of unconventional measures. The term structure of interest rates is used to find which policy rate would generate the observed yield curve if the policy rate could be taken to negative values. The "shadow rate" curve is obtained from calculating the value of a call option to hold cash at the ZLB and subtracting it from the actual yield curve. Our source for those rates was Kripnner (2016).
(ii) Real Global GDP growth (% YoY). Our source was the IMF IFS database.
(iii) Commodity price: All Commodity price index, compiled by the IMF. It is composed of weighted averages US dollar prices (2005=100) of non-fuel (edible, industrial inputs) and energy commodities.
(iv) VIX: Index of expectations of US stock market (S&P 500) volatility over the next 30-day period, calculated by the Chicago Board Options Exchange (CBOE). Proxy for market sentiment/global risk aversion, as described by several authors such as Rey (2015).

Model Specification and Methodology

Regarding the model specification, our main panel regression is the following:

$$\Delta \log Leverage = c + \Delta \log CountryFactors + \Delta \log GlobalFactors + \varepsilon$$

This specification broadly follows the one used by the IMF (2015). The dependent and independent variables are all presented in quarterly log changes, and we also do proper stationarity tests to make sure there are no unit roots in the series. In order to control for omitted variable bias, we make the option to use first differences, as we aim to control for unobserved heterogeneity among selected countries across time. To address a possible endogeneity problem on microeconomic factors (higher firm leverage influencing contemporaneous balance sheet indicators – profitability, liquidity, solvency, asset tangibility), the variables that measure them are lagged by one quarter, so that balance sheet indicators in the previous quarter will eventually explain leverage.

On an alternative specification, we also include an interaction term between two important variables, namely Commodity Price and the Real Effective Exchange Rate, so we can analyze how the introduction of this interaction term affects the model results.

$$\Delta \log Leverage = c + \Delta \log CountryFactors + \Delta \log GlobalFactors + \Delta \log Interaction + \varepsilon$$

The interaction term captures a singular relationship that exists between commodity prices and exchange rate movements, particularly in commodity-exporting emerging countries. The idea is that an increase in global commodity prices would result in an improvement in the terms of trade of commodity exporters, increasing prospective currency inflows and leading to an appreciation of foreign exchange in those countries, therefore reinforcing easing borrowing conditions for firms, especially abroad. This special link between commodity prices and exchange rates is documented by Kohlscheen et al (2017), who affirm this link goes beyond the global risk appetite (i.e. the one driven by the simultaneous movement of investors into/out of commodity markets and high-yielding currencies during risk-on/risk-off episodes), but do not use it with the purpose of explaining the rise in corporate debt. The introduction of an interaction term between two explanatory variables could raise a question about the presence of multicollinearity in the model. However, multicollinearity is not considered an issue for the model as a whole when using interaction terms, once the p-value for the interaction is not affected by the multicollinearity, according to authors such as Allison (2012).

The methodology employed was a Feasible Generalized Least Squares (FGLS) estimation of the previous regressions. In the panel estimation, we add weights that follow the Cross Section Seemingly Unrelated Regression (SUR) method, to include robustness to groupwise heteroskedasticity, autocorrelation and cross-section dependence. On the coefficient covariance, we also use the Cross Section SUR method, but with a modified specification (Panel-Corrected Standard Errors – PCSE), which has increased accuracy in hypothesis testing. Table 10.1 presents a summary of the expected signs of the relationships between the dependent variable with each one of the explanatory variables.

Table 10.1 Expected sign for relationship between leverage and explanatory variables

Explanatory variable	Expected sign	Reference in literature
	Microeconomic factors	
Profitability: return on assets	Positive/ Negative	Adair and Adaskou (2015) IMF (2015)
Solvency ratio: free cash flow per share/short- and long-term debt	Positive/ Negative	Adair and Adaskou (2015) IMF (2015)
Liquidity: current ratio	Positive/ Negative	IMF (2015)
Asset quality: tangible assets per share	Positive/ Negative	Adair and Adaskou (2015) IMF (2015)
	Macroeconomic factors	
Real GDP growth	Positive	Feyen et al (2015) IMF (2015)
Monetary policy rate	Negative	IMF (2015) Lo Duca et al (2016)
Real effective exchange rate	Positive	Feyen et al (2015) IMF (2015)
	Global factors	
Monetary policy rate of FED, ECB, BOE, BOJ	Negative	Feyen et al (2015) IMF (2015) Lo Duca et al (2016)
Real global GDP growth	Positive	Feyen et al (2015) IMF (2015)
Commodity price	Positive	IMF (2015) Kohlscheen et al (2017)
VIX	Negative	McCauley et al (2015b) Serena and Moreno (2016)
	Interaction	
Commodity Price*REER	Positive	—

Results

Table 10.2 summarizes our estimation output results.

Analyzing the results of the table as a whole, we observe that the signs of the coefficients are according to previously expected in Table 10.1. For microeconomic factors, the signs are positive, in accordance with the trade-off theory of corporate finance (firms with better balance sheet indicators face lower expected costs of financial distress and find interest

Table 10.2 Panel estimation output baseline results

Independent variables	Dependent variable: debt to equity					
	2000 Q1–2016 Q4		2000 Q1–2007 Q4		2009 Q1–2016 Q4	
	No Interaction	Interaction	No Interaction	Interaction	No Interaction	Interaction
Country						
Return on assets (1 lag)	**0.029***** (0.011)	**0.029***** (0.011)	**0.045***** (0.013)	**0.048***** (0.013)	0.011 (0.010)	**0.020**** (0.010)
Free cash flow/ Short- and long- term debt (1 lag)	0.002 (0.003)	0.002 (0.003)	**0.010*** (0.005)	**0.009*** (0.006)	0.002 (0.002)	0.003 (0.002)
Tangible assets per share (1 lag)	**0.024*** (0.013)	**0.024*** (0.013)	0.006 (0.013)	0.005 (0.014)	**0.028*** (0.017)	0.024 (0.017)
Current ratio (1 lag)	**0.109***** (0.023)	**0.108***** (0.023)	0.038 (0.027)	0.037 (0.027)	**0.188***** (0.021)	**0.199***** (0.020)
Real GDP growth	0.001 (0.004)	0.001 (0.004)	0.006 (0.007)	0.005 (0.007)	**0.009***** (0.003)	**0.007***** (0.002)
Monetary policy rate	−0.015 (0.018)	−0.015 (0.018)	−0.024 (0.023)	−0.027 (0.024)	−0.004 (0.016)	−0.001 (0.016)
REER	**0.396***** (0.068)	**0.381***** (0.069)	**0.591***** (0.095)	**0.587***** (0.098)	**0.131***** (0.047)	**0.185***** (0.050)
Global						
US shadow short rate	**−0.009*** (0.005)	**−0.009*** (0.005)	−0.004 (0.033)	−0.002 (0.036)	**−0.008***** (0.002)	**−0.006***** (0.002)
UK shadow short rate	−0.000 (0.003)	−0.001 (0.003)	−0.300 (0.088)	−0.309 (0.094)	**−0.003*** (0.001)	**−0.002*** (0.001)

Table 10.2 *(continued)*

	Dependent variable: debt to equity					
Independent variables	**2000 Q1–2016 Q4**		**2000 Q1–2007 Q4**		**2009 Q1–2016 Q4**	
	No Interaction	Interaction	No Interaction	Interaction	No Interaction	Interaction
EUR shadow short rate	−0.002	−0.002	−0.222	−0.236	−0.006	−0.009
	(0.012)	(0.012)	(0.085)	(0.091)	(0.005)	(0.004)
Japan shadow short rate	−0.013	−0.013	−0.017	−0.017	−0.041	−0.054
	(0.007)	(0.007)	(0.006)	(0.006)	(0.008)	(0.007)
Global GDP growth	0.008	0.009	0.022	0.014	0.004	**0.008****
	(0.010)	(0.010)	(0.037)	(0.039)	(0.004)	(0.004)
Commodity price	0.065	0.003	0.109	0.106	0.020	**0.335*****
	(0.041)	(0.088)	(0.063)	(0.096)	(0.026)	(0.049)
VIX	**−0.034*****	**−0.033*****	**−0.068***	**−0.068***	**−0.024*****	**−0.024*****
	(0.009)	(0.010)	(0.015)	(0.016)	(0.005)	(0.004)
	Interaction					
Commodity Price*REER	–	0.053	–	0.006	–	**0.265*****
		(0.062)		(0.067)		(0.035)
	Other information					
Number of quarters	66	66	30	30	32	32
Observations	913	913	373	373	480	480
R2 (GLS weighted)	0.092	0.094	0.204	0.196	0.316	0.401

Notes: All variables are measured in log changes. P values: *, **, ***, denote statistical significance at the 10, 5 and 1 percent level, respectively. Robust standard errors are in parenthesis.

tax deductions more valuable, thus having higher incentives to take on more debt). One of the main explanatory factors for leverage would be the real effective exchange rate (REER), once this variable is significant in all specifications, and it has the largest coefficient in most samples (except 2009–2016). Its positive sign means an exchange rate appreciation in EMEs is linked to an increase in firms' debt/equity ratios.

Observing the full sample (2000 Q1–2016 Q4), we see that beyond the REER, other variables that presented statistical significance were: (i) at the microeconomic level, the ones related to firms' profitability (return on assets), liquidity (current ratio) and asset tangibility (tangible assets per share), all positively related to leverage; (ii) at the global level, the variable which represents US monetary policy stance (US shadow short rate) and the VIX (proxy for global risk aversion), both negatively related to leverage, meaning leverage tends to increase when those variables are lower.

In the sample 2000 Q1–2007 Q4, the most significant variables are at the country level: exchange rate (REER) and firms' profitability (return on assets). Other variables are also significant: at the micro level, firms' solvency ratio (free cash flow per share/short- and long-term debt); at the global level, the VIX. Even so, the degree of significance of those two last variables is lower (p-values closer to 10%).

In the sample 2009 Q1–2016 Q4, several variables are significant: at the micro level, firms' liquidity and asset tangibility indexes; at the macro level, REER and real GDP growth; at the global level, the VIX and US shadow short rates are strongly significant; the UK shadow short rate is also significant, albeit at a lower level. In the specification with the interaction term, also appear as significant firms' profitability at the micro level, and Global GDP growth at the global level. Most importantly, in this specification Commodity Price and the interaction Commodity Price*REER are strongly significant and have the largest coefficients. Their positive signs mean an increase in commodity prices and the interaction between higher commodity prices and exchange rate appreciation in EMEs are linked to an increase in firms' leverage. This finding is in accordance with data which shows that a large share of EMEs corporate debt after 2008 was taken by commodity sector industries, as was previously described in the section "Features of Corporate Debt in EMEs."

In order to better analyze the changes in the determinants of corporate debt expansion between the time periods of the study, we perform Wald tests to check the joint significance of independent variables' coefficients. We divide the coefficients into two big groups: country coefficients and global coefficients. Country coefficients are then split into two smaller groups: Micro (firm factors) and Macro (aggregate economic factors). Global coefficients are also divided into two groups: one that gathers main central banks' monetary policy rates (US, Euro, UK and Japan shadow short rates), and a second that accounts for other global variables in the model (global GDP growth, commodity price and VIX). In the specification that considers the interaction term Commodity Price *REER, the term was included in the domestic macro factors (as the REER), due to its particular influence according to each country. In order to verify the statistical significance of each coefficient block, we test two hypotheses: (i) if the coefficients are different in the 15 countries; (ii) if the coefficients are different from zero in the 15 countries. Thus, an answer "Yes" implies the joint coefficients have statistical significance as a group, while an answer "No" means they do not have joint statistical significance. The results are reported in Table 10.3.

The results in both specifications (without and with the interaction term) are similar, and analyzing them one can reach the following conclusions. Before the 2008 crisis, the main determinants of debt expansion were in the group of *country* factors (as shown by the high significance of the return on assets in domestic microeconomic factors, and the REER in domestic macroeconomic factors). Conversely, after the 2008 crisis, while country factors remain important, factors in the *global* group also gain ground, both in the block related to international interest rates (e.g. US shadow short rate), as well as in the block related to other global variables (VIX, commodity price, Global GDP growth). Those results are consistent with other studies available in the literature previously mentioned above.

As a robustness analysis, we removed China from the country sample, in order to test if its faster pace of credit growth when compared to other countries and its profile more reliant on local currency debt were introducing some bias on the results. However, the results kept broadly similar to the full country sample, with the same variables appearing as significant and in the same degree of significance, as reported in Table 10.A1 (see Appendix).

Overall, our findings suggest that the exchange rate has been one of the most important determinants that explain the increase in EMEs companies' debt through the period 2000–2016, and also in the period before the 2008 crisis. But after 2008, beyond some country-level factors (exchange rate, national GDP growth, firms' higher liquidity levels), other factors that have global origins (more accommodative monetary policy stance in the USA, lower financial market volatility, global GDP growth, higher commodity prices and its interaction with the exchange rate appreciation) have become increasingly important to explain emerging market corporate debt expansion.

Table 10.3 Joint significance of independent variables' coefficients (Wald test)

Coefficient group	2000 Q1–2016 Q4		2000 Q1–2007 Q4		2009 Q1–2016 Q4	
	No Interaction	Interaction	No Interaction	Interaction	No Interaction	Interaction
Domestic Microeconomic Factors						
Different in all countries	Yes***	Yes***	Yes***	Yes***	Yes***	Yes***
Different from zero in all countries	Yes***	Yes***	Yes***	Yes***	Yes***	Yes***
Domestic macroeconomic factors						
Different in all countries	Yes***	Yes***	Yes***	Yes***	Yes***	Yes***
Different from zero in all countries	Yes***	Yes***	Yes***	Yes***	Yes***	Yes***
Domestic micro & macro factors						
Different in all countries	Yes***	Yes***	Yes***	Yes***	Yes***	Yes***
Different from zero in all countries	Yes***	Yes***	Yes***	Yes***	Yes***	Yes***
US, UK, Euro Area, Japan shadow short rates						
Different in all countries	Yes*	Yes*	No	No	Yes***	Yes***
Different from zero in all countries	No	No	No	No	Yes***	Yes***
World GDP, Commodity Price, VIX						
Different in all countries	Yes**	Yes**	Yes*	Yes*	Yes***	Yes***
Different from zero in all countries	Yes***	Yes***	Yes*	Yes*	Yes***	Yes***
All global factors						
Different in all countries	Yes***	Yes***	Yes*	Yes*	Yes***	Yes***
Different from zero in all countries	Yes***	Yes***	Yes*	Yes*	Yes***	Yes***

Note: P values: *, **, ***, denote statistical significance at the 10, 5 and 1 percent level, respectively.

CHALLENGES FOR EMERGING COUNTRY FIRMS AND ECONOMIC POLICY IMPLICATIONS

The analysis in the previous section showed that debt expansion in EMEs companies turned those firms more sensitive to the movements of the international economy. Hence, if firms are more sensitive to those movements, a reversal of international favorable conditions (i.e. monetary policy tightening in advanced economies, increase in risk aversion) may generate adverse effects in countries (e.g. currency depreciation, lower liquidity), increasing firms' borrowing costs and worsening their debt rollover conditions, turning their balance sheets weaker. Those facts were already observed in previous episodes – in 2013, the "taper tantrum" in the USA; in 2014, the fall in commodity prices (especially oil/minerals); in 2015, uncertainties in China's foreign exchange/stock markets; in 2016, after the election of the new US president – and could occur again.

Challenges Faced by Emerging Country Firms

Beyond the international scenario surrounded by uncertainties, other challenges faced by emerging country companies are: (i) currency mismatch problems; (ii) susceptibility to the interests of creditors, banks and institutional investors; and (iii) macroeconomic volatility.

Currency mismatch

Currency mismatch occurs when there is a discrepancy between agents' financial commitments and revenues denominated in foreign currency, due to uncertainty in the behavior of foreign exchange rates. In this context, companies could be in better financial health if they had enough *hedge* – funds in exchange for liabilities in foreign currency. It is known that many of them have "natural" hedges, once most of their revenues are denominated in foreign currencies, which in principle would make them less vulnerable to local currency depreciation. Another possibility would be to manage currency exposures through financial derivatives. However, it is difficult to measure the existing amount of those derivative instruments due to the lack of transparency of this information in many emerging economies. International data regarding non-financial companies' hedge is not disclosed in a clear and timely form, especially in EMEs. Indeed, many firms acquire loans through their subsidiaries abroad, turning more difficult to know in which degree their net foreign exchange exposure is really found. Moreover, hedging guarantees are not static. In the case of exporting firms, there may be a drop in revenue due to a reduction in their products' price or in the amounts exported. Furthermore, the hypothesis that having access to developed financial markets would ensure proper hedging can be refuted by the case of exporting companies from South Korea, Brazil, and Mexico. Those companies incurred in heavy losses in the 2008 financial crisis because they were involved in foreign exchange derivative transactions with the intention to speculate, as Chui et al (2014) report. In fact, they made hedge contracts that had lower costs, but were more risky, once they would be forced to sell their dollars at below market prices if domestic currency depreciated. As these companies were betting on a continued appreciation of local currencies, they engaged in several of those contracts, but once their domestic currency depreciated after 2008, they were forced to execute their positions, incurring in losses. Thus, companies which adopt a strategy to increase balance sheet exposure to foreign currency, but hope that hedge contracts will provide full insurance, may be taking a risky step. This uncertainty occurs because future expectations may not be fulfilled, and in occasions of foreign exchange volatility, market liquidity shrinks and it is more difficult to roll over hedge contracts. Therefore, the availability of funds for hedge is reduced at occasions they are most needed.

Susceptibility to the interests of creditors, banks and institutional investors

Another critical element for emerging market companies is their susceptibility to creditors', banks' and institutional investors' interests. As discussed in the section "Features of Corporate Debt in EMEs," non-financial corporate debt profile has changed over the last years: although bank loans remained the main source of funding, resources obtained through bond markets had a significant increase in their share. This fact adds more complexity to companies' decisions.

Concerning bank loans' funding, banks had to adapt to the new supervisory and regulatory framework after the 2008 crisis, which required, among other things, an increase in capital requirements. According to BIS (2015), banks' core tier 1 expanded on average from 7% in 2011 to 11% in 2014, mainly through retained earnings. However, the scenario of low global interest rates reduced net interest income over the period. In this context of increased capital requirements and downward pressure in profitability, banks, when observed an increase in emerging firms' default ratios, tended to tighten their lending conditions: reduced terms, increased interest rates, and rationed credit. This tightening would further aggravate the problems of indebtedness and defaults among companies.

About companies financing through bond market funding, its expansion in the period did not occur by accident. It is known that raising funds through bond markets has some advantages when compared to bank loans, among which the following: (i) the possibility of issuing debt on better terms (longer maturities, lower interest rates, in some cases in domestic currency); and (ii) a more diversified investor base. However, this form of financing has a particularly volatile nature, since it is characterized by: (i) the influence of investors' procyclical behavior, which may induce herd effects in bond prices; (ii) the presence of collective action problems, since it is more difficult to control capital outflows from a diversified scope of market investors than from a more limited and regulated set of international banks.

Additionally, it is worth mentioning that the rise of finance and institutional investors linked to non-financial corporations' portfolios has strongly influenced their behavior. Within a broader movement of financialization (observed since the 1970s but with increasing importance in more recent decades), it has been shaped a new framework for the structure and management of corporations, the shareholder value. The shareholder value framework submitted corporate governance decisions to financial markets' purposes, and encouraged exacerbation of risky positions by increasing speculation and leverage, according to Lazonic (2004). In this context, corporations increasingly engaged in share buybacks, mergers/acquisitions, dividend payouts, and other strategies to prop up their stock prices and fulfill shareholders' interests. Stock options and other types of incentive-based compensation plans were also implemented in order to align the interests of companies' shareholders and managers. Thus, complying with CEOs' and institutional investors' requests for high earnings in the short term, firms were encouraged to expand financial transactions and riskier operations. Hence, this behavior has left firms more exposed to fluctuations in macroeconomic indicators, financial markets, and asset prices.

Most of the bonds issued by firms were acquired by institutional investors such as insurance funds, pension funds, hedge funds, mutual funds, usually controlled by asset management companies. In general, asset management companies' business models (i.e. the adoption of benchmarks and the importance given to market peers' performance), as well as the investment structures they offer (e.g. collective investment vehicles) encourage short-term behavior that may be disruptive in the face of adverse shocks. In the case of EMEs' asset management companies, this short-term bias is even more pronounced, since the funds they operate have a smaller number of benchmarks and a more correlated profile than their counterparts in advanced economies. As a result, financial shocks are more likely to affect a wide range of investors in EMEs funds simultaneously. Hence, one of the main risks for corporations would be a sudden withdrawal of those investors.

Macroeconomic volatility
Regarding the adversities posed by macroeconomic volatility, it can be noted that emerging economies are more susceptible to shocks and instability, due to their structural characteristics. First, it is clear that emerging firms have higher funding costs in international markets. BIS data (2016a) shows that corporate spreads paid by emerging firms are consistently higher than those paid by US and European companies when compared to their peers in high-yield and investment-grade markets. This fact is generally associated with their nations' sovereign spreads, which impose them a clear competitive disadvantage in international markets. Another sign of deterioration in emerging countries firms' credit perspective is the increase in the number of downgrades performed by rating agencies in recent years. They may face higher losses because spreads/credit ratings of similar sectors/countries were negatively affected, even if their own conditions have not changed. Actually, at a time of many uncertainties in the international economy, it is expected that emerging markets are more subject to large movements in capital flows and, consequently, to exchange rate volatility. Once we compare data from foreign exchange volatility (VXY Index) for emerging currencies and for G7 currencies, we note that emerging market currencies are more volatile on most occasions during the period 2000–2016. It is important to mention that such a scenario is riskier for emerging market companies, because it may increase their debts' amounts and service payments, and also affect loans' refinancing conditions.

Economic Policy Implications

Since financial crises experienced in the 1990s, emerging countries have sought to implement a number of defense mechanisms to prevent external crises. From companies' point of view, they expanded their amount of private assets held abroad. However, in times of instability, the main shortcoming of this mechanism is its low liquidity.

From governments' point of view, they have also made an effort to create a series of sovereign lines of defense against potential external macroeconomic and financial risks. One set of lines of defense that can be mentioned was the accumulation of foreign reserves – which increased as an average in EMEs from 10% of GDP in the mid-1990s to 30% in 2014, according to BIS (2015) – as well as currency swap agreements between central banks and precautionary lines with multilateral institutions (e.g. the IMF). However, there are problems with this set of mechanisms: (i) the difficulty in directing official foreign exchange reserves to solve liquidity shortages in the private sector; (ii) governments' reluctance to use official reserves, for reasons of not wanting to convey wrong incentives to agents or to run out of tools in case of a deeper crisis; (iii) resistance to signing assistance programs with the IMF, once those programs are generally associated with tough conditionalities.

A second set of safeguards was a reform in the macroeconomic framework, which incorporated in many countries monetary policy with an inflation targeting regime, fiscal rules, and a flexible exchange rate system. On the one hand, this new macroeconomic framework has turned emerging markets more solid under international investors' view, as they perceived emerging countries with more tools and flexibility to deal with problems arising from external shocks. Note that on such occasions, the usual policy recommendations would be: (i) more restrictive monetary policy; (ii) countercyclical fiscal policy; and (iii) more flexible exchange rates.

On the other hand, it is known that macroeconomic policies are only partial shields to crises episodes. In particular, in the case of monetary policy, although it can be tightened to prevent asset price booms and an increase in leverage, this tightening is not a good alternative when is done very quickly, because the forced contraction could result in losses in output/employment and a higher foreign debt level. Moreover, it can become ineffective in occasions of adverse international financial conditions and strong capital outflows, with the rise in interest rates turning indebted companies even more vulnerable. Regarding fiscal policy, emerging countries at the moment do not have the same "fiscal space" for countercyclical policies they had right after the 2008 crisis, as governments are dealing with issues related to the increase in public deficits/debts since then. Moreover, fiscal instruments usually have more obstacles to be implemented, once they require parliamentary approval. Nevertheless, some authors suggest changes in tax laws that may inhibit an excessive increase in agents' debt levels. First, removing tax incentives for companies to raise funds through debt rather than equity, which exist in several countries (BIS, 2016b). Second, in times of economic growth, the imposition of higher tax rates for more leveraged companies and lower tax rates for less leveraged firms. The resources collected with such taxes should be destined to a fund that would serve as a liquidity buffer to be used in times of financial adversity (BIS, 2015). However, in this second case, the real effectiveness of this measure cannot be ensured, once it has not been tested yet. Therefore, emerging countries have the challenge – beyond traditional macroeconomic policies to prevent external and domestic vulnerabilities – to adopt actions to mitigate currency mismatch and high leverage in their firms. These actions should be implemented not only through monetary and fiscal policies, but also with an improvement in regulatory frameworks, as well as macro- and micro-prudential measures, preferably on a coordinated basis, as it will be argued in the sequence.

Improvement in regulatory frameworks

Recognizing the existence of regulatory shortcomings is a key factor to try to solve problems that became clear since the 2008 crisis. Regulatory actions adopted since then (i.e. Basel III rules) have not been able to properly address problems such as excessive leverage growth and procyclical behavior of the whole financial sector. In this sense, there is a demand for additional reforms on regulatory frameworks. In order to monitor systemic risks more appropriately, one has to consider the increasing interconnectedness between the various participants in the financial system. Hence, the potential range of regulation needs to be broadened to all financial activities, especially in the non-banking sector. As suggested by Auvray, Dallery and Rigot (2016), more regulation is needed over institutional investors (insurance companies, pension funds, hedge funds, mutual funds), generally controlled by asset management companies. For the case of asset management companies, it would be advisable to adopt the following measures, according to BIS (2015): (i) impose restrictions on fast redemptions and sudden changes in funds' portfolio composition, that would reduce liquidity risks and serve as stabilizers in temporary adverse shocks; (ii) establish limits on leverage, seeking to contain the amplification of shocks; and (iii) encourage the extension of managers' investment horizon and the implementation of precautionary buffers, which would increase the capacity of these companies to absorb losses.

Another issue to be developed is the improvement of financial/non-financial institutions' resolution schemes, in order to establish proper roles for public/private participation in such schemes, to mitigate financial stability risks/moral hazard with government support. Regulators need to be able to enforce restructuring or closure of institutions which face financial problems or bankruptcy. According to the IMF (2015), legal frameworks should be improved, so that regulatory agencies have mandates and tools consistent with their objectives. Their duties and responsibilities need to be clear for future accountability. Obviously, many corporate interests can be challenged in a reform of resolution frameworks, so that political lobbies may create obstacles for the implementation of the necessary reforms (i.e. limits for "too big to fail" institutions).

Macroprudential actions

Macroprudential actions can be implemented with two primary objectives: enhancing the resilience of the financial sector (measures to avoid the buildup of financial imbalances and significant exposure against financial shocks), or smoothing the credit cycle (countercyclical actions to mitigate an expected credit boom or bust). There is a wide variety of macroprudential tools, but for each one of those objectives, there would be some set of measures that would be more appropriate. In the case of enhancing the resilience of financial sector, authors such as Claessens et al (2014) and Boar et al (2017) argue in favor of: (i) capital-based instruments (countercyclical capital requirements, leverage restrictions, general or dynamic provisioning) and (ii) liquidity-based requirements. When the goal is to smooth the credit cycle, those authors support: (i) asset-side instruments (credit growth limits, maximum debt-service-to-income ratios, limits to bank exposures to individual agents, such as maximum loan-to-value ratios); (ii) changes in reserve requirements; and (iii) currency instruments (limits on foreign exchange exposure, net open positions and differential treatment of deposit accounts in foreign currency).

Evidence in the literature is broadly in favor of the use of macroprudential policies, when implemented in a proper way. Boar et al (2017) show that countries that implement macroprudential policies have stronger and less volatile GDP growth. Claessens et al (2014) show that measures destined to control credit growth over borrowers (debt-to-income, loan-to-value ratios) and financial institutions (limits on credit growth, foreign currency lending) are effective on preventing excessive asset growth. Gambacorta and Murcia (2017) show that macroprudential policies are effective in stabilizing credit cycles, with propagation effects for measures aimed at smoothing the credit cycle (average of one quarter) more rapid than for measures aimed at enhancing the resilience of the financial sector (average of one year). However, those actions are not perfect and can generate distortions when not implemented in an adequate way. Still, one can affirm that when properly implemented, those policies are important tools for monitoring risks in the economy from a systemic point of view. They also turn companies' balance sheets more solid, as well as their interactions with banks and other agents of the economy.

As each country has its own institutional framework and economic condition, one cannot prescribe a "single book" of recommendations, valid for all countries at the same time, or even for emerging countries as a whole, due to their very diverse nature. However, some researchers, such as the authors of IMF (2015), point to a general set of guidelines for macroprudential initiatives that would be interesting to be taken by emerging countries on a preventive basis, in order to avoid excessive risk-taking by EMEs companies. In the short term, the proposed actions would be to limit corporate risks with leverage and foreign exchange exposure, and their impacts on other interrelated sectors, such as banks. For example, reserve requirements/risk weights over certain assets could be increased, as well as limits for leverage in real estate markets (debt-to-income and debt-service coverage ratios) and foreign exchange positions could be introduced. Capital flow management measures, to deal with excessive flows that pose systemic financial risks, could also be considered. In the long term, other measures would be recommended, among which: (i) changes in tax codes, removing tax benefits in favor of excessive debt growth; (ii) promoting the development of local financial markets with proper regulation, and encouraging greater participation of domestic investors.

Micro-prudential actions

At the micro-prudential level, supervisory authorities should improve data collection mechanisms from financial and non-financial companies. In particular, promote an improvement in the measurement and disclosure of data related to foreign exchange exposure, hedge and offshore issuances, which in many emerging countries are still inadequate. Monitoring should also include stress tests, where interest rate/exchange rate volatility and currency mismatches are considered, according to IMF (2015). Supervisory authorities should increase the accuracy of their tools of control and analysis, because as seen in the 2008 crisis, the opacity of balance sheets led to an increase in financial system's instability. Those authorities need to consider in their analysis that liquidity risk can become insolvency risk for each individual institution. Aspect to be highlighted is that more attention should be given to tail risk. The 2008 crisis demonstrated that VaR (Value at Risk) models have failed to determine the magnitude of the losses observed.

In terms of incentives, there is a need to reduce stimulus to excessive borrowing/lending of certain types. For instance, avoid incentives for companies in non-tradable sectors to borrow in foreign currency. In these situations, those companies have local currency revenues, but liabilities in foreign currency, which render them more exposed to default risks in occasions of domestic currency depreciation.

Coordinated actions

Despite the efforts to improve the efficiency and reduce the asymmetries of the global financial regulatory framework, each country has its particular institutional arrangement and current economic situation, and hence implements its own set of regulations and macro-/micro-prudential measures. Regarding macroprudential policies, one of the shortcomings they present is that, when adopted on an ad hoc and temporary basis, to act on specific market segments, those policies allow agents to discover ways to evade/circumvent them, opening the doors for regulatory arbitrage. Moreover, their improper use can lead to distortions in other economic sectors in the same country or other countries.

Therefore, a first recommendation would be to seek greater coordination in countries' regulatory frameworks, in order to avoid loopholes, and that macroprudential policies targeted to a specific sector or country do not harm other sectors/countries. Second, instead of adopting macroprudential measures on a reactive, ad hoc, and temporary basis, choose to implement them preventively, jointly and on a medium-/long-term basis. Thus, such measures could act on an ex-ante way (preventing imbalances), and be continuously monitored and assessed to correct eventual distortions and ensure proper calibration, so that their overall objectives are achieved in the long term (IMF, 2013).

Besides, due to the close relationship between macroprudential and financial supervision with antitrust, fiscal and monetary policies, it is advocated for improvement in the coordination among those policies. In particular, with appropriate coordination between monetary and macroprudential policies, central banks and financial supervision authorities could take balanced decisions in the two spheres, being able to ensure macroeconomic and financial stability at the same time (BIS, 2016b). Another good example of properly coordinated actions would be the creation of mechanisms that drive companies' incentives to less short-term/speculative actions, and more towards medium-long term/real investments. A way to do so would be to implement proper industrial policies, with the support of institutions such as national/multilateral development banks, which can provide more adequate conditions for financing development in the long term. Policies should target strategic sectors: infrastructure, health, education, SMEs, "decent jobs" creation, innovation/technology, energy/ecological transition. Such policies could reduce financial stability concerns, and at the same time foster more private/public investments in the real economy, towards sustained economic growth.

CONCLUSIONS

This study explored corporate debt expansion in emerging markets after the 2008 crisis, its profile, main determinants, the challenges faced by firms related to this issue, and discussed economic policy implications for those countries. Some of the main features of this expansion in EMEs corporate debt were the increase in leverage, net foreign exchange exposure, later leading to a deterioration of debt repayment capacity in a significant share of firms. Those features would have as a common point agents' procyclical behavior, being in accordance with theoretical approaches that have been well described both in the mainstream and heterodox literature, related to concepts such as the risk-taking channel of monetary policy, herd behavior, animal spirits, Keynesian "beauty contest", and financial instability hypothesis.

Our contributions to the literature are to investigate the determinants of EMEs corporate debt expansion by using a dataset which goes from 2000 Q1 up to a more recent period (2016 Q4), and with subsamples before and after the 2008 crisis, so we identify the main changes in the factors that explain EMEs corporate debt expansion before and after this event. Most importantly, we identify a factor which was not previously used in the literature for that purpose: the interaction between higher commodity prices and more appreciated exchange rates. Our findings suggest that the exchange rate has been one of the most important determinants that explain the increase in EMEs companies' debt through the period 2000–2016, and also in the period before the 2008 crisis. But after 2008, beyond some country-level factors (exchange rate, national GDP growth, firms' higher liquidity levels), other factors that have global origins (more accommodative monetary policy stance in the USA, lower financial market volatility, global GDP growth, higher commodity prices and its interaction with the exchange rate appreciation) have become increasingly important to explain emerging market corporate debt expansion.

Hence, if EMEs companies are more sensitive to the movements of the global economy, a reversal of international favorable conditions may generate adverse effects, increasing firms' borrowing costs, worsening debt rollover conditions and weakening their balance sheets. In this context, difficulties posed by the international economic scenario – uncertainties in major economies (the USA, China, Europe) as well as large swings in emerging currencies and commodity prices – together with problems related to currency mismatch; susceptibility to the interests of creditors/institutional investors/banks and macroeconomic volatility may put into question the financial sustainability of these companies. Moreover, it was seen that, although in recent decades several macroeconomic lines of defense have been developed by EMEs governments to combat economic/financial crises, the capacity of such lines to fulfill private firms' needs in occasions of crises is uncertain, due to the problems mentioned.

Ultimately, we draw attention to the need for policies oriented not only to enhance macroeconomic fundamentals, but also to improve regulatory frameworks, as well as micro and macroprudential instruments. They should be implemented in a coordinated way, in order to strengthen the monitoring of individual and systemic risks, increasing balance sheets resilience. Therefore, emerging countries would have better tools to face new financial crises, attenuating the moments of greater instability, and could pursue better strategies towards sustainable growth in the medium-/long-term.

REFERENCES

Adair, P. and M. Adaskou (2015), "Trade-off-theory vs. pecking order theory and the determinants of corporate leverage: evidence from a panel data analysis upon French SMEs (2002–2010)," *Cogent Economics & Finance*, 3 (1), 1–12.

Allison, P. (2012), "When Can You Safely Ignore Multicollinearity?," accessed 20 November 2017 at https://statisticalhorizons.com/multicollinearity.

Alter, A. and S. Elekdag (2016), "Emerging Market Corporate Leverage and Global Financial Conditions," IMF Working Paper Series No 16/243, Washington, December.

Auvray, T., T. Dallery and S. Rigot (2016), *L' Entreprise Liquidée. La finance contre l'investissement*, Paris, France: Michalon.

Avdjiev, S., M. Chui and H.S. Shin (2014), "Non-financial corporations from emerging market economies and capital flows," *BIS Quarterly Review December 2014*, Basel, December.

Bank for International Settlements – BIS (2015), "85th Annual Report, 1 April 2014–31 March 2015," Basel, June.

Bank for International Settlements – BIS (2016a), "Uneasy Calm Gives Way to Turbulence," *BIS Quarterly Review March 2016*, Basel, March.

Bank for International Settlements – BIS (2016b), "86th Annual Report, 1 April 2015–31 March 2016," Basel, June.

Bank for International Settlements – BIS (2017), "BIS Statistical Bulletin June 2017," Basel, June.

Boar, C., L. Gambacorta, G. Lombardo and L.A.P. Silva (2017), "What are the effects of macroprudential policies on macroeconomic performance," *BIS Quarterly Review September 2017*, Basel, September.

Bruno, V. and H.S. Shin (2015), "Capital flows and the risk taking channel of monetary policy," *Journal of Monetary Economics*, 71 (C), 119–32.

Chui, M., I. Fender and V. Sushko (2014), "Risks related to EME corporate balance sheets: the role of leverage and currency mismatch," *BIS Quarterly Review September 2014,* Basel, September.

Claessens, S., S. Ghosh and R. Mihet (2014), "Macro-Prudential Policies to Mitigate Financial System Vulnerabilities," IMF Working Paper No 14/155, August.

Feyen, E., S. Ghosh, K. Kibuuka and S. Farazi (2015), "Public Global Liquidity and External Bond Issuance in Emerging Markets and Developing Economies," World Bank Policy Research Working Paper WPS No 7363, Washington, July.

Gambacorta, L. and A. Murcia (2017), "The impact of macroprudential policies and their interaction with monetary policy: an empirical analysis using credit registry data," BIS Working Papers No 636, May.

International Monetary Fund – IMF (2013), "Key Aspects of Macroprudential Policy," Washington, June.

International Monetary Fund – IMF (2015), "Global Financial Stability Report – Vulnerabilities, Legacies and Policy Challenges: Risks Rotating to Emerging Markets," Washington, October.

International Monetary Fund – IMF (2016), "Global Financial Stability Report – Fostering Stability in a Low-Growth, Low-Rate Era," Washington, October.

Keynes, J.M. (1936), *The General Theory of Interest, Employment and Money*, London, UK: Macmillan Publishers.

Kohlscheen, E., F. Avalos and A. Schrimpf (2017), "When the walk is not random: commodity prices and exchange rates," *International Journal of Central Banking*, 13 (2), 121–58.

Kripnner, L. (2016), "Comparison of international monetary policy measures," RBNZ Additional Research, accessed 1 November 2017 at http://www.rbnz.govt.nz/research-and-publications/research-programme/additional-research/measures-of-the-stance-of-united-states-monetary-policy/comparison-of-international-monetary-policy-measures.

Lazonic, W. (2004), "Corporate restructuring," in Ackroyd, S., R. Batt, P. Thompson and P. Tolbert (eds), *The Oxford Handbook of Work and Organization*, Oxford, UK: Oxford University Press.

Lo Duca, M., J. Nicolleti and A.V. Martinez (2016), "Global corporate bond issuance: what role for US quantitative easing?," *Journal of International Money and Finance*, 60 (C), 114–50.

McCauley, R., P. McGuire and V. Sushko (2015a), "Dollar credit to emerging market economies," *BIS Quarterly Review December 2015*, Basel, December.

McCauley, R., P. McGuire and V. Sushko (2015b), "Global dollar credit: links to US monetary policies and leverage," BIS Working Papers No 483, January.

Minsky, H. P. (1978), "The financial instability hypothesis: a restatement," in *Thames Papers in Political Economy*, London, UK: North East London Polytechnic.

Organisation for Economic Co-operation and Development – OECD (2017), "Resilience in a time of high debt," *OECD Economic Outlook*, Volume 2017 Issue 2, Paris: OECD Publishing, pp. 55–96.

Rey, H (2015), "Dilemma not trilemma: the global cycle and monetary policy independence," NBER Working Paper No 21162, May.

Serena, J.M. and R. Moreno (2016), "Domestic financial markets and offshore bond finance," *BIS Quarterly Review September 2016*, Basel, September.

APPENDIX

Table 10.A1 Results for model with full country sample and model without China specification without interaction

	Dependent variable: debt to equity					
Independent variables	**2000 Q1–2016 Q4**		**2000 Q1–2007 Q4**		**2009 Q1–2016 Q4**	
	Full country sample	Without China	Full country sample	Without China	Full country sample	Without China
	Country					
Return on assets (1 lag)	**0.029*****	**0.024*****	**0.045*****	**0.049*****	0.011	0.003
	(0.011)	(0.012)	(0.013)	(0.014)	(0.010)	(0.012)
Free cash flow/ short- and long- term Debt (1 lag)	0.002	0.001	**0.010***	**0.010***	0.002	0.001
	(0.003)	(0.003)	(0.005)	(0.006)	(0.002)	(0.002)
Tangible assets per share (1 lag)	**0.024***	**0.037***	0.006	0.023	**0.028***	**0.039***
	(0.013)	(0.014)	(0.013)	(0.017)	(0.017)	(0.017)
Current ratio (1 lag)	**0.109*****	**0.112*****	0.038	0.018	**0.188*****	**0.180*****
	(0.023)	(0.025)	(0.027)	(0.030)	(0.021)	(0.023)
Real GDP growth	0.001	0.002	0.006	0.010	**0.009*****	**0.005*****
	(0.004)	(0.004)	(0.007)	(0.007)	(0.003)	(0.003)
Monetary policy rate	−0.015	−0.015	−0.024	−0.015	−0.004	−0.017
	(0.018)	(0.018)	(0.023)	(0.025)	(0.016)	(0.015)
REER	**0.396*****	**0.421*****	**0.591*****	**0.568*****	**0.131*****	**0.181*****
	(0.068)	(0.071)	(0.095)	(0.107)	(0.047)	(0.058)

Table 10.A1 (continued)

Independent variables	**Dependent variable: debt to equity**					
	2000 Q1–2016 Q4		**2000 Q1–2007 Q4**		**2009 Q1–2016 Q4**	
	Full country sample	Without China	Full country sample	Without China	Full country sample	Without China
			Global			
US shadow short rate	**−0.009****	**−0.009****	−0.004	−0.015	**−0.008******	**−0.007******
	(0.005)	(0.005)	(0.033)	(0.040)	(0.002)	(0.002)
UK shadow short rate	−0.000	−0.001	−0.300	−0.224	**−0.003****	**−0.002****
	(0.003)	(0.003)	(0.088)	(0.110)	(0.001)	(0.001)
EUR shadow short rate	−0.002	−0.008	−0.222	−0.227	−0.006	−0.003
	(0.012)	(0.012)	(0.085)	(0.105)	(0.005)	(0.004)
Japan shadow short rate	−0.013	−0.016	−0.017	−0.013	−0.041	−0.033
	(0.007)	(0.007)	(0.006)	(0.007)	(0.008)	(0.008)
Global GDP growth	0.008	0.006	0.022	0.039	0.004	0.001
	(0.010)	(0.010)	(0.037)	(0.045)	(0.004)	(0.004)
Commodity price	0.065	0.077	0.109	0.113	0.020	0.046
	(0.041)	(0.043)	(0.063)	(0.079)	(0.026)	(0.026)
VIX	**−0.034******	**−0.027******	**−0.068****	**−0.096****	**−0.024******	**−0.018******
	(0.009)	(0.010)	(0.015)	(0.018)	(0.005)	(0.004)
			Other information			
Number of quarters	66	66	30	30	32	32
Observations	913	847	373	343	480	448
R2 (GLS weighted)	0.092	0.098	0.204	0.209	0.316	0.275

Note: P values: *, **, ***, denote statistical significance at the 10, 5 and 1 percent level, respectively.

11. From trilemma to dilemma: monetary policy after the Bretton Woods world[1]

Hasan Cömert

INTRODUCTION

The gold standard implemented in the 19th century collapsed at the beginning of World War I. After 1918, several attempts to return to the gold standard failed. The Great Depression and the succeeding developments made the return to the gold standard impossible.

With the end of World War II, a new international institutional structure was sought under the leadership of the US and the United Kingdom. This search resulted in a treaty signed in 1944 in the town of Bretton Woods (BW). With the BW treaty, a new phase began in the Western world economy.

In this chapter, we will investigate factors affecting the independence (effectiveness) of monetary policies during and after the BW system. We use the concept of independent monetary policy to include the effects of central bank policies on key macroeconomic variables.[2] In this respect, we use monetary policy independence and effectiveness synonymously throughout the text.

The main arguments of the chapter are as follows: It is possible to talk about the relatively independent (effective) monetary policy under the BW system. The concept of trilemma (impossible trinity), suggesting that out of three concepts of independent monetary policy, free movement of capital, and fixed exchange rate regime only two can exist at the same time, may be useful to understand the BW period. Conventional interpretation implies that under fixed exchange rate regimes, capital controls made independent monetary policy possible during the BW period. However, if independent monetary policy prevailed under the BW system, besides controls on capital movements, it is necessary to mention two more factors that made independent monetary policy possible:

(a) Domestic financial markets were relatively under tight controls and,
(b) Central banks utilized multiple instruments.

The effectiveness of monetary policy in the post-BW system suffered considerable damage both in developed and developing countries whereas conventional theory suggests that the transition to flexible exchange rate regimes in response to the liberalization of capital movements was sufficient for monetary policy independence. In other words, according to this view, the concept of the trilemma retains its explanatory power in the post-BW period. However, contrary to this view, the process after BW can be interpreted as a convergence process to dilemma, implying that exchange rate regimes became irrelevant, especially in developing countries. While financial markets and capital movements have reached enormous sizes, central bank policy choices based only on overnight interest rates have contributed to the reduction of central banks' effectiveness in both developed and developing countries. The unorthodox policies implemented after the global financial crisis in both advanced and developing countries can be considered a partial realization of the dilemma by central banks.

There has been growing number of studies on trilemma and dilemma (Obstfeld et al. 2005; Aizenman et al. 2008; Aizenman, 2011; Georgiadis and Mehl, 2015; Klein and Shambaugh, 2015; Obstfeld, 2015; Rey 2015) some of which will be discussed in the text in detail. This study tries to interpret the BW period and afterwards from a different perspective based on the findings of existing literature and the author's previous studies. Our study has many affinities with Rey (2015). She (2015) states that central banks in developing countries under the influence of financial flows cannot follow independent monetary policy. She claims that it is dilemma rather than trilemma. We highlight that even under the BW system, monetary policy independence was related to the institutional structure in addition to the capital controls. Dramatic changes in central banking practices and in domestic financial markets have contributed to the post-BW developments significantly alongside capital liberalization. Financial flows have played a central role in this process in developing countries. However, it is increasing capacity of financial institutions to expand their balance sheets almost without limit has been the driving force in advanced countries. In this sense, although the dilemma has been much more apparent for developing countries, advanced countries have not been insulated from this process.

Furthermore, Rey (2015) puts too much emphasis on the Fed rate as an important determinant of global cycles. However, the Fed rate has also gradually lost its power to influence developments in the US markets. Our perspective is a more evolutionary, institutional and Post-Keynesian. We argue that the effectiveness (either short- or long-term) of a central bank mainly depends on the institutional framework in which the central bank operates. The institutional framework is largely determined by the interaction among the regulatory framework, the central bank's choice of tools, international conditions and other dynamic forces within the financial system. Under different combinations of these forces, the degree of the influence of a central bank over the domestic economy can vary. Therefore, monetary policy discussions should be institutionally and historically specific. As Minsky (1957:171) puts it aptly: "[. . .] if a period of rapid changes in the structure or in the mode of functioning of financial markets occurs, then the efficacy of central bank actions has to be reexamined."[3] There is no such a theory that can equip economists to understand monetary policy and its interaction with the financial system in all periods. Indeed, As Hicks (1967:156) stated, "monetary theory is less abstract than most economic theory. It cannot avoid a relation to reality [. . .]. It belongs to monetary history, in a way that economic theory does not always belong to economic history."

It is necessary to examine some of the claims of the chapter in more detail, both theoretically and empirically. However, there is a significant amount of evidence that directly or indirectly supports the main argument of the article.

The outline of the chapter is as follows. In the second part, briefly, the emergence of the BW, how it functioned and how monetary policy during the BW period can be investigated by the concept of trilemma will be explained in detail. The third section will explain the collapse of the BW system and changes in central banking, financial markets and financial flows after the BW. Then, focusing on developments in the period after the BW, the fourth section will try to assess the changes in the effectiveness of central banking. The last part will conclude.

BW AND MONETARY POLICY

Emergence and Functioning of the BW System

During the 19th century, the gold and silver system (bimetallism) and the silver system were abandoned by many countries and the gold standard became a complete international monetary system between 1880 and 1914. During this period, especially England did not hesitate to take the necessary steps to support this system. The economic and financial strength of the United Kingdom led other countries to follow its policies. The main driver of this system was England while the other countries followed Britain.

In addition, since it was perceived as a necessary condition for attaining international credits to comply with the gold standard, other countries were generally loyal to the gold standard under the leadership of the United Kingdom. Some studies claim that some of the countries violated the rules by manipulating discount rates even under the gold standard (Bloomfield, 1959). However, other studies suggest that until 1914, discretionary policies were not used extensively to threaten the system and, if used in an emergency, they soon returned to the old rules (Schwartz, 1984).

The efforts to return to the gold standard in the 1920s did not succeed due to various reasons. These include the existence of two reserve currencies, lack of leadership, and lack of coordination between strong countries. These can be added to the fact that France and the United States had been supporting deflationary pressures around the world by sterilizing their balance of payment surpluses (Bordo, 1993).

The system in this period can be called the gold-exchange standard. The difference between this system and the gold standard was that some currencies could be converted at a fixed price to another currency that is convertible in gold. In this system, less gold reserves were supposed to be needed than the classical gold standard.

At the end of the Second World War, efforts for a new international monetary system began. The aim is to avoid the uncertainties and crises that occurred after 1914. The treaty was signed on July 1, 1944, in the town of Bretton Woods, USA. With this agreement, the foundations of the IMF and the World Bank were laid as well. The new system aimed at the stability of the exchange rates as in the case of the gold standard. However, capital controls were one of the backbones of the new system, whereas the gold standard was based on free financial flows. According to this system, the participating countries will set parity and apply the monetary policy to allow this parity to fluctuate upwards and downwards by only one percent. The parity may be changed by participants up to 10 percent after consulting the IMF for serious imbalances or by prior notice.

According to the BW agreement, while capital controls are possible, member states must allow convertibility of their currencies after a certain period of time. Exchange controls may continue during the transition period. Member countries can use funds from the IMF to help resolve short- and medium-term balance of payments problems. To this end, a common pool of funds has been established in which all member states participate at certain levels. According to the treaty, the value of 35 US dollars was fixed to an ounce of gold. The other members' currencies are practically fixed in terms of dollars. This system can be called a pegged exchange rate system, since member countries have the ability to change exchange rates in times of major problems.

It is possible to separate the BW system into two main periods. The first period covers 1946–1958 (pre-convertible) years, while the second period covers 1959–1971. The full convertibility was achieved in 1958. For a long time, currencies outside of the US dollar were not convertible. This was related to the fact that two thirds of the world's gold reserves were concentrated in the US and other countries did not have enough dollar reserves due to their current account deficits. In the midst of the 1950s, Marshall's plan played an important role in the overcoming of this situation as the European countries began to have current account surpluses.

After 1958, the BW system became fully functional. During the BW period, many countries maintained restrictions on capital movements. However, after the mid-1960s, capital controls were being used more widely in the United States, while the frequency of controls in other countries gradually decreased (Bordo, 1993).

Understanding the Monetary Policy Under the BW System

As can be seen, the two basic backbones of the BW system were fixed exchange rate regimes and capital controls. The general belief is that central banks can implement an independent monetary policy under the BW system (Obstfeld et al. 2005). This is illustrated by the concept of trilemma (impossible trinity) (Figure 11.1). According to the literature, in the period of the "classical gold system" (1880–1914), capital mobility and fixed exchange rate regime (the two points at the base of the triangle) were preferred. In the BW period, while the capital mobility was abandoned, fixed exchange rate and independent monetary policy (left two corners)

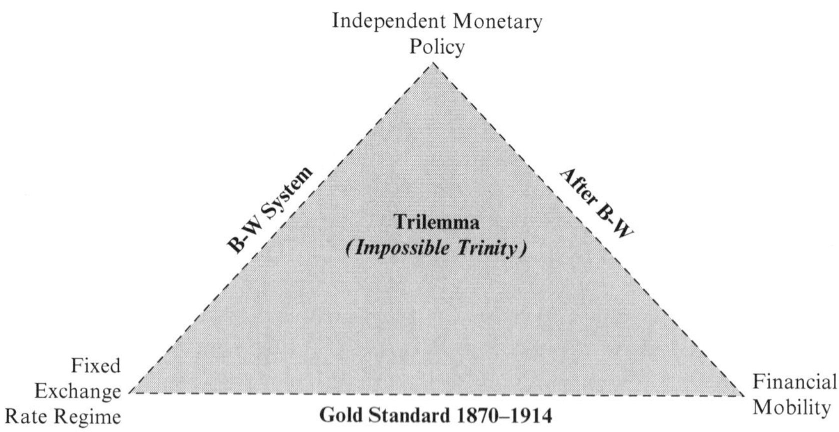

Figure 11.1 Original trilemma framework

were preferred. Thus, monetary policy independence is assumed to be provided simply by the controls on capital movements under fixed exchange rate regimes.

Similarly, as will be discussed in detail below, the trilemma implies that after the BW system period, the fixed exchange rate regime is abandoned at the expense of capital mobility. In this approach, there is no distinction between independent monetary policy and monetary policy effectiveness. Independent monetary policy is defined as the ability to set the interest rates (short-term) independently of foreign interest rates. This is considered enough to reach domestic targets. Accordingly, in general, the independence of the monetary policy is basically measured by looking at the correlation between the domestic interest rates and foreign interest rates (Aizenman et al. 2008). Low correlation between the domestic policy rate and Fed/ECB interest rate is considered as an indication of independent monetary policy. High correlation means lack of monetary independence.

This framework implies that under the right combination of capital mobility and exchange rate regimes, central bank instruments (in particular interest rates) have a capacity of influencing the ultimate targets such as inflation and national income (even if in the short-run) through determining market interest rates, credit expansion and expectations. Theoretically, the classical Mundell-Fleming (MF) model (IS/LM model) or the variants of this model have been used to support the trilemma. In this model, it is possible to determine the domestic interest rates differently from the world interest rates under the fixed exchange rate regimes with capital controls. When capital movements are free, domestic interest rates should be equal to world interest rates. International interest rates are affected by mainly very advanced countries.

The mechanism operates as follows: If a central bank wants to implement an expansionary monetary policy, domestic interest rates will decline. If financial flows are free, when the domestic interest rates fall below the foreign interest rates, ceteris paribus, there will be a reversal in financial flows due to the fact that the returns on foreign financial assets are higher than those of domestic assets. This situation put downward pressure on the value of the domestic currency. Central banks aiming at keeping exchange rates constant have to use foreign exchange reserves. In theory, it is expected that foreign exchange sales will reduce the money supply in the domestic market and bring interest rates back to world interest rates. In other words, monetary policy is not effective when there is a fixed exchange rate regime with free capital mobility. The effectiveness of monetary policy takes place only by giving up free capital movements or fixed exchange rate regime. Under the BW system, capital mobility is the parameter given up. Alternatively, under the assumption that domestic interest rates can be strongly and predictably influenced by central banks, different versions of uncovered interest rate parity which has been one of the backbones of current international macroeconomics imply trilemma as well. Although this framework has its own problems, one does not have to assume exogenous money supply within this framework.[4]

However, as Minsky and Hicks imply, without paying enough attention to the institutional structure and actual functioning of central banks, the trilemma framework can only give an incomplete and sometimes misleading picture. If central banks followed an independent monetary policy under BW, there are two other important factors that might have complemented capital controls. First, central banks used a multi-tool set during the BW period. Second, domestic capital markets were relatively under tight control during the same period.

Central banks concentrated not only on short-term interest rates such as overnight interest rates in the BW period but also on a wide range of policy instruments. For example, in the United States, as part of the "Regulation Q," ceilings on interest rates were actively used (Volcker, 2002). Similarly, credit controls were implemented in the United States and many other countries whenever it was deemed to be necessary. Margin requirement was another tool used to influence the dynamics of financial markets. According to Shiller (2000), margin requirements were one of the most active means used by the Fed before the 1980s. In addition, reserve requirements were actively used to influence banks' credit expansion decisions (Feinman, 1993; Cömert, 2013). Discount rates were the preferred means of influencing the liquidity demand in the banking sector. European countries and Japan did not lag behind the United States in using multi-monetary policy instruments. In a series of studies, Gerald Epstein (2006 and 2013), shows that many developing countries after 1945 also resorted to various monetary policies to influence financial markets and reach developmental goals in an institutional framework in which state run banks were the dominant financial actors in these countries.

During BW, central banks did not use only a large set of tools; they also conducted monetary policies in relatively more regulated national financial markets. For example, the Glass–Steagall Act introduced in the United States in 1933, separated investment banks and commercial banking with strict lines. Thus, US authorities tried to prevent commercial banks from directly or indirectly dealing with assets such as bonds and stocks (Barth et al. 2000). During this period, the banking system in the US and Western countries focused on collecting deposits and providing real sector loans. During the period state-owned banks, which can be more easily affected by central banks, made up an important part of the financial system, especially in many European countries (Eichengreen, 2005). In addition,

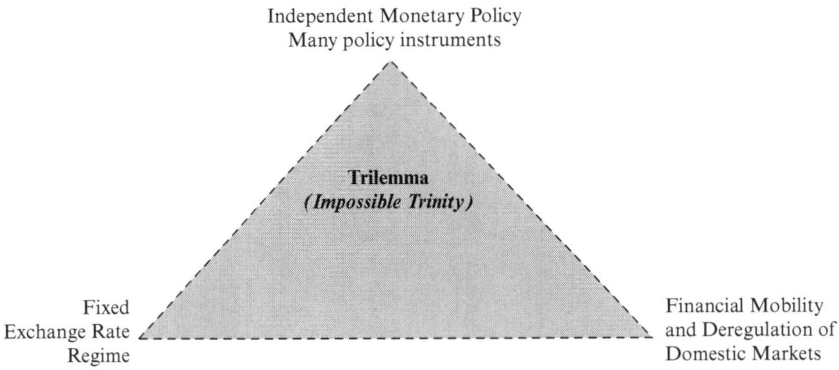

Figure 11.2 Modified trilemma under the BW system

central banks and other relevant institutions have implemented the existing rules more stringently than in the post-BW period (Cömert, 2013).

Given the central banks' use of multiple instruments and tighter supervision of the financial markets, trilemma under BW can be revised as in Figure 11.2. The common point between this figure and the previous one is that the fixed exchange rate regime and capital controls were implemented although the effectiveness of capital controls decreased gradually. Figure 11.2, in addition to Figure 11.1, emphasizes multiple central bank instruments and regulated financial markets. This figure implies that under the BW period when capital flows were relatively limited and internal markets were tightly controlled; central banks have more possibilities to effectively use multiple policy instruments in their hands to reach national macro targets.

THE COLLAPSE OF THE BW SYSTEM AND MONETARY POLICY IN POST-BW ERA

The Collapse of the BW System

However, the BW system, which provided an institutionally more favorable framework for the implementation of the monetary policy, began to erode over time. Various reasons for this have been put forward in the literature. Here we will briefly mention some of the main factors.

Many authors (Triffin, 1960; Kenen, 1960; Gilbert, 1968) argue that the gold-dollar system could not be stable because world gold production was below the total production of goods and services. In cases where the gold supply is insufficient, it is expected that the price of an ounce of gold (35 dollars) will increase. However, the BW system gradually became a fixed exchange rate system due to concerns regarding the trust and cost problems of frequent adjustments in exchange rates (Bordo, 1993).

The dollar supply must increase in order for the system to function properly. The increase in dollar supply depends on the current account deficit or overall balance of payments deficits (excluding reserves) of the main reserve currency country. Although the US gave the current account surplus, US net financial account was negative from 1958 to the end of the BW system, due to massive capital outflows. This implies an increase in the supply of dollars outside the US. However, the Triffin Dilemma suggests meeting the liquidity needs of the world markets through US deficits cannot be the long term solution to the problem caused by low gold supply. The Triffin Dilemma claims that even if it is necessary to increase the dollar supply, giving high current account deficits for a long time can undermine confidence in the reserve currency. In such an environment, if a flight to gold starts, a fixed exchange rate cannot be sustained.

The ratio of the US dollar supply outside the US to the total US gold reserves gradually increased after the mid-1950s. In 1959, while total dollar obligations were equal to US gold reserves, the total gold reserves of other countries in the same year exceeded US gold reserves. In 1964, official US dollar obligations held by the foreign monetary authorities surpassed the US dollar stock (Bordo, 1963). The likelihood that the US dollar could be converted into gold reserves, which is relatively low against the dollar supply, hung over the BW system like the sword of Damocles.

One of the reasons behind the increase in dollar supply in world markets is considered as US expansionary monetary policy to boost domestic production. This contrasts with the attitude of the UK between 1880 and 1914. For some, utilizing US monetary policy to address exclusively domestic needs meant that the US monetary policy was not suitable for the base currency.

The BW system is basically a system built upon commitments (promises). There is no official sanction under the BW system except for the reputation related concerns. In this system, it was assumed that the US was obliged to sustain price stability after the value of the dollar was stabilized against the gold. By accepting the fixed exchange rate regime, other countries are assumed to be accepting US price levels as the main determinants of their own price levels. At the same time, it is expected that the US will also provide the necessary dollar supply.

In such a case, the continuation of the fixed exchange rate regime depends on the coordination between the countries and the existence of a strong leader country. Coordination between countries within the BW system gradually decreased. In fact, some countries took steps directly against the system by either converting their dollar reserves into gold or threatening to convert their reserves into gold. For example, in 1965, Charles de Gaulle of France, who was not pleased with the dominance of the US dollar, started to convert the dollar reserves into gold reserves which began to put the United States in a difficult situation (Eichengreen, 1998). In addition, during this period, the US's ability to lead was increasingly eroded due to factors such as the Vietnam War and the fast recovery in Europe and Japan.

Increased international capital flows and growing national financial markets exacerbated the structural problems of the BW system. Capital movements, along with the controls on financial markets, were gradually deregulated throughout the period. At the same time, a number of financial innovations, such as Euro-dollar accounts, reduced the effectiveness of controls over capital movements and financial markets.

Increasing dollar supply may create inflationary pressures and may deteriorate confidence in an environment where the coordination between countries declines, the leadership capacity of the leading country diminishes and capital movements and financial markets reach considerable sizes. The first symptom of the confidence crisis emerged in the 1960s when the demand for gold increased suddenly. Soon after, to tackle this problem, the Fed and seven major central banks came together to form the London gold pool. In the 1960s, alongside the creation of a gold pool, the United States took extra measures to protect its gold reserves. Swap agreements, Roosa[5] bills and moral suasion were among them. Although these efforts contained the impacts for a while, they did not prevent the gold reserves of the United States from diminishing.

In April 1971, the US had a trade deficit for the first time in a very long time. This meant that the pressure on already existing US gold reserves increased. Allowing the dollar to depreciate started to be discussed in the US. The intention of the UK and France to convert their dollar reserves into gold at the beginning of August worsened the situation. In response to these developments, the US suspended the convertibility of the dollar to the gold on August 15, 1971. As a result, the BW system collapsed. Although there were some attempts to modify BW and implement a similar international monetary system for a while, the oil shocks of the 1970s directly and indirectly affected employment adversely, and growth and inflation in non-oil exporting countries put the final nail in the coffin of BW.

Monetary Policy After BW

As in the case of the end of the BW period, increasing role of financial movements may limit central banks' ability to implement independent/

effective monetary policy. In such a case, the trilemma framework suggests either abandoning the independent monetary policy or not defending the exchange rate.

The US stopped defending the fixed exchange rate system and the convertibility. Many consider it an inevitable implication of trilemma. The pressure on the Fed diminished with the adoption of the floating exchange rate regime and with abandoning the gold standard. Since there was no other reserve money to replace the US dollar, the US dollar maintained its reserve currency position even in the post-BW period. As in the US, most of the developed countries started to follow floating exchange rate regimes. In Europe, efforts to reduce the volatility of exchange rates continued after the BW. After some trials and errors, the European monetary system was established in 1979. Although it had a big crisis in 1992, the system survived and converged to Eurozone in 2002. While the Euro replaced local currencies, it was left to fluctuate against other world currencies. Developing countries tried to fix or heavily managed their exchange rates for a while. Indeed, multiple exchange rates were implemented, especially as part of industrialization strategy in Latin America and many other countries during the 1970s. After the 1980s, in response to high inflation and other problems, many IMF-led programs were based on exchange rate pegs.[6] However, along with financial liberalization, fixed or exchange rate pegs ended up with devastating currency crises in almost all countries that implemented these policies. As a result, the majority of developing countries started to follow flexible exchange rate regimes after the beginning of the 2000s.

All capital control policies in developed countries were completely lifted after the early 1980s. Developing countries removed capital controls after the late 1980s. In particular, the IMF has played a very pivotal role in promoting full capital mobility in developing countries. In parallel with this, the US also pushed for capital mobility in these countries by making free capital mobility part of bilateral commercial treaties with them.

As discussed above, the choices regarding capital mobility and exchange rate regimes changed in the post-BW period. In parallel with these changes, there have also been fundamental changes in central banking over time. Under the influence of the monetarist approach, the central banks of advanced countries used monetary aggregates as a basic tool for a short time. After a while, they started to use only short-term interest rates.[7] Monetary policy instruments such as margin requirements, credit controls, required reserve ratios, moral suasion, discount rates, etc., which were actively used previously by many central banks, were removed from active use.

Along with the changes in the instruments of central banks, the aims of monetary policy have also changed significantly. Inflation has been adopted as either the sole or the main target. In this context, formal or informal inflation targeting regimes have become the policy framework for many central banks in developed countries. The conventional economic theory came to the conclusion that central banks don't have the power to influence variables such as growth and unemployment in the long run, and that expansionary monetary policies will only generate more inflation. These ideas and practice have been followed by most of the developing countries, albeit with some lags.[8]

While the obstacles on capital movements were lifted during the 1980s and central banks abandoned many of their previous instruments, financial markets also experienced a very considerable transformation. Financial innovations such as securitization and derivatives have gained importance in advanced countries. Financial innovations have been supported without any scrutiny with the assumption that they will reduce risks and increase productivity. The existing regulations on financial markets have either been lifted or applied very loosely. For example, in the United States, between 1980 and 1986 and as a part of the liquidation of the "Regulation Q," interest rate ceilings were lifted (Gilbert, 1986). Similarly, the Glass–Steagall Act, separating commercial banking and investment banking, gradually lost its importance (Barth et al. 2000) due to financial innovations and a number of previous changes, and was completely abolished in 1999. Changes in the legal framework in the US and elsewhere have determined the institutional transformation in the financial system to a significant extent. However, the interpretation of existing legislation in favor of financial institutions also contributed to this process (Cömert, 2013). For instance, in 1986, by taking advantage of wholes and vague definitions in the Glass–Steagall Act, the Fed permitted bank holding companies to have subsidiaries which could conduct some security operations, if the revenue regarding these operations is not making more than 5 percent of the bank's gross revenue. Indeed, the Fed and many other institutions tried to do their best to stop all regulatory attempts. At the end of the 1990s, when Commodity Future Trading Commission (CFF) attempted to bring a new set of rules for derivatives including Credit Default Swaps (CDSs), it was the Fed who used all its prestige and power to stop this attempt. Levine (2010:18) aptly points out that "the Fed's decision to maintain its regulatory stance toward CDSs was neither a failure of information, nor a shortage of regulatory power. It was the result of the belief that financial markets can self-regulate itself." Other regulatory institutions followed suit. "In 2005, the SEC even closed its risk management office and did not inspect a single investment bank. These activities took place about two years before the most recent crisis" (Labaton, 2008, cited in Levine, 2010:24).[9]

Due to deregulations of financial flows and financial markets, the importance of financial flows increased and the size and the impacts of financial markets reached unprecedented levels. In such an environment, as explained above, central banks began to solely rely on short-term interest rates too. How did these developments influence the ability of central banks to implement independent/effective monetary policy? According to many economists, conducting monetary policy with short-term interest rates is sufficient for both inflation and financial stability (Woodford, 2002). In the international context, it is considered that the free exchange rate regime is sufficient to implement an independent monetary policy. In other words, choosing the right corner of the trilemma configuration is enough to implement effective monetary policy. For example, according to Papademos (2008), former deputy European Central Bank vice-president, even in a fully integrated world economy, central banks of relatively small economies may have an impact on domestic demand, as long as they follow a flexible exchange rate regime. In general, the conventional view in economics is that the developments in national and international financial markets have only slightly complicated the work of central banks and force them to think more carefully (Geithner, 2006; Bernanke, 2007).

Some explicitly utilized the concept of trilemma and attempted to demonstrate the existence of effective/independent monetary policy under flexible exchange rate regimes and capital mobility. For example, researchers from ECB, Georgiadis and Mehl (2015) claim that financial globalization has amplified "monetary policy effectiveness in the typical advanced and emerging market economy." They argue that due to financial globalization, contractionary monetary policy has been more powerful by 40 percent. Therefore, according to them, "classical trilemma is valid."

Some others are more cautious in their assertions although, at the last instance, they defend the validity of the trilemma for BW and post BW period in different configurations. For instance, Klein and Shambough (2015:36) claim that "countries with pegged exchange rates and open capital accounts have less monetary autonomy than those floating exchange rates and or capital controls." In a similar vein, constructing a monetary independence index, Aizenman et al. (2008) argue the existence of trade-offs.[10] They claim that when a country chooses more exchange rate flexibility and more capital mobility, it needs to give up some of its capability of independent monetary policy. According to this trade off approach, different degree of capital mobility, exchange rate flexibility and monetary autonomy can exist at the same time. For example, if a country chooses exchange rate flexibility and capital mobility, this country can still have both some degree of autonomy and exchange rate peg unless it prefers full fixed exchange rate regime. Considering reserve accumulation of developing countries, Aizenman (2011) argues that an extended Trilemma framework can be a useful tool to understand developments, especially after 2002 in developing countries. According to him, a higher level of accumulated reserves can be used to ease the trade off at least in the short run. Investigating the determinants of short term and long-term interest rates, Obstfeld (2015:2) is clearer about the constraints on monetary policy in developing countries.[11] He argues that those countries with relatively flexible exchange rate regimes have more influence on the short end of the term structure "but long-term interest rates are more highly correlated across countries irrespective of the exchange rate regime." However, although Aizenman and others in this group accept the decline in the space of monetary policy by accepting the possibility of non-corner solutions, they highlight opportunities rather than a structural constraint and convergence to dilemma imposed upon (in some cases supported by) central banks.

There have been counter voices as well. Rey (2015) states that the situation in developing countries is a complete dilemma. She investigates the co-movement of gross flows and assets prices and reports that these global co-movements are closely related to the risk aversion and uncertainty, which has been very sensitive to interest rates in the center countries. As a result, she (2015:21) argues that "fluctuating exchange rates cannot insulate economies from the global financial cycle, when capital is mobile." The "trilemma" morphs into a "dilemma" – independent monetary policies are possible if and only if the capital account is managed, directly or indirectly, regardless of the exchange rate regime." Focusing on institutional and structural changes in financial markets and central banking in the US, Cömert (2013) calls developments in the US as a dual decoupling between the Fed rate and market interest rates and balance sheets of financial firms. He claims that central banks have gradually lost their power to influence relevant market interest rates and especially balance sheets of financial institutions.

Following Cömert (2013) and partially Rey (2015), we argue that, the developments since the 1980s have gradually reduced the capacity of central banks to implement effective monetary policy. It would be more accurate to say that the post-BW system has evolved to "dilemma" gradually along with changes in both central banking, financial markets and financial flows. Dilemma refers that central banks have largely lost the ability to implement effective/independent monetary policy regardless of existing exchange rate regimes (Figure 11.3). However, this situation shows some differences in developed and developing countries. The main macroeconomic variables are more sensitive to capital movements in developing countries due to relatively shallow financial markets. In the advanced countries, endogenous processes in domestic financial markets

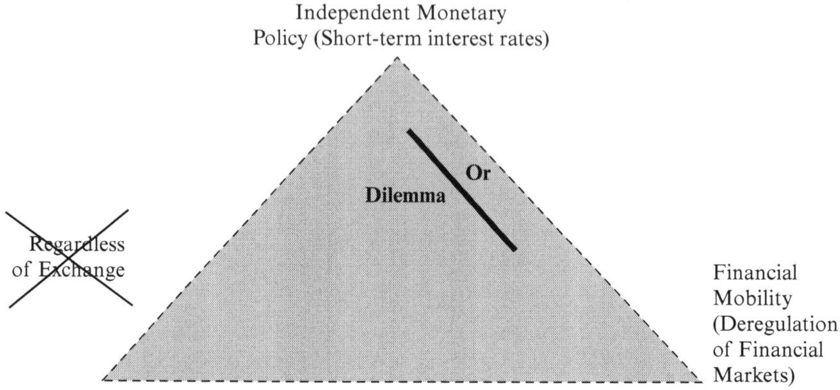

Figure 11.3 Dilemma

seem to have been much more decisive relative to financial flows although financial flows started to influence asset prices even in the US.

By the same token, asset prices have become less affected by central bank policies in advanced countries. Thornton (2010) shows that the theoretically expected relationship between the Fed interest rate and the Treasury bond deteriorated by the end of the 1980s. Cömert (2012, 2013) went one step further and econometrically showed that the relationship between Fed's interest rates and all long-term interest rates in the US financial markets decreased gradually. In other words, it seems that the responsiveness of long-term interest rates to the changes in Fed rate decreased gradually. These findings significantly overlap with the findings of Warnock and Warnock (2009) on capital movements affecting long-term interest rates even in the United States. On the other hand, there are signs that the central banks have become less influential on the balance sheets of financial firms as a result of unprecedented changes in both central banking and financial markets. In this sense, these signs imply increasing endogeneity of balance sheet expansions, especially in developed countries. Increasing the degree of endogeneity of balance sheets of financial markets, ceteris paribus, means that the central banks have less leverage on the credit expansion in the financial markets. Adrian and Shin (2009) and Cömert (2013) demonstrate how balance sheets can expand endogenously in response to an increase in asset prices. In such an environment, it is expected that the effects of the central banks' instruments on the expansion of the balance sheets will diminish. For the US economy, Esterella (2002) reports that "[s]ecuritization has likely weakened the impact of any policy move." Similarly, Altunbas et al. (2009) by using

Table 11.1 Fed rate and balance sheet expansion in US

	1982(IV)–2008(IV)	1982(IV)–1990(IV)	1991(I)–2000(IV)	2001(I)–2008(IV)
	Fed	Fed	Fed	Fed
All sectors	−0.6493	−0.3289	0.5168	0.6647
Finance	−0.6811	−0.3259	0.518	0.5629
Commercial banks	−0.6579	−0.3202	0.5498	0.5981
Brokers and dealers	−0.6197	−0.2891	0.3374	0.6016

Source: Cömert, 2013.

micro data on 3000 euro-zone banks, documents that banks which utilize more securitization are less responsive to changes in official rates.

Table 11.1 shows that the correlation between Fed interest rates and the balance sheet expansion gradually decreased after 1980. Surprisingly, as seen in the recent period (after 2001), even the expected positive relationship between interest rates and balance sheets disappeared; when interest rates increased, there was not even a contraction in the balance sheets of US financial firms in the last period. This result implies that the expected effect of the Fed's monetary policy on balance sheets has not taken place, or/and it has been overcome by a number of other factors.

While in the post-BW period even the effectiveness of central banks in advanced countries was influenced by developments in national and international financial markets, the main macroeconomic indicators were determined significantly by external factors in developing countries.

The General Macroeconomic Implications of Financial Flows in Developing Countries

Financial movements directly affect the growth and inflation in a significant way through mainly influencing intermediate food prices, interest rates, credit expansion and foreign exchange rates in developing countries. There are various transmission channels linking main macroeconomic variables to financial flows in these countries. Here, we will shortly explain these mechanisms under the broad headings of credit and asset price channels. An obvious direct mechanism works through credit creation capacity of financial flows. This mechanism can be simply labeled as the credit channel. Benefiting from the discussion on the transmission mechanism, three strands of the credit channel can be investigated. First, some of the big, non-financial sector firms can directly borrow from international financial markets, which can contribute to the investment capacity of the firms and GDP growth. The second strand of the mechanism works through the banking system. Financial flows in the form of borrowings of domestically operated banks can increase the capacity of the banks to give more credit to domestic consumers and firms. Those banks with access to cheap credit from international financial markets can generate more credit domestically (Igan and Tan, 2017). Third, as elaborated on below, net high positive (negative) financial flows can cause improvements (deterioration) in the balance sheets of banks/other firms through appreciation (depreciation) of the domestic currency. As a result, on the one hand, banks would be eager to give more credit; on the other hand, due to strong balance sheets, non-financial firms would be more eligible to borrow. This link can be labeled as the *balance sheet effect* of financial flows within the credit channel. High credit growth can stimulate high economic growth. Signaling prospects for a healthy economy, high GDP growth may also ease credit constraints on domestic firms to borrow from the rest of the world. Therefore, in general, high financial flows and high GDP growth can create a virtuous credit circle and feed each other until an external or endogenously driven shock hits the economy.

The second channel works through domestic asset prices. Financial flows may exert pressure on the prices of domestic assets by altering supply and demand conditions in financial markets. The asset prices channel can be broadly further divided into interest rates, stock prices, and exchange rate channels. With regard to the interest rate channel, high net positive financial flows may increase demand for domestic bonds, which can drive the price of domestic assets up. Large amounts of purchases of domestic securities by foreigners may contribute to a big decrease in the interest rates on these assets by driving up their prices. Furthermore, if domestically operated banks find cheap funding from international financial markets, they can decrease their lending rates at home without jeopardizing their overall profits. This may imply a decline in overall interest rates, which may induce demand for credit and, in turn, consumption and investment expenditures. Furthermore, lower interest rates can strengthen balance sheets by decreasing the operational cost of firms, which can increase their net worth and collaterals.

Financial flows may exert some influence on an economy through stock prices too. Portfolio flows include the purchase of domestic stocks by foreigners. In addition to this, if, due to high financial flows, there is an overall decrease in interest rates in the economy, domestic stock markets may also attract domestic investors, which can cause a further increase in stock prices. This may generate a lucrative funding source for the firms issuing stocks at the domestic stock exchange markets. As a result, investment expenditures of these firms may expand. In the countries where there is widespread public participation in stock exchange markets, high stock prices may also cause a *wealth effect*: economic entities holding high amounts of domestic stocks may feel richer, thereby encouraging them to spend more during times of high stock prices.

Recently, the importance of gross financial flows has rightly highlighted by many authors (Borio and Disyatat, 2011). However, net financial flows can be still a very important indicator for many developing countries for its impact, especially on the availability of foreign exchanges, which influences directly exchange rates (Cömert and Düzçay, 2016). In developing countries, exchange rates are among the most important asset prices. An increase in the supply of foreign currencies resulting from higher net financial flows brings about a nominal appreciation of the currency of these countries against major foreign currencies. Changes in exchange rates can have impacts on an economy through balance sheets, inflation, and the current account. If the agents operating in an economy have different foreign assets and foreign liabilities structures, any significant movement in exchange rates may either deteriorate or improve the balance sheets of the agents considerably.

For example, if the majority of firms have more liabilities denominated in foreign currencies relative to their assets, a considerable appreciation of the domestic currency resulting from high net financial flows may improve the balance sheet by decreasing the value of the liabilities in terms of the domestic currency. In other words, this process leads to an increase in net worth (the difference between assets and liabilities). As discussed in the balance sheet effect as a part of the credit channel, an increase in net worth can induce more investment by either easing credit constraints and/or creating extra available funds. Nominal appreciation of currencies of developing countries in the periods after 2002 might have induced more credit and investment. As opposed to the case of appreciation, as documented by the third-generation crisis literature, a significant depreciation of domestic currency resulting from financial reversals (abrupt, large slowdowns) may generate a balance sheet crisis (Krugman, 1999). The Asian crisis of 1997 can be considered as an example of a balance sheet crisis.[12]

Changes in exchange rates can also directly influence inflation through its impact on imported intermediate goods. In the case of depreciation of the domestic currency, consumption goods imports can decrease significantly. Although this can decrease competition in domestic markets (by increasing the price of foreign goods) and enable domestic producers producing substitutes for foreign goods to charge higher prices for their own final goods, may not contribute to inflation much if domestic content of the production is high or/and domestic substitutes for foreign goods can be found easily. However, many developing countries have to import a significant amount of intermediate goods for domestic production.

Particularly, those countries without many natural resources have to import oil, natural gas and many raw materials. As a result, depreciation means an increase in inflation rate. Indeed, inflation in these countries is very sensitive to developments in exchange rates.[13] In fact, as Benlialper and Cömert (2015a) show, the main determinants of inflation in emerging countries such as Turkey are external conditions rather than interest rates set by central banks. Similar findings were reported for developing countries in general (Mohanty and Klau, 2001). These findings mean that the tasks of central banks trying to prevent inflation by influencing the demand side through overnight interest rates are not easy. On the one hand, central banks in developing countries may not easily influence financial variables such as market interest rates, credit expansion and exchange rates because these variables are very sensitive to financial flows through many channels. On the other hand, inflation in these countries is not associated with demand side considerably.

Apart from very rare cases that are mostly related to adverse developments in inflation expectations, the appreciation of the domestic currency is mostly translated into real appreciation. The appreciation of the real exchange rates mostly related to financial flows makes exports more expensive and import prices lower, which can induce current account deficits.[14] Besides this, whenever the growth of these economies coincides with high financial inflows, current account deficits reach record levels. Therefore, financial flows may also widen current account deficits by suddenly easing credit conditions, leading to a demand boom, partially boosting imported goods expenditures.

Overall, as detailed above, financial flows exert a substantial influence on developing countries by affecting very important macro variables such as exchange rates, interest rates, credit conditions and stock prices. As a result, GDP growth, inflation, unemployment and the current account balance have been exposed to boom–bust cycles of financial flows. Indeed, as well established in the literature during the boom periods, the developing economies experience relatively high growth while the growth either becomes negative or slows down considerably during the bust periods.

Figure 11.4 shows the correlation between financial flows and economic growth, loan growth and real exchange rate for the 16 major developing countries in the 1990–2014 period. The correlation between financial flows and other variables is too high to be neglected. In the studied countries, the average of the correlations is between 0.4 and 0.5. In some individual countries, this coefficient exceeds 0.7. Despite the need for further study, these data support the assertions that at least capital movements and significant macroeconomic indicators are highly related.

In cases where the magnitude and direction of financial flows can be

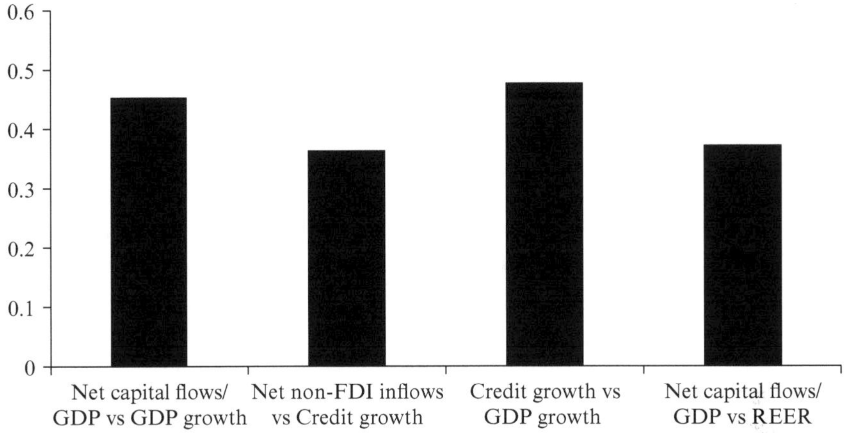

Source: Benlialper and Cömert, 2016.

Figure 11.4 The average of correlations among financial flows and main macroeconomic variables in selected developing countries (1990–2014)

determined by policy instruments, it may not be a problem to have major macroeconomic variables significantly affected by capital movements. If policy makers could influence the direction and the magnitude of financial movements to a predictable extent, capital movements could even turn into an instrument of monetary policy. However, capital movements are largely influenced by global risk perception (Rey, 2015). Developments in domestic policy or changes in fragility indicators of certain developing countries may affect financial flows to these countries more than their peers. However, as the global risk appetite begins to decline, capital flows into these countries slow down and even reverse, regardless of the macroeconomic fundamentals and other indicators. While when the VIX (the global risk perception) is high, financial flows in developing economies slow down, in the periods of lower VIX, a significant increase in capital inflows to developing countries was observed.

It is not possible to talk about effective monetary policy when central banks rely on very indirect tools, domestic financial markets reach unprecedented levels, and key macroeconomic variables such as growth and inflation are under the influence of financial flows to a significant extent and financial flows are not very sensitive to monetary policy. In this situation, interest rates of central banks become empty signifiers and exchange rate regimes implemented in developing countries become irrelevant. This has been a worldwide phenomenon; however, much more apparent in developing countries. Under these conditions, it can be argued that the trilemma of the BW system converges to the dilemma as in the case of the period after the BW.

CONCLUSION

Controls on capital movements and domestic financial markets as well as multiple instruments used by central banks contributed to the relative independence of monetary policy during the BW system. In this respect, with some modification, the concept of the trilemma can be used to explain this period. However, financial markets have been deregulated while capital movements have been completely freed in the post-BW period. Existing rules have not been implemented effectively. Short-term interest rates have come to the forefront as the only means of central banks. In this process, the central bank's ability to implement effective monetary policy in both emerging and developed countries has increasingly eroded. However, although developments in domestic financial markets can be much more decisive in advanced countries, developing countries have been much more exposed to boom–bust cycles in financial flows.

This can also be thought of as a convergence process from trilemma to dilemma. While capital movements are free and parallel to that, financial markets have reached a very large size, the capacity of central banks to affect credit expansion, interest rates, exchange rates and stock prices will be very limited by using only overnight interest rates. After the 2008 crisis, central banks in both developing and advanced countries have started to use many heterodox policies. These policies can, in fact, be interpreted as an effort to gain effective monetary policy capability. Besides interest rates, many other instruments were introduced after the recent financial crisis. At the same time, financial stability and similar concerns became important parts of the new central banking. The capital controls that many authors (Crotty and Epstein, 1999; Stiglitz, 2002; Rey, 2015) have long argued have even begun to be applied in some countries (Benlialper and Cömert, 2015b). However, it is very difficult for the central banks to have independent monetary policy capacity in today's conditions unless serious steps are taken to address fundamental structural/institutional changes eroding their capacity.

NOTES

1. This chapter draws heavily on my previous book and papers such as Cömert 2013, 2016, 2017. I am very grateful for the comments and suggestions of the par-

ticipants of the Grenoble Conference 2017 and Louis-Philippe Rochon and Virginie Monvoisin.

2. In my framework monetary policy independence does not only imply the ability of central banks to set their interest rates independent of foreign interest rates.
3. In the same spirit, Minsky concludes his 1986 article as follows: "[T]he further evolution of the financial structure and the relationships between finance, money, investment and employment are likely to diminish our ability to contain turbulence" (Minsky 1986:352).
4. Under a fixed exchange rate regime with capital controls, considering that central banks can determine market interest rates by setting its overnight interest rates and investment/consumption is sensitive to interest rates is enough to justify existing of independent monetary policy. When one relaxes the assumption of capital controls but retains the fixed exchange rate regime, as in the case of trilemma, domestic interest rates cannot be different than world interest rates. The burden of the adjustment will be fully carried by interest rates. Under flexible exchange rate regimes with capital mobility, some part of the adjustment will take place through changes in exchange rates. As a result, in general, independent monetary policy will retain its validity.
5. Roosa bills were US treasury bills launched on the initiative of US Treasury Counsel Robert Roosa to reduce gold demand. This plan aimed at replacing the US dollar with reliable long-term US papers. It can also be considered as a method of international sterilization process (Makin, 1971).
6. The IMF was established as a part of the BW system, together with the International Bank for Reconstruction and Development (IBRD, now the World Bank). Under BW, to be able to defend the system the IMF was supposed to provide temporary finance to those countries with a balance of payment problems. The IMF was also tasked for the approval of significant exchange rate adjustments by member countries. However, from the beginning, the IMF was significantly influenced by the IMF due to structure of its voting system allowing the countries with higher quotes to have more say in the decision making process. The US with one third of all quotes had de facto veto power over all the decisions of the IMF. After the collapse of the BW system, the IMF became much more instrumental and active in pushing for the US and its close allies' agenda worldwide.
7. According to Thornton (2004:489) "sometimes between October 1982 and late 1980s the Fed began explicitly targeting the federal funds rate, but the market was unaware of it." It was only at the beginning of the 1990s that the market started to realize it (Poole et al. 2002). The Fed has only officially announced the Federal Funds rate targets since 1995, although it started explicitly announcing changes in its policy stance in 1994.
8. As explained above developing countries implemented exchange rate based programs even in the form of currency boards in order to tackle with especially high inflation. In many countries, central banks were tasked to follow structural adjustment programs mainly composed of a package of domestic financial deregulations and financial mobility. Paradoxically, under these circumstances, in many cases, they were also mandated to keep variants of a pegged exchange rate regime.
9. In a similar way, in 2004, the Security Exchange Commission (SEC) allowed the five largest investment banks to use their own models to determine how much capital they should keep for their operations. According to Nadauld and Sherlund (2009:4), this would enable the largest investment banks to reduce their capital needs by 30 to 40 percent.
10. In Aizenman's words (2011:3) "a lingering challenge is that in practice, most countries rarely face the binary choices articulated by the Trilemma. Instead, countries chose the degree of financial integration and exchange rate flexibility."
11. Although Obstfeld (2015) does not elaborate on it, he is among a few who recognizes the fact that independent/effective monetary policy cannot be reduced to capability of setting official interest rates independent of foreign rates. According to him (2015:2) "independent monetary policy is feasible for financially open EMEs, but limited in what it can achieve."
12. In the Turkish case, the severity of the crisis of 2001 can be partially explained by the balance sheet effect resulting from a sudden and big depreciation of TL (Özatay, 2009).

13. Therefore, even under the inflation-targeting regime, central banks in developing countries might benefit from the nominal appreciation or the slowdown in the depreciation of their currencies to bring inflation under control (Benlialper and Cömert, 2015a). Indeed, inflation shows a considerable declining trend during the periods of abundance of financial flows, causing domestic currency to appreciate relative to other currencies.
14. The importance of exchange rates for the trade balance has been a contested topic for a long time. There has not been a consensus on the magnitude and even on the sign of the impacts. However, a long period of a significant depreciation/appreciation of a currency can sooner or later impact on the trade.

REFERENCES

Aizenman, J. (2011), "The impossible trinity-from the policy trilemma to the policy quadrilemma," (No. 678). Working Papers, UC Santa Cruz Economics Department.

Aizenman, J., M.D. Chinn and H. Ito (2008), "Assessing the Emerging Global Financial Architecture: Measuring the Trilemma's Configurations Over Time," (Working Paper No. w14533), *National Bureau of Economic Research.*

Adrian, T. and H.S. Shin (2009), "Money, Liquidity, and Monetary Policy," *FRB of New York Staff Report*, No. 360.

Altunbas, Y., L. Gambacorta and D. Marques-Ibanez (2009), "Securitisation and the bank lending channel," *European Economic Review*, 53(8), 996–1009.

Barth, J.R., R.D. Brumbaugh and J.A. Wilcox (2000), "Policy watch: the repeal of Glass–Steagall and the advent of broad banking," *The Journal of Economic Perspectives*, 14(2), 191–204.

Benlialper, A. and H. Cömert (2015a), "Implicit asymmetric exchange rate peg under inflation targeting regimes: the case of Turkey," *Cambridge Journal of Economics*, doi:10.1093/cje/bev073, first published online November 12, 2015.

Benlialper, A. and H. Cömert (2015b), "Central Banking in Developing Countries after the Crisis: What Has Changed?," (Working Paper No. 395), *Political Economy Research Center*.

Bernanke, B.S. (2007), "Globalization and Monetary Policy." Remarks by the Chairman of the Board of Governors of the US Federal Reserve System, at the Fourth Economic Summit, *Stanford Institute for Economic Policy Research*, (2 March), Stanford, California.

Bloomfield, A.I. (1959), "Monetary Policy under the International Gold Standard: 1880–1914," *Federal Reserve Bank of New York*.

Bordo, M.D. (1993), "The Bretton Woods International Monetary System: a historical overview," in M. D. Bordo and B. Eichengreen (eds), *A Retrospective on the Bretton Woods System: Lessons for International Monetary Reform*, Chicago: University of Chicago Press, 3–108.

Borio, C. and P. Disyatat (2011), "Global imbalances and the financial crisis: link or no link?," (Working Paper No. 346), *Bank for International Settlements*.

Bruno, V. and H.S. Shin (2015), "Capital flows and the risk-taking channel of monetary policy," *Journal of Monetary Economics*, 71, 119–32.

Calvo, G.A. and C.A. Végh (1994), "Inflation stabilization and nominal anchors," *Contemporary Economic Policy*, 12(2), 35–45.

Cömert, H. (2012), "Decoupling between the Federal Funds Rate and Long-Term

Interest Rates: Decreasing Effectiveness of Monetary Policy in the US," (No. wp295), *Political Economy Research Center*.
Cömert, H. (2013), *Central Banks and Financial Markets: The Declining Power of US Monetary Policy*, Cheltenham: Edward Elgar Publishing.
Cömert, H. (2016), "İmkansız Üçleme'den İmkansız İlilem'e: Bretton Woods Dönemi ve Sonrası Para Politikası," *Hacettepe Üniversitesi İktisadi ve İdari Bilimler Fakültesi Dergisi*, 34(1), 115–36.
Cömert, H. (2017), "The financial flows and the future of EU–Turkey relations," *FEUTURE Online Paper*, No. 9.
Cömert, H. and G. Düzçay (2015), "Understanding developments in current accounts and financial flows in light of discussions on global imbalances and recent crises," *Ekonomik Yaklasim*, 26(96), 59–90.
Crotty, J. and G. Epstein (1999), "A defense of capital controls in light of the Asian financial crisis," *Journal of Economic Issues*, 33(2), 427–33.
Eichengreen, B.J. (1998), *Globalizing Capital: A History of the International Monetary* System, Princeton: Princeton University Press.
Eichengreen, B. (2008), *The European Economy Since 1945: Coordinated Capitalism and Beyond* (Vol. 23). Princeton University Press.
Epstein, G. (2006), "Central Banks as Agents of Economic Development," (No. 2006/54), UNUWIDER, *Research Paper*, United Nations University (UNU).
Epstein, G. (2013), "Developmental central banking: winning the future by updating a page from the past," *Review of Keynesian Economics*, 1(3), 273–87.
Estrella, A. (2002), "Securitization and the efficacy of monetary policy," *FRBNY Economic Policy Review*, 8(1), 1–13.
Feinman, J.N. (1993), "Reserve requirements: history, current practice, and potential reform," *Federal Reserve Bulletin*, 79, 569–89.
Gambacorta, L. (2009), "Monetary policy and the risk-taking channel," *BIS Quarterly Review*, December, 43–53.
Geithner, T. (2006), "Global Economic and Financial Integration: Some Implications for Central Banking," *Remarks at the Columbia Business School Center on Japanese Economy and Business 20th Anniversary Conference*, (26 October), Columbia University, New York City.
Gilbert, M. (1968), "The Gold-Dollar System: Conditions of Equilibrium and the Price of Gold," (No. 70), *Essays in International Finance*, Princeton University.
Gilbert, R.A. (1986), "Requiem for regulation Q: what it did and why it passed away," *Federal Reserve Bank of St Louis Review*, February, 22–37.
Georgiadis, G. and A. Mehl (2015), "Trilemma, not dilemma: financial globalisation and monetary policy effectiveness," Globalization and Monetary Policy Institute Working Paper 222, Federal Reserve Bank of Dallas.
Greenspan, A. (2005), "Federal Reserve Board's Semiannual Monetary Policy Report to the Congress," *Testimony: Before the Committee on Banking, Housing, and Urban Affairs*, US Senate, 21 July.
Igan, D. and Z. Tan (2017), "Capital inflows, credit growth, and financial systems," *Emerging Markets Finance and Trade*, 53(2), 2649–71.
Kenen, P.B. (1960), "International liquidity and the balance of payments of a reserve-currency country," *The Quarterly Journal of Economics*, 74(4), 572–86.
Klein, M. W. (2013, January 17), "Capital controls: Gates vs walls." Retrieved from http://www.voxeu.org/article/capital-controls-gates-versus-walls.
Klein, M. W. and J. C. Shambaugh (2015), "Rounding the corners of the policy

trilemma: sources of monetary policy autonomy," *American Economic Journal: Macroeconomics*, 7(4), 33–66.
Krugman, P. (1999), "Balance sheets, the transfer problem, and financial crises," *International Tax and Public Finance*, 6(4), 459–72.
Makin, J. H. (1971), "Swaps and Roosa bonds as an index of the cost of cooperation in the crisis zone," *The Quarterly Journal of Economics*, 85(2), 349–56.
Minsky, H.P. (1957), "Central banking and money market changes," *The Quarterly Journal of Economics*, 71(2), 171–87.
Minsky, H.P. (1986), "The evolution of financial institutions and the performance of the economy," *Journal of Economic Issues*, 20(2), 345–53.
Mohanty, M.S. and M. Klau (2001), "What determines inflation in emerging market economies?," (No. 8), *BIS Working Papers*, Bank for International Settlements.
Obstfeld, M. (2015), "Trilemmas and trade-offs: living with financial globalisation," No. 480, Bank for International Settlements.
Obstfeld, M., J.C. Shambaugh and A. Taylor (2005), "The Trilemma in History: Tradeoffs among Exchange Rates, Monetary Policies, and Capital Mobility," (No. 10396), *NBER Working Paper*, NBER.
Papademos, L. (2008), "Globalisation and Central Bank Policies," *Speech at the Bridge Forum Dialogue*, Luxembourg, 22 January.
Poole, W., R.H. Rasche and D.L. Thornton (2002), "Market anticipations of monetary policy actions," *Review–Federal Reserve Bank of Saint Louis*, 84(4), 65–94.
Rey, H. (2015), "Dilemma not Trilemma: The Global Financial Cycle and Monetary Policy Independence," (No. w21162), *National Bureau of Economic Research*.
Schwartz, A.J. (2009), "Introduction," in M.D. Bordo and A. J. Schwartz (eds), *A Retrospective on the Classical Gold Standard, 1821–1931*, Chicago: University of Chicago Press, 1–22.
Shiller, R.J. (2000), "Margin Calls: Should the Fed step in?," *Wall Street Journal*, 10 April 2000.
Stiglitz, J.E. (2004), "Capital-market liberalization, globalization, and the IMF," *Oxford Review of Economic Policy*, 20(1), 57–71.
Tew, B. (1982), *The Evolution of the International Monetary System, 1945–1981*, London: Hutchinson.
Thornton, D.L. (2004), "The Fed and short-term rates: is it open market operations, open mouth operations or interest rate smoothing?," *Journal of Banking and Finance*, 28(3), 475–98.
Thornton, D.L. (2007), "The unusual behavior of the Federal funds and 10-year treasury rates: a conundrum or Goodhart's law?," Federal Reserve Bank of St. Louis, R. Triffin (ed.), (1960), *Gold and the Dollar Crisis*, New Haven: Yale University.
Volcker, P. (2002), "Monetary policy transmission: past and future challenges," *Federal Reserve Bank of New York Economic Policy Review*, 8(1), 7–11.
Warnock, F.E. and V.C. Warnock (2009), "International capital flows and U.S. interest rates," *Journal of International Money and Finance*, 28(6), 903–19.
Woodford, M. (2002), "Financial market efficiency and the effectiveness of monetary policy," *Federal Reserve Bank of New York Economic Policy Review*, May, 85–94.
Woodford, M. (2003), "Optimal interest-rate smoothing," *The Review of Economic Studies*, 70(4), 861–86.

12. Shifting frames of the expert debate: quantitative easing, international macro-finance and the potential impact of post-Keynesian scholarship

Max Nagel and Matthias Thiemann

INTRODUCTION

Given close international linkages via trade and financial markets, domestic monetary policies produce spillovers to foreign countries via effects on macro-economic variables (real policy spillovers) as well as on financing conditions and capital flows (financial policy spillovers). Whereas the former spillover channel received attention in policy debates and academia over the last decades in the "currency war" literature (Eichengreen and Sachs 1986; Corsetti et al. 2000), the latter was largely left aside in expert discourses. This changed when volatilities on global financial markets during and after the "taper tantrum" in May/June 2013 clearly visualized how accommodative policy stances in advanced economies led to the buildup of financial risks domestically but also abroad, primarily in emerging market economies.[1] How do the policy institutions in the field make sense of these adverse developments on the stability of the international monetary and financial system stemming from unconventional and highly accommodative monetary policies?

To tackle this question, this chapter looks at the discursive developments in the debate about international financial policy spillovers among three key policy institutions in the transnational realm (Federal Reserve Board, International Monetary Fund and Bank for International Settlements). We sought to trace the debate, using document analysis and expert interviews to understand the shifting evaluation of unconventional monetary policy in the transnational expert discussion from 2007–2017. In particular we base ourselves on an in-depth analysis of various types of documents that were issued by the three-policy institution from 2007 onwards and that were addressing the domestic conduct of monetary policies and its international ramifications.[2] These entail:

- 29 working papers, 85 FOMC minutes, 44 speeches, 5 Staff Reports by the Fed.
- 79 working papers, 7 Staff Discussion Notes, 2 Spillover Notes, 3 Spillover Reports, 20 Global Financial Stability Reports, 12 Policy Papers and 6 speeches by the IMF.
- 44 working papers, 42 Quarterly Reviews, 7 BIS Papers, 11 Annual Reports and 16 speeches by the BIS.

In these papers, these institutions discuss unconventional monetary policies, entailing asset purchase programmes ("quantitative easing"), negative interest rate policies and forward guidance, which are the main novelty of the conduct of monetary policies after the financial crisis 2007. Whereas the aim, the achievement of domestic macro-economic objectives, is clearly set out, we show that central bankers increasingly focus on adverse side effects stemming from these policies, particularly regarding their effect on domestic (and global) financial stability as well as on the economy and financial system of other countries. This chapter analyzes developments in the expert debate regarding these effects, focussing on the Federal Reserve, International Monetary Fund and Bank for International Settlements, and identifies central changes in their analytical frames of monetary policy effects. It furthermore relates these findings to the post-Keynesian literature and discusses to what extent post-Keynesians could make use of these changes to increase their leverage in monetary policy debates. Particularly their insistence on the inseparability of macro-economics and finance and hence about macro-financial linkages, both domestically and globally, could support changes in monetary policymaking.

To explain (possible) policy changes among central bankers, it is of relevance to understand how central bankers make sense of the effects that monetary policy have on global financial stability and on other countries. Understanding how economics alters the framing of the effects of monetary policy is therefore central to explain conduct of monetary policy and possibility of policy change. Change in economics is thus a possible venue to bring about change of monetary policies.[3] The reduction of uncertainty through new economic models that allow for the framing of unintended consequences can therefore lead to the improvement of monetary policymaking. This points to the question to which extent mainstream economics, which undergirds monetary policymaking, is able to provide analytical frameworks that allow for macro-economic and financial stability? Its deficiencies in this regard lead us to argue that post-Keynesianism is a particularly qualified alternative. It hence argues that there is a window of opportunity regarding the influence of Post-Keynesians on policymakers, where an increased focus on the interlinkages between price stability and financial stability and the derivation of improved monetary policy frameworks may increase the leverage of Post-Keynesians. This window of opportunity is however rapidly closing, as neoclassical economists increasingly account for the role of financial instabilities, also on the international level (see Korinek 2018).

This chapter proceeds as follows: Section 2 presents a brief literature review. Section 3, the analytical part, focusses on our findings concerning how economics shapes analytical frameworks deployed by central banks and therefore the conduct of monetary policy. Implications are derived from this regarding possible alleys through which monetary policy frameworks could become adjusted to the realities that are imposed by an international monetary and financial system. It is doubtful that current analytical frameworks are sufficient to reduce negative externalities to global financial stability and the financial and economic systems of other countries. that are produced by central banks. Since economics is the base on which analytical frameworks are developed, implications regarding alleys for rethinking of economics are derived. Section 4 discusses post-Keynesian contributions and links to the debate among central bankers. Section 5 concludes.

LITERATURE REVIEW

Although the change of monetary policies after the financial crisis and its real and financial effects continue to be a highly studied topic in both mainstream and heterodox economics in the pursuit of optimal monetary policy frameworks, the developments in the debate among policymakers themselves remain understudied. This is striking, assuming that these economists' interventions aim at changing monetary policy frameworks, since the literature on capital controls shows the important influence that changing ideational outlooks of technocrats have on policy evolution (cf. Hall 1993). In particular, the literature on changes in capital flows post-crisis received plenty of attention by scholars interested in policy changes (Gabor 2012; Moschella 2015a; Gallagher 2015a; Chwieroth and Sinclair 2013), particularly so with regard to the shift of the IMF in its stance towards capital flows (Moschella 2015b; Gallagher 2015b; Grabel 2015; Chwieroth 2008; Abdelal 2009).

A noteworthy example is the contribution by Jeffrey Chwieroth (2010), in which he traces the ideational processes within the IMF and how they led to discursive and institutional shifts of the IMF's position towards capital controls. Chwieroth finds that norm entrepreneurs within policy institutions are not completely subject to structural pressures but are endowed with strategic agency, namely the capacity to exert discursive influence by framing problems and problem resolutions in a way that challenges competing framings. While challenging hegemonic frames within the institution, norm entrepreneurs can benefit from outside allies and their economic models, such as was the case for capital controls (Gallagher 2015b).

In contrast to this literature, changes in ideational views on monetary policies in the aftermath of the financial crisis as well as the role of financial stability concerns in driving these changes in monetary policies remain largely unaccounted for.[4] This neglect seems little warranted, as scholars analyzing the interactions among central bankers over the course of the last 30 years argue for the existence of a transnational epistemic community (Kapstein 1989; Haas 1992), increasingly based on the formal language of economics (Marcussen 2006). They show how central bankers debate issues of concern and aim to find policy solutions bilaterally but also via platforms like the BIS and IMF. The analysis of the debate about adverse effects of monetary policies requires therefore the study of these transnational platforms. Particularly Marcussen (2006) shows how only few central bankers make up the core of the transnational epistemic community and have a decisive impact. Their ideational influence is of particular importance to bring about the possibility of cooperation, "as the responses policy-makers formulate to address those challenges cannot be understood without attention to ideational factors, in particular policy-makers shared beliefs about the nature of monetary policy." (McNamara 1999: 56).

Nevertheless, change with respect to monetary policy is unlikely to occur from inside of the epistemic community alone. On the one hand, central bankers across the globe are sharing a common mindset, on the other hand central bank mandates have a clear domestic scope. Emanating from this is a potentially destabilizing impact within the epistemic community of central bankers when policy spillovers affect foreign peers. A question that arises is in how far common ties that make up the epistemic community can cope with tensions that arise due to negative policy spillovers due to the domestic macro-economic scope of monetary policies. The abundance of literature regarding monetary policy frameworks with domestic macroeconomic objectives and their international ramifications (Haberis and Lipinska 2012; Ahmed and Zlate 2013; Clark et al. 2016), as well as ongoing international debates among technocrats within a homogeneous policy field (Bernanke 2005; Rajan 2014), indicate discursive tensions between the twofold embeddedness of central bankers, simultaneously embedded in a transnational epistemic community based on economics and in their domestic mandates. This chapter investigates in how far discursive dynamics, emanating from the debate on the effects of quantitative easing lead or do not lead to discursive repositioning by central banks, in this case by the Federal Reserve.

In our analysis, we have taken our cues from Actor Network Theory (ANT) and its insistence on the social construction of analytical frames to evaluate policy spillovers – focusing in particular on the possible channels which are left out and the ones that are included in these frames (Callon 2014). Particularly the relevance of the problem framing is highlighted in ANT, as it requires for the exclusion of various entities that could also be entailed in the frame (Callon 2006: 61–62). This conceptualization of problem framing therefore emphasizes its political character of framing actions on the micro level (see also Latour 2006: 120–121, 131).[5] Importantly for the construction of frames and the internalization of spillovers, it is required to identify source, target and the overflowing itself. In the field of economics, "spaces of calculability" (ibid.: 256) are hence to be produced by economists to allow for target-oriented policy actions. Economic models are an important factor in the construction of frames. For the case of "monetary policy spillovers," the discourse thus needs to identify which monetary policy causes what type of spillover to which countries and through which channels so that the assessment costs and benefits as well as the deduction of policy implications become possible. In the central bank policy field, these identifications are still debated, an issue which we turn to now.

ANALYSIS

It emerges from the analysis that, until the taper tantrum of 2013, the analytical frames deployed by Fed, IMF and BIS to guide monetary policies were structured by a clear division between macro-economics and finance. Adverse effects of domestic monetary policies on domestic and global financial stability and on economies abroad were not part of the analytical frames that guide the setting of optimal monetary policy. The separation between macro-economics and finance has a decisive impact on financial and monetary policymaking as it underpins the division of labor between financial regulation and monetary policies: Whereas the latter is supposed to target macro-economic variables, the former should safeguard the stability of the financial system and offset possible risks emerging from monetary policies. In how far macro-financial linkages are accounted for in analyses of monetary policies affects whether the division of labor can be upheld or whether the case for the integration of financial stability concerns in monetary policy frameworks is strengthened.

After the "taper tantrum," the three institutions increasingly accounted for financial variables in monetary policymaking, albeit to varying degree. Particularly the BIS switched from an analytical frame underpinned by pure macro-economics to one undergirded by international macro-finance. This led to a significant change in the identification of problems in the conduct of monetary policies, from too low inflation rates to too loose financing conditions, and the policy advice derived from them, from deploying new policy instruments for reaching inflation target to integrating (global) financial stability objectives.[6]

Concepts

In the following, in order to facilitate the better understanding of our results we present the discursive concepts, which structure the two predominant frames we found in our analysis regarding the possible effects of Quantitative Easing, one which is based on a neoclassical view and can be described as neoclassical macro-economics and one based on a new view that has been called "international macro-finance" (Obstfeld and Taylor 2017).

Macro-economics versus international macro-finance

Two main frames emerged since the financial crisis, one that is informed by macro-economics with a focus on current accounts and one that is informed by international macro-finance with a focus on capital accounts (Obstfeld and Taylor 2017). Based on these frames, different policy implications are derived. This emphasizes the role of economics in the formulation of monetary policy. Only the separation between macro-economics and finance allows for neatly dividing policy instruments and policy objectives in the sense that monetary policies should solely focus on domestic macro-economic objectives, while financial stability is to be safeguarded by prudential regulation. If the separation collapses, it depends on the specific framing of the linkages between macro-economics and finance as well as on the effectiveness of prudential tools to what degree monetary policy needs to consider financial stability concerns. This "leaning-against-the-wind" debate gained significant traction after the financial crisis and is still unresolved (see Svensson 2017).

On the international dimension, the specific framing of the linkages determine to what extent international coordination of monetary policies becomes necessary to produce globally efficient outcomes. Coordination as suggested by a purely macro-economic framework in form of monetary policies focus solely on domestic inflation targets does not suffice when an international macro-finance framework is adopted. As the international scope of financial regulation implies, the framing of the interaction between monetary policy and financial stability does not halt at jurisdictional borders. Therefore, macro-financial frameworks come with international implications. The extent to which international macro-financial frames destabilize central bank mandates with domestic macro-economic objectives is affected by their specific framing. In any case, the externalization of unintended effects from monetary policies on financial stability would be difficult to be upheld in monetary policy discourses.

Capital accounts versus current accounts

Focusing on the macro-economic side in analyses of monetary policies makes the adoption of a current account perspective a logical step when it comes to the implications of monetary policies for the stability of the international monetary and financial system. The focus on transactions that stem from the exchange of goods, which materialize in net capital flows, results in a focus on variables that affect the free trade of goods, particularly exchange rate interventions to strengthen a country's international competitiveness. Focusing on international macro-finance, in contrast, makes capital accounts the prime indicator for tracing global imbalances. Purely financial transactions are accounted for, increasing the dimension of complexity in the assessment of global imbalances. Financial risks may not only stem from exchange rate interventions, but also from global push factors such as monetary policies in advanced economies.

The current account, however, entails only net financial flows caused by the exchange of real goods and services. Against this backdrop, financial imbalances build up due to differentials in global savings and consumption. Countries that have higher saving ratios export demand to other countries that receive capital from these surplus countries to finance the imports of their goods. A "global saving glut" (Bernanke 2005), according to the current account perspective, can therefore cause asset price bubbles and credit booms as capital inflows finance the deficits of other countries. The main risks to domestic financial and macro-economic stability as well as the international monetary and financial system stem from exchange rate interventions by countries that resist upward pressure of their currencies to defend the international competitiveness of their export industry. These exports are in turn financed by net capital inflows to deficit countries and become possible since surplus countries have higher savings-to-investment ratios.

If surplus countries flexibilize their exchange rates, their appreciating currencies would reduce net capital outflows. On the other hand, currencies of deficit countries would depreciate and their exports would increase, leading to reduced net capital inflows. When exchange rates of all countries are flexibilized and savings-to-investment ratios adjust, the international financial and monetary system will be stabilized by equilibrating market forces. This perspective is adopted by the Fed, which argues that monetary policies should solely be focused on domestic macroeconomic objectives, identifying exchange rate interventions as currency manipulation to promote growth at the expense of other countries. The scope of coordination and the guarantee of global financial stability therefore hinges on the idea that every country abstains from exchange rate interventions. From this current account perspective, the international risk-taking channel is infeasible to observe as net capital flows are driven by fundamentals, manipulative exchange rate interventions and savings-to-investment differentials.

The self-stabilization of the international monetary and financial system through flexible exchange rate regimes does not get to the core of the problem when a capital account perspective is adopted. The current account perspective misses out core features of the buildup of financial imbalances in the context of "excess financial elasticity." This is related to the confounding of saving and financing by the current account perspective since it frames investments as financed solely via savings (Borio 2012: 12).[7] Given the relevance of international financial markets in the financing of investments, this is an odd conceptualization. Bracketing out "finance" from the current account perspective leads to the veiling of financial imbalances that materialize in gross capital flows and stocks of debt and can produce financial risks. By taking finance seriously, the capital account perspective acknowledges the interactions of monetary policies and financial conditions across countries, as framed by the "excess financial elasticity" concept.

Accounting for interdependencies between monetary policies and between monetary policies and global financing conditions in monetary policy frameworks is therefore inevitable to prevent the buildup of global financial risks. Financial imbalances in the capital account perspectives build up not as a result of exchange rate interventions and differentials in savings and consumption. Instead, they are affected by the complex interconnections between monetary policies and between monetary policies and financing conditions. Looking at net capital flows does not entail information about what kind of financing is occurring in which country. Only by focusing on capital accounts and balance sheets of economic entities, it becomes possible to comprehensibly assess global imbalances and financial risks. In contrast to the current account perspective, policy implications from a capital account perspective become more complex.

Imbalances stemming from net capital flows are only one indicator for a possible buildup of financial risks. Financial risks can furthermore stem from various factors; for example, different types of currency or maturity mismatches. The origin of the problem lies therefore not in savings-to-investment ratios and currency manipulations, but can emerge from various entities in the web of central banks and financial markets, which are interdependent and interconnected via the current international monetary and financial system. For the post-crisis period, U.S. monetary policy was identified as a main driver of global liquidity that leads to the buildup of financial risks on the balance sheets of corporates in emerging market economies, traced in the BIS Quarterly Reviews. Based on the identification of problems and origins via the capital account perspective, policy implications aim for a more comprehensible account for entities that may be source and targets of risks. While some entities like banks and nonbanks can be regulated, central banks are unconstrained in their pursuit of domestic inflation targets and solely need to legitimize their actions according to their domestic mandate. Central banks that pursue only domestic macro-economic objectives are therefore a potential risk to the stability of the international monetary and financial system. Only if central banks acknowledge their interdependent position in the complex system and internalize the potential damaging effect of their monetary policies, the global system can be stabilized.

The case for integrating financial stability objectives in monetary policy is therefore much more compelling given an analytical framework informed by macro-finance. Financial stability in this perspective hinges fundamentally on global finance conditions that are significantly affected by loose monetary policy stances of central banks in advanced economies after 2007. Taking into account the international linkages between monetary policies and global financing conditions means that the integration of financial stability in monetary policy frameworks will entail an international dimension. For the current account perspective, the case is much stronger for keeping monetary policy and financial stability separated, with the latter being safeguarded by financial regulation.

The international risk-taking channel and capital flows

The concept of the risk-taking channel is decisive for understanding the separation between macro-economics and finance. This channel plays literally no role in the Fed's analytical framework but is central to the ones of the BIS and the IMF post-2010, as they identify capital flows that are not driven by fundamentals and exchange rate interventions which are aimed to strengthen the competitiveness of surplus countries. The risk-taking channel transmits yield-searching activities of banks and nonbanks which are not fundamentals-based but purely driven by the need to produce profit. Whether this channel is analyzed from a domestic or an international scope generates different implications. Domestically the channel comes with implications for domestic financial stability concerns. Yield-searching activities on the international level materialize in capital flows to countries that offer favorable returns to investors. Particularly emerging market economies were targets of these speculative flows in the post-crisis period due to higher interest rate environments they offered.

This in turn leads to the buildup of financial risks in emerging market economies. Due to the speculative nature of these flows, they are considered as particularly volatile. As soon as policy rates in advanced economies will be increased again, financial imbalances will unravel and international investors will return to safer investments. Since these capital flows can cause significant market volatilities, like experienced during the "taper tantrum," financial stability concerns are inevitably entailed in the framing of the international risk-taking channel. Lacking the international risk-taking channel in its analytical framework, the Fed frames capital flows as driven by pull factors in emerging market economies. The IMF notes that the risk-taking channel has some influence, which is indicated in the identification of both fundamentals-driven pull factors and speculation-driven push factors in driving capital flows. The BIS fully embraced the risk-taking channel in its analytical framework and argues that capital flows in the post-crisis era are driven mainly by push factors, particularly unconventional monetary policies in advanced economies. The size of the impact of the international risk-taking channel on capital flows is determining in how far monetary policy can be held responsible for creating risks in the international monetary and financial system.

Based on the respective analytical framework, different policy implications are proposed. When the international risk-taking channel is not taken into account, the burden of adjustment is externalized to countries that face speculative capital inflows. They are called to improve their fundamentals and regulatory frameworks if they cannot cope with these capital flows. When the risk-taking channel is integrated in the analytical framework, the burden of adjustment shifts towards source countries, i.e. advanced economies, which endanger the stability of the international financial and monetary system by recklessly focusing their monetary policies on domestic macro-economic objectives.

Spillovers

Adopting either a perspective informed by macro-economics or one informed by international macro-finance gives different meanings to what is meant by "policy spillovers." In the current account perspective, which is adopted by the Fed, spillovers are located on the macro-economic side, where demand is shifted abroad and net capital flows are the indicator for the buildup of global imbalances. Since, according to this view, the objective of monetary policy is to achieve domestic macro-economic stability, policy spillovers are identified as inevitable by-product. Spillovers, from this perspective, occur on macro-economic variables, e.g. reduced output due to increased demand of imports that are driven by exchange rate manipulations in other countries. In that sense, monetary policy spillovers are negative if the demand-shifting effect is bigger than the combined effect of increasing demand in the country that employs accommodative policies and the easier access to credit which will increase investment and output. If international capital flows are causing problems in emerging market economies, they have to adjust their fundamentals and prudential frameworks.

By adopting a capital account perspective, the focus shifts towards financial policy spillovers. Due to the abstraction from domestic macro-economic objectives, the accommodative policy stances in advanced economies may be identified as unjustified given the costs that are caused by real and financial policy spillovers. This is particularly the case if these financial spillovers cannot be sufficiently targeted by prudential frameworks and capital controls in capital-receiving countries. While the current account perspective frames the financial policy spillover channel as the ease of access to credit that is used for growth-enhancing investments, the capital account perspective is more granular and zeroes in on how financial risks begin to materialize on balance sheets of financial and non-financial entities. The stock of debt or currency and maturity mismatches may indicate risks that fundamentally stem from yield-searching flows through the international risk-taking channel which are triggered by unconventional monetary policies in advanced economies. Only to the extent that easy financing conditions are used for productive investments, these spillovers can be positive. Given the significant increase of dollar-denominated debt that circulates in emerging market economies in the post-crisis period, monetary policy spillovers may have led to a buildup of financial imbalances that are prone for a disorderly unwinding when policy rates in advanced economies are normalized.

DISCOURSE TRAJECTORIES: FED – IMF – BIS 2007–2012

In the time between the financial crisis 2007 and the taper tantrum in 2013, the analytical frameworks deployed by Fed, IMF and BIS were all underpinned by a purely macro-economic perspective. They therefore converged regarding the identification of policy problems and the implications for improving monetary policies. According to these frameworks, monetary policies do not affect financial systems and they do not have a negative impact on other economies when all central banks target their monetary policies exclusively on domestic inflation targets. Capital flows therefore are simply reflect the global exchange of goods. Only when countries intervene in foreign exchange markets to foster competitiveness and deploy monetary policies for this purpose, global imbalances may build up due to the shifting of demand abroad. These deficits are financed by capital inflows from surplus countries. This is why the shared problem resolution frames contained advices to flexibilize exchange rate regimes, deploy monetary policies exclusively for achieving domestic macro-economic objectives and to improve fundamentals and regulatory frameworks. The latter should further safeguard the financial stability of each country, underpinning the separation between macro-economics and financial stability. If every country follows this recipe, there would be no buildup of global imbalances and global output can be maximized.

The analytical framework informing the policymaking of the Fed before 2013 was the one with the lowest degree of change after the taper tantrum. The focus of monetary policies on domestic macro-economic objectives and the need for exchange rate flexibilization to rebalance the international monetary and financial system did not change in the post-crisis period. Emerging market economies are called on to continue to improve the quality of their policy frameworks and their financial systems (Brainard 2016; Fischer 2014). The sole, albeit significant, change is that Yellen's tenure is characterized by a clearer communication of its conduct of monetary policy, particularly to her central bank colleagues in other countries.

The general agreement on this macro-economic analytical framework slowly weakened when central bankers grew increasingly aware that

Table 12.1 Discourse – pre-2013

	FED	IMF	BIS
Spillovers	Real	Real	Real
Risk-taking channel	No	No	No
Global imbalances	Current account	Current account	Current account
Scope of analysis	Net capital flows	Net capital flows	Net capital flows
Scope of monetary policy	Domestic macroeconomics	Domestic macroeconomics	Domestic macroeconomics
Adjustment	EMEs	EMEs	EMEs
Coordination	House in order	House in order	House in order

post-crisis monetary policies do have a (negative) impact on financial stability after all and that these effects are spread globally. The final collapse of the consensus coincided with the taper tantrum in 2013, after which the three institutions adopted analytical frameworks that are, at least partially, mutually inconsistent. While general ideas of the pre-taper tantrum consensus still prevail (focus on inflation targets), there is a growing adoption of macro-financial aspects in the analytical frameworks.

This reflects a shift of a focus from imbalances on the current account to those on the capital account (that take into account speculative financial flows, and not only those used to finance the global exchange of goods). Monetary policies have therefore an impact on financial stability and the focus of central banks on domestic inflation targets is insufficient to safeguard the stability of the international monetary and financial. Particularly the BIS emerged as an institution that adopted and actively promoted their newly adopted analytical framework underpinned by macro-finance. The adoption of financial stability-oriented monetary policy frameworks, the internalization of negative policy spillovers and closer monetary policy coordination are main demands posed by the BIS. The preparation of this framework from the early 2000s onwards allowed for its adoption in 2013, when a window of opportunity emanated due the unexpected events during the taper tantrum. Particularly Claudio Borio and Hyun Shin are names linked to the change of the framework.

The IMF moved from a rigid macro-economic framework to one that accounts for the existence of macro-financial linkages, primarily in the form of the international risk-taking channel. It thereby acknowledges that financial imbalances are not completely identifiable on the current account. Nevertheless, current account imbalances remain central in the IMF framework, invoking policy implications that focus on exchange rate flexibilization and macro-economic adjustments in emerging market economies. Financial risks from capital flows that are triggered by yield-searching activities are to be reduced by the employment of prudential tools and, in emergency situations, capital controls. In contrast to the BIS, the IMF argues that prudential frameworks allow to sufficiently counter these financial risks. Monetary policies should maintain their focus on domestic macro-economic variables. The BIS states that prudential frameworks are insufficient to prevent the buildup of financial imbalances so that monetary policy frameworks need to take into account financial stability concerns and policy spillovers to other countries. Particularly this breakdown of the separation between macro-economics and finance is highly problematic for the hegemonic international monetary policy discourse as it inevitably relativizes the domestic macro-economic scope of monetary policy frameworks.

Table 12.2 Discourse Trajectories after the taper tantrum

	FED	IMF	BIS
Spillovers	Real	Real	Financial
Risk-taking channel	No	Yes	Yes
Global imbalances	Current account	mixed	Capital account
Scope of analysis	Net capital flows	mixed	Balance sheets
Scope of monetary policy	Domestic macroeconomics	Domestic macroeconomics	International macro-finance
Adjustment	EMEs	EMEs	AEs
Coordination	House in order	House in order	Monetary policy

There is hence a cacophony in the transnational discourse on the effects of QE, with BIS the most opposed to QE, the Fed firmly defending its policies and the IMF seeking an intermediating position. This lack of clarity is strongly bounded up with a reference to vepistemic uncertainty by all agents in the discoursive field.

Epistemic Uncertainty

Fed, BIS as well as IMF referred to the epistemic uncertainty revolving around the issue of negative, unintended effects of monetary policies on financial stability and on other countries. Either analytical frameworks do not reach so far to account for some entities and mechanisms, like financial policy spillovers, or they are not yet sufficiently developed to the extent that they can directly inform policy decisions (Interview former U.S. policymaker, 23 May 2017 in Washington D.C.). Uncertainties revolve around the effects of particularly monetary policies on global financing conditions and capital flows as well as the effects of capital flows on emerging market economies. To the present day, it only became consensus among the analyzed institutions that spillovers are affected differently by different types of monetary policies (e.g. monetary policies at the zero lower bound are different than "conventional" interest rate policies) and that spillover effects may diverge across countries. While all three policy institutions show awareness regarding the uncertainty that emanate from difficulties to disentangle and identify different international effects of monetary policies, they all draw on epistemic uncertainty as a resource to promote their particular frames.

THE POTENTIAL FOR POST-KEYNESIAN CONTRIBUTIONS

Post-Keynesians are traditionally aware of the inherent instability of the international monetary and financial system, its adverse impact on the economy if not sufficiently regulated and the implications of macro-financial linkages for the conduct of monetary policy (Minsky 1986). The need for coordination in the international monetary and financial system was emphasized early on by Keynes (see e.g. Keynes 1919). It is therefore not surprising that the financial crisis 2007 led to a surge of contributions that picked up these two issues. This section identifies contributions made in the *Review of Keynesian Economics, Journal of Post Keynesian Economics, Cambridge Journal of Economics*, *Review of Political Economy* and *Journal of Economic Issues* since 2007 which account for the macro-financial dimension of monetary policies as well as implications for the global governance of the international monetary and financial system.

Conduct of Monetary Policy

Criticisms of inflation-targeting frameworks, which were the largely uncontested hegemonic until the financial crisis 2007, are not surprising to occur from the side of post-Keynesianism. The inherent macro-financial perspective and the implications of financial instabilities for the governance of the international monetary and financial system are traditionally centerpiece of (post-)Keynesianism. Nevertheless, contributions from this side differ in the degree to which monetary policies should be reformed. Older contributions made only minimal changes to the original inflation-targeting framework and do not account for the financial dimension of monetary policy (Kriesler and Lavoie 2007). Contributions after the crisis became more sweeping. Vernengo (2016) argues that the unidimensional focus on inflation objectives impedes economic development. He does not account, however, for financial stability aspects and therefore suggests that capital inflows are unambiguously good for development. Aquanno and Brennan (2016) similarly criticize distributional effects of inflation-targeting regimes. Seccareccia (2017) shows how sectoral interests affect monetary policy and how this affects distributional effects of quantitative easing.

Taking into account the impact of financial instability on the economy automatically entails a distributive dimension, strengthening the venture point of critics that adopt a macro-financial perspective. This is convincingly shown by Knibbe (2015), who criticizes inflation-targeting policy frameworks and argues for the integration of price and financial stability objectives, since the focus on price stability of consumer goods is insufficient to guarantee monetary and financial stability. Tokucu (2014) shows how the Turkish central bank adjusted its policy framework to account for changes in financial markets, emphasizing how financial stability concerns need to be integrated in monetary policy frameworks. Arestis and Sawyer (2010) find that that financial stability, not inflation targeting, should be the prime rational for the conduct of monetary policy. It is particularly this link between monetary policy and financial stability that is in the center of debates of central bankers about monetary policy frameworks.

Dow (2017) discusses the need for integrating financial stability concerns in monetary policy frameworks since, based on the changing structure of financial system, only this allows to safeguard macro-economic and financial stability. Further, Le Maux (2017) shows how changing structures of financial markets underpinned the change in monetary policy frameworks after the financial crisis, increasingly focussing on financial stability. Reforming the monetary policy framework by integrating financial stability concerns will reduce the buildup of financial imbalances and financial risks that were largely unnoticed in the years before the financial crisis. Post-Keynesian approaches could help promote this change of policy frameworks which gained momentum in the debates of Fed, IMF and BIS. But what about possible contributions to the debate about the governance of the international monetary and financial system?

The Governance of the International Monetary and Financial System

A number of contributions analyze the problems posed by destabilizing international capital flows. Particularly the difference between the current account perspective (as adopted by the Fed) and the capital account perspective (as adopted by the BIS in 2013) is well articulated. Liang (2012a) provides an interesting contribution as he explicitly questions the usefulness of the current account perspective for analyzing global financial imbalances. She nicely shows how coordination under current account perspective will neither reduce global financial risks nor global economic growth (only beggar-thy-neighbor). In a follow-up paper, Liang (2012b) shows how the international monetary and financial system fuels both financial imbalances and financial instabilities and argues, in Keynes' tradition, for the implementation of a clearing union to reform the international monetary and financial system. This builds on the Keynesian insight that financial flows and economic development are tightly interlinked.

Bonizzi's study (2017) sheds light on how capital flows are not triggered by macro-economic considerations but instead are speculative and profit-driven, which have implications for financial stability. His insights resemble those of Borio at the BIS, who also identifies a conceptual confusion of savings and finance that underpin the separation between the current account and the capital account view of international capital flows. Tokunaga and Epstein (2018) show that the current account view is insufficient in explaining the financial crisis as the focus needs to be shifted to the aspect of finance, for which the U.S. dollar is the central currency. Their insights allow for strengthening the argument for integrating macro-financial aspects in the conduct of monetary policy. Gallagher (2015a), who points to Keynes' contribution in the debate to global financial regulation, namely that international capital flows need to be regulated to safeguard economic and financial stability shows how welfare economics made a breakthrough in this respect. He further identifies similarities of new welfare economics to post-Keynesian approaches (ibid.: 59–60). Although drawing on different theories, both focus on the nature of international capital flows and their implications for financial stability, and find that these flows need to be regulated nationally and/or multilaterally.[8]

A second aspect of international governance highlighted in the literature concerns the role of asymmetries that are produced by the existence of reserve currencies, particularly the U.S. dollar. D'Arista (2009) emphasizes the shortcomings of the current currency systems and offers an overview of possible alternative regimes that could supplant the centrality of the U.S. dollar. Also, Garcia Banchs and Mata Mollejas (2010) point out the fundamental asymmetry in the international monetary system, divided into countries that issue reserve currencies and countries that build up reserves in these currencies. This has implications on the independence of monetary policy (reserve currency issuing countries are more independent) and the exchange rate regime (see also, Kaltenbrunner and Painceira 2017).

This brief overview of post-Keynesian contributions to the debate about negative externalities posed by monetary policies indicates that they could also offer relevant insights for policymakers. Until now, mainstream economists adapted to recent criticisms by integrating financial frictions into standard DSGE models and by developing new thoughts in welfare economics (see Korinek 2018). The capital account view is closely interlinked with post-Keynesian approaches, focussing on the role of finance and its role in the international monetary and financial system. Post-Keynesian focus on fundamental uncertainty and speculation, reflecting the opposing approach in the governance of international monetary and financial system as well as the conduct of monetary policy. A main thrust is how to ensure that monetary policies can be conducted independently, pointing to the need for global monetary governance (similar concerns have been raised in the debate on the global financial cycle, mostly stemming from empirical work, see Coimbra and Rey 2018; Aggripino and Rey 2015).

CONCLUSION

Recalling the main findings of this chapter: firstly, there is a consensus among the three institutions that national monetary policies lead to international spillovers, although their sign, quality and quantity are still a matter of debate. Secondly, the 2013 taper tantrum coincides with a significant change in the analytical frames deployed by the three institutions. The Fed changed the communication of its conduct of monetary policy. The IMF increasingly studied and discussed effects as well as provided policy implications for emerging market economies concerning financial policy spillovers. And the BIS embraced a discourse that emphasizes the linkages between monetary policies and financial markets and asks advanced economies, particularly the U.S., to internalize negative policy spillovers they produce. Thus, the change of the Fed's discourse correlates with a general shift in the international discourse among policymakers about international effects of monetary policies.

The shift in analytical frameworks which we detected by 2013 resulted in the destruction of the congruence and harmony of the joint outlook on Quantitative Easing by the three investigated policy institutions. The inflow of international macro-financial conceptual variables in these analyses led to diverging policy assessments, the relevance of the risk-taking channel serves as a prime example. The Fed still focusses on the achievement of domestic macro-economic objectives, while being increasingly mindful of the need to communicate with market actors and peers from abroad to prevent unrests as well as to reduce tensions within the central bank community. The IMF changed its understanding of policy spillovers and the role of monetary policies in driving capital flows. These efforts resulted in an analytical framework that mainly entailed ways how emerging market economies can cope with destabilizing capital flows, whereas the domestic macro-economic focus of monetary policies remained unquestioned.

Also the BIS significantly changed its analytical framework regarding these issues, which result in policy implications that contrast starkly with the one of the IMF or the Fed. Monetary policies in advanced economies are identified as a main source of risks to the stability of the international monetary and financial system; hence the role of advanced economies was positioned in the center of the derived policy implications. Post-Keynesian ideas show remarkable similarities to ideas that were adopted by the BIS and the IMF over the last couple of years. The mutual indifference is hence all the more striking. While post-Keynesians at least partially cite norm entrepreneurs at the BIS and IMF, namely Borio, Disyatat, Claessens or Korinek, the other way is even less so. The integration of financial frictions in DSGE models, the adoption of the capital account view by the BIS, the rethinking in the IMF and the debates among central bankers about the integration of financial stability concerns in monetary policy frameworks are links that can be used by post-Keynesians to strengthen their influence in policy debates. Post-Keynesians have a head start in these debates and could use this momentum to strengthen their position.

The large advantage of post-Keynesian approaches is that they do not presume that financial markets are inherently efficient. From this vantage point it is much easier for post-Keynesian to identify problems of monetary policies, particularly in its macro-financial dimension. Their approach is hence less convoluted and driven by auxiliary assumptions, as is the case for neoclassic economics, for which, since the financial crisis, financial frictions are increasingly discussed and integrated in mainstream DSGE models, a trend followed by central bankers. Post-Keynesians could enrich the debate by opening up the frames of analysis and offering macro-financial analyses and models that deviate from assumptions of equilibrium which could broaden the debate and inform future policy decision-making by central bankers.

NOTES

1. Due to the low interest rate environment in advanced economies, market actors increasingly made short-term investments in higher-yielding emerging market economies, leading to a boom in short-term dollar-denominated debt and unsustainable currency mismatches. An increase in the policy rate can lead to a disorderly unwinding of these positions, as it happened during the taper tantrum (see Thiemann and Nagel 2018).
2. The relevance of documents for the analysis was assessed via their titles and abstracts. If these did not give sufficient indication for the content of the document, the introductions, headings and conclusions were analyzed. If keywords that regularly occur in the debate like spillovers, coordination, capital flows, global imbalances, etc. were mentioned, the documents were analyzed in-depth. This analysis was conducted by coding the content and subdividing the coded statements into problem frames and policy resolution frames. Due to the size of the data set, it is not attached in the Annex. Instead, it is provided electronically at request.
3. Evidently, such change is only a necessary, but not sufficient condition (see Hall 1989).
4. Manuela Moschella's analysis of the Swiss National Bank's change of its exchange rate policy due to discursive shifts within the central bank community towards taking financial stability more seriously (Moschella 2015a) presents an outlier.
5. Framing is hence the foundation through which meanings are ascribed to the entities (actors, mechanisms, outcomes), by which institutions can position themselves as "obligatory passage points" and the policy field itself is constructed. Framing actions, in this sense, are the internalization of spillovers, resulting in the equilibration of costs and benefits among actors and the renewed closure of the frame (see Callon 2014).
6. We do not imply that the taper tantrum was the main causal driver for the changes in the debate. Instead, it functioned as a catalyst for ideas that were present already before, allowing existing, but neglected ideas to become prominent.
7. "Financing is a gross cash-flow concept, and denotes access to purchasing power in the form of an accepted settlement medium (money), including through borrowing.

Saving, as defined in the national accounts, is simply income (output) not consumed. Expenditures require financing, not saving" (Borio 2012: 12).

8. In this vein, Ferrari-FIlho and De Paula (2008) argue that capital controls and managed exchange rate regimes need to be implemented to protect emerging market economies and developing countries from destabilizing short-term capital flows (see also Kaltenbrunner and Painceira 2017).

REFERENCES

Abdelal, Rawi. 2009. *Capital Rules: The Construction of Global Finance*. Cambridge, Mass.: Harvard Univ. Press.

Ahmed, Shaghil, and Andrei Zlate. 2013. "Capital Flows to Emerging Market Economies: A Brave New World?" IFDP 1081 (June 2013).

Aquanno, Scott, and Jordan Brennan. 2016. "The Politics of Canadian Monetary Policy: Reassessing Canadian Inflation, Part II." *Journal of Economic Issues* 50(3): 814–33.

Arestis, Philip, and Malcolm Sawyer. 2010. "What Monetary Policy after the Crisis?" *Review of Political Economy* 22(4): 499–515.

Baker, Andrew. 2013. "The New Political Economy of the Macro-prudential Ideational Shift." *New Political Economy* 18(1): 112–39, doi:10.1080/13563467.2012.662952.

Banchs, Angel G., and Luis M. Mollejas. 2010. "International Monetary Asymmetries and the Central Bank." *Journal of Post Keynesian Economics* 32(3): 467–96.

Bernanke, Ben S. 2005. *The Global Saving Glut and the U.S. Current Account Deficit*. Remarks at the Sandridge Lecture, Virginia Association of Economists. April 14, 2005. St. Louis, Missouri.

Bonizzi, Bruno. 2017. "An Alternative Post-Keynesian Framework for Understanding Capital Flows to Emerging Markets." *Journal of Economic Issues* 51(1): 137–62.

Borio, Claudio. 2012. "The Financial Cycle and Macro-economics: What have we Learnt?" *BIS Working Paper* 395(December 2012).

Brainard, Lael. 2016. *What Happened to the Great Divergence?* Remarks at the "2016 Monetary Policy Forum" annual conference, sponsored by University of Chicago Booth School of Business. February 26, 2016. New York, New York.

Callon, Michel. 2006. "Die Sozio-Logik der Übersetzung: Auseinandersetzungen und Verhandlungen zur Bestimmung von Problematischem und Unproblematischem." Pp. 51–74 in *ScienceStudies, ANThology: Ein einführendes Handbuch zur Akteur-Netzwerk-Theorie*, edited by A. Belliger and D. J. Krieger. Bielefeld: Transcript-Verl.

Callon, Michel. 2014. "An Essay on Framing and Overflowing: Economic Externalities Revisited by Sociology." *The Sociological Review* 46(1): 244–69, doi:10.1111/j.1467-954X.1998.tb03477.x.

Chwieroth, Jeffrey M. 2008. "Normative Change from Within: The International Monetary Fund's Approach to Capital Account Liberalization." *International Studies Quarterly* 52(1): 129–58, doi:10.1111/j.1468-2478.2007.00494.x.

Chwieroth, Jeffrey M. 2010. *Capital Ideas: The IMF and the Rise of Financial Liberalization*. Princeton, N.J: Princeton University Press (http://lib.myilibrary.com/detail.asp?ID=247319).

Chwieroth, Jeffrey M., and Timothy J. Sinclair. 2013. "How You Stand Depends on How We See: International Capital Mobility as Social Fact." *Review of International Political Economy* 20(3): 457–85, doi:10.1080/09692290.2012.675875.

Clark, John, Nathan Converse, Brahima Coulibaly, and Steven Kamin. 2016. "Emerging Market Capital Flows and U.S. Monetary Policy." IFDP Notes (October 18, 2016).

Coimbra, Nuno, and Helene Rey. 2018. "Financial Cycles and Credit Growth Across Countries." *American Economic Review Papers and Proceedings*.

Corsetti, Giancarlo, Paolo Pesenti, Nouriel Roubini, and Cédric Tille. 2000. "Competitive Devaluations: Toward a Welfare-Based Approach." *Journal of International Economics* 51(1): 217–41, doi:10.1016/S0022-1996(99)00043-4.

D'Arista, Jane. 2009. "The Evolving International Monetary System." *Cambridge Journal of Economics* 33(4): 633–52.

Dow, Sheila. 2017. "Central Banking in the Twenty-first Century." *Cambridge Journal of Economics* 41(6): 1539–57.

Eichengreen, Barry, and Jeffrey Sachs. 1986. "Competitive Devaluation and the Great Depression." *Economics Letters* 22(1): 67–71, doi:10.1016/0165-1765(86)90144-8.

Fischer, Stanley. 2014. *The Federal Reserve and the Global Economy*. Remarks at the Per Jacobsson Foundation Lecture, 2014 Annual Meetings of the International Monetary Fund and the World Bank Group. October 11, 2014. Washington, D.C.

Gabor, Daniela. 2012. "Managing Capital Accounts in Emerging Markets: Lessons from the Global Financial Crisis." *Journal of Development Studies* 48(6): 714–31, doi:10.1080/00220388.2011.649257.

Gallagher, Kevin P. 2015a. *Ruling Capital*. Ithaca, NY: Cornell University Press.

Gallagher, Kevin P. 2015b. "Contesting the Governance of Capital Flows at the IMF." *Governance* 28(2): 185–98, doi:10.1111/gove.12100.

Grabel, Ilene. 2015. "The Rebranding of Capital Controls in an Era of Productive Incoherence." *Review of International Political Economy* 22(1): 7–43, doi:10.1080/09692290.2013.836677.

Haas, Peter M. 1992. "Introduction: Epistemic Communities and International Policy Coordination." *International Organization* 46(1): 1–35, doi:10.1017/s0020818300001442.

Haberis, Alex, and Anna Lipinska. 2012. "International Policy Spillovers at the Zero Lower Bound." FEDS 2012–23 (April 2012).

Kaltenbrunner, Annina, and Juan Pablo Painceira. 2017. "The Impossible Trinity: Inflation Targeting, Exchange Rate Management and Open Capital Accounts in Emerging Economies." *Development and Change* 48(3): 452–80.

Kapstein, Ethan B. 1989. "Resolving the Regulator's Dilemma: International Coordination of Banking Regulations." *International Organization* 43(2): 323–47, doi:10.1017/s0020818300032938.

Keynes, John Maynard. 1919. *The Economic Consequences of the Peace* (1st ed.). London: Macmillan.

Knibbe, Merijn. 2015. "Metrics Meta About a Metametric: The Consumer Price Level as a Flawed Target for Central Bank Policy." *Journal of Economic Issues* 49(2): 355–71.

Korinek, Anton. 2018. "Regulating Capital Flows to Emerging Markets: An Externality View." *Journal of International Economics* 111: 61–80, doi: 10.1016/j.jinteco.2017.12.005.

Kriesler, Peter, and Marc Lavoie. 2007. "The New Consensus on Monetary Policy and its Post-Keynesian Critique." *Review of Political Economy* 19(3): 387–404.

Latour, Bruno. 2006. "Gebt mir ein Laboratorium und ich werde die Welt aus den Angeln heben." Pp. 103–34 in *ScienceStudies, ANThology: Ein einführendes Handbuch zur Akteur-Netzwerk-Theorie*, edited by A. Belliger and D. J. Krieger. Bielefeld: Transcript-Verl.
Le Maux, Laurent. 2017. "Financial Structure Changes and the Central Bank Policy." *Journal of Economic Issues* 51(4): 1054–73.
Liang, Yan. 2012a. "Global Imbalances as Root Cause of Global Financial Crisis? A Critical Analysis." *Journal of Economic Issues* 46(1): 101–18.
Liang, Yan. 2012b. "Global Imbalances and Financial Crisis: Financial Globalization as a Common Cause." *Journal of Economic Issues* 46(2): 353–62.
Marcussen, Martin. 2006. "The Transnational Governance Network of Central Bankers." Pp. 180–204, in *Transnational Governance*, edited by M.-L. Djelic and K. Sahlin-Andersson. Cambridge: Cambridge University Press.
McNamara, Kathleen R. 1999. *The Currency of Ideas: Monetary Politics in the European Union*. Ithaca, NY: Cornell Univ. Press.
Miranda-Agrippino, Silvia, and Hélène Rey. 2015. *US Monetary Policy and the Global Financial Cycle*. NBER Working Paper No. 21722.
Moschella, Manuela. 2015a. "Currency Wars in the Advanced World: Resisting Appreciation at a Time of Change in Central Banking Monetary Consensus." *Review of International Political Economy* 22(1): 134–61, doi:10.1080/09692290.2013.869242.
Moschella, Manuela. 2015b. "The Institutional Roots of Incremental Ideational Change: The IMF and Capital Controls after the Global Financial Crisis." *The British Journal of Politics and International Relations* 17(3): 442–60, doi:10.1111/1467-856X.12049.
Obstfeld, Maurice, and Alan M. Taylor. 2017. "International Monetary Relations: Taking Finance Seriously." NBER Working Paper No. 23440. May 2017.
Rajan, Raghuram. 2014. *Competitive monetary easing: is it yesterday once more?* Speech at the Brookings Institution. April 10, 2014. Washington, D.C.
Seccareccia, Mario. 2017. "Which Vested Interests do Central Banks Really Serve? Understanding Central Bank Policy Since the Global Financial Crisis." *Journal of Economic Issues* 51(2): 341–50.
Svensson, Lars E. 2017. "Cost-benefit Analysis of Leaning Against the Wind." *Journal of Monetary Economics* 90: 193–213.
Thiemann, Matthias, and Max Nagel. 2018. "The Allure and Pitfalls of Market Based Finance for Sustainable Development: Financial Sector Policy and the Addis Ababa Action Agenda." *Bread for the World Analysis* 80.
Tokucu, Erkan. 2014. "Appraising the Effectiveness of the Recent Turkish Monetary Policy: A Minskian Perspective." *Journal of Economic Issues* 48(3): 787–820.
Tokunaga, Junji, and Gerald Epstein. 2018. "The Endogenous Finance of Global-Dollar-Based Financial Fragility in the 2000s: A Minskyan Approach." *Review of Keynesian Economics* 6(1): 62–82.
Vernengo, Matias. 2016. "Kicking Away the Ladder, Too: Inside Central Banks." *Journal of Economic Issues* 50(2): 452–60.

13. Linking the real and financial sectors of the economy: the major contribution of post-Keynesians

Joëlle Leclaire

Nothing makes the link between the financial sector and the real sector clearer than a financial crisis. When the financial system is running smoothly and supporting the activities of the real sector, creating a decent number of good jobs, supporting aggregate demand adequately, providing a fair store of value for current and future retirees, then the link between the sectors seems almost invisible. For the most part, it takes a financial crisis to highlight the fact that there is a deep and necessary bond between finance and real production.

The roots of this link, between the financial and real productive sides of the economy, form one of the most foundational pillars of discussion for post-Keynesian economists. Understanding this nexus is potentially the most significant contribution that post-Keynesian economists can bring to the table. These models, based on the work of Keynes, Robinson, Kalecki, and Kaldor, and more, integrate the idea that money is essential to production (c.f. Lavoie 1984, 772–773; Lavoie 2014, 183; Kregel 1984, 139; Graziani 1989, 2; Rossi 2006, 121). The way money is integrated in post-Keynesian models provides an important starting point. There are two ways this is done in post-Keynesian models. The first is the superimposition of monetary values on multi-sectoral models. Money in the Keynesian, Robinsonian, Kaleckian, and Kaldorian models is not taken as an input into production, per se, but monetary values are superimposed onto a multi-sector model. Perhaps the best example of this branch is Kregel's work. He depicts Keynes' *General Theory* as a financial model where monetary values determine the level of private investment (Davidson 1972, 102; Minsky 2008, 195; Kregel 1983, 1984, 142, 1998; Wray 1993, 544). Like other post-Keynesian models, Kregel integrates a structural component where the distribution between the investment and consumption goods sectors determines output, employment, and growth. In this way, post-Keynesian models take financial-monetary values as a starting point. These nominal values change over the course of the production cycle and impact the distribution of income between the investment and consumption sectors.

The second and more recent way money is integrated into post-Keynesian models is via money's role as an input into production. Keynes alluded to the role of money as an input into production (c.f. Keynes 1973[1936], 173) but the monetary circuit originally proposed by Parguez, Graziani, and Schmitt, and brought to us in large measure via Seccareccia and Lavoie's work, introduced a new level of precision and understanding to the linkages between the real and financial sides of the economy (c.f. Graziani 1989; Bellofiore and Passarella 2016; Parguez 1984; Rossi 2006). The circuit approach suggests that money should be taken as an input into production, just like labor and physical capital. With the exception of the Dijon-Fribourg branch, the monetary circuit also has a feature which complements and further supports Davidson's and Kregel's discussion of Keynes' *General Theory*. The monetary circuit model incorporates time into the production process (Davidson 1972; Kregel 1983, 1984, 1998; Graziani 1989, 4–5; Lavoie 2014, 269; Rossi 2006, 124). Now money and time are incorporated in an expanded and more precise conception of the macroeconomy. This chapter will look at the nexus between the financial and real sectors, from the perspective of the work of some of the major post-Keynesians to highlight their significant contribution to our understanding of financial crises. Specifically, we will look at circuit theory, endogenous money and the determination of the overnight target rate, federal government deficit spending, employment, and economic growth. The focus will be on how a deeper understanding of money's role in these areas of the economy improves our knowledge of financial crises.

Post-Keynesians have developed a useful discussion of the interaction of the financial side and real side of the economy which helps us understand how their relationship is symbiotic in nature, and essential to understanding financial crises. Specifically, the ideas of the Franco-Italian circuitists – Parguez, Schmitt, and Graziani in particular – show that production is financed by banks, which are explicit in their models (Graziani 1989, 4–5; Bellofiore and Passarella 2016; Rossi 2006, 122). Seccareccia and Lavoie's work, which is part of the Franco-Italian school, supports the idea that production is financed directly by banks which create deposit balances *ex-nihilo* and they hold the position that central banks determines the overnight rate exogenously (Lavoie and Seccareccia 2013, 75–78).

Post-Keynesians strongly support a positive relationship between government deficit spending and its impact on the state of financial sector balances. Seccareccia and others use the financial sector balances approach to show that household debt now plays a significant role in offsetting non-financial business surpluses (Seccareccia 2012, 71). As he explains, that position is not sustainable and is likely to lead to a financial crisis. A second threat to financial stability relates to the securitization of household debt. Lavoie indicates that securitization of household debt threatens the stability of the financial structure and should not be permitted (Lavoie 2013b, 232). Taken together, these two positions on household debt's link to financial stability express the post-Keynesian view which is that the financial and economic system operate as one unit which needs to be supported by government spending and better regulated.

THE MONETARY CIRCUIT

The theory of the monetary circuit was developed in the late 1950s in France, most notably by Alain Parguez (1984) and Bernard Schmitt (1996), and in Italy by Augusto Graziani (1989, 1994); (Graziani 1989, 1, also mentions François Poulon of Bordeaux and Alvaro Cencini of Dijon, while Rossi 2006, mentions Le Bourva 1962 as potentially the first circuitist). Graziani explains that, until his 1989 English-language article, the literature on the monetary circuit is exclusively in French and Italian. The latter articles are written by French, Italian, and Canadian scholars (Graziani 1989, 2). Current branches of the circuit school would be Italian and French as before, with a French-Canadian contingent, and Modern Monetary Theory (MMT), and despite their reluctance in being associated with the circuit, the Fribourg-Dijon school as well. We now also see more English-language work.

Part of the reason that circuit theory is known to English language scholars has to do with Lavoie and Seccareccia. With his discussion of the monetary circuit in Lavoie's 1992 *Foundations of Post-Keynesian Economic Analysis* (among other articles and book chapters), his work was instrumental in bringing this French and Italian perspective to Canada, and making it well-known in the US and the UK post-Keynesian circles (Lavoie 1992, 151, 2014). American post-Keynesians with Italian links, Wray and Kregel, were also involved in the development of the circuit approach (c.f. Kregel (1984) in the first number of *Monnaie et Production*, and Wray (1991)). Lavoie and Seccareccia facilitated the creation of long-lasting connections between the French, Italian and English-speaking Keynesian economists working on money and production. The three groups of circuit theorists – the Italian and the two French schools – had very similar conceptions of how money enters the economy. The goal of firms is to recapture the wage bill to repay their debt to banks. Firms take back the wage bill by selling the proceeds of production back to workers and selling financial securities to get any remaining saving (Lavoie 2014, 269–270; Seccareccia 2013, 280–281; Wray 1993, 547–550; Graziani 1989, 4–5; Rossi 2006, 124). The circuit approach considers financial markets as an intermediary where household saving offsets firms' capital accumulation (Graziani 1989, 7; Seccareccia 2013, 281; Lavoie 2014, 269–270; Wray 1993, 550). Debates exist between the three circuit schools. The most important points of discussion include whether banks provide loans for both capital goods and the wage bill, the time dimensions of production, lending and debt repayment, and also the creation and existence of profit and value (Graziani 1989, 4–12; Bellofiore and Passarella 2016, 244–245; Parguez and Seccareccia 2000, 105, 108–109; Rossi 2006, 124). Of all the insights brought forward by the circuit, the most problematic seems to be the conditions under which loans, thus money, nets out to zero for the economy as a whole (Graziani 1989, 18; Parguez and Seccareccia 2000, 102, Bellofiore and Passarella 2016, 244–245, Rossi 2006, 126). Indeed, Parguez and Seccareccia write: "Credit money, as a rule, is thus created only to be destroyed in the circulatory process and not to be held (2000, 102)." When all bank loans are repaid, no profit exists, and, most importantly, no money exists either (Rossi 2006, 128). This leaves a net lack of money in the system. The way circuitists (again, except the Fribourg-Dijon school) resolve this dilemma is by integrating time. Not all loans are repaid at any given point in time. This makes profit and net monetary balances in the system possible at each point in time. Net monetary balances exactly equal total outstanding loan balances. Another problem is that the monetary circuit cannot close when money balances are demanded as a store of value in the face of uncertainty (Graziani 1989, 19; Bellofiore and Passarella 2016, 244). Existing monetary balances are thus offset by loan balances (Parguez and Seccareccia 2000, 105). As a result, households' or firms' liquidity preference can prevent closure of the circuit because as households and firms hold onto cash balances, those balances are not recaptured by the firms to be used to extinguish debt, and thus the monetary circuit cannot close, and may also face a value problem (Graziani 1989, 19; Seccareccia 2013, 281; Bellefiore and Passarella 2016, 244; Rossi 2006, 130–131). Firms may choose to sell financial assets to households in order to recapture the saving and this would close the circuit. However, the circuit will not close if cash balances are not entirely taken back by the sale of securities.

In the late 1990s, neo-chartalists provided an alternative way to close the circuit by adding government net money creation (Wray 1998; Parguez 2002). Now, government spending adds balances to the economy which do not need to be backed by a loan. Bond sales are used in this model to maintain interest rates rather than finance government spending. Here, net monetary creation, thus the funding of profit, or net private sector saving, is possible due to government deficit spending (see also Graziani's model, as discussed in Bellofiore and Passarella 2016, 245; Parguez 2002). Neo-chartalists call this the vertical circuit: government spends first, then a certain proportion of the expenditure refluxes back to the government in the form of taxes (Wray 1998, 111–115; Parguez 2002, 89–90; Lavoie 2013a, 8). Within this context, the bank money circuit developed by the French and Italian schools is expressed as a horizontal circuit. With respect to the horizontal circuit, when all loans are repaid no new money exists in the economy to account for private sector saving (Wray 1998; Lavoie 2013a, 6; Parguez and Seccareccia, 2000, 102; Graziani 1989, 18; Bellofiore and Passarella 2016, 245; Rossi 2006, 128–129). Clearly, if all loans were repaid and no government debt existed, no money would exist in the system either.

Parguez, creator of the French monetary circuit approach, adopted the majority of the elements of the neo-chartalist conception of the circuit. He also helped to refine and integrate the ideas of the state money approach with those he had spearheaded in the original circuit approach (c.f. Parguez and Seccareccia 2000, 102; Parguez 2002). For instance, Parguez and Seccareccia indicate that debt is always the other side of spending in a capitalist economy: "At the macroeconomic level, spending in a monetary economy is always and everywhere in the nature of debt financing" (2000, 102). From this statement, among others, it's not clear whether Parguez and Seccareccia believe that government deficit spending must be offset by a bond issue, or by the not-yet-refunded commercial bank loan balances (see also, Parguez and Seccareccia 2000, 111; Parguez 2002, 89–91). Lavoie's view is that government deficit spending is always funded by Treasury bond sales to the central bank (Lavoie 2013a, 9–10). The only reason this is important is that neo-chartalists such as Wray, Kelton, Fulweiler, and Parguez, contend that net new government spending needs not be offset by new bond issues (Wray 1998, 75; Lavoie 2013a, 9–10; Parguez 2002, 91). In reality, it doesn't really matter whether bank loans or bond issues offset deficit spending. What matters theoretically is to understand that the deficit is offset by a liability, which may be held either by the private sector, or the public sector – or both. Parguez and Seccareccia (2000, 119) indicate that neo-chartalists place more importance on taxes than do circuitists in general (see also Parguez 2002). But in line with the neo-chartalist position, they indicate that government spending that creates new production of public goods or gives rise to new private investment is not inflationary, unless the expenditure is wasteful (Parguez and Seccareccia 2000, 120; Parguez 2002, 93). This is also exactly what Keynes argues in the *General Theory*. He stated that new government spending creates new jobs, or new goods or services, is beneficial, while expenditures that bid up existing prices are inflationary, whether this spending originates from the government or from private sector spending (Keynes 1973[1936], 118–119; see also Wray 1998, 84).

The monetary circuit helps us better understand a number of elements that underlie financial crises. For example, increases in households' liquidity preference may prevent firms from recapturing the entire wage bill via household purchases of goods, services, and financial securities. The ensuing inability of firms to validate production, and repay their loans to banks, could lead to a breakdown of the incentives for banks to continue financing production (c.f. Graziani 1989, 19; Seccareccia 2013, 281). This in turn, could lead to a financial crisis. Also, if taxes are too high relative to government spending, then there may not be enough money in the system to close the circuit. Thus, both liquidity preference and government deficit spending relative to taxation are key to understanding the causes of financial crises. The next question, then, is to ask what determines liquidity preference and net government deficit spending.

ENDOGENOUS MONEY AND THE EXOGENOUSLY DETERMINED OVERNIGHT RATE

The ideas of the French and Italian circuitists were connected with the endogenous money approach taken by post-Keynesians such as Seccareccia and Lavoie (Lavoie 2013a, 5–7, 2014, 182–183; Parguez and Seccareccia 2000, 116). The post-Keynesian endogenous money approach simply indicates that banks create deposits by granting loans. Therefore, loans create deposits, a position which is also expressed as investment creates savings: as opposed to the neoclassical position where deposits are used to create loans, or savings creates investment. Kalecki was the first to state this position expressly (Kalecki 1971, 83; Kaldor 1955, 96). For post-Keynesians, which is also true for circuitists, money is created *ex nihilo* by banks to finance production (Lavoie 2014, 193; Parguez and Seccareccia 2000, 105; Bellofiore and Passarella 2016, 244; Rossi 2006, 122). Money creation occurs for the purpose of production in response to creditworthy loan requests and does not depend on existing central bank reserves, and is therefore endogenous, or internal to the economic and financial system, rather than an add-on to that same system.

In the late 1980s, post-Keynesians elaborated the endogenous money position arguing two opposing points of view (Moore 1988). The first point of view, called structuralist, was that the overnight interest rate was determined at the intersection of supply and demand of reserves (Pollin 1991, 374, 393; Palley 1996, 106). The opposing point of view, called horizontalist, was that the overnight rate was determined exogenously by the central bank and could be set at any level the bank deemed met social needs (Moore 1988). Seccareccia and Lavoie identify themselves with the horizontalist position indicating that central banks set targets for the overnight rate and are able to hit those targets without fail, under all but the worst conditions (Lavoie 2011, 5, 12). Lavoie (2011) argues that when the Fed neutralizes, and even when it does not (cannot neutralize), it still hits the target or nearly so, except temporarily, under conditions of severe financial crisis (Lavoie 2011, 10, 12).

Briefly stated, the horizontalist position is that banks make loans to creditworthy borrowers, regardless of whether the bank has the reserves necessary to make loans. Reserve requirements needed to comply with federal regulations are calculated after loans are made. If required reserves are needed, the bank will borrow those reserves on the open market, or, when no reserves can be obtained on the open market, banks will borrow from the discount window (Lavoie 2014, 231). The supply and demand for reserves by banks on the open market determines the effective overnight interest rate which will fall closely within range of the target overnight rate determined exogenously by central bank officials (the FOMC in the US). The reason this position is called horizontalist is because reserves will be supplied as needed at any given interest rate determined by the central bank, whether via bond sales/purchases in the open market, repurchase agreements, or from direct discount loans to banks. Operationally, the central bank must meet all creditworthy demands for reserves, or it will jeopardize the stability of the financial system (see also Lavoie 2011, 5; Minksy 2008[1986], 49; Wray 1998, 105). By way of contrast, the structuralist position is that the greater the demand for reserves by banks, the more the overnight interest rate will increase (Palley 1996, 105–106; Pollin 1991, 374, 393). This position assumes a fixed level of reserves.

Federal government deficit spending reduces the overnight interest rate (Lavoie 2013a, 11, 2011, 20–21; Wray 1998, 85–86). The overnight interest rate target is always determined exogenously, but the effective rate fluctuates to reflect the supply/demand of Treasury securities and reserves in the economy which are determined by government deficit spending, and, central bank open-market purchases/sales of Treasury/Government securities and/or commercial bank assets. While in all monetary systems the target interest rate is determined exogenously, the effective rate is determined differently depending on the operational system adopted by the monetary authorities. For example, in Canada a corridor system exists where the target overnight interest rate sits at the center of a range with the upper bound at the rate commercial banks pay on reserve balances, and the lower bound at the rate paid on balances commercial banks keep at the central bank (Lavoie and Seccareccia 2013, 76). Lavoie and Seccareccia (2013) explain that the American monetary system started to move toward a corridor system in 2003 when the Fed set the discount rate above the Federal Funds Rate target (2013, 78). They indicate that this transition to a corridor system was completed in 2008 when the Federal Reserve started to pay interest on reserves (Lavoie 2011, 11; Lavoie and Seccareccia 2013, 78–79).

Lavoie (2011) argues that the corridor system in the US surfaced out of necessity at the time of the 2007–2008 financial crisis in the US because the central bank faced a large amount of excess reserves and could no longer neutralize (meaning sell bonds to offset) the large injections of cash into the economy which occurred as a result of large purchases of assets by the central bank (Lavoie 2011, 4, 8). He argues that at first, the Fed sought to sop up excess reserve balances and thereby get the Fed Funds Rate near its target by selling Treasury securities, and thus replacing cash with interest-earning bonds (Lavoie 2011, 8). Liquidity preference was so high, however, that commercial banks kept excess reserves beyond the amount that normally would have been offset by a supposed "normal" amount of Treasury bond sales, and the Fed stopped selling Treasury securities to offset its liquidity injections caused by purchases of non-performing assets from commercial banks. Instead of selling Treasury bonds to offset its purchases of assets, the central bank shifted to purchasing the non-performing assets directly and started paying interest on reserves (Lavoie 2011, 9). As Lavoie explains, the overnight interest rate would have fallen precipitously given this build-up of reserves given the scale of Fed asset purchases, so the Fed started paying interest on reserves kept at the central bank, instead of selling bonds. Thus, according to Lavoie, the Fed switched to paying interest on reserve balances directly instead of selling bonds to establish a positive interest rate.

My understanding of the argument, however, is that a floor to the interest rate might not be required, and that even under the worst conditions the interest rate would not tend to fall to zero if there were a positive demand for cash balances as expressed by a strong degree of liquidity preference. Given that the effective Federal Funds Rate is determined at the intersection of the supply and demand for reserves in general, rather than for required reserves specifically, the interest rate need not be set exogenously.

Hence, Lavoie (2011) and Lavoie and Seccareccia (2013) contend that the version of the corridor system that emerged in the US was a floor system, where the overnight Federal Funds target rate is equal to the Federal funds deposit rate, or to zero if the central bank does not pay interest on reserves (Lavoie 2011, 18). Regardless of the operational specifications from one country or monetary system to another, it is always the case that banks make loans when creditworthy borrowers ask for them, and purchase required reserves as needed at an interest rate that is targeted by the central bank. Hence, money is endogenous and the interest rate is determined exogenously.

Conditions of financial crisis increase liquidity preference such that central bank open-market sales of Treasury securities may need to be really high if the central bank is aiming to offset all liquidity injections by the government and the central bank. The alternative to offsetting injections with bonds is to offset injections with undervalued securities directly as the Fed did in the US during the 2008 financial crisis. If the overnight rate is determined at the intersection of the supply and demand for reserves, it would fall as more reserves were injected into the system. The high levels of liquidity preference which prevail when we have a financial crisis would suggest that higher levels of reserves would be demanded by the commercial banks seeking to cushion themselves against potential future blows. This higher demand for reserves could act as an offsetting feature to the increases in reserves made by government deficit spending and/or central bank purchases of assets. Establishing a corridor system, where banks pay a discount rate as the top boundary and another rate paid to banks on reserves being the lower bound, is another way the central bank can conceive to hit its overnight interest rate target. When they're deficient, banks are not going to pay more for reserves than the central bank discount rate. Certainly, banks with excess reserves might seek to make a higher interest rate than the interest rate the central bank pays on reserves. Thus, the corridor system establishes a range for the interest rate, but this range is effectively brought into being, and the actual Federal Funds rate is determined, at the intersection of the supply and demand for reserves in the open market.

Regardless of the specificity of the determination of the overnight interest rate, the endogenous money approach contends that the central bank provides reserves on demand. Reserves are provided to commercial banks after loans are made. Banks are not limited in the number or value of loans made, but they are limited to making loans to creditworthy borrowers who are likely to be able to repay the loans. Providing unlimited reserves as needed creates financial stability and is a fundamental part of the lender-of-last resort function of the central bank.

HOUSEHOLD DEBT AND SECURITIZATION: SOLUTIONS TO GROWING FINANCIAL INSTABILITY

A significant branch of post-Keynesian work focuses on the functioning of the banking system and the changing landscape of its lending practices, which are now more dependent on household lending and less on the indebtedness of business (c.f. Seccareccia 2012, 71; Lavoie 2013b, 231). These changes in the financial structure have led many economists to promote the use of deficit spending to restore a positive net financial position to households. Another suggestion is that the securitization of household debt should be forbidden, which would make banks responsible for the risks associated with increased household lending (Lavoie 2013b, 232).

As Seccareccia explains, there have been two movements that have destabilized the current financial landscape. The first is the constant attack on deficit spending, and the second is the redirection of existing private sector surpluses toward the business sector and away from households (Seccareccia 2012, 71–73; Seccareccia 2013, 282; Seccareccia 2014, 568; Lavoie 2013b, 217–218, 224). Macroeconomic stability, thus stability in production, employment and economic growth, is supported by the working of automatic stabilizers, federal budget items that grow during downturns to offset declines in private spending. Automatic stabilizers have been eroded over the last 40 years with the attack on deficit spending. As a result, the foundation of the macroeconomy has been compromised (Seccareccia 2012, 73; Seccareccia 2014, 574).

The second trend is that private sector surpluses have been accumulating as business rather than household balances. This causes concern for the wellbeing of middle and lower-income households whose expenditures are increasingly being funded by large amounts of debt (Seccareccia 2012, 72; Seccareccia 2013, 282–283; Lavoie 2013b, 217–218). Lavoie indicates that the current accumulation regime is "a regime based on high consumption spending and ever-rising household debt, justified by high prices in the stock-market and real estate market . . ." (2013b, 2017). Household debt is offset by the new growing nonfinancial private business surpluses (Seccareccia 2013, 283; Lavoie 2013b, 216, 217–218). What this means is that traditional nonfinancial firms are making a growing proportion of their income from the sale of financial assets to household, and/or indebting households. Seccareccia writes: "In this hyperfinancialized system, the dynamics of credit creation have been sustained not by business indebtedness but by household indebtedness . . ." (2013, 283). These trends create a new degree of instability for the macroeconomy because they make a large part of debt repayment and nonfinancial private business profitability dependent on the stagnating employment income of households, rather than growing business profits. Stagnating household incomes result from weak and extinct labor unions that make it possible for firms to pay low wages (Lavoie 2013b, 218, 220). Households' financial position is further compromised by increasing debt loads used to feed a growing marginal propensity to consume (Lavoie 2013b, 217). Lavoie explains that governments and central banks, faced with globalization and financialization, have not supported the maintenance and strengthening of unions, or regulated the banking and non-bank sector adequately. The result is low wages, weak households, and unstable financial relationships between banks, households, and private business (Lavoie 2013b, 220, 222, 231).

Prior to financialization, banks were responsible for holding private sector debt, most of which was held by the business sector. It was a credit–debit relationship between business and banks, which was heavily determined by government regulations, and accordingly backed up by government guarantees and the central bank's lender-of-last-resort function. Post-financialization, we find ourselves in a world where a large and growing number of the credit–debit relationships are between business and the household, with banks playing a new role (Seccareccia 2013, 283–284; Seccareccia 2014, 573). While banks still originate loans, they now package and sell the loans to non-bank financial actors. This process of securitization created a rift between the interests of the lender, whose main interest is to make as many loans as possible, and those of the final investor, whose main concern is the profitability of the asset. Bank capital requirements that would normally have supported new loans on bank balance sheets are evaded when loans are packaged and sold to non-bank actors. This leads banks to generate loans beyond what used to be considered safe leverage guidelines because the loans are no longer on the books of the banks (Lavoie 2013b, 229–230). The risk of this additional leverage is transferred to the financial market with the purchase of the packaged loans. Thus, a failure to make payment on loans will reverberate, not initially through banks as had been the case in the past, but through holders of the packaged loans: pension funds and other institutional investors. Because households and nonfinancial business are the ultimate holders of these loans (via pension funds and institutional investments), both bear the risk that was originally borne by financial businesses (banks) and protected by government guarantees and especially by the lender of last resort function of the central banks (Lavoie 2013b, 231–232). Lavoie advocates for regulation on non-bank financial businesses and the abolition of securitization (Lavoie 2013b, 232).

Seccareccia proposes the idea that re-establishing and strengthening automatic stabilizers via federal deficit spending would improve the stability of the macroeconomy (Seccareccia 2012, 74). Even more than strong automatic stabilizers, he argues (as did Keynes, Minksy and others) that government deficit spending in the form of public investment should take up a great enough share of total investment, up to three quarters of total investment, such that it would offset fluctuations in total investment enough to maintain permanently robust levels of productivity and employment (Seccareccia 2012, 80; Keynes 1980, 322–323, quoted in Seccareccia; see also Keynes 1973[1936], 320, 325, 376–378; Minsky 2008[1986], 330–333). Here, Seccareccia explicitly links the wellbeing of the real economy to fluctuations in the financial side of the economy. He states: "If public investment were strong enough, the greater 'make-weight' provided by the higher amount of public investment would ensure that it would be more difficult for future financial shocks to drag down the 'real' economy" (Seccareccia 2012, 80).

There are several different elements to a public investment strategy such as the one recommended by Seccareccia and formerly endorsed by Keynes, some of which are specific to our current financial landscape. For instance, one element of a large public investment program is that federal government deficit spending could be directed to create net surpluses in the household sector, restoring household savings, which would make households more resilient to shocks in employment levels, and to changes in interest rates on household debt (Seccareccia 2013, 297). Another related element would be that public investment could be directed to maintain high levels of employment and productivity. In this scenario, public investment could take up a greater or lesser share of total investment with the goal of keeping employment and/or production levels stable. Here, a public jobs program offers an excellent tool for achieving employment and price stability, as discussed elsewhere (Minsky 2008[1986], 343–349; Wray 1998, 122–154; Tcherneva 2013, 291–292; Leclaire 2007, 58–60).

Ideally, the program could be set up such that the federal government current account would actually show surpluses from returns made on public investment, such as increased tax revenue offsetting much more stable employment income earnings, or profits on publicly funded government enterprises, like the post office, or public day care, senior care, and/or medical care programs (Keynes 1980, also quoted by Seccareccia, 2012, 76; c.f. Tcherneva 2013, 294–295; Leclaire 2015, 307–308). Surpluses could be used to "pay off"/offset any bonds (if any exist) held on capital account that were used to "finance" long-term public investments (Keynes 1980, 366–367, quoted in Seccareccia 2012). Alternatively, as Keynes argued, current account surpluses could be used to "fund" new public investment, generating ever greater returns to the current account, albeit at a new higher debt-to-GDP level. This process could continue until the business cycle is wiped out (Keynes 1980, quoted in Seccareccia 2012, 76). A policy of high publicly directed investment that focuses on providing goods and services that are not being provided adequately by the private sector compliments and enhances the existing economy and provides for more stability for households and firms with respect to fluctuations in employment and, financial sector flows, including profits, prices, and interest rates (c.f. Parguez 2002, 93).

The post-Keynesian position explicitly describes the important role of government deficit spending in creating net financial surpluses in the private and/or the external sectors (Kalecki 1971, 85; Lavoie 2014, 310; Godley and Lavoie 2007, 36–37; 95, Wray 1998, 75; Seccareccia, 2012, 71, 2013, 297; Godley 1999, 10–11). Currently, these financial balances show that households are heavily indebted, especially to non-financial business, a position which is unstable. As part of a solution to this dilemma, Seccareccia, among others, seeks to increase deficit spending via automatic stabilizers to restore a positive balance to households. Lavoie and others propose a ban on the securitization of household debt by banks, and the regulation of the shadow banking sector. Simultaneously then, we find that post-Keynesians consider that the financial and economic system, as it is currently structured, requires a much greater level of investment and should be better regulated. Investment would potentially take the form of government directed investment in socially useful programs, most specifically when the level of private investment is not great enough to bring stability to household balances. New regulation of non-bank financial firms would remove securitization of household debt from the table.

CONCLUSION

When it comes to understanding financial crises, how we organize the link between the real and financial sectors of the economy is crucial. Many post-Keynesians use a financial Keynesian model like the one elaborated by Davidson, Kregel, Minsky, and Wray, in which financial values determine the investment decision. Employment, output, and economic growth result from the decision to invest, and the decision to invest is a financial choice based on the relative rates of return (Davidson 1972, 102; Minsky 2008, 195; Kregel 1983, 1984, 142, 1998; Wray 1993, 544). Incorporating the ideas of the monetary circuit into the post-Keynesian endogenous money framework enhances our ability to understand and appropriately deal with financial crises. More precisely, the monetary circuit model shows where money enters the economy and how banks and financial institutions are at the center of financial crises and the decision to invest in financial assets or production (Parguez and Seccareccia 2000). Liquidity preference and its impact on the economy is made clear within the monetary circuit model, and underlines the monetary shortfall that makes liquidity preference a significant factor in financial crises.

Post-Keynesians also link the concept of endogenous money creation with exogenous interest rate determination. This relationship highlights the role that the central bank plays in its relationship with the federal government in maintaining financial stability, specifically during times of crisis by providing reserves on demand. They also discuss the role of securitization in promoting household debt growth within the wider context of financialization. Naturally, they oppose the separation of the loan from the originator, favoring a ban on securitization of household debt in order to remove the growing systemic risk with which it is associated. Financialization has also meant a change in the nature of financial relations. The business sector now offsets its surpluses with household debt. This puts households and businesses, hence the economy, in a precarious position which Lavoie and Seccareccia, among others, maintain could be improved by increasing federal government deficit spending via increasing public investment to restore our deteriorated automatic stabilizers. Ultimately, a public investment strategy would continue until household sector were brought back to a relative financial surplus position.

By zeroing in on the relationship between the real and financial sectors of the economy, the work of post-Keynesians has brought us a much stronger understanding of financial crises. In particular, their work on the monetary circuit highlights the role of banks during a crisis. Their discussion of the endogeneity of money and the determination of the interest rate shows that during a financial crisis, the central bank's lender of last resort function maintains liquidity in essentially the same way it does during periods of relative calm: by providing reserves on demand. Finally, their work on financialization has promoted the support of household financial balances by banning securitization of household debt and increasing government spending on public investment on automatic stabilizers. The purpose overall is to strengthen households so they can better weather the next financial storm.

BIBLIOGRAPHY

Bellofiore, Riccardo and Passarella, Marco V. 2016. Introduction: the theoretical legacy of Augusto Graziani, *Review of Keynesian Economics* 4(3), Autumn: 243–49.

Davidson, Paul. 1972. Money and the real world, *Economic Journal* 82(325): 101–15.

Godley, Wynne. 1999. Seven Unsustainable Processes: Medium Term Prospects and Policies for the United States and the World. *Levy Institute Special Report.* Annandale-on-Hudson: Levy Economics Institute.

Godley, Wynne and Marc Lavoie. 2007. *Monetary Economics: An Integrated Approach to Credit, Money, Income, Production and Wealth.* New York: Palgrave Macmillan.

Graziani, Augusto. 1989. The Theory of the Monetary Circuit. *Thames Papers in Political Economy.* Spring: 1–26.

Graziani, Augusto. 1994. *La Teoria monetaria della produzione.* Firenze: Banca Popolare dell'Etruria e del Lazio.

Kaldor, Nicholas. 1956. Alternative theories of distribution, *Review of Economic Studies* 23(2): 83–100.
Kalecki, Michàl. 1971. *Selected Essays on the Dynamics of the Capitalist Economy 1933–1970*. Cambridge: Cambridge University Press.
Keynes. John Maynard. 1973[1936]. *The Collected Writings of John Maynard Keynes, Vol. 7, The General Theory of Employment Interest and Money*. London: Macmillan.
Kregel, Jan. 1983. The multiplier and liquidity preference: two sides of the theory of effective demand, in A. Barrère (ed.), 1985 (1983). *Keynes Today: Theories and Policies*. London: Macmillan.
Kregel, Jan. 1984a. Théorie de l'économie monétaire de production et politique monétaire. *Economies et Societés*, Série Monnaie et production, no.1.
Kregel, Jan. 1984b. Constraints on the expansion of output and employment: real or monetary?, *Journal of Post-Keynesian Economics* 7(2): 139–52.
Kregel, Jan. 1998. Aspects of a post-Keynesian theory of finance, *Journal of Post-Keynesian Economics* 21(1): 111–133.
Lavoie, Marc. 1984. The endogenous flow of credit and the post-Keynesian theory of money, *Journal of Economic Issues* 18(3), September: 771–97.
Lavoie, Marc. 1992. *Foundations of Post-Keynesian Economic Analysis*. Brookfield: Edward Elgar.
Lavoie, Marc. 2011. Changes in central bank procedures during the subprime crisis and theory repercussions on monetary theory, *International Journal of Political Economy* 39(3), Fall: 3–23.
Lavoie, Marc. 2013a. The monetary and fiscal nexus of neo-chartalism: a friendly critique, *Journal of Economic Issues* 47(1), March: 1–31.
Lavoie, Marc. 2013b. Financialization, neo-liberalism, and securitization, *Journal of Post-Keynesian Economics* 35(2): 215–33.
Lavoie, Marc. 2014. *Post-Keynesian Economics: New Foundations*. Cheltenham, UK and Northampton, USA: Edward Elgar.
Lavoie, Marc and Mario Seccareccia. 2013. Reciprocal influences: a tale of two central banks on the North American continent, *International Journal of Political Economy* 42(3), Fall: 63–83.
Leclaire, Joëlle. 2008. US Deficit control and private-sector wealth, *Journal of Post-Keynesian Economics* 31(1): 139–49.
Leclaire, Joëlle. 2015. Women and investment: the role of fiscal policy, *International Journal of Political Economy* 44: 296–310.
Minsky, Hyman. 2008 [1986]. *Stabilizing and Unstable Economy*. New York: McGraw Hill.
Moore, Basil. 1988. *Horizontalists and Verticalists: The Macroeconomics of Credit Money*. Cambridge: Cambridge University Press.
Palley, Thomas. 1996. *Post-Keynesian Economics: Debt, Distribution and the Macro Economy*. New York: St. Martin's Press.
Parguez, Alain. 1984. La dynamique de la monnaie, *Economies et Sociétés*, Cahiers de l'ISMEA, Tome XVIII(4), April: 84–118.
Parguez, Alain. 2002. A monetary theory of public finances: the new fiscal orthodoxy: from plummeting deficits to planned fiscal surpluses, *International Journal of Political Economy* 32(3): 80–97.
Parguez, Alain and Mario Seccareccia. 2000. The credit theory of money: the monetary circuit approach, in John Smithin (ed.). *What is Money?* New York: Routledge, pp. 101–23.

Pollin, Robert. 1991. Two theories of money supply endogeneity: some empirical evidence, *Journal of Post Keynesian Economics* 13(3), Spring: 366–96.
Rossi, Sergio. 2006. The theory of money emissions, in P. Arestis and M. Sawyer (eds), *A Handbook of Alternative Monetary Economics*. Cheltenham, UK and Northampton, USA: Edward Elgar, pp. 121–38.
Schmitt, Bernard. 1996. A new paradigm for the determination of money prices, in G. Deleplace and E. Nell (eds), *Money in Motion: The Post-Keynesian and Circulation Approaches*. Houndsmills: Macmillan, and New York: Palgrave, pp. 105–38.
Seccareccia, Mario. 2012. The Role of public investment as principal macroeconomic tool to promote long-term growth, *International Journal of Political Economy* 40(4), Winter: 62–82.
Seccareccia, Mario. 2013. Financialization and the transformation of commercial banking: understanding the recent Canadian experience before and during the international financial crisis, *Journal of Post Keynesian Economics* 35(2), Winter: 277–300.
Seccareccia, Mario. 2014. Banking sector viability and fiscal austerity: from Rhetoric to the reality of bank behavior, *Journal of Economic Issues* 48(2), June: 567–74.
Tcherneva, Pavlina. 2013. Fiscal policy for the great recession and beyond, in Barry Cynamon, Steven Fazzari and Mark Setterfield (eds), *After the Great Recession*. New York: Cambridge University Press, pp. 291–99.
Wray, L. Randall. 1993. Money, interest rates, and monetarist policy, *Journal of Post Keynesian Economics* 15(4): 541–69.
Wray, L. Randall. 1995. Keynesian monetary theory: liquidity preference or black box horizontalism, *Journal of Economic Issues* 29(1): 273–82.
Wray, L. Randall. 1990. *Money and Credit in Capitalist Economies: The Endogenous Money Approach*. Cheltenham, UK and Northampton, USA: Edward Elgar.
Wray, L. Randall. 1991. The inconsistency of monetarist theory and policy, *Economies et Sociétés*, Série Monnaie et production, no. 8.
Wray, L. Randall. 1998. *Understanding Modern Money: The Key to Full Employment and Price Stability*. Cheltenham, UK and Northampton, USA: Edward Elgar.

PART 4

Some notes on the dual economy

14. Notes on dual economy conceptions in economic analysis

David Leadbeater

INTRODUCTION

As it has been used in Economics in differing contexts since the 1950s, economic dualism has referred to the existence within a given economy of two sectors, one which is leading, more developed, or wealthier, and the other which is generally subordinate, less developed, or poorer. The second is treated as being an autonomous or divergent subsystem, or as being subject to a different set of structural economic forces and having inferior conditions of well-being. My argument is that the conception of dual economy (or economic dualism) might have some value as a heuristic or a point of entry for the analysis of complex and pressing economic issues; there are often elements of truth and a capacity to focus attention in analyses of duality. However, in social scientific terms, there have usually been substantial flaws in dualism coupled with a dependence on neoclassical theory that has reduced its effectiveness as an alternative to neoclassical theory or neoliberal policy. Further, economic dualism can obscure more radical critiques of capitalist development and deflect debate from fundamental but contentious policy questions. Here I illustrate the argument with a few instances of economic dualism and some of its conceptual problems, then conclude with a brief comment on the policy implications of dual economy analysis.

The earliest use in mainstream economics of the dual economy conception is most commonly identified with Arthur Lewis's 1954 paper "Economic Development with Unlimited Supplies of Labour."[1] Lewis's model, which became a foundational element in Development Economics, is based on the view that certain poor capitalist economies can be analyzed as having such large and persistent quantities of surplus labour that it depresses wages and living conditions. In contrast to the neoclassical full-employment assumption or the more temporary surpluses of labour in the Keynesian approach, Lewis positioned his model as being in the "classical framework in solving problems of distribution, accumulation, and growth" (Lewis, 1954:1).

Lewis argued that the unlimited surplus labour assumption referred to unskilled labour and that it was applicable in particular to certain "underdeveloped" countries such as Egypt, India, and Jamaica. By contrast, Lewis claimed, "It is obviously not true of the United Kingdom, or of North West Europe" (1954:2). Lewis analyzed such poorer countries as having two sectors, a "capitalist" sector and a "subsistence" sector. The surplus labour, which has negligible, zero, or negative marginal productivity, is maintained at a subsistence level in the subsistence sector which supplies labour to the capitalist sector. The capitalist sector hires labour to the point where its marginal productivity equals the wage, and the wage level is held near or at the subsistence level by the surplus supply of labour available.[2] In this latter regard, the capitalist sector has an interest in maintaining conditions in the subsistence sector at subsistence levels in order to keep wages low in the capitalist sector: "The fact that the wage level in the capitalist sector depends upon earnings in the subsistence sector is sometimes of immense political importance, since its effect is that capitalists have a direct interest in holding down the productivity of the subsistence workers" (1954:6).

In certain ways, particularly in recognizing the persistence and role of surplus labour, the Lewis model appears to break from neoclassical orthodoxy and assert a more realistic view of economic development, at least in colonial conditions. However, the Lewis conception of the two sectors has a lot of empirical imprecision in its definition. At times, particularly in later interpretations, the subsistence sector is viewed as being a "traditional" agricultural sector motivated by subsistence, not primarily profit-making production, in contrast to a "modern" sector, and, hence, as an autonomous system or mode of production with its own dynamics and rules.[3] But Lewis himself expanded the subsistence sector to include casual workers (dockworkers, porters, or gardeners), petty traders, domestic and commercial retainers (servants and messengers), wives and daughters in households, and net population increase.[4] In the end, there is no distinguishing and consistent characteristic to the subsistence sector other than its being the repository of surplus labour that acts to hold down wages in the capitalist sector.

Critics have questioned the implied lack of dynamism in Lewis's subsistence sector, the extent of its labour redundancy and lack of productivity, and the secondary and imbalanced role for agriculture that the model implies, among other things. The key point here, however, is that while the two sectors are often viewed as being different systems or modes of production, the sectors are in the end defined by their interacting functions, the capitalist sector by capital accumulation and growth in labour demand, and the subsistence sector by supplying labour and depressing wages.

Lewis was well aware of Marx's theory (Tignor, 2006), and the subsistence sector appears little more than a version of Marx's industrial reserve army of labour (or relative surplus-population) though in a form emphasizing "disguised unemployment" or Marx's latent reserve. On the other hand, Lewis's theory was a step backwards from Marx's more critical and sophisticated treatment, for example, in rejecting the existence of technological or productivity-induced unemployment in the capitalist sector. While Lewis's work raised important concerns about the conditions of colonized areas, the theory actually contains very little about the ownership or class structures characteristic of colonialism in general or about the specific countries for which he deems the model applicable. Without a more rigorous empirical discussion of the subsistence sector one is left with a conception of surplus labour, which could as much exist – and does, such as in the household – in developed capitalist economies. Further, the model still holds to a fundamental of neoclassical theory, the marginal productivity theory of distribution and wage determination.[5]

In the US, dualism has grown out of Institutionalism and as a critical reaction to neoclassical and Keynesian orthodoxy (for example, Averitt, 1968). In the field of labour economics, in particular, economic dualism appeared from the 1960s in discussions of persistent inequality in labour markets including by race and gender. In the most prominent original dualism, Doeringer and Piore (1971) argued that the labour market is divided into a primary and a secondary labour market, in theory, by job characteristics.[6] Jobs in the primary labour market possess "high wages, good working conditions, employment stability, chances of advancement, equity, and due process in the administration of work rules," while jobs in the secondary labour market were characterized by "low wages and fringe benefits, poor working conditions, high labour turnover, little chance of advancement, and often arbitrary and capricious supervision" (165). The Doeringer and Piore argument viewed the US labour market as reflecting both a general dualism in the economy and a specific institutional evolution within the labour market, particularly an increased importance of skill training.

This early version of labour market dualism evolved iteratively, including notably by Reich, Gordon, and Edwards (1973), who saw dualism defined more by worker characteristics and capitalist power: labour market inequality persisted because, when faced with a historically increasing power of workers, "employers actively and consciously fostered labour market segmentation in order to 'divide and conquer' the labour force." The primary labour market, relative to the secondary labour market, had disproportionately more white to non-white workers, and more male to female workers. Other worker characteristics such as native-born to immigrant, and high-education to low-education also found their way into characterizations of the dualism. Generally, whether there exist two or multiple sectors or segments in the labour market, the conception is that: (1) the primary market is separated or segregated and not subject directly to the competition of the secondary market (or of a labour reserve), and (2) this dualism is associated with a dualism in market structure, particularly between monopoly capitalist and competitive capitalist sectors or, as sometimes characterized, "core and peripheral" sectors.

Labour market dualism can be seen as a more realistic effort to contend with the problem of the persistence of inequality in labour markets, and hence a break from the neoclassical approach and its underlying belief in convergence. But like developmental dualism, the typology of primary and secondary labour markets has been criticized as inconsistent and empirically inadequate. As noted by Botwinick (1993, Ch 2) in his critique of labour market dualism, empirical evidence continued to challenge the dual categories. For instance, there exist some primary labour markets in peripheral (competitive) industries like construction and longshoring that do not share any of Doeringer and Peore's structural characteristics. For Botwinick, labour market dualism was an extension of Institutionalism and never an effective replacement to the neoclassical approach to the labour market or to a consistent theory of wage determination. Albelda and Drago (2013, 152) too question the accuracy of a dualism that includes in the primary sector higher paid manufacturing workers, as such jobs have been disappearing due global competition and reduced job security. They suggest that the "old form of segmentation" might be disappearing though taking a new form. While one can introduce new or varying types of dualism or segmentation, dualism appears inadequate to explain the transformation of labour market institutions by capitalist competition in the direction of lower or stagnating average wages and conditions, without introducing a labour reserve and its role in impoverishment.

From his field of economic history, Peter Temin (2016) has recently applied dualism to the contemporary US economy to analyze not simply persisting but increasing inequality since the 1980s. Citing Lewis's subsistence and capitalist economies, Temin creates the duality of a finance, technology, and electronics (FTE) sector and a low-wage sector. While his primary evidence is based on income, Temin says he distinguishes the two sectors by skills and occupations. "The first and most familiar sector consists of skilled workers and managers who have college degrees and command good and even very high salaries in our technological economy" (89). By contrast, the low-wage sector "consists of low-skilled workers who are suffering the ills of globalization in its various aspects."[7] He estimates the FTE sector has 30 percent of the population and low-wage sector has 70 percent. For Temin, the transition from the low-wage to FTE sector is made through education, though this transition has become more difficult due to inadequate expenditures in education as well as racial and class barriers in the college system.

Several elements in Temin's analysis deserve detailed discussions in their own right, particularly his claimed interrelations between occupation, industry, education, and incomes. But for present purposes I want to note how his dualism turns in the end around identifying what are the polarizing forces in the economy, who is impacted, and the relation between the two. It is not at all clear from the analysis that Temin's duality by occupation and skill is actually stable, let alone that it has a stable correspondence with low or falling incomes versus higher rising incomes, or how precisely these levels or trends are defined, or how this relates to persisting segregation by rate or gender.[8]

For instance, his own article notes low pay in teaching yet this is not usually seen as a low-skill occupation. Further, in the face of such evidence as the impoverishing of education workers or certain skilled work, Temin's dualism still does not appear to break with the neoclassical human capital doctrine or the marginal productivity theory of distribution. One wonders what is the evidence Temin uses to claim that higher education or skill, particularly in finance, leads to higher marginal productivity (hence, such high incomes) – or even if education or skill has much to do with the increased incomes in finance.

Temin does raise important concerns about social polarization and the roles of globalization and systemic white supremacy (not simply racial "discrimination"). But in terms of analysis, his dualism, like others, founders on problems in the clarity, consistency, and stability of its typology and the fundamental issue of the competitive force of the labour reserve in polarization and impoverishment. In drawing on the legacy of the Lewis model, Temin mischaracterizes the Lewis model as a rural-urban duality (though this is not uncommon) and in so doing occludes the more critical Marxist element in Lewis's analysis of the subsistence sector: the subsistence or low-wage sector acts to depress wages in the capitalist sector, hence, drives generally lower *average* conditions across the economy. Further, Lewis's model was geared to explain a transformation in growth appropriate to a colonial country. Temin's version is about a developed capitalist country that turns to dualism beginning in the 1980s, largely triggered by policy decisions. In itself, the appearance of such a dualism, especially given the long history of white supremacy, should raise the question of whether the present dualism is simply a unique period of disparity in the neoliberal era or whether the existence of the low-wage sector or such disparity has a previous history and persisting economic function.

Lastly, I will give an example of a popular dualism from on my research on mining towns in urban and regional development. Since the 1980s the conception of "rust belt" regions has appeared in the popular media and even academic discourse to characterize some US and Canadian areas of primary and manufacturing industry suffering employment and civic decline.[9] One common implication of this characterization and related stereotypes is that the industries of these towns or regions have been economically backward, outmoded, or even unproductive by comparison to the modern, leading, or "post-industrial" sectors (such as perceived of Temin's FTE). The resulting "deindustrialization," which is often associated with a general decline of employment and population in hinterland areas, is viewed with a metropolitanist bias as being the problem (and sometimes fault) of the region itself and not more fundamental conditions of the capitalist economy.[10]

But the evidence, for instance for mining, is that the industry is actually highly productive and technically advanced, to the point that much less labour is demanded to sustain production; in reality, the decline has been associated not with backwardness but its opposite, high productivity, and the decline is tied, often exploitatively, with conditions outside the area.[11] Of course, some views of "rust belt" areas are sympathetic to the areas and even critical of neoliberal policies, but the general dualism applied to such areas, reinforced by stereotyped characterizations, undermines analyses of such areas that are both more realistic and radical, including their often colonial and environmental dimensions.

As a whole, I would argue that the rise of dual economy models in the post-Second World War period dominated by the Cold War was a response to the glaringly evident disparities present in colonial and former colonial areas and, later, in the wealthier capitalist countries. The approach was critical of capitalist development patterns but still within the acceptable ambit of neoclassical and Keynesian economics. In its initial Lewis form, dualism was clearly influenced by Marxist theory, particularly the labour reserve analysis. In this respect, the Lewis model stepped outside the neoclassical full-employment doctrine, and Lewis also acknowledged explicitly both that the subsistence sector depressed wages in the capitalist sector and that the capitalist sector had an interest in maintaining subsistence conditions. Further, Lewis carried this critical view into the international sphere, considering it "one of the worst features of imperialism" (Lewis, 1954: 6–7): "The imperialists invest capital and hire workers [in the colonial countries]; it is to their advantage to keep wages low, and even in those cases where they do not actually go out of their way to impoverish the subsistence economy, they will at least very seldom be found doing anything to make it more productive."

This said, Lewis also expressed the view that there exists no labour reserve either in the capitalist sector of the model or in actual developed capitalist economies, and he ruled out unemployment from technological change or productivity-enhancing growth (such unemployment was only "theoretically" possible).[12] However, denying persisting unemployment in the capitalist sector can go only so far, unless one is prepared to rule out technological or productivity impacts on unemployment, the unemployment-reducing role of the non-market state sector, and, beyond the closed economy model, negative employment impacts of globalization (such as suggested by Temin).

Unfortunately, the more critical elements of the Lewis model, particularly around the fundamental role of the labour reserve, are often muted if not absent in later dualisms, whether seen as a domestic labour reserve or as an extended internationalized labour reserve. As well, while later dualisms do recognize the role of differential bargaining power between labour and capital within the capitalist sector, the role of the labour reserve and its racial and gendered evolution is not usually seen as a key factor determining that bargaining power, including in defining and valuing skill and its productivity.

What are the implications of dualism for policy? Economic dualism generally arose in the context of social democratic or reformist critiques of capitalism. In the early decades after the Second World War, a wide range of labour and progressive political forces in the developed capitalist countries generally emphasized full employment and a break with *laissez faire* policies that had led to and worsened the Great Depression. Since then, the states in developed capitalist countries, gripped by neoliberalism, have largely abandoned full employment or redefined it downwards, privatized the "mixed economy," reduced Welfare State programme standards, and hardened actions against labour and democratic rights. In the present context, it is not surprising to see a rise of more critical views of capitalism and, in particular, a renewed interest in dual economy analyses of capitalism.

However, the political economic situation today makes it more difficult to break with dualism in distribution without a more fundamental change in power, particularly to achieve a robust full employment if not over-full employment, eliminate the labour reserve, and expand social programs. Policies now have to contend more directly with growing environmental crises, and expanded globalization and militarism. Given sharper environmental constraints, impoverishment cannot be solved simply by higher rates of material growth. Nor can there be a major redistribution internationally without ending the highly concentrated corporate ownership and power driving the neoliberal order, including its enormous waste of resources on militarization and war. Eliminating the dualistic structures of capitalism today will require structural changes and redistribution. Some believe this is still possible within capitalism. I suggest that economic dualism, taken to its roots in the analysis of the labour reserve, leads to a fundamental critique of capitalism itself and the need for a serious discussion of socialism.

NOTES

1. Besides Lewis (1954), Boeke (1953) is also mentioned but given less attention.
2. "Earnings in the subsistence sector set a floor to wages in the capitalist sector, but in practice wages have to be higher than this, and there is usually a gap of 30 percent. or more between capitalist wages and subsistence earnings" (Lewis, 1954: 7). It is not clear if the surplus labour must all be living at the same subsistence level because, for Lewis, the subsistence level can be either as determined by the average product of peasant farmers or "subjectively in terms of a conventional standard of living" (6).
3. Lewis himself later shifted his own terminology for the two sectors to "modern" and "traditional" (Lewis, 1979).
4. Further, the capitalist sector is subdivided, and Lewis (5) allows that his conception is present in earlier stages of capitalist development generally: the capitalist sector, like the subsistence sector, can also be subdivided. What we have is not one island of expanding capitalist employment, surrounded by a vast sea of subsistence workers, but rather a number of such tiny islands. This is very typical of countries in their early stages of development."
5. Lewis makes this explicit: "Our present task is not to supersede neo-classical economics, but merely to elaborate a different framework for those countries which the neo-classical (and Keynesian) assumptions do not fit" (2).
6. See Ryan (2008) for a useful overview of primary and secondary labour markets.
7. Elsewhere (98) he notes that "Low wages are the result of increased supply coming from globalization – trade, immigration, moving production offshore – and decreased labour demand coming from improving technology" and that these were largely policy-initiated. In terms of function, Temin sees the low-wage sector as supplying services to the FTE sector: "Rural people sold food to cities in the Lewis model; members of the low-wage sector sell services to the FTE sector in this modern reincarnation."
8. Temin moves between income and education in ways which themselves question how empirically clear or stable are his two categories, particularly in defining the FTE sector: "However, a college education does not by itself guarantee a high and rising income. The choice of major, the state of the business cycle, and other less intangible personal characteristics affect the relation between education (or human capital) and income" (89). One can legitimately ask what are the effects of such major factors on Temin's categories and claims.
9. Among more serious historical discussions of the "rust belt" are High (1984), Neumann (2016), and High et al. (2017).
10. Those conditions include extraterritorial capitalist ownership and control of resources, and resource-export dependency and the political-state framework that maintains them.
11. See, for example, Leadbeater (2014, 2009).
12. Lewis (1954, 4) asserted: "It is clear that the effect of capital accumulation in the past has been to reduce the size of the reserve army, and not to increase it, so we have lost interest in arguments about what is 'theoretically' possible."

BIBLIOGRAPHY

Albelda, Randy and Robert Drago (2013), *Unlevel Playing Fields: Understanding Wage Inequality and Discrimination*, Boston, MA: Economic Affairs Bureau.

Averitt, Robert T. (1968), *The Dual Economy: The Dynamics of American Industry Structure*, New York: Norton.

Boeke, J.H. (1953), *Economics and Economic Policy of Dual Societies*, New York: Institute of Pacific Relations.

Botwinick, Howard (1993), *Persistent Inequalities: Wage Disparity Under Capitalist Competition*, Princeton, NJ: Princeton University Press.

Doeringer, Peter B. and Michael J. Piore (1971), *Internal Labour Markets and Manpower Analysis*, Armonk, NY: M.E. Sharpe.

High, Steven (2003), *Industrial Sunset: The Making of North America's Rust Belt, 1969–1984*, Toronto: University of Toronto Press.

High, Steven, Lachlan MacKinnon and Andrew Perchard (eds) (2017), *The Deindustrialized World Confronting Ruination in Postindustrial Places*, Vancouver: University of British Columbia Press.

Kumar, Arun (2014), "India's Black Economy: Causes, Implications and Remedies," in B. Vivekandan (ed.), *India Today: Issues Before the Nation*, New Delhi: Gyan Publishing House.

Leadbeater, David (2009), "Single-industry Resource Communities, 'Shrinking,' and the New Crisis of Hinterland Economic Development," in Karina Pallagst et al. (eds), *The Future of Shrinking Cities: Problems, Patterns and Strategies of Urban Transformation in a Global Context*, Monograph 2009–2001, Berkeley: Institute of Urban and Regional Planning, University of California Berkeley.

Leadbeater, David (2014), "Metropolitanism and Hinterland Decline," in David Leadbeater (ed.), *Resources, Empire and Labour: Crises, Lessons and Alternatives*, Halifax: Fernwood Publishing.

Lewis, W. Arthur (1979), "The Dual Economy Revisited," *The Manchester School*, 47 (3): 211–29.

Lewis, W. Arthur (1954), "Economic Development with Unlimited Supplies of Labour," *The Manchester School*, 22: 139–91, https://la.utexas.edu/users/hcleaver/368/368lewistable.pdf.

Neumann, Tracy (2016), *Remaking the Rust Belt: The Post-industrial Transformation of North America*, Philadelphia: University of Pennsylvania Press.

Ranis, Gustav (1988), "Analytics of Development: Dualism," (Ch 4) in Hollis Chenery and T.N. Srinivasan (eds), *Handbook of Development Economics*, Vol.1: 73–92, New York: Elsevier.

Reich, Michael, David M. Gordon and Richard C. Edwards (1973), "A Theory of Labour Market Segmentation," *American Economic Review*, 63 (2), May: 359–65.

Ryan, Paul (2008), "Primary and Secondary Labour Markets," in Steven N. Durlauf and Lawrence E. Blume (eds), *The New Palgrave Dictionary of Economics*, Houndmills, UK: Palgrave Macmillan.

Seccareccia, Mario (2017), "Dualism and Economic Stagnation: Can a Policy of Guaranteed Basic Income Return Mature Market Economies to *les Trentes Glorieuses*?" New York: Institute for New Economic Thinking (INET), https://www.ineteconomics.org/uploads/papers/Seccareccia-INET-Dualism-GI-01.pdf.

Smith, Murray E.G. (2009), "Against Dualism: Marxism and the Necessity of Dialectical Monism," *Science and Society*, 73 (3), July: 356–85.

Temin, Peter (2016), "The American Dual Economy: Race, Globalization, and the Politics of Exclusion," *International Journal of Political Economy*, 45: 85–123.

Tignor, Robert L. (2006), *W. Arthur Lewis and the Birth of Development Economics*, Princeton, NJ: Princeton University Press.

Vines, David and Andrew Zeitlin (2008), "Dual Economies," in Steven N. Durlauf and Lawrence E. Blume (eds), *The New Palgrave Dictionary of Economics*, Houndmills, UK: Palgrave Macmillan.

15. Do the robots come to liberate us or to deepen our inequality? The uncertain macrostructural foundations of the robotic age

Arpita Bhattacharjee and Gary Dymski[1]

INTRODUCTION

How will the increasing presence of robots and artificial intelligence (AI) affect production and consumption processes? Do they constitute a threat to the human workers whose roles and tasks they increasingly replace, or a source of liberation from drudgery? Debate over these questions in journals and policy forums the world over has exposed contradictory views, and led to still further questions. Do robots create the conditions for a new human renaissance (Quattrucci, 2017) or endanger the rights of humans (van Est and Gerritsen, 2017)? And do robots threaten 'us' because we don't know precisely what they can do (Wohl, 2017), because of what they can do that we can't (Nair, 2017)? The profound uncertainty thus exposed, as we argue below, constitutes a key aspect of this area of inquiry.

Most economic research on the questions posed above has taken an empirical approach. Wildly divergent estimates of how the robotic revolution might affect employment have been proposed. One widely cited study (Frey and Osborne, 2013) asserted that 47% of US jobs are at risk. A 2017 report by McKinsey Global Institute (2017) asserted that this estimate was excessive, for while AI and robotics make routine processing easier, growth will happen in 'jobs that require interpersonal, creative, and entrepreneurial skills.' Acemoglu and Restrepo (2017) similarly found a significant but quantitatively small adverse effect of introducing robots into head-to-head competition with human workers. However, a subsequent OECD study (Nedelkoska and Quintini, 2018) reinforced the conclusions of the Frey/Osborne (2013) study, indicating that a high proportion of jobs were at risk from robotics.

The theoretical implications of AI and robotics have received less attention, and have been examined through very constricted lenses. Dynamic one- and two-sector models have been used to model the replacement of humans by robots (see, for example, Sachs, Benzell, and LaGarda, 2015); the focus is on how the 'human-labour replacement' aspect of robotics directly impacts profits and worker wages in the context of the representative firm. The economics of AI is less mature than that on robots.[2] Varian (2018), a leading thinker in this area, treats AI as equivalent to other new advances in the digital revolution which began in the 1980s. As Agrawal, Gans, and Goldfarb (2018) elaborate in one of a series of studies, AI's dispersion across industries will replace both human labour and less efficient machines, as well as augmenting productive capacity across the economy. In sum, both the robotics and AI transitions have thus far been treated as linear extensions of well-understood trajectories of technological change. As Robert Gordon (2018, p. 18) put it, 'Robots are nothing new,' having first been incorporated into manufacturing in 1961.

But what if robots *are* something new? This chapter explores the theoretical foundations of the human-robot transition beyond the microeconomics of human-labour replacement per se. We start with microfoundations, focusing not just on robots' expanding *mechanical* capabilities but on the implications of their emerging *autonomous decision* (AI) capacities. We first argue that introducing AI and robotics into production processes generates new dimensions of uncertainty, more akin to (but not reducible to) the concept of fundamental uncertainty introduced by Keynes (Chapter 12, 1936) than to probabilistic risk. We then argue that AI and robotics can be expected to drastically alter the terms of principal–agent power relations in the workplace and labour market. These two explorations permit us to examine an aspect of the robotics revolution that is front and centre in public debate, but ignored by economists: the fear that robots generate as a perceived threat to human society.

Macro-structural aspects of the human-robot-AI transition are also centrally important. To illustrate this point, we take up the idea featured in Paul Mason's *PostCapitalism* (2015) that the information revolution – including robotics and AI – will enable individuals and communities to withdraw from the market. This claim ignores the continuing need for maintaining and governing what might be termed 'macrostructural balances' among the spatial areas that people use to coordinate their economic activity. Insuring the adequacy of goods and service provision (the aggregate demand problem that Keynes explored) requires an entity with the legitimacy to both monitor cross-border flows facilitating that provisioning and to assure wellbeing through redistribution for those who grant it that legitimacy. The need for an entity – a state – capable of playing this role will, if anything, be greater in the post-robotic world than at present.

In essence, this chapter argues that the shrinking zone of human control in productive work, or for that matter in social life, is not the crux of the matter. Considered only as accelerated labour-replacement, the robotic revolution as such simply follows the arc of technological change established at the dawn of the Industrial Revolution. Rather, the threat to economic (and human) reproduction implicit in the robotic revolution arises at the systemic level. And the fear and uncertainty generated by this revolution at the microfoundational level leads people to doubt the capacity of government to confront this problem. This, in turn, leads to the election of political leaders whose platforms disregard the effectiveness of state action, thus removing the state's capacity at precisely the moment it is most needed.

UNCERTAINTY AND THE ROBOTIC AGE

Perhaps the defining feature of the robotic revolution thus far is the profound uncertainty it generates about whether our current systems of provision are future-proof. This feeds the fear and sense of threat discussed above, and represents an uncomfortable starting point for economic analysis. John Maynard Keynes highlighted the coercive effect on calculations in financial markets of our ignorance of the longer-term implications of investment commitments that might be made today. He emphasized 'the extreme precariousness of the basis of knowledge on which our estimates of prospective yield have to be made' in his *General Theory* (Keynes, 1936, p. 149), using as an example the value of a liner or a building in the City of London in five years' time (*ibid*., p. 150). A year later he clarified his intentions in that chapter, adding further examples and a famous four-line precis of his argument:

> The sense in which I am using the term is that in which the prospect of an European war is uncertain, or the price of copper and the rate of interest twenty years hence, or the obsolescence of a new invention, or the position of private wealth-owners in the social system in 1970. About these matters there is no scientific basis on which to form any calculable probability whatever. We simply do not know. (Keynes, 1937, pp. 113–14)

This is 'Keynesian' or 'fundamental' uncertainty, which when it interacts with fear or loss of confidence can cause investment – and economic growth – to sink like a stone. This said, the introduction of AI and robotics into production and consumption leads to a further stage of uncertainty.

Profound technological change forces adaptation for all those it affects. When that change is epoch-making, older patterns of living and working are displaced so violently that entire life-trajectories are remade, and cities take new shapes. Skills once highly prized in the market are rendered worthless; some are shunted off to the margins, as economic rents are redistributed according to still-emerging principles and practices.

The coming robotic age threatens at least this level of dislocation: whenever the rate of technological advancement outpaces the rate of job creation, technological unemployment displaces some workers. In effect, more labor with certain characteristics is on offer than is demanded. Keynes' *General Theory* (Chapter 2, 1936) categorizes this as one type of 'involuntary unemployment.' This certainly is an emergent tendency when the rate of technological advancement outpaces the rate of job creation. But as Keynes noted, involuntary unemployment can arise for other reasons too, notably deficiencies of aggregate demand. And in any event, the notion that 'the machines are coming' has happened before: the steam engine, the repeating rifle, the airplane (and so on), all substituted machine power for human power, and opened new capabilities in transportation, transit, and killing (and so on).

But what robotic machines represent, and the threat they pose, stir deeper – and possibly new – concerns: the redundancy of autonomous human control, of experienced workers' judgement in the face of expanding machine capacity. Epochal inventions such as the airship and the gun were controlled by human masters or human designers. Now, machines are becoming not only more dexterous, but more capable of complex, real-time 'decisions.' That is, they are 'artificially intelligent.'[3] Nearly every human quality previously required in producing a material outcome is no longer strictly necessary. It is the fact that no skill set can be definitionally exempted from the existential crisis associated with this profound wave of technological change. I can no longer take comfort in the fact that my skills protect me from the fate of those inside the technological frontier. With enough time, engineers will surely produce robots capable of perfect waltzes and rhumbas. There is no clear divide between hunter and prey, between master and servant, once this divide has been crossed; redundancy stalks any human in any field.

ASYMMETRIC POWER AND THE MICROFOUNDATIONS OF ROBOTICS AND AI

We now turn to the microfoundational structure of the workplace. We build on Piketty and Saez' (2003) insight that all income-earners do not fit into one category; it includes managers as well as more-skilled and less-skilled workers.[4] These distinctions between categories of 'worker' matter. As Erik Olin Wright (Chapter 7, 2015) has shown, the 'ambiguity' of Piketty's categories hides more traditional class categories, in which more privileged income-earners – managers and owners – exert control over the pace of work and allocation of resources in production processes. We have already seen that the profound uncertainty associated with AI and robotics can generate fear and a sense of threat on the part of those engaged in production. The fear of robots and AI, and the perception that they constitute a threat, not a liberator, is reinforced by the way that these phenomena are incorporated into the structures of control (that is, on power relations) in production.

Insofar as robots and AI represent the latest manifestation of technological change, building this argument requires that we deviate from economists' benchmark approach to technology. In the core Walrasian model (Katzner, 1988), the level of technology is one of the three elements of agents' endowments, along with preferences and wealth; and these endowments establish the constraints on agents' ability to maximize their utility in decentralized market equilibria. In this context, technological change offers opportunities to relax knowledge and resource constraints that have constituted barriers to wellbeing. This, in principle, levels the playing field by forcing all economic agents engaging with that change to retrain. So technological change should expand choice sets while reducing the disutility of work, and even suggesting more efficient ways to deliver public services. In the case of encroaching robotics, jobs within the 'digital divide' will be lost; but investment by affected agents in their human capital (education and training) will insure that gains from robotic technology are more widely shared. Further, such investments should be self-financing.

Working from first principles in this way, then, any adjustment problems associated with the dawning of the robotic age, such as the 'productivity gap,' can be laid to three factors: inadequate provisions for training and education; perverse market incentives or perverse agent responses to market signals; mechanism problems in capturing robots' spillover benefits. If there is a 'digital divide,' its boundaries will be shifting continually as technology changes, so households will have recurring opportunities to jump across it. Thus, evidence that some portion of the population remain marginalized as technology marches on evidently reflects choice rooted in preferences.

Many markets, however, deviate substantially from Walrasian first principles – especially markets for the factors of production. All agents are not created equal, in terms of the resources and information they bring to the market, and in terms of the quality of public goods (education, access to transportation, jobs, healthcare, and so on) to which they have access. Markets, then, create winners and losers: principals who control resources such as financial wealth and access to employment, and the agents whose survival depends on selling their services to principals.

A recent paper by Dekker, Salomons, and van der Waal (2017) found, for a sample of respondents in 20 European countries, that fear of robots is more pronounced for those whose employment is more likely to be negatively affected by robots, and for those living in countries with adverse economic conditions and with fewer protections for workers from market forces. This reaction of economically vulnerable agents to this new wave of technological change is readily described by the analytical syntax that has been developed in microfoundational theory over the past forty years: the problematics of asymmetric information (Stiglitz, 1987) and contested exchange (Bowles and Gintis, 1993) explain how signalling and screening processes leave some agents struggling to hang on, while others prosper. Geographic and social divides can arise and persist, reinforced and not eliminated by market mechanisms.[5]

Fear and the sense of threat will then readily arise in these circumstances of structurally differentiated opportunity. The inattention of economic models to this aspect of the robotic age can be attributed to two factors. One is that the modelling literature on robotics and AI referenced above has used explicitly dynamic models, whether continuous-time (as in general-equilibrium frameworks) or periodic-time (as in overlapping generations models). The Occam's Law principle followed in mainstream theory dictates that the best explanation is that which makes the fewest deviations from the reference case – and that case is the Walrasian equilibrium (Dymski, 2014). The social-power implications of principal–agent relations in factor markets, because they are not strictly necessary, are ignored.

However, the fear noted above can be explained if differential social power is incorporated into, not excluded from, models of robotic transition. For one thing, unequal resources and location generate dynamic spillovers: being able to take advantage of training for a new wave of technical change depends on prior training and still prior education, and that in turn is conditional on the location, social conditions, and public resources available in every agent's area of origin.

Beyond this, the incursion of robotic machines into the realm of human decision poses an even deeper challenge than their mechanical superiority in many tasks. As robotic machines become self-reflexive, they can take over decision-spaces previously reserved to human beings. When the production space involves not just [human–machine], but [human (principal)]–[machine + human(agent)], developments in this (AI) direction can squeeze principals, not just agents. Indeed, Autor (2015) has documented evidence that those in middle-level jobs – including some employers with managerial (directing) roles – have been most likely to experience losses from technological advance.

The continuing evolution of AI promises to destabilize this game of positional power, however. At present, some relatively privileged agents can avoid redundancy in workspaces by maintaining their edge over less-prepared agents. In game-theoretic terms, they are able to react better in the wake of moves by 'nature' in what is essentially a rigged zero-sum game. Thus, the agents who control autonomous decision-making in work settings have, until the advent of AI, been immunized against technological advance: they decide where the machines should go, and who should run them. This 'edge' is threatened once that part of the labor process reserved to autonomous decision-making – the [human(principal)–[machine] part of the above chain – is squeezed by AI machines. Now the game changes. No longer can those able to attain the 'right skills' in economically strategic sectors rely on market forces to demonstrate their evolutionary fitness and enhance their wellbeing, leaving less well-positioned or less well-adapted workers to fall behind. What constitutes the 'right skills' changes too fast, and backup systems such as government provisioning for social welfare or more sophisticated retirement systems cannot keep up.

CAN THE ROBOTIC AGE GUIDE US TO POST-CAPITALISM?

We now turn to the macro implications of robotics and AI: how will their growing use affect, and be affected by, the structure of the economy as a whole? Here we do not consider the state's role in stabilizing the macroeconomy or encouraging its growth; we focus on the compositional implications of adding up across individual economic units engaging with robotics and AI. It is helpful to recall that macroeconomic activity is distributed across space – firms and workers do not all occupy the same space but are distributed across space. Also note that aggregate activity is divided into smaller units – nation states or regions.

Here we can only briefly explore the macro-structural aspects of the robotics/AI revolution. We begin with the notion that the information revolution marks a step in the direction of a post-capitalist society. This thesis has been put forward most forcefully by journalist Paul Mason. He pointed the way to post-capitalism in a *Guardian* article reviewing the Frey-Osborne study cited above:

> The automation revolution is possible, but without a radical change in the social conventions surrounding work it will not happen. The real dystopia is that, fearing the mass unemployment and psychological aimlessness it might bring, we stall the third industrial revolution. Instead we end up creating millions of low skilled jobs that do not need to exist.
>
> The solution is to begin to de-link work from wages. (Mason, 2016)

This passage captures the main thematics of Mason's *PostCapitalism* (2015): the critique of capitalism and the view that an information/digital revolution for which robotics is crucial will liberate society from the grip of this unfair system. In his book, he argues that 'the main faultline in the modern world is between networks and hierarchies' (Mason, 2015, p. 212); to move from the latter to the former, and thus accomplishing this liberation, requires a transformative role for the state as a 'Wiki-state,' which 'has to act more like the staff of Wikipedia: to nurture the new economic forms to the point where they take off and operate organically. As in the old vision of communism, the state has to "wither away" . . . [and to] reshape markets to favour sustainable, collaborative and socially just outcomes' (*ibid.*, p. 273).

Mason's vision of 'the network unleashed' (*ibid.*, p. 286) is based on the premise that much economic activity can be moved outside the purview of the market and the state, on the basis that many goods are now delivered at zero marginal cost through the internet, and that other goods can be produced and consumed locally (food, energy, and so on). In this book and elsewhere he has advocated experiments with universal basic income as a means of easing the transition from a situation of depending on capitalism to deliver needed goods and services to a situation in which capitalism has been bypassed.

While Mason's visionary work gives its readers much to ponder and admire, the jump it proposes from where *we* are now to a networked humanity overlooks the indispensable role of macrostructures in the flows of goods and services. Who is this 'we'? The claim that this community of 'we' can be built organically, ignores the spatial structure of the economy: every community, no matter how circular, is spatially interconnected with the outside world, and individuals are embedded in communities. This 'macrostructural' aspect of economic communities' reproduction will not disappear as robots replace humans: to the contrary, it will be more important than ever.

The root of macrostructures is that all economic activity occurs in space. Space divides into spatial areas, according to a logic of 'nationhood,' 'region,' or 'community.' Every spatial area has a balance (surpluses or deficits) with the rest of the world: if it sells more goods and services to the rest of the world than it buys, it will build up a surplus or an ownership stake in assets located elsewhere; and vice versa. People have locations in space too, belongings. The link between the location of people and of economic activity is dramatically illustrated via a multi-sectoral input-output model such as that of Sraffa (1960).

Sraffa's model, by specifying simple linear relations in production and identifying input and output requirements, focuses attention on the distributional implications of different patterns of production. Labour, in his model, is reduced to a standard commodity, with uniform standards for social reproduction. This simplification allows the closure of this model to be determined by a 'social' decision on the division of income between the real wage and the rate of profit.

Here we can work with whatever split has been decided between wages and profits. For our purposes, we are interested in what happens – under whatever wage/profit split exists – when the amount of labour required for production is cut drastically by the introduction of robots. If the demand for labour in a given spatial area were to decline – by half, for example – any area's output would decline by half. Consequently, half the wages previously paid to workers in that area would disappear. But those workers – and their dependents – still need to live, and presumably they would need more than half-wages.

But this would require transfers from those accruing the gains from this technological advance to those working – either through raising wages or through redistribution of surplus. This will require allocation rules – governance – and the agreement of the governed to make the requisite increases to wages or transfers. And this agreement would plausibly turn on the answer to two questions: first, the locus of control over revenues (taxes and fees) of the government responsible for redistributing income; second, the geographic areas of origin of the workers who supply labour in this area.

If all the workers impacted by robotics originate from within this spatial area, and if all the capitalists accruing profit from production processes in that area are located there as well, then redistributions from capitalist profit to workers' subsistence would be intra-national (or intra-regional). But even supposing such a political post-robotic compensation arrangement were feasible given these circumstances, consider the viability of such an arrangement if the workers originated 'abroad': shouldn't they just be sent home, rather than being granted supplemental income support (universal basic income)? And consider, further, the viability of this arrangement if the capitalists controlling production in this spatial area do not 'receive' their profits there – that is, if they make use of tax shelters. If they are asked to pay in a portion of the surplus to support subsistence needs for this area's workers – thus possibly reducing their profit rate below the 'global average,' will they not disinvest (or threaten to) and invest in production facilities elsewhere?

In short, the political plausibility of required transfers depends on conditions regarding the spatial origins of workers and the spatial location of profits that are unlikely to be met in the world as it exists today. In this case, solutions involving income transfers to the needy may not pass any jurisdiction's political test; and the consequence is that those who have voting rights in that jurisdiction may not only be unwilling to vote for a government that would promise to protect their living standard: they may be willing to vote for a government that at least punishes and restricts those who, having originated from outside the spatial area in question, now would require the same transfers as would 'native' workers if they are to remain there.

CONCLUSION: LEARNING FROM THE IPCC

This chapter has critically examined the nature of the economic threat to human society posed by the increasing use of robots, and of more autonomous robots. Our analysis helps to explain why such a wide range of empirical estimates about how robotization will affect employment. First, robots in all their dimensionality into economic models cannot be fully represented in economic models anything like those in current use. Second, there is invariably a macrostructural dimension to the incorporation of robots that feeds back on the purely micro dimensions of the use of labour with capital (some of it robotic) in any given spatial area. Acknowledging the existence and implications of the macrostructural dimension immediately raises all the unresolved questions about the fit between micro and macro logics that John Maynard Keynes and Piero Sraffa, among others, brought into view; and these are issues that still remain unresolved in the very core of economic theory.

The threat to economic (and human) reproduction implicit in the robotic revolution arises at the systemic level. It must be addressed at the systemic level – not solely by market forces, nor by waiting for market forces to starve to death. Instead, a Polanyian double movement – wherein states react to and create manageable channels for market initiatives – combined with a Keynesian state with the capacity to provide for their residents' wellbeing, might have a chance to reverse the pull toward steadily rising inequality that has destabilized social reproduction across the globe.

Achieving social and economic conditions of the sort envisioned in Keynes' essay on the economic possibilities 'for our grandchildren' (Keynes, 1930, pp. 358–73) will require both sustained activism in macroeconomic policy-making and, as the previous section shows, a sustainable solution to the insider/outsider problem of those who supply labour and those who generate surpluses on the basis of that labour.

The need to solve the problem of aggregate demand and supply imbalances in his day led Keynes to propose a global mechanism for imbalanced flows among nation states. This problem remains unsolved. In our day we must add to it a further global challenge. The ongoing technological revolution, combined with the cross-border mobility of labour, is heightening the tension between what machines can do, what and where the 'capital' behind those machines resides, and the capacity and political will of national governments. The demand on governments to both care for their residents and to maintain global competitiveness is exposing the impossibility of squaring this circle, and feeding frustrations that, when expressed, further weaken remaining mechanisms for macrostructural control.

The immediacy of these dilemmas already exposes the need to rethink the basis of value and the principles of distribution. In a world interconnected both by supply-chains and by mobile labour, the ultimate solutions are evidently global. As in the Depression conditions that inspired Keynes' *General Theory*, the coming of the robots puts humanity face to face with the need to reimagine the boundaries of existing systems of provision. A lesson might be taken from the global effort to stop global warming – the Intergovernmental Panel on Climate Change (IPCC). As with the robotic revolution, the climate-change problem is replete with spillover problems. Clearly, climate change has not been stopped or reversed; but nation states' willingness to declare a global crisis and to begin taking responsibility for addressing it has been a crucial step forward. If we concede that the macrostructural spillovers exceed the capacity for compensatory action by any one government in a world of mobile capital and labour, then a parallel to the IPCC – a global panel on the threat to human sustainability implicit in the robotic revolution – is overdue.

NOTES

1. The impetus for this chapter is a UK research initiative in which both authors are involved, the EPSRC Self-Healing Cities project, which is aiming at using robotics and AI to make urban infrastructure – from roads and streets to pipeways to cable systems – self-maintaining. The authors wish to give special thanks to project members Andrew Brown, Netta Cohen, Raul Fuentes, Gary Graham, Mark Miodownik, Phil Purnell, Rob Richardson, and Chris Rogers for many insightful discussions on the topics considered here. They also thank Riccardo Bellofiore and participants in the December 2017 Grenoble Post-Keynesian Conference for their comments on a preliminary version of this chapter. The authors bear full responsibility for any errors of fact or attribution in these pages.
2. The AI research agenda still under formation (Aghion, Jones, and Jones 2017). Furman and Seamans (2018) provide a useful overview of this nascent literature.

3. Of course, this raises the further questions of what is artificial intelligence, and indeed, what is intelligence itself – conundra that have haunted humankind over the millennia.
4. The term 'microfoundational theory' is used here rather than 'microeconomic theory.' For while the latter term encompasses the broad terrain of studies of the behaviour of firms and individuals in resource allocation, the former term refers to frameworks that center on firm and individual behaviour with the intention of generalizing analytical conclusions to the economy as a whole.
5. An example here is racial redlining; see Stiglitz and Weiss (1981) and Dymski (1995).

REFERENCES

Acemoglu, Daron, and Pascual Restrepo, 2017. 'Robots and Jobs: Evidence from US Labor Markets,' NBER Working Paper No. 23285, Cambridge: National Bureau of Economic Research, March.

Aghion, Philippe, Benjamin F. Jones, and Charles I. Jones, 2017. 'Artificial Intelligence and Economic Growth,' NBER Working Paper No. 23928, Cambridge: National Bureau of Economic Research, October.

Agrawal, Ajay K., Joshua S. Gans, and Avi Goldfarb, 2018. 'Economic Policy for Artificial Intelligence,' NBER Working Paper No. 24690, Cambridge: National Bureau of Economic Research, June.

Autor, David H., 2015. 'Why Are There Still So Many Jobs? The History and Future of Workplace Automation,' *Journal of Economic Perspectives* 29(3), Summer: 3–30.

Benzell, Seth G., Laurence J. Kotlikoff, Guillermo LaGarda, and Jeffrey D. Sachs, 2016. 'Robots Are Us: Some Economics of Human Replacement,' NBER Working Paper No. 20941, Cambridge: National Bureau of Economic Research, March.

Bowles, Samuel, and Herbert Gintis, 1993. 'The Revenge of Homo Economicus: Contested Exchange and the Revival of Political Economy,' *Journal of Economic Perspectives* 7(1), Winter: 83–102.

Dekker, Fabian, Anna Salomons and Jeroen van der Waal, 2017. 'Fear of Robots at Work: The Role of Economic Self-interest,' *Socio-Economic Review* 15(3): 539–62.

Dymski, Gary A., 1995. 'The Theory of Bank Redlining and Discrimination: An Exploration,' *Review of Black Political Economy* 23(3), Winter: 37–74.

Dymski, Gary A., 2014. 'Neoclassical Sink and Heterodox Spiral: Political Divides and Lines of Communication in Economics,' *Review of Keynesian Economics* 2(1), Spring: 1–19.

Frey, Carl Benedikt, and Michael A. Osborne, 2013. 'The Future of Employment: How Susceptible are Jobs to Computerisation?,' Oxford University, September 17.

Furman, Jason, and Robert Seamans, 2018. 'AI and the Economy,' Working Paper No. 24689, Cambridge: National Bureau of Economic Research, June.

Gordon, Robert J., 2018. 'Why Has Economic Growth Slowed When Innovation Appears to be Accelerating?,' NBER Working Paper No. 24554, Cambridge: National Bureau of Economic Research, April.

Katzner, Donald, 1988. *Walrasian Microeconomics: An Introduction to the Economic Theory of Market Behavior*, Reading: Addison-Wesley.

Keynes, John Maynard, 1930. *Essays in Persuasion*, London: Macmillan.

Keynes, John Maynard, 1936. *The General Theory of Employment, Interest, and Prices*, London: Macmillan.

Mason, Paul, 2015. *PostCapitalism: A Guide to Our Future*, London: Allen Lane.

Mason, Paul, 2016. 'Automation may mean a post-work society but we shouldn't be afraid,' *The Guardian*, 17 February.

McKinsey Global Institute, 2017. *A Future That Works: Automation, Employment, and Productivity*, January.

Nair, Leena, 2017. 'In the robot age, are you sure you're a human?' *World Economic Forum*, January 17. Accessed at https://www.weforum.org/agenda/2018/01/in-the-robot-age-are-you-sure-youre-a-human/.

Nedelkoska, Ljubica, and Glenda Quintini, 2018. 'Automation, skills use, and training,' Working Paper No. 202, Organization for Economic Co-Operation and Development (OECD), Directorate for Employment, Labour, and Social Affairs, DELSA/ELSA/WDSEM(2018)3.

Quattrucci, Leonardo, 2017. 'The age of robots could be a new Renaissance. This is why,' *World Economic Forum*, October 18. Accessed at https://www.weforum.org/agenda/2017/10/ai-renaissance/.

Piketty, Thomas, and Emmanuel Saez, 2003. 'Income Inequality in the United States, 1913–1998,' *Quarterly Journal of Economics* 118(1), February: 1–41.

Sachs, Jeffrey D., Seth G. Benzell, and Guillermo LaGarda, 2015. 'Robots: Curse or Blessing? A Basic Framework,' NBER Working Paper No. 21091, Cambridge: National Bureau of Economic Research, April.

Sraffa, Piero, 1960. *Production of Commodities by Means of Commodities: Prelude to a Critique of Economic Theory*, Cambridge: Cambridge University Press.

Stiglitz, Joseph E., 1987. 'The Causes and Consequences of The Dependence of Quality on Price,' *Journal of Economic Literature* 25(1), March: 1–48.

Stiglitz, Joseph E., and Andrew Weiss, 1981. 'Credit Rationing in Markets with Imperfect Information,' *American Economic Review* 71(3), March: 393–410.

van Est, Rinie and Joost Gerritsen, 2017. 'Human rights in the robot age: Challenges arising from the use of robotics, artificial intelligence, and virtual and augmented reality,' Rathenau Instituut Parliamentary Assembly of the Council of Europe, The Hague, The Netherlands.

Varian, Hal, 2018. 'Artificial Intelligence, Economics, and Industrial Organization,' NBER Working Paper No. 24839, Cambridge: National Bureau of Economic Research, July.

Wohl, Benjamin, 2017. 'How Artificial Intelligence and the robotic revolution will change the workplace of tomorrow,' *The Conversation*, March 16. Accessed at https://theconversation.com/how-artificial-intelligence-and-the-robotic-revolution-will-change-the-workplace-of-tomorrow-72607.

Wright, Erik Olin, 2015. *Understanding Class*, London: Verso.

Name index

Subject index